s are fueling
ent. Doctrinal
ndermining the
a while spiritual
i-rected into new
s and cults. These
e our current
nty-first-century
apply equally to

e Civil War, the
nting press had
erce dispute. Just
arlier, during the
evolutionary War
the Constitution,
universally seen
ogy that was the
the American
the late antebel-
effects seemed a
culated news and
he nation, and it
and regional
ffused the Bible,
ectarian divides;
ific discoveries,
nacy to quack
Confidence-Man,
ool's Day 1857,
ges an exchange
contemporary
technologies.

e raises his glass
ric on the press,"
enthusiastically
miracle-working
arlie's panegyric
aken aback, for
a different press
"Praise be unto
s, but Noah's; let
fy the press, the
h, from which
orning. Praise be
e black press but
and magnify the
of Noah, from
nspiration." As
urls, its biblical
wine as the
tion and tyranny
gnorance: "Who
d contentions?
ause, inflicteth
nto the press, the
a, which knitteth
th foes." This
clumsily and

A con man himself, Frank is not buying Charlie's praise of this press. He thinks it is the printing press, not the wine press, that is the antidote to polarization and tyranny and ignorance. Frank acknowledges, however, that some people criticize the printing press, and he summarizes the arguments of these "sour sages" with a particularly vivid analogy: While under dynastic despotisms, the press is to the people little but an improvisatore, un-der popular ones it is too apt to be their Jack Cade. In fine, these sour sages regard the press in the light of a Colt's revolver, pledged to no

deaf-and-dumb man—who may be the titular confidence man and who may reappear later in the guise of the cosmopolitan Frank and who may be the devil himself (Melville suggests these connections without confirming them)—boards a steamship named Fidèle ("faith"). He threads his way through a crowd, which includes several pickpockets, and positions himself next to a sign advertising an "impostor" or confidence man who is wanted by the law. This deaf-and-dumb man then inscribes statements from 1 Corin-thians 13 on a small slate: "Charity thinketh no

deaf-and-dun
statements fro
a small slate
evil," "Chari
and so on. A
scene, the shi
declaring "N
The contras
written phras
"No Trust"—
Textual techn
and beneficia
levels of trus
tend to erode
communities
It is in des
Melville's na
the wolves a
increase." In
the statemen
as America h
the bandits a
Wild West b
pickpockets
broadly, tho
suggests th
predators ar
breeds of pre
that rely on
Under certain
press can in
populace fi
ties—the mo
are the two
cited by pri
doing so, it re
to foxy pred
trickery and
men, hoaxe
abounded in
nineteenth-ce
als struggled
of strangers,
made them v
and deceptio
destabilized
structures,
individuals v
voices. Whil
at least in A
dismantlir
forcefull
authori
recor
reli
sh

England is titular, I hold the press to be actually—Defender of the Faith!—defender of the faith in the final triumph of truth over error, metaphysics over superstition, theory over falsehood, machinery over na-ture, and the good man over the bad.
So which is it? Is the printing press an iron Paul, an Advancer of Knowledge, and a Defender of the Faith? Or is it an erratic revolver, a mob boss like Jack Cade, and a cheap diffuser of amusing drivel?
Melville, as is typical for him, does not settle the question, but he places

populace from wolfish authori-ties—the monarchy and the papacy are the two paradigmatic examples cited by print's advocates—but in doing so, it renders people vulnerable to foxy predators, ones that rely on trickery and sleight-of-hand. Con men, hoaxes, and other scams abounded in the urbanizing, mo-bile nineteenth-century society; individu-als struggled to navigate this "world of strangers," and weak social bonds made them vulnerable to hypocrisy and deception. Insofar as print destabilized traditional authority

Words for Conviviality

Media Technologies and Practices of Hope

Jeffrey Bilbro

BAYLOR UNIVERSITY PRESS

Cover and book design by Elyxandra Encarnación
Cover image: modification of Currier & Ives, *The Progress of the Century – The Lightning Steam Press. The Electric Telegraph. The Locomotive. The Steamboat* (1876). Bequest of Adele S. Colgate, 1962. The Met Museum.

Library of Congress Cataloging-in-Publication Data

Names: Bilbro, Jeffrey, author.
Title: Words for conviviality : media technologies and practices of hope / Jeffrey Bilbro.
Description: Waco, Texas : Baylor University Press, 2024. | Includes bibliographical references. | Summary: "Retrieves reading practices from major American authors as a guide to more communal approaches to the consumption of media in a digital age"-- Provided by publisher.
Identifiers: LCCN 2024004289 (print) | LCCN 2024004290 (ebook) | ISBN 9781481319829 (hardback) | ISBN 9781481319850 (adobe pdf) | ISBN 9781481319843 (epub)
Subjects: LCSH: Books and reading--United States--History--19th century. | Literature and society--United States--History--19th century. | Mass media--Technological innovations--United States--History--19th century. | Metaphor. | American literature--19th century--History and criticism.
Classification: LCC Z1003.2 .B55 2024 (print) | LCC Z1003.2 (ebook) | DDC 428.4088/818309--dc23/eng/20240610
LC record available at https://lccn.loc.gov/2024004289
LC ebook record available at https://lccn.loc.gov/2024004290

To my mother who read aloud to me, my wife who reads with me, and my daughter who lets me read aloud to her.

Contents

III Hope

Or, *What alternative metaphors might orient more convivial reading?*

Acknowledgments

The genesis of this book, inasmuch as books have an identifiable genesis, occurred in 2014 in Louisville, Kentucky, where thousands of English teachers were gathered to grade AP exams. Two friends from graduate school—Steven Petersheim and Daniel Train—sat patiently in a hotel room while I sketched out the argumentative arc of a book project I had in mind, one I had been ruminating on during the week in order to stay sane while deciphering the handwriting of countless high school students. They asked some tough and necessary questions and encouraged me in the belief that this project was worth pursuing. Over the years, many other colleagues and friends read portions of the manuscript and offered helpful commentary—in particular, Eric Miller, Robert Moore-Jumonville, Gracy Olmstead, Jason Peters, and Matt Stewart. Others wrote recommendation letters for various research grants and course releases: Tim Burbery, Hal Bush (who was endlessly generous and supportive before his untimely death in 2021), David Lyle Jeffrey, and Chris Phillips. When the Spring Arbor University English department was disbanded, I never expected to work in such a congenial department again, but the Grove City College English faculty embody the arts of conviviality, and I am deeply grateful to work and learn among them.

As a teacher, I regularly have opportunities to learn from dedicated and thoughtful students, and I'm grateful for the many students who have read the authors featured in this book with me and deepened my own understanding of them by asking thoughtful questions, engaging in vigorous conversation, and writing perceptive essays. Many of my students are initially daunted by the prospect of reading *Moby-Dick* and are then surprised to find it one of their favorite books when we read nineteenth-century American literature. But few students have been as moved by Melville's novel as Scout Dennings was. After the semester ended, she asked me to do an independent study on Melville's other writings. As we were settling on the reading list, I told her she could pick between *Pierre* and *Clarel*. She chose *Clarel*, and though I think she may have regretted it by the end of those eighteen thousand lines, that was the provocation I needed to read the whole poem carefully. What a gift. I'm also particularly grateful to my student assistants Janna Lu, Sarah Reardon, and Josh Sutter, who helped with research and served as initial readers for drafts of these chapters.

Spring Arbor University granted me a sabbatical and several course releases to work on this book, and Grove City College was likewise very supportive with course releases and summer research grants. It's a great gift to serve under capable and supportive academic leaders such as Pete Frank, Paul Kemeny, and Josh Mayo. Thanks also to the invaluable librarians at the Hugh and Edna White Library (Robbie Bolton and Kami Moyer are extraordinary), the Henry Buhl Library, the William Clements Library at the University of Michigan, and the American Antiquarian Society.

List of Images

Introduction

Trust, Watersheds, and America's Industrial Print Culture

Radical innovations in communications technologies are transforming culture and disrupting journalism and publishing. Fierce partisan and geographic divides are fueling political realignment. Doctrinal disputes are undermining the institutional church while spiritual energy is being redirected into new religious movements and cults. These statements describe our current situation in twenty-first-century America, but they apply equally to 1850s America.

On the eve of the Civil War, the effects of the printing press had become a topic of fierce dispute. Just a few generations earlier, during the excitement of the Revolutionary War and the drafting of the Constitution, printing was almost universally seen as a good, a technology that was the sine qua non of the American experiment. But by the late antebellum period, print's effects seemed a mixed bag: print circulated news and stories throughout the nation, and it inflamed partisan and regional differences; print diffused the Bible, and it hardened sectarian divides; print spread scientific discoveries, and it lent legitimacy to quack medicine. In *The Confidence-Man*, published on April Fool's Day 1857, Herman Melville stages an exchange that encapsulates contemporary disputes about print technologies.

When Charlie Noble raises his glass to declaim a "panegyric on the press," his friend Frank enthusiastically stands to honor this miracle-working invention. But as Charlie's panegyric unfolds, Frank is taken aback, for Charlie is praising a different press than Frank expects: "Praise be unto the press, not Faust's, but Noah's; let us extol and magnify the press, the true press of Noah, from which breaketh the true morning. Praise be unto the press, not the black press but the red; let us extol and magnify the press, the red press of Noah, from which cometh inspiration." As Charlie's toast unfurls, its biblical cadences proclaim wine as the panacea for polarization and tyranny and injustice and ignorance:

2 | Words for Conviviality

"Who hath babblings and contentions? Who, without cause, inflicteth wounds? Praise be unto the press, the kindly press of Noah, which knitteth friends, which fuseth foes."[1] This press heals—albeit clumsily and indiscriminately—a fragmented world. Of course, if you actually believe Charlie's over-the-top claims about the powers of the red press, then—in the words of that great American con man George C. Parker—I have a bridge to sell you.

A con man himself, Frank is not buying Charlie's praise of this press. He thinks it is the printing press, not the wine press, that is the antidote to polarization and tyranny and ignorance. Frank acknowledges, however, that some people criticize the printing press, and he summarizes the arguments of these "sour sages" with a particularly vivid analogy:

> While under dynastic despotisms, the press is to the people little but an improvisatore, under popular ones it is too apt to be their Jack Cade. In fine, these sour sages regard the press in the light of a Colt's revolver, pledged to no cause but his in whose chance hands it may be; deeming the one invention an improvement upon the pen, much akin to what the other is upon the pistol; involving, along with the multiplication of the barrel, no consecration of the aim. The term "freedom of the press" they consider on par with *freedom of Colt's revolver*.[2]

Frank nonetheless disagrees with this assessment. He sees the printing press not as an indiscriminate revolver but as a mechanized, infallible proclaimer of the gospel[3]:

> I hold the press to be neither the people's improvisatore, nor Jack Cade; neither their paid fool, nor conceited drudge. I think interest never prevails with it over duty. The press still speaks for truth though impaled, in the teeth of lies though intrenched. Disdaining for it the poor name of cheap diffuser of news, I claim for it the independent apostleship of Advancer of Knowledge:—the iron Paul! Paul, I say; for not only does the press advance knowledge, but righteousness. . . . In a word, Charlie, what the sovereign of England is titular, I hold the press to be actually—Defender of the Faith!—defender of the faith in the final triumph of truth over error, metaphysics over superstition, theory over falsehood, machinery over nature, and the good man over the bad.[4]

So which is it? Is the printing press an iron Paul, an Advancer of Knowledge, and a Defender of the Faith? Or is it an erratic revolver, a mob boss like Jack Cade, and a cheap diffuser of amusing drivel?

Melville, as is typical for him, does not settle the question, but he places this exchange between Charlie and Frank in a story that wrestles with one of the central paradoxes of a culture shaped by mass print: "Where the wolves are killed off, the foxes increase."[5] This phrase appears in the opening scene of *The Confidence-Man*. An apparently deaf-and-dumb man—who *may* be the titular confidence man and who *may* reappear later in the guise of the cosmopolitan Frank and who *may* be the devil himself (Melville suggests these connections without confirming them)—boards a steamship named *Fidèle* ("faith"). He threads his way through a crowd, which includes several pickpockets, and positions himself next to a sign advertising an "impostor" or confidence man who is wanted by the law. This deaf-and-dumb man then inscribes statements from 1 Corinthians 13 on a small slate: "Charity thinketh no evil," "Charity endureth all things," and so on. Across from this unusual scene, the ship's barber puts up a sign declaring "No Trust" in his window. The contrast between these two written phrases—"Charity . . ." and "No Trust"—frames Melville's story.[6] Textual technologies can be powerful and beneficial in a culture with high levels of trust, yet such technologies tend to erode the kinds of charitable communities that foster trust.

It is in describing this scene that Melville's narrator remarks, "Where the wolves are killed off, the foxes increase." In its immediate context, the statement refers to the way that, as America has become more settled, the bandits and armed robbers of the Wild West have been replaced by pickpockets and con men. More broadly, though, Melville's adage suggests that when powerful predators are eliminated, different breeds of predators proliferate, ones that rely on deceit and distraction. Under certain conditions, the printing press can indeed help to liberate a populace from wolfish authorities—the monarchy and the papacy are the two paradigmatic examples cited by print's advocates—but in doing so, it renders people vulnerable to foxy predators, ones that rely on trickery and sleight-of-hand.[7] Con men, hoaxes, and other scams abounded in the urbanizing, mobile nineteenth-century society; individuals struggled to navigate this "world of strangers," and weak social bonds made them vulnerable to hypocrisy and deception.[8] Insofar as print destabilized traditional authority structures, it rendered liberated individuals vulnerable to predatory voices. While industrial printing has, at least in America, contributed to the dismantling of overtly oppressive, forcefully imposed systems of authority, it has a much more mixed record cultivating healthy political, religious, and economic relationships. And if the steam-powered printing press is a Colt's revolver, then, as we shall see, the Internet is a fleet of heavily armed drones. Technologies that spread pixelated words around the world may provide a "multiplication of the barrel," but those of us inundated with AI-generated deep fakes, misinformation, and endless drivel can attest that they ensure "no consecration of the aim."

So although the printing press and other textual technologies can at times act like an "iron Paul," spreading the gospel of liberty, they just as often spread anarchy and mistrust. Confidence men like Frank are symptomatic of a society where strangers have to rely on printed identification and affidavits rather than personal knowledge, and in this context trusting others makes individuals vulnerable. As C. S. Lewis observes, "That demand for our confidence which a true friend makes of us is exactly the same that a confidence trickster would make. That refusal to trust, which is sensible in reply to a confidence trickster, is ungenerous and ignoble to a friend, and deeply damaging to our relation with him."[9] When we trust, we make ourselves vulnerable. Yet without this vulnerability, friendship and rich relationships are impossible. Fostering trust requires textual technologies and practices that promote conviviality, thick relationships, and the give and take of conversation and friendship. The industrialization and digitization of textual technologies, however, erodes convivial verbal practices and makes trust an increasingly risky proposition.

Frank and Charlie, then, are a fit pair as neither of them trusts the other. Frank repeatedly praises "trust" and "confidence"; these are the characteristics required for society to function in a mobile, print-mediated world. But they're also, of course, the qualities that enable Frank's cons to succeed. Similarly, for all his praise of the wine press, Charlie drinks almost nothing during their long conversation, preferring to press more port on Frank while toying with his own glass. Charlie aims to use wine's powers to soften up Frank before soliciting funds from him. As Charlie says at one point, "Up, fill up! Be we convivial. And conviviality, what is it? The word, I mean; what expresses it? A living together. . . . And how delightful to think that the word which among men signifies the highest pitch of geniality, implies, as indispensable auxiliary, the cheery benediction of the bottle. Yes, Frank, to live together in the finest sense, we must drink together."[10] Charlie's proposed conviviality, one lubricated with alcohol, is clearly a faux conviviality; instead of living together genially, both men are trying to trick the other into handing over money, and when they come to a standoff, they part. Frank and Charlie represent the two figures that dominate public discussion of digital technologies today: the techno-optimist who thinks AGI is around the corner and will save humanity, and the romantic pessimist who thinks a digitally induced dystopia is imminent.

But we do not have to choose between these unpalatable alternatives. In the last third of this book, I will draw on Melville's long poem *Clarel* and other literary works to describe how textual technologies and practices might be truly convivial—in Ivan Illich's sense of that word rather than Charlie's. In the remainder of this introduction, however, I want to briefly sketch the technological and cultural conditions that led to these deeply ambivalent feelings regarding print in antebellum America. The industrialization of print technologies in the early nineteenth century transformed print culture in ways that parallel the transformation of reading wrought by the digital revolution. Understanding how a previous era was shaped—and in some ways warped—by the assumptions that industrial print technology engendered may enable us to recognize more clearly how our own verbal habits and practices are formed and deformed by our enmeshment in digital technologies. Perhaps the convivial reading practices that some antebellum literary authors imagined can guide us toward more healthy ways of reading today.[11]

Industrializing Print, Fragmenting Union

During the revolutionary and constitutional periods, Americans were almost uniformly optimistic about the effects of the printing press. Assessing the Revolutionary War in 1793, David Ramsay famously claimed that "in establishing American independence, the pen and the press had merit equal to that of the sword."[12] In 1821 the Philadelphia Typographical Society expressed this conventional attitude when it celebrated its nineteenth anniversary with "conviviality and good humor." The members were quite satisfied with the good work of their institution, "founded as it is upon benevolence and charity." The gathering concluded with a series of toasts that punningly linked the print industry with the American experiment, the Constitution, and the military; printing was declared "the tombstone of ignorance and superstition" (see fig. 1). Throughout these toasts, all words relating to the printing process were italicized. One example gives a sense of the dad joke flavor: "*The United States.— Imposed* in the chase of liberty by Jefferson, Hancock, and the sages of the revolution; *locked up* by Washington, Warren, and the patriots of '76; *corrected* by the representatives of the people; and *revised* by the heroes of the late war, they exhibit an *original form* of government, from which all nations may *copy*."[13] This series of toasts indicates the way in which

Philadelphia Typographical Society.

The *Nineteenth Anniversary* of the society was celebrated on Saturday evening the 3d inst with the usual conviviality and good humor. Great harmony prevailed throughout the evening; and a full share of sentiments were expressed, such as the occasion is always calculated to elicit. In looking back for a period of twenty years, and reflecting upon the usefulness of the institution, founded as it is upon benevolence and charity, there is good cause for rejoicing at the past, and strong hopes for the future and permanent usefulness of our exertions.

After the annual election for officers had taken place, the cloth being removed, the following toasts were drunk, interspersed with songs.

TOASTS.

1. *The Day.*—Again celebrated in festive mirth by the brethren of the type. May friendship and good-will be the *rule* of our conduct, and moderation *guide* us in our social intercourse.

2. *The United States.*—*Imposed* in the *chase* of liberty by Jefferson, Hancock, and the sages of the revolution; *locked up* by Washington, Warren, and the patriots of '76; *corrected* by the representatives of the people; and *revised* by the heroes of the late war, they exhibit an *original form* of government, from which all nations may *copy.*

3. *The Federal Constitution.*—Foreign *impressions* cannot *batter* its face, nor party *squabbles* throw it in *pie.*

4. PRINTING: *the Art, preservative of all arts.*—The tombstone of ignorance and superstition; let those who *impose* upon it *plain down* lightly, and *lock* up in silence, lest they awake the dead.

5. *The Liberty of the Press.*—A *nonpareil form* of old *English* character; may it always be in *register,* and its appearance never be *spoiled* by *monks* or *friars.*

6. *Franklin.*—Though death has *erased* his name from among the living, memory will write *stet.* in the margin.

7. *Our deceased Brethren.*—Laid aside for a time, to wait *justification* at the general *revise.*

8. *Our absent Brethren.*—May they never want *sorts,* nor a disposition to *distribute,* when charity demands them.

9. *The Heroes of '76*—Who *set up* the *form* of liberty at the *point* of the bayonet, and *registered* it on the *tympan* of fame.

10. *The Army.*—May they always have good *balls,* quick *pulls,* and deep *impressions,* for our enemies' *imposition.*

11. *The Navy.*—Though nearly *out of work,* may they never be *out of sorts.*

12. *The State.*—A *fount case* of the American republic, from which *sorts* can always be obtained when necessity requires them.

13. *The Fair*—May *cramps rack* the base *form* that would *soil* nature's *frontispiece.*

FIGURE 0-1. *Long-Island Patriot.* "Philadelphia Typographical Society." November 14, 1821.

print technology and the formation of the United States were intertwined in the early American imagination. Granted, a typographical society, and particularly one based in Philadelphia, would be predisposed to subscribe to this narrative; nonetheless, this link was so strong that print technology could supply a whole network of metaphors for understanding the American experiment.

Indeed, such optimism about the unifying power of textual technologies had some warrant. In part, it was fueled by the general American faith in the power of technology to fuel progress.[14] More particularly, though, the American revolutionaries bequeathed a potent myth to subsequent generations about the power of print to unify the nation and diffuse republican virtue.[15] Neil Postman summarizes the prevalence of this myth when he states that Americans in the early national period "were as committed to the printed word as any group of people who have ever lived. . . . [Their] religious sensibility, political ideas and social life were embedded in the medium of typography."[16] The supreme authorities in the early republic were printed texts, and in the relative absence of authoritative institutions, print took on an outsized importance. But steam-powered printing technologies made texts cheaper and more abundant, and the printed word that had once unified the colonies became an atomizing force, one that served to fragment culture, church, and union.

The Protestant heritage of the American colonists predisposed them to see printed texts as authoritative, perspicuous, and unifying. The Protestant Reformation depended for its success on the power of the printing press to spread the biblical text and religious arguments to a broad audience, bypassing the institutional structures of the Catholic Church. In America, this valuation of the printed word in religious contexts transferred to the political sphere. Mark Noll argues that "trust in the Bible was a religious analogue to political trust in the Constitution. . . . [C]onfidence in the Bible as an authoritative written document from which one could understand practical questions of life may have been one of the impulses that transformed the notion 'constitution' from its British meaning of an inherited body of precedents to its American sense of a written document."[17] In both religious and political spheres, then, authority shifted away from traditions and institutions and toward printed texts.

Because we take the Constitution for granted today, it can be hard to recognize the audacious innovation the nation's founders made when they based the legitimacy of the new nation on a printed document.[18] Thomas Paine, in his *Rights of Man*, realizes this is an unusual arrangement and draws on religious practices to explain it. He emphasizes that a constitution takes precedence over a government and hence "a government is only the creature of a constitution." This textual authority depends, however, on a relatively widespread print culture. Paine describes how the Pennsylvania convention drafted a constitution and then "ordered it to be published, not as a thing established, but for the consideration of the whole people, their approbation or rejection." When the "whole people" (clearly, this is a rather optimistic claim on Paine's part) approved it, the convention ratified it. The result of this widespread dissemination of the printed constitution was that the constitution became "the political bible of the state. Scarcely a family was without it. Every member of the government had a copy; and nothing was more common, when any debate arose on the principle of a bill, or on the extent of any species of authority, than for the members to take the printed constitution out of their pocket, and read the chapter with which such matter in debate was connected."[19] Paine draws on the reading practices associated with the Bible to describe and shape those developing around written constitutions; in both cases, readers would settle differences by referring to a common, authoritative text. Indeed, the preamble to the United States Constitution indicates that one of the purposes of this document was to "form a more perfect Union."[20]

This need for a textually mediated union was acute during the early national era. As the Revolution dismantled traditional and institutional authorities, it created a political and cultural vacuum. What common authority could unify this newly decreed national community, one that was quite culturally and geographically diverse? In a word, print. Nathan Hatch, borrowing a phrase from John Murrin, notes that "the federal government, a 'midget institution in a giant land,' had almost no internal functions" in the early nineteenth century.[21] In ratifying the Constitution, the founders erected, to borrow another phrase from Murrin, "a roof without walls."[22] Noll expands on this point, claiming, "the Constitution secured the promise of a stable political framework, but it did not create a national culture."[23] The relative absence of other forces of social cohesion put an immense burden on texts.[24]

Thus appeals to biblical, and later constitutional, authority grew increasingly widespread. Noll points out that before the 1790s, the Bible was rarely cited in political or social debates. In the following decades, however, it became the key authority. "The principle of *sola Scriptura*," Noll concludes, became "an anchor of religious authority in a churning sea of demographic, social, and political turmoil."[25] This mode of arguing by reference to an authoritative text transferred to the use of political texts as well.[26] So even though the Constitution arose out of fierce debate and deep disagreements, Cathy Davidson observes that "popular history—and especially our legal system's continual reference back to Constitutional precedence—has made the Constitution a monument, not the result of a process, representing only a fraction of those living in what would become the United States, that was sometimes divisive, contentious, and even cynical."[27]

Even monumental texts do not interpret themselves, but appeals to these authoritative texts proved persuasive because most participants in the early national print culture shared a basic philosophy and hermeneutic. This philosophy was rooted in Scottish common sense, which essentially held that every person had the basic capacity to interpret and reason.[28] This way of thinking gave early Americans great confidence in the ability of common people to discern truth for themselves and act ethically on the basis of this truth; all that was needed was to disseminate information to the people, hence the importance of print. Along with this belief in common sense, most early American readers followed a Baconian, inductive hermeneutic.[29] The plain meaning of texts would become clear by "simply looking carefully at the evidence, determining what were 'the facts,' and carefully classifying these facts."[30] It was Baconian induction that justified the commonly held belief in biblical perspicuity; if each individual reader follows the proper method, the text's meaning will be clear. The upshot of this combination of common sense philosophy and an inductive hermeneutic was a belief that individuals could read texts on their own and that the result would be agreement and "a more perfect union."

Given these centripetal forces—shared, authoritative texts and a common hermeneutic approach—print culture did play a key role in forging a disparate conglomeration of colonists into a national community. Many historians have shown how the colonial print culture was essential to the success of the revolution. Pamphlets, most famously Thomas Paine's *Common Sense*, spread the arguments of patriots, and newspapers circulated news of political and military developments.[31] Significantly, there were only about fifty printing presses in the American colonies during the revolutionary period, and these presses produced thirty-five to forty-five newspapers.[32] Even these numbers inflate the diversity of voices as newspapers relied heavily on republishing reports first printed by other papers. "By publishing accounts from throughout the colonies," Carol Humphrey explains, "the newspapers helped foster a sense of unity and solidarity of purpose that was essential if Americans were going to win their fight for liberty and independence."[33]

Print's unifying effects continued after the Revolutionary War. Congress authorized a postal system in 1792, which established postal routes and stations, subsidized the delivery of newspapers, and stitched together the sprawling towns and villages of the new union.[34] Taverns, coffee shops, library societies, and lyceums functioned as a kind of embodied social media; despite the romantic image of the individual reader, reading remained a deeply communal activity.[35] And for the most part, people read the same texts: in addition to the Bible, a limited number of books, what David Hall terms "steady sellers," dominated publisher's lists and formed a shared base of knowledge.[36] Thus, in the words of Joyce Appleby, reading became "the principal activity of nation-building."[37] Swaths of the population were of course excluded from this activity: while women increasingly took active roles in publishing and reading, enslaved people were prohibited from learning to read, and schools and newspapers were less common throughout the South than they were in the North.[38] Yet even populations with less access to literacy saw print as a vital means of participating in politics and religion, and they were creative and determined in their efforts to read and publish.[39] Printed texts were trusted authorities, and print culture in the first decades of the nineteenth century played a key role in constructing—or at least imagining—a unified nation.[40]

This potent mythology of print as a unifying, democratizing force generated great excitement around the incredible advances in print technologies during the first forty years of the nineteenth century. The irony, as we will see, is that these technological developments in turn exposed the fragility of this myth. The printing presses used in colonial America were not much different from the one that Gutenberg used, but between 1800 and 1840, printing technology advanced rapidly: first came iron presses, then the steam-powered Adams press and steam-powered rotary presses, then stereotyping and electrotyping. Alongside these improvements, steam-powered paper mills and new methods to produce paper from wood fiber dramatically decreased the cost of paper.[41] Steam power represented a rupture in the production and dissemination of texts that was at least as radical as that generated by digital technologies.[42]

Visitors to the 1876 Centennial Exhibition in Philadelphia were treated to a vivid display of these technological improvements. In a speech given to the American Book Trade Association, which held its annual meeting in conjunction with the exhibition, the chairman of the reception committee highlighted a display in Machinery Hall. There, visitors could see "the old printing-press of Franklin, upon which, by hard labor he could produce perhaps 150 impressions per hour, side by side with the Messrs. Hoe & Co.'s latest invention, the Web perfecting-press, printing 32,000 copies of a newspaper, on both sides, in the same time. . . . Steam, the telegraph, and the power printing-press, what have they not accomplished, and how have they changed the condition of the civilized world!"[43] A 42,666 percent increase in efficiency is quite remarkable, and those who lived through these changes acutely felt this disruptive power.

Furthermore, as the chairman's remarks indicated, it was not just the steam-powered printing press that transformed the nation's communication infrastructure. The telegraph and the railroad also shrank the world dramatically. Indeed, the difference between words printed by hand and carried by horse and sail and words printed by steam and carried by wires and rails is at least as vast—if not more so—as the difference between 1876 technologies and the digital technologies of our day. A Currier & Ives print, published in 1876, portrays the potent combination of these innovations. Its title sums up its optimistic attitude: "The Progress of the Century – The Lightning Steam Press. The Electric Telegraph. The Locomotive. The Steamboat" (see fig. 2).[44] In this image, these marvelous inventions work together to spread words throughout the vastly expanded nation. And the text unspooling from the telegraph's reel depicted in the print conveys the messianic, redemptive effect these technologies were presumed to have: "Glory to God in the highest. On earth peace. Good will toward men."[45] This biblical passage was the one that Samuel Morse chose to send out through all the telegraph lines in the United States during an 1871 celebration of his invention.[46] The print adds a statement of the political results that will follow from this salvific peace and good will: "Liberty and union now and for ever[.] One and inseparable."[47] These are lovely sentiments, but coming barely ten years after a bloody Civil War, they ring rather hollow: the lady doth protest too much, methinks.

While the Currier & Ives print clearly sides with Frank's optimistic view of the printing press as "an iron Paul," an apostle of knowledge and righteousness, after midcentury more and more Americans experienced the press as a Colt's revolver, a Jack Cade spreading anarchy and confusion. In brief, as print technologies industrialized, print became a centrifugal force that undermined the nation's unity and fragmented its culture. David Hall summarizes this process as "the journey . . . from scarcity to abundance" and traces how "the structure of traditional literacy unraveled,

FIGURE 0-2. "The Progress of the Century – The Lightning Steam Press. The Electric Telegraph. The Locomotive. The Steamboat." Currier & Ives, 1876.

as print became abundant."[48] The central irony—registered so powerfully in Melville's *Confidence-Man*—is that although print was essential in unifying disparate colonists and forging a common national culture, *amplifying* print had opposite effects: as printing technologies improved and texts became cheap and widespread, American politics, religion, and culture fragmented.[49]

In her perceptive book on this shift, *The Republic in Print: Print Culture in the Age of U.S. Nation Building, 1770–1870*, Trish Loughran comments on the centennial Currier & Ives print, noting that these supposedly unifying inventions actually contributed to an era of "*dis*integration and national fragmentation."[50] Still, this optimistic image bolstered the prevalent belief in the unalloyed good of print technologies: "print is," as Loughran states, "American nationalism's preferred techno-mythology." The period of the American Revolution

> bequeathed to its heirs a profound belief in the possibilities of a more perfect, more material union—a union made increasingly "real" through the spread of post roads, canals, railroad tracks, and national periodicals that hailed an ever more reachable American public to recognize itself as a community in print. Cross-regional communication is, in fact, the fiction on which the founding based itself, and the antebellum period would serve as both the fulfillment of that founding fantasy and its undoing.[51]

When this eighteenth-century dream of the power of print was realized by nineteenth-century industrial technologies, the result was not union but civil war. Differences reified and hardened. As Loughran argues, gaps in the colonial communication network were key to consensus building and ratification. Eighteenth-century Americans could *imagine* a print-based national conversation in part because it was not yet a reality. When industrial print and transportation technologies arose to fulfill this dream, underlying political divisions became more apparent and in fact deepened.[52]

A similar irony developed in the context of religious discourse. Even though most Americans acknowledged biblical authority, and even though the Second Great Awakening intensified the commitment to this authority, theological and denominational disputes proliferated in the early nineteenth century. Cheap print was a chief culprit. As Hatch claims, "A profound irony, in fact, surrounds the success of religious printing. Instead of the press serving as truth's herald, it often amplified a welter of competing voices, proving, if anything, that no truth had inherent power. Instead of erasing the distinction between leaders and followers, the press gave ample opportunity for religious demagogues to expand their influence."[53] Whether it proves that no truth had inherent power, the industrialization of print certainly cast doubt on print's ability to render truth accessible and perspicuous.

Industrial printing technologies in the first half of the nineteenth century finally realized the promise of Gutenberg's invention—texts were actually becoming reliable, standardized, and accessible—and yet the consequences of this realization were unexpectedly mixed: misinformation spread, discourse fragmented, and readers suffered from information overload.[54] Today, we tend to think such problems are the result of the digital revolution, but antebellum Americans experienced them first.[55] The printing press amplified charlatans, cult leaders, and sensational stories more than it diffused republican virtue. "Under [the] fluid conditions" created by industrialized print, Hatch explains, "it was increasingly difficult to differentiate between science and superstition, naturalism and supernaturalism, medicine and quackery. It was a golden age both of empiricism and of imposters and counterfeiters."[56] Improving print technologies did not improve the signal-to-noise ratio; it amplified *noise*.[57] Given this confused state, Charlie's panegyric on the wine press seems appropriate. Being drunk on wine has similar effects as being drunk on misinformation. And both create fertile ground for confidence men, authoritarian leaders, and opportunistic capitalists.

Two Watersheds

Many who lived through these seismic changes felt the disruption acutely. The *experience* of reading had fundamentally changed. The author and publisher Samuel Griswold Goodrich, writing in 1856, vividly contrasts the reverential reading practices he observed at the end of the eighteenth century with the careless skimming that now predominated:

> The amusements were then much the same as at present—though some striking differences may be noted. Books and newspapers—which are now diffused even among the country towns, so as to be in the hands of all, young and old—were then scarce, and were read respectfully, and as if they were grave matters, demanding thought and attention. They were not toys and pastimes, taken up every day, and by everybody, in the short intervals of labor, and then hastily dismissed, like waste paper. The aged sat down when they read, and drew forth their spectacles, and put them deliberately and reverently upon the nose. These instruments were not as now, little tortoise-shell hooks, attached to a ribbon, and put off and on with a jerk; but they were of silver or steel, substantially made, and calculated to hold on with a firm and steady grasp, showing the gravity of the uses to which they were devoted. Even the young approached a book with reverence, and a newspaper with awe. How the world has changed![58]

Instead of carefully, reverentially reading texts, Goodrich laments, people now consume them thoughtlessly and then throw them away. To some extent, Goodrich's account is an example of what Raymond Williams memorably terms the "escalator" effect, whereby each generation tends to look back nostalgically on an idyllic past that is being destroyed.[59] If he were writing his memoir today, Goodrich would be airbrushing the age of cheap print; *those* were the glory days before smartphones, social media, and clickbait ruined reading. And yet, as Williams acknowledges, sometimes these accounts bear witness to genuine inflection points.

I contend that even if you discard the "kids these days" husk of Goodrich's description, there remains an important kernel of truth. The introduction of steam power to the production of texts did indeed constitute a cultural and political watershed. And in the decades following this divide, Americans experienced a sort of vertigo as the earlier optimism regarding the power of print became less and less plausible. In response, some—like the con man Frank or the boosters at the 1876 Centennial Exhibition—doubled down on their insistence that the printing press could magically unify the nation. Others, like the con man Charlie, succumbed to despair. But still others took the opportunity to reimagine textual technologies and readerly practices in search not of greater power and control but of genuine conviviality.

Ivan Illich's understanding of technological change can help us locate this watershed in communications technologies within the broader context of industrialization. Illich claims that when industrial technologies replace traditional tools, there is an initial inflection point at which industrialization introduces significant improvements. However, at some later point, the industrialized tools begin causing new problems and "the marginal utility of further" professionalization and industrialization declines.[60] After this second watershed is passed, the application of industrial technologies causes more harm than good. In the context of medicine, Illich locates the first watershed around 1913, as germ theory and new medicines led to marked improvement in people's health. But by the 1950s, iatrogenic diseases—those induced by the medical system—were on the rise, and "the cost of healing was dwarfed by the cost of extending sick life."[61] Illich traces a similar trajectory in many spheres of life, including "education, the mails, social work, transportation, and even civil engineering."[62] In each of these spheres, the second watershed is characterized by a violation of human, biological limits. Late industrial technologies are experienced as oppressive to the extent that they treat people as machines rather than as persons.[63] Industrial print (and, of course, digital technologies) produces more text than human communities can read or digest profitably.[64]

As Illich's metaphor is meant to suggest, these "watersheds" are often not noticed when they are crossed. You can be driving through an apparently flat cornfield in northern Indiana and cross over an imperceptible rise, from one side of which water flows to the Gulf of Saint Lawrence and from the other side to the Gulf of Mexico. This dividing line can be subtle, yet its consequences are drastic. In the context of industrial technologies, it is the second watershed that is particularly difficult to discern. This is because the optimism generated by the early benefits of new technologies blinds people to the inflection point at which these technologies begin generating more problems than they solve.

If, in the context of textual technologies, Gutenberg's press represents the first watershed, the second watershed may have been the application of steam power to printing.[65] Similarly, if the first watershed of digital texts was crossed at some point in the early 1990s, the second one may be marked by the 2007 release of the iPhone. As smartphones became ubiquitous, a few companies—Facebook, Google, and Amazon in particular—consolidated and monetized the more decentralized flow of information that marked the early days of the Internet. Earlier assumptions that "a widespread adoption of computers and communications systems along with easy access to electronic information will automatically produce a better world for human living" have become laughable.[66]

An example might clarify the disorientation felt when crossing over this second watershed. In March 2011, just a month after Egyptian president Hosni Mubarak was forced to resign, Wael Ghonim gave a TED talk extolling the power of what he termed "Revolution 2.0."[67] Ghonim, a Google executive, created the Facebook page "We Are All Khaled Said," which became a hub for protestors, and the success of the January 25 Revolution seemed to promise an "Arab Spring," in which democracy would bloom in the Middle East. In 2015, though, Ghonim opened a second TED talk with a retraction: "I once said, 'If you want to liberate a society, all you need is the Internet.' I was wrong."[68] While social media effectively coordinated dramatic protests, it failed to facilitate the deliberation needed to turn a movement into democratic governance. As Ghonim puts it, "the post-revolution events were like a punch in the gut. The euphoria faded, we failed to build consensus, and the political struggle led to intense polarization. Social media only amplified that state, by facilitating the spread of misinformation, rumors, echo chambers and hate speech. The environment was purely toxic."[69] In 2011 Facebook and Twitter were going to inaugurate democracy around the world. By 2017 commentators declared that social media had eroded the "informational underpinnings of democracy."[70] The second watershed is somewhere in our rearview mirror, but many activists and analysts hadn't realized this until the very technologies they once lauded as salvific—a silicon Paul, as it were—were sowing chaos.

In applying Illich's two watersheds theory, I want to be careful to avoid an excessive technological determinism. The disorienting transition from optimism to pessimism that characterizes a society's journey beyond the second watershed also occurs on more personal or subjective scales. When an individual feels that he is in control of a new communications technology, he is likely to be optimistic about its effects; but when he feels that others are beginning to wield the technology against him, pessimism ensues. Martin Luther is perhaps the most famous example of a person who experienced this disorienting trajectory.

When Luther nailed his ninety-five theses to the church door in Wittenberg, he had no reason to expect them to receive attention beyond his small university town.[71] But they were quickly mailed to other cities, reprinted, translated into German, and printed again. The result was that this document, quite literally, "went viral."[72] As Luther noted the following spring, "what is happening is unheard of."[73] Luther quickly adapted his writing to take better advantage of the new media ecology: he crafted edgy, German prose, he wrote short pamphlets that could be set and printed in a single day, and he benefited from Lucas Cranach's woodcuts that created eye-catching title pages.[74] Thanks in large part to the innovative methods of the Reformers, they dominated the print battle: "In the years between 1521 and 1525, when the pamphlet war was at its height, Luther and his supporters out published their opponents by a margin of nine to one."[75]

Yet the printing press and Luther's doctrine of the priesthood of all believers took on lives of their own. When the Peasants' War broke out in 1524, the rebels employed the logic of the Reformation: "The Bible proves that we are free and want to be free."[76] And, like the Reformers, they used the printing press to spread their demands and make their case to the German-speaking public. They were using Luther's own rhetoric and methods for political aims with which Luther disagreed. Luther's initial response was to publish the irenic *Admonition to Peace*, but this failed to reconcile the parties and Luther's political patrons pressured him to do something to prevent the Reformation from descending into anarchy. The notorious *Against the Robbing and Murdering Hordes of Peasants* was the result, in which Luther urged Germans to butcher any peasant prone to unrest. Luther never gave up his use of the printing press, but he increasingly combined rhetorical persuasion with authoritarian tactics to maintain control over the movement he had unleashed.[77] In less than a decade, Luther experienced a burst of optimism—I can use this new communications technology to spread my message and transform the church!—followed by deep pessimism regarding this technology—only superior military force can control unauthorized users of the printing press.

The two watersheds, then, are psychological as well as technological. They are personal as well as societal. Throughout this book, I use "optimism" and "pessimism" as a shorthand for these two related but distinct phenomena that happen when communication technologies are industrialized. The first is the societal shift that Ivan Illich describes: at first more people benefit from the technology; later, it causes more harm than it prevents. The second is related but more subjective: those who use and benefit from the technology tend to be optimistic; those who are used or oppressed by the technology become pessimistic. As a technology moves further past the second watershed, more and more people find themselves in the category of those used and abused rather than those benefiting from a technology.

The fact that Illich's two watersheds—a theory he developed to describe the effects of technological industrialization—describe these dysfunctional dynamics suggests that the root problem is not a particular textual technology in and of itself but our very human tendency to treat reading as a technique, a way to get something that we want. When scholars discuss the activity of reading, they often differentiate between different modes of reading: deep or shallow reading; or fiction, nonfiction, and poetry; or reading as entertainment, political deliberation, instruction, or religious devotion. Such taxonomies can be helpful, but they tend to obscure the more fundamental distinction between reading as a technique aimed to derive some individual benefit, or reading as a mode of participating in a community oriented toward understanding and practicing truth.

When we read in the mode of technique, we are using texts to get something that we want—perhaps personal pleasure or perhaps information that will enable us to accomplish a task. The only standard for reading in a technological mode is whether or not it is effective.[78] Jews and Christians, as People of the Book, have a long history of reflection upon the dangers that ensue when reading-as-technique becomes dominant, and these theological traditions of reflection can be fruitful in understanding political and cultural dynamics as well as religious ones. At root, reading-as-technique is an activity of what Saint Augustine terms the curious soul. Theologian Paul Griffiths summarizes the posture of this soul, explaining that what the curious soul wants "is new knowledge. . . . And what it seeks to do with that knowledge is control, dominate, or make a private possession of it."[79] Studious souls, on the other hand, do "not seek to sequester, own, possess, or dominate what they hope to know; they want, instead, to participate lovingly in it, to respond to it knowingly as gift rather than as potential possession, to treat it as an icon rather than as spectacle. A preliminary definition of studiousness, then, is: appetite for closer reflexive intimacy with the gift."[80] For the studious soul, reading is not a technique by which we will get something; it is an act of loving participation in the lives of others.[81] Studious readers do not look for new technologies to make words more effectively serve their individual interests. Instead, they aspire to convivial practices and arrangements, which Ivan Illich defines as "individual freedom realized in personal interdependence" enjoyed through "creative intercourse among persons, and the intercourse of persons with their environment."[82] These arrangements may involve any number of technologies and media, but they are characterized by virtuous, self-disciplined participants who seek to use words to sustain healthy relationships and communities. As Illich concludes, "convivial reconstruction" remains possible in a highly technological society; it depends not on "the regression to inefficient tools [but] on the degree to which society protects the power of individuals and of communities to choose their own styles of life through effective, small-scale renewal."[83]

I will return to these distinctions, but at this juncture the point is simply that bad reading is a human problem before it is a technological one. There is not an app you can download that will make you into a studious person who reads convivially. In fact, apps and other technological tools predispose us to approach texts in a curious, selfish manner. If we feel like the tools we use are expanding our control or power over others, we will be optimistic about textual technologies. If they prove inadequate—or if we find ourselves being dominated and controlled by others—we will be pessimistic. Technologically empowered curiosity leads to these dysfunctional cycles of optimism and pessimism. It leads to two con men spouting extravagant language to deceive each other. But, as we will see in the last third of this book, other ways of reading remain possible; no matter the technological situation, we can practice studious modes of reading that lead to conviviality, to reading and writing that aim to transform lives by bringing them into harmonious participation with truth.

Consciousness, Metaphors, and Practices

When powerful new verbal technologies come along, then, our only options are not either booster optimism or resigned pessimism. We have alternatives to seeing print—and now pixels—as either an iron Paul or a Colt's revolver. And some of the most helpful guides in charting a path toward genuinely convivial modes of reading are the literary authors who lived through the industrialization of print in nineteenth-century America. These authors experienced the power and peril of the steam-powered printing press, the telegraph, and mass media, and they sought to understand their effects through the most fundamental reality of language: metaphor.

It may seem strange to argue that new metaphors, and the heightened awareness they can bring to our encounters with textual technologies, are adequate responses to industrial-scale communication media. But even a scholar like Marshall McLuhan, who is often labeled a techno-determinist, argues that it is the *unconscious* use of media that gives them their total-izing power. He writes, "The point is . . . how do we become aware of the effects of alphabet or print or telegraph in shaping our behaviour? . . . Knowledge does not extend but restricts the areas of determinism. And the influence of unexamined assumptions derived from technology leads quite unnecessarily to maximal determinism in human life."[84] Thus, near the end of *The Gutenberg Galaxy*, McLuhan states, "The theme of this book is not that there is anything good or bad about print but that unconsciousness of the effect of *any* force is a disaster, especially a force that we have made ourselves."[85] This is why McLuhan insists that "there is absolutely no inevitability as long as there is a willingness to contem-plate what is happening"; our technologies do not doom us or save us, and we retain the freedom to use them wisely as long as we have the courage to examine them.[86]

Neil Postman takes a similar position, arguing near the end of *Amus-ing Ourselves to Death* that "no medium is excessively dangerous if its users understand what the dangers are. It is not important that those who ask the questions arrive at my answers or Marshall McLuhan's (quite dif-ferent answers, by the way). This is an instance in which the asking of the questions is sufficient. To ask is to break the spell."[87] Asking questions of our textual technologies begins to open a space for imagining alternative, more convivial forms of conversation. So although simply understanding how a given technology shapes our assumptions about truth and authority and community is, on its own, inadequate, such awareness is a vital first step. We're always going to be dependent on verbal technologies, but we need to recognize the ways such technologies warp and bend our percep-tions so that we are not locked into their predispositions.

Evocative metaphors may be the most potent way to raise our aware-ness of the hidden affordances and subtle nudges that are latent within dominant communication technologies. Postman gestures to this possibil-ity when he crucially revises McLuhan's famous adage, "the medium is the message." Postman tweaks this claim, arguing that "the forms of our media . . . are rather like metaphors, working by unobtrusive but powerful implication to enforce their special definitions of reality. Whether we are experiencing the world through the lens of speech or the printed word or the television camera, our media-metaphors classify the world for us, sequence it, frame it, enlarge it, reduce it, color it, argue a case for what the world is like."[88] Thus the media through which a culture conducts its conversations powerfully shape that culture's imaginary:

> Every medium of communication, I am claiming, has resonance, for resonance is metaphor writ large. . . . Because of the way it directs us to organize our minds and integrate our experience of the world, [any given medium] imposes itself on our consciousness and social institutions in myriad forms. It sometimes has the power to become implicated in our concepts of piety, or goodness, or beauty. And it is always implicated in the ways we define and regulate our ideas of truth.[89]

In other words, the textual technologies we use supply the metaphors we live by.

That phrase, "the metaphors we live by," is the title of a perceptive book by George Lakoff and Mark Johnson. They argue that a culture's metaphorical concepts undergird its conceptual system: "Our concepts structure what we perceive, how we get around in the world, and how we relate to other people. Our conceptual system thus plays a central role in defining our everyday realities."[90] Because our fundamental metaphors so powerfully structure our social imaginary, the only way to think beyond a given metaphor is to propose a new metaphor: "Metaphors are not merely things to be seen beyond. In fact, one can see beyond them only by using other metaphors."[91] Hence when literary authors tried to think outside the dominant metaphors imposed by words as printed text, they did so through other metaphors.[92]

Metaphors are a vital first step, but on their own, they are an inadequate response to steam-powered rotary presses or server farms. As Alan Jacobs rightly notes, "the point of any truly valuable critique of technology is not merely to understand our tools but to change them—and us."[93] Hence the space opened by questions and metaphors needs to be filled with practices and institutions that reinforce convivial metaphors. Lakoff and Johnson identify the reciprocal link between metaphors and rituals as the source of cultural formation: "The metaphors we live by, whether cultural or personal, are partially preserved in ritual. Cultural metaphors, and the values entailed by them, are propagated by ritual. Ritual forms an indispensable part of the experimental basis for our cultural metaphorical systems. There can be no culture without ritual."[94] Metaphors carry entailments; they orient us toward the world in ways that imply certain actions and obscure other possibilities. And as we enact metaphorical concepts through rituals, we also need to form the communities and institutions that can sustain those practices that make up a convivial culture.[95] In what follows, then, I lay out a suggestive array of metaphors from literary artists and consider the practices and rituals to which these metaphors may point.

Polyphonic Pilgrimage

It is hard to overstate the extent to which the metaphor of the "bookish text" formed and continues to form America's cultural understanding of the word. Some, like Postman, exalt the bookish text in contrast to the electronic media that have undermined its monopoly on our imagination of the word.[96] As Goodrich's narrative suggests, though, many antebellum writers recognized that the book is not a perfect technology. In brief—and this sketch will be fleshed out in the chapters that follow—the bookish text presents meaning as visual, spatially arranged content. Hence, as Lakoff and Johnson argue, it has historically contributed to an objective notion of meaning that relies on a "building-block" theory of a world composed of discrete objects. When printed in books, "words and sentences . . . can be readily looked upon as objects. . . . As objects, they have parts—they are made up of building blocks."[97] Walter Ong traces a complementary narrative, arguing that printed books changed the way readers imagined truth itself: "In lieu of merely telling the truth, books would now in common estimation 'contain' truth, like boxes."[98] Books appear to us as containers within which bits of meaning can be manipulated to grant solitary readers greater control over the world. With the right method of analysis, the bookish text will provide perspicuous, reliable, universal truth.[99]

Pixels, for all their transformative effects, in many ways simply extend the metaphor embodied in moveable type and printed books. From the alphabet to punctuation, to spaces between words, to moveable type, to pixels—each of these developments further atomizes language. Divided into ever smaller bits of content, language can be manipulated in ever more granular detail. Our digital culture continues to rely on technologies that imply meaning can be visually arranged, fixed in place, and then packaged, commodified, and sold. So although our digital age does introduce new challenges and opportunities, those of us who are living through these changes often overstate the newness of our situation.

In the following pages, I endeavor to listen to the metaphors and insights of nineteenth-century American authors to hear what wisdom they might have for those of us who inhabit a digital culture. While I like linear, perspicuous arguments—I am myself deeply formed by the bookish text—I would like to imagine this book not as a box that contains a set of truths but as a score that orchestrates different voices into a polyphonic harmony; not as a map that clearly lays out a single idea but as a pilgrimage that leads readers through a multifaceted, ecologically complex landscape.[100] My focus will remain on the industrial print culture, but to enrich this composition and highlight its relevance to digital concerns, I will introduce each chapter with a contemporary technology or phenomenon that parallels nineteenth-century dynamics. Each chapter will then draw on a particular literary metaphor to invite a reappraisal of the promise and peril inherent in our textual technologies.

To kick the pilgrimage off, I offer twenty-six theses about textual technologies, one thesis for each letter of the alphabet. These are not meant as summative declarations but as provocations to further thought and discussion. Following these theses, I have broken the rest of the book's pilgrimage into three stages, each of which considers a set of metaphors that antebellum authors deployed to answer three underlying questions: What does industrial print tempt optimistic readers to imagine themselves as? What does it lead its victims to fear they will become? And what alternative metaphors and practices might orient more convivial reading?

In the first two stages, we will see what happens as powerful new textual technologies amplify individual atomization—they increase negative freedom. They can liberate individuals from wolfish authorities, but the fracturing that results in turn empowers foxy predators. Despots, celebrities, and technocrats thrive, but the rest of us are rendered what Melville terms "loose fish," vulnerable individuals prone to become distracted consumers, commodities, or even slaves. In other words, the fracturing of meaning tends to exaggerate both optimism or pessimism; it leads individuals to imagine they are on the cusp of either utopia or dystopia.

In the final stage, I turn to practices that sustain hope—walking, conversing, befriending, and cross-bearing—to suggest that to wield textual technologies well, we need to develop cultural practices that strengthen our relationships and our commitment to a common good. We need to be tied more deeply to others and to our places in order to respond to the atomizing pressures of print and pixel. Instead of developing new technologies to solve the problems that technologies have caused, the authors I examine here propose that we develop better readers—readers who are more attuned to the power of the textual technologies they use and disciplined in the virtues necessary to imagine and practice healthy, convivial forms of discourse.[101] These metaphors of hope, then, are ways of reimagining texts, practices, and institutions so that they might contribute to more studious ways of reading and the formation of more convivial textual cultures. These authors obviously did not eschew industrialized print; they did not simply give up on the technologies of their day. Rather, they cultivated metaphors that might inspire us to beat swords—or Colt revolvers—into ploughshares or to "make do" on the margins of an increasingly technocratic world.[102]

As we have seen, such convivial cultures are oriented toward love, toward participating in the life and flourishing of others. And as Melville's references to the words of Saint Paul remind us, if our words—whether spoken, printed, or pixelated—lack charity, they are as "sounding brass" or "tinkling cymbal." Hence these practices of hope challenge us to wield words in ways that foster loving participation in the marvelous gift of life. They undermine the default plausibility structures of print or pixel and remind readers that meaning cannot be selfishly possessed, mastered, or controlled—as powerful textual technologies may tempt us to believe—but rather is a gift exchanged in community and cherished by studious readers. And in listening to the wisdom of these nineteenth-century literary authors, we may find prescient guidance for how screen-reading might also be subordinated to practices of love.

Twenty-Six Theses on
Textual Technologies

Presenting a set of theses for disputation is an old form, with Martin Luther's "Disputation on the Power and Efficacy of Indulgences" being the most famous instance.[1] As Luther's title reminds us, these theses were printed to set the stage for a verbal disputation (though it appears that Luther's ninety-five theses were never formally debated in Wittenberg). Similarly, the theses that follow are not summative declarations so much as provocations to thought and discussion. As Francis Bacon notes, aphorisms, because they represent "only portions and as it were fragments of knowledge, invite others to contribute and add something in their turn; whereas methodical delivery, carrying the show of a total, makes men careless, as if they were already at the end."[2] So if these raise questions or stir fierce disagreement, my hope is that readers will have a keener appetite for the pilgrimage that follows.

These theses are by no means original to me, but rather than including references here, I will more fully acknowledge my sources in the subsequent pages. To make it easier for interested readers to trace these connections, I will refer back to these theses throughout the book (e.g., see thesis 22). Given the primary role the alphabet plays in all subsequent textual technologies, I thought it fitting to include the same number of theses as there are letters in the modern English alphabet. Finally, in keeping with a digital disputatious technology, these aphorisms are all fewer than 280 characters, the limit on tweets after 2017. While arranging theses for a disputation is an old genre, it is also a contemporary one.

(1) Language is primarily a relational (rather than a representational) technology. Words articulate our relationships to God, other humans, our environment, and even ourselves.

(2) Because meaning arises from relationships, metaphor and analogy are at the heart of language.

(3) In the Christian tradition, Christ's role as mediator and reconciler between God and Creation flows from his identity as the Word. The Word mediates. This mediating Word is the one who declares himself the Truth.

(4) Beauty and truth and goodness name harmonious forms of relationships.

(5) Truth is ultimately dramatic or symphonic, not propositional.

(6) To know the truth is to be in tune with a complex, polyphonic reality. One might say that a "fact" is "true" if it helps us relate to the world in a more proper, harmonious, beautiful, healthy, or just manner.

(7) Harmony is experienced more fully in artistic or poetic forms rather than in rational exposition. Metaphor, poetry, and narrative invite readers to participate in a harmonic order rather than to map it analytically.

(8) The highest use of language is to serve friendship, and the kinds of conversations our textual technologies encourage will shape the kinds of friendship that are imaginable.

(9) Cultures develop the technologies they desire, and the technologies a culture uses shape its desires. One might call this recursive causation.

(10) Convivial technologies and practices cultivate friendships—they foster harmonious relationships among different members (including other humans, creatures, God, and the self).

(11) The history of textual technologies in the West—the alphabet, punctuation, spaces between words, moveable type, digital pixels—is a history of atomization.

(12) These textual technologies have caused words to migrate from an aural habitat to a visual one.

(13) These textual technologies have also led readers to imagine ideas as objects that are extended in space. Like type and pixels, ideas become bits (or bytes) that can be manipulated and rearranged to form new meanings.

(14) Print and pixels do have certain differences: Print renders ideas as solid—they feel graspable, reliable, fixed. Pixels render ideas as ephemeral—they appear from a distant cloud or web, and we surf them as they float away.

(15) Both, however, contribute to a spatial view of language and reality that leads us to imagine reason as a faculty for the perception and manipulation of objects. However, the highest mode of reason is an imaginative participation in reality.

(16) The atomization of language makes discrete bits of information appear increasingly interchangeable and manipulable.

(17) Powerful textual technologies can spread ideas widely, but insofar as they render meaning atomized and fungible, they threaten the intelligibility of truth and beauty and goodness.

(18) Atomization can free individuals from diseased bodies or communities, but the atomizing effects of print and pixel are like the toxins of chemotherapy—better than cancer, but not, in themselves, healthy.

(19) The recombinations that atomization makes imaginable fragment old syntheses and lead to new forms of meaning.

(20) The introduction of new textual technologies dissolves old communities and forms new ones (nations, denominations, political parties, factions, fandoms, interest groups).

(21) As textual technologies mature, they diversify and fragment conversations they sustained in their youth.

(22) The tension between the liberative power of atomization and meaning's dependence on relationships defines the paradoxes inherent in the disparate effects of textual technologies.

(23) There is always an analogy between our dominant way of imagining words and our dominant metaphors for the mind and the self.

(24) If words are imagined spatially, the human self becomes a bounded container with manipulable contents, and other selves appear to be objects, commodities, or avatars ("Its" rather than "Thous").

(25) The Enlightenment subject, the buffered self, is a creature of print. The postmodern subject, the anxious, lonely, identity-morphing self, is a creature of pixels.

(26) In an atomized world inhabited by commodified subjects, convivial friendship—loving, intimate participation in the life of other creatures, humans, and God—is deeply longed for, yet elusive.

I
Utopia

Or, What does industrial print tempt optimistic readers to imagine themselves as?

1
Transparent Eyeballs

Near the beginning of his 1836 manifesto, *Nature*, Ralph Waldo Emerson uses a startling metaphor to describe a sublime experience. On an evening walk, he feels himself caught up into the Universal Being and transformed into a transparent eyeball:

> Crossing a bare common, in snow puddles, at twilight, under a clouded sky, without having in my thoughts any occurrence of special good fortune, I have enjoyed a perfect exhilaration. . . . In the woods, we return to reason and faith. There I feel that nothing can befall me in life,—no disgrace, no calamity, (leaving me my eyes,) which nature cannot repair. Standing on the bare ground,—my head bathed by the blithe air, and uplifted into infinite space,—all mean egotism vanishes. I become a transparent eye-ball. I am nothing. I see all. The currents of the Universal Being circulate through me; I am part or particle of God. The name of the nearest friend sounds then foreign and accidental. To be brothers, to be acquaintances,—master or servant, is then a trifle and a disturbance.[1]

Louisa Thomas rightly calls this "one of the weirdest . . . passages in American literature."[2] Does Emerson really think of himself as a *transparent* eyeball, one with no body or history or tradition to inflect his gaze? Does he really believe that he can slough off all human relationships and become godlike, occupying a panoptic vantage?[3] This dense passage, with all of its strange details, reveals many of the key attributes of Emerson's fundamental interpretive posture.[4]

On one level, his visual metaphor has autobiographical roots. Eleven years earlier, Emerson feared he was losing his sight. He twice had surgery to puncture his cornea and relieve inflammation, and in the wake of these procedures, he had to stop reading and writing.[5] Although he eventually recovered, "an anxiety over blindness and an obsession with sight subsequently haunts Emerson's work," as Thomas rightly notes.[6]

FIGURE 1-1. "Standing on the bare ground, – my head bathed by the blithe air, & uplifted into infinite space, – all mean egotism vanished. I become a Transparent Eyeball." From Christopher Pearse Cranch (1813–1892), *Illustrations of the New Philosophy: Drawings* [ca.1837–1839] (MS Am 1506). Houghton Library, Harvard University, Cambridge, Mass.

On a deeper level, Emerson's sensation of being a transparent eyeball stems from his immersion in a particular kind of print culture, one that privileges the visual to the detriment of the body and its other senses, elevates the present at the expense of memory and tradition, and promises direct, unmediated access to truth. *Nature* begins with Emerson critiquing a "retrospective" stance and longing for "an original relation to the universe."[7] He goes on to claim that the poet or idealist who lives "a life in harmony with nature" will develop eyes to read and control its secrets: "By degrees we may come to know the primitive sense of the permanent objects of nature, so that the world shall be to us an open book, and every form significant of its hidden life and final cause. . . . That which was unconscious truth, becomes, when interpreted and defined in an object, a part of the domain of knowledge,—a new weapon in the magazine of power."[8] As his reference here to weaponry foreshadows, Emerson ends *Nature* with a sweeping vision of the power that can be wielded by those who answer his call and join him in becoming "part or particle of God."

Emerson's panoptic, visual posture is only plausible and imaginable because of industrial print and its affordances. Today a similar stance, one rooted in pixels rather than print, can be seen in the reliance on algorithms to interpret and shape reality. If printed texts allowed Emerson to imagine himself as a "transparent eye-ball" who scans and controls the "open book" of the world, digital technologies invite us to imagine an ideal reader algorithmically extracting meaning from "raw" data and controlling immense computing power with the swipe of a finger. Like Emerson's imagined viewer who discards his body, his traditions, and his relationships in order to gain a godlike vantage, algorithms promise to strip away all the noise in order to reveal the signal that lies hidden beneath the irrelevant particulars.

Algorithms hold out the promise of objective knowledge that sees through all the clutter that clouds individual perception. Algorithmic forms of knowledge are attractive because they appear to reveal the inner needs and desires of others. We turn to algorithms because we think they will enable us to peer inside other persons and make them perspicuous and malleable to our will. Hence corporations invest huge sums of money to develop algorithms that can predict and shape consumer behavior, tech companies train LLMs on vast data sets so they can generate text or images in response to any prompt, sports teams create analytics departments to build winning teams, politicians and governments rely on algorithms to better allocate public funds or to "nudge" citizens toward preferred choices.[9] All these purport to offer authoritative answers, free from limited human perspectives and subjective biases.

The reality, of course, is more complicated. Algorithmic meaning-making has been subject to criticisms that have also been leveled at Emerson's transparent eyeball: it neglects fraught histories; it minimizes the messy particulars of human bodies; it legitimates oppressive forms of power and control; it evades accountability.[10] To take just one example, when Arkansas switched its Medicaid needs assessment from a "human-based system" to an algorithmic one, many recipients found their allotments dramatically cut. They had little recourse and no explanation for the decision. When asked whether these algorithms were working properly, the man who designed them simply replied, "You're going to have to trust me that a bunch of smart people determined this is the smart way to do it."[11] Algorithms may amplify an individual or system's decision-making power, but they do not necessarily make it more discriminating or just. As Melville's Frank might put it, they involve, "along with the multiplication of the barrel, no consecration of the aim."

While Emerson's intuitive transcendentalism and the digital era's obsession with algorithmic power may seem vastly different, these interpretive postures are eerily similar. Both grow frustrated with the messy, fleshy complexity of analogue reality and reduce it—either to an apparition to see through or to a set of abstract data points; they claim such means will allow them to know other people better than people know themselves. Both hold that a detached and elevated perspective will yield perspicuous knowledge and magical control.[12] Both dismiss embodied, material mediation in their quest for an idealized, perfect truth.

In the remainder of this chapter, I focus on two facets of Emerson's interpretive stance: his rejection of various mediating relationships and the power he thinks this stance will grant him. Ironically, though not surprisingly, Emerson also found this posture eventually led to a profound loneliness. Readers should not mistake this chapter for a complete overview of Emerson's thought, which is famously complicated. As Emerson declares in "Self-Reliance," "A foolish consistency is the hobgoblin of little minds, adored by little statesmen and philosophers and divines. With consistency a great soul has simply nothing to do."[13] Instead of trying to summarize Emerson's thought, I am going to sketch the shape of his famous (or infamous) self-reliant posture and show how it derives from, and in turn legitimates, a particular kind of print culture. Emerson, to use Whitman's famous phrase, contains multitudes, and there is much in his writing that I find bracing and admirable, but I am focusing on a set of tendencies and metaphors in his thought that are, I think, troubling and that continue to shape our expectations for digital tools.

An Original Relation

Emerson's affirmation of a transparent, pure perceiving subject entails a set of significant rejections or refusals. He must slough off his body, his community and tradition, and his enmeshment in unchosen relationships. In sum, Emerson rejects various forms of mediation in hopes of attaining direct or "original" access to truth (see thesis 3). These tendencies were already apparent several years before the publication of *Nature*; they mark, for instance, his famous 1832 sermon on the Lord's Supper, in which he resigns his pulpit after explaining why he can no longer administer that sacrament. And in many respects, these rejections are only plausible because of the print culture that had so powerfully shaped Emerson's imagination.

Emerson certainly participated in vibrant oral cultures. He was a sought-after orator and a compelling public speaker. And his sermon on the Lord's Supper was of course first delivered orally to a church congregation. Robert Mark Smith, however, rightly claims that "a close examination of Emerson's texts reveals certain psychological, epistemological, and stylistic influences indicative of a profound influence of typographic literacy."[14] In particular, Emerson shared his culture's underlying confidence that printed texts could provide individual readers direct, unmediated access to truth.

When Alexander Campbell, one of the founders of the Restoration Movement, stated, "I have endeavored to read the Scriptures as though no one had read them before me," he voiced a hermeneutic impulse that was relatively common among his contemporaries. One might expect that a theological liberal like Emerson would have little in common with a biblicist like Campbell, but in fact they shared much in common: a common foe and a common hermeneutic. As Nathan Hatch explains, it was heterodox liberals who led the biblicist charge in eighteenth-century America: "To gain leverage against the entrenched Calvinism of the Great Awakening, theological liberals redoubled their appeal to depend on the Scriptures alone. . . . Charles Chauncy, pastor of Boston's First Church for sixty years (1727–1787), is the most prominent example of an exclusive appeal to Biblical authority in order to unravel theological orthodoxy. . . . Well into the nineteenth century, rationalistic Christians—many of them Unitarians and Universalists—argued against evangelical orthodoxy by appealing to the Bible."[15] Emerson's insistence on staking out an "original relation" to God and nature, one unencumbered by the accretions of theological or cultural reflection, shares in these American theological trends.

And these American trends are themselves part of broader tendencies within print culture more generally. Marshall McLuhan observes that "the new homogeneity of the printed page seemed to inspire a subliminal faith in the validity of the printed Bible as bypassing the traditional oral authority of the Church, on one hand, and the need for rational critical scholarship on the other. It was as if print, uniform and repeatable commodity that it was, had the power of creating a new hypnotic superstition of the book as independent of and uncontaminated by human agency."[16] In contrast to oral traditions (or even handwritten manuscripts and earlier, more artisanally printed books) mass-produced books present ideas in more objective, bloodless terms; ideas seem graspable apart from their human knowers.

To the extent that books offered "uncontaminated" access to truth, they also devalued cultural memory and led to a new emphasis on original ideas and innovative practices. In an oral culture, the collective past must be rehearsed and preserved through living memory, but a print culture can afford to celebrate innovative individuals because the past is safely stored in widely available books. As Walter Ong puts it, "By storing knowledge outside the mind, writing, and even more, print downgrade the figures of the wise old man and the wise old woman, repeaters of the past, in favor of younger discoverers of something new."[17] Elizabeth Eisenstein traces similar dynamics, concluding that "the preservation of the old . . . launched a tradition of the new."[18] In disregarding memory, tradition, and community as necessary mediators between himself and truth, Emerson shared the typographical biases and tendencies of many of his contemporaries.

What was unusual was Emerson's boldness in pushing these tendencies toward their logical conclusion. This radical streak is on full display in his 1832 sermon, in which he explains why he can no longer administer the Lord's Supper and is, therefore, resigning his position as minister. Emerson's rejection of this act of bodily, communal memory is predicated on a simple fact: the sacrament is "disagreeable to my own feelings." He elaborates on this feeling by stating simply that it is "repuls[ive]" to him, and he has no "sympathy" with the institution.[19] His opposition to the sacrament is rooted in an ingrained, fundamental dislike of embodied memory and mediation.

When Emerson endeavors to justify his visceral distaste for this ordinance, he does so by claiming to speak for an unspecified "we": "The use of the elements" is "foreign and unsuited to affect us. We are not accustomed to express our thoughts or emotions by symbolic actions." Emerson's "we" remains vague here; he defines it only by contrasting "our" emotions with the "Jewish prejudices" held by the writers of the New Testament.[20] He appears to imagine that he is speaking for his fellow countrymen, as he later makes the very American, Protestant claim that "freedom is the essence of Christianity."[21] It is the American affinity for freedom—at least as defined by Emerson—that results in a deep-seated antipathy to material mediation, to being joined to God through bread and wine.

In addition to declaring his freedom from this embodied act, Emerson also declares his freedom from the traditions of the "primitive Church." While Saint Paul's "mind had not escaped the prevalent error" of his culture, Emerson breezily claims, "I think we may see clearly enough" now why early Christians needed this primitive ceremony.[22] Hence he concludes, "I think [the supper] was good for [early Christians]. I think it is not suited to this day. . . . On every subject we have learned to think differently" from those early Christians who "were obstinately attached to their Jewish prejudices."[23] Such bodily acts may have been appropriate in past times, but they are not congenial to contemporary tastes. This attitude flows, as Ong and Eisenstein point out, from the presentist bias fostered by print and American print culture in particular.

In some respects, Emerson's insistence on freeing himself from the physical elements and ecclesiastic tradition is part of his effort to be free from any kind of mediation. He wants to be a transparent eyeball with direct access to the divine, and so he refuses anything that would mediate between the self and God or others. He acknowledges that the Bible calls Jesus the "Mediator," but he assures his auditors that "He is the Mediator in that only sense in which possibly any being can mediate between God and man, that is an Instructor of man. He teaches us how to become like God." Drawing on the Unitarian rejection of the Trinity, Emerson asserts that "the soul stands alone with God, and Jesus is no more present to the mind than your brother or your child."[24] In proclaiming his freedom from all mediation—even the mediation of the incarnate Christ, which is central to orthodox understandings of Christianity—Emerson foreshadows his desire in *Nature* to behold "God and nature face to face."

Yet despite Emerson's longing for a transparent self that can enjoy an immediate relationship with the divine, Buell points out the irony implicit in the form of *Nature*'s opening question: "Why should not we also enjoy an original relation to the universe?" Even in formulating his desire for an original relation, Emerson has recourse to the mode of relation he thinks "the foregoing generations" enjoyed. As Buell writes, "The position is illogical (how can a recapturing, a 'we also' mode of aspiration, be 'original'?)."[25] And indeed, while Emerson's rejection of the Lord's Supper was unusual, his motives for doing so were very much part of his broader cultural milieu: no matter how much he tried to escape the mediation of previous generations, the rituals of church tradition, or the particularities of his physical body, Emerson's perceptions and "sympath[ies]" remained profoundly shaped by his antebellum print culture.

Like many of his contemporaries, he thought books and texts could provide access to truth unmediated by messy and frustrating human institutions. And yet words themselves—like the elements in the Lord's Supper—are history-laden mediators of meaning and presence. Emerson responds to the frustrations of verbal mediation by seeking to transcend the signs and get at the elusive presence to which they point. In "The American Scholar," Emerson imagines an ideal book, one that perfectly "transmut[es] life into truth." Of course this ideal remains unrealizable: "As no air-pump can by any means make a perfect vacuum, so neither can any artist entirely exclude the conventional, the local, the perishable from his book, or write a book of pure thought, that shall be as efficient, in all respects, to a remote posterity, as to contemporaries, or rather to the second age." Thus it is that Emerson's lecture condemns "the book-learned class" who get their ideas from tainted books rather than actively pursuing original thought.[26] Impossible though it may prove to be, this book of pure thought remains Emerson's ideal.

In seeking to escape the frustrations of mediation, Emerson endangered the possibility of communication and communion. Words and traditions and bodies are fallible. They slip and falter. Yet they also enable the very thing that Emerson claims to desire: a meaningful relation with God and nature. In describing why most Christians did not adopt foot washing as a sacrament, even though Christ commanded that more explicitly than he did the keeping of the Supper, Emerson writes this is "because it was typical and all understand that humility is the thing signified."[27] Emerson endorses this practice of keeping the internal trait signified and dropping the material signifier. He thinks we can discard the bodily reality and keep only the spiritual meaning. This is how algorithmically sorted big data claims to work as well; it enables us to shuck off the noise and keep the signal.

But what if we discriminate wrongly? What if the body is the form of the soul? What if what we judge to be noise is, in fact, signal? What if that which is meaningful in relation is meaningless by itself?[28] On the traditional Christian account, for instance, the Lord's Supper is meaningless if it is merely bread and wine or merely a disembodied spiritual feeling. Its sacramental meaning lies in the incarnational union of body and spirit, signifier and signified. In a parallel vein, many critics have noted the shortcomings of an epistemic posture that ignores one's tradition, body, and community: Hans-Georg Gadamer insists we cannot know outside of a tradition, Michael Polyani defends the importance of our bodies in forming knowledge, and Raymond John Pierotti shows how we always make meaning as members of ecological communities.[29] Overlooking these inescapable dimensions of knowledge has serious consequences: all too often visualist epistemologies akin to Emerson's transparent eyeball undergird oppressive modes of surveillance and control.

A Tyrannous Eye

In his sermon on the Lord's Supper, Emerson casually remarks that "I think we may see clearly enough how" Saint Paul could have been confused about the imminent second coming of Christ. He goes on to explain his own purportedly clear-eyed understanding of the spiritual reality this myth obscured. Emerson's metaphor for the superiority of his modern understanding—"we may see clearly" where earlier generations were blinded by cultural biases—is so common and clichéd that it almost does not register as a metaphor. For while sight has long been a common analogue for knowledge, print makes this sense particularly dominant (see thesis 12). And for Emerson (and many others), this visualist understanding of knowledge leads him to imagine reason as a faculty of manipulation and control (see thesis 15). When Emerson imagines himself as a "transparent eye-ball," he feels himself to be "part or particle of God." Quite simply, he imagines himself as a panoptic deity.

While analyses of print culture often focus on what Walter Ong calls "external" effects—"printing 'spread ideas,' made the text of the Bible 'available,' put the Bible 'into the hands of the people,' or 'encouraged more people to read'"—its more imperceptible effects are also far-reaching. As Ong argues, "the interior change in psychological structures tied in with the shift of the word from a written to a printed culture is at least as important as the physical spread of inscribed texts, for changes in sociological structures are the interior coefficients of developments in exterior history."[30] In the second decade of the twenty-first century, Nicholas Carr and others drew on developments in neuroscience to show how our interactions with screens actually alter our brains.[31] Ong's point is much the same, and Emerson's reliance on sight as a master metaphor for knowing is an instance of the deep psychological effects that print culture can have.

Emerson deploys this visual metaphor in striking and sometimes disturbing ways. In "The Poet," he outlines a way for poets (who are also the protagonists in *Nature*) to not merely see but to see *through* the physical world and so exercise a profound and fundamental power: "As the eyes of Lyncaeus were said to see through the earth, so the poet turns the world to glass, and shows us all things in their right series and procession."[32] By turning the world to glass, the poet's x-ray vision penetrates to the true nature of things. It sees beneath mere appearance to discern reality's inner nature. In many respects, the power Emerson describes is akin to the power that algorithms promise—they will reveal underlying patterns and meaning that are opaque to superficial observation. Emerson admits, however, that his ideal poet does not exist, at least not yet: "We have yet had no genius in America, with tyrannous eye, which knew the value of our incomparable materials, and saw, in the barbarism and material-ism of the times, another carnival of the same gods whose picture he so much admires in Homer; then in the middle age; then in Calvinism."[33] The poet's eye is tyrannous because it imposes meaning on a world—in this case nineteenth-century American life—that seems to weaker eyes to be banal and insignificant.

In *Nature*, Emerson figures this tyrannous eye in terms derived from print technology, declaring that "the eye is the best composer."[34] A com-poser or compositor is, of course, the person who arranges type for print-ing. Emerson suggests that the eye can manipulate and organize bits of reality in order to create the meaning it desires. This is a deeply subjective view of meaning; drawing on another print analogy, Emerson writes that mere "sensual man conforms thoughts to things; the poet conforms things to his thoughts. The [sensual man] esteems nature as rooted and fast; the [poet], as fluid, and impresses his being thereon. To him, the refractory world is ductile and flexible."[35] For the poet with his transforming vision, nature has become a blank page upon which the self *impresses* its words, a figure also drawn from the printing press. When Emerson promises that, to this poet, "the world shall be . . . an open book," he does not mean that the poet will learn to read and understand the given meaning of the world. Rather, the world will become a blank page upon which he can impress or imprint his own meaning; hence Emerson claims this understanding of language is "a new weapon in the magazine of power."[36] This claim seems to echo Francis Bacon's famous declaration that "the art of printing, gun-powder and the nautical compass, have changed the face and condition of things all over the globe."[37] Understood in this fashion, printing's power is akin to the coercive and explosive power of gunpowder.

Such a claim may seem overblown, but Emerson is right that the power to create meaning is the root of power over other creatures. Emerson takes pains to show how the idealist poet can impose his will on the material world: "Nature is thoroughly mediate. It is made to serve. It receives the dominion of man as meekly as the ass on which the Saviour rode . . . More and more, with every thought, does [man's] kingdom stretch over things, until the world becomes, at last, only a realized will,—the double of man."[38] For this poet, nature does not mediate between the self and others; it mediates between his will and its instantiation. Emerson's transparent eyeball, like modern algorithms, ultimately enables the poet to exercise panoptic control.

This posture leads to Emerson's famous (or infamous) conclusion in *Nature* that those who embrace his idealism will wield a magical power:

> A correspondent revolution in things will attend the influx of the spirit. So fast will disagreeable appearances, swine, spiders, snakes, pests, madhouses, prisons, enemies, vanish; they are temporary and shall be no more seen. The sordor and filths of nature, the sun shall dry up, and the wind exhale. . . . [T]he advancing spirit . . . shall draw beautiful faces, warm hearts, wise discourse, and heroic acts, around its way, until evil is no more seen. The kingdom of man over nature, which cometh not with observation,—a dominion such as now is beyond his dream of God,—he shall enter without more wonder than the blind man feels who is gradually restored to perfect sight.[39]

Instead of a merely mechanical power over Nature, Emerson promises a spiritual power. It may seem strange to modern readers to link poetry with spiritualist magic, but these arts have long been intertwined. Abracadabra seems to be derived from a Latin word for alphabet, and glamor, with its original meaning of enchantment or spell, derives from grammar.[40] The poet who masters the alphabet and language masters meaning itself. In *Nature*, Emerson references Shakespeare's *Tempest* as an example of these connections, and he also cites Christ's miracles, the "miracles of enthusiasm" practiced by Swedenborg and others, and "animal Magnetism" as instances of the kind of power he thinks the idealist can attain.[41]

While most people today would eschew the mesmeric practices that were popular in the nineteenth century, we experience a similar whiff of the uncanny at the hands of algorithmic technologies.[42] How does Netflix know you might want to watch that film? How does Amazon know you were thinking about buying a garden rake? How does Target know you are pregnant and might want baby clothes?[43] LLMs such as ChatGPT can be even more eerie: Cal Newport notes that it is easy to be "caught off guard by a moment of uncanny humanity, or left awestruck by the sophistication of a response."[44] Whether it is a computer that seems to intelligently converse with you, or companies trying to sell you products you actually want, or paternalistic corporations or governments trying to "nudge" you to behave in a certain way, algorithms make it seem that computers know us better than we know ourselves, and they empower others to steer our choices, often in ways we are not fully conscious of.[45] Algorithmic programmers—like the grammarian mage of an earlier era or Emerson's transcendental poet—wield uncanny power to create their version of reality. And such modes of perception and relation are of course dangerous. They encourage us to see Thous as Its and to treat persons as avatars whose actions we can predict and manipulate (see thesis 24).[46] So even though there is a vast difference between the way Emerson imagines a poet bringing about a "revolution in things" and the means by which digital algorithms empower their users, my aim is to delineate the surprisingly similar assumptions that lie behind these endeavors.

Several critics have warned about this insidious side to Emerson's epistemic posture, noting that it can lead to oppression and—in his own words—tyranny. Allen Tate calls him the unwitting "prophet of a piratical industrialism."[47] Lawrence Buell, more demurely, admits that Emerson's "essays do in fact sometimes treat feats of entrepreneurial rapacity or imperial conquest with a certain gusto," though he concludes that "the inner logic of Emerson's thinking is more complicated than such sweeping generalizations sound."[48] Christina Bieber Lake likewise recognizes the ambivalence inherent in Emerson's posture. She praises the social reforms that his idealism helped motivate, but she worries that "contemporary biotechnological advances make Emerson's 'revolution in things' more literally possible than ever."[49] While she focuses her warnings on biotechnologies and the lure of the posthuman, big data and its accompanying algorithms are also realizing Emerson's longed-for revolution. Yet a revolution based on the imprinting self, the realized will, always carries the risk of blotting out those who might frustrate our desires. As Bieber Lake asks of the Emersonian, "If I value my personal freedom highest, what happens to my neighbor?"[50]

Emerson himself, in *Nature*, seems willing to sacrifice his neighbors and friends in order to realize his rarefied vision. When he feels himself to be a transparent eyeball, he writes that "the name of the nearest friend sounds then foreign and accidental. To be brothers, to be acquaintances,— master or servant, is then a trifle and a disturbance."[51] And yet less than ten years later, in the aftermath of his young son's death, Emerson admits that his earlier aspiration to be a transparent, all-seeing self may not be possible or desirable:

> It is very unhappy, but too late to be helped, the discovery we have made that we exist. That discovery is called the Fall of Man. Ever afterwards we suspect our instruments. We have learned that we do not see directly, but mediately, and that we have no means of correcting these colored and distorting lenses which we are, or of computing the amount of their errors. Perhaps these subject-lenses have a creative power; perhaps there are no objects.[52]

These lenses shut "us in a prison of glass which we cannot see."[53] Experience has taught Emerson that the original, unmediated vision he aspired to will always remain out of reach. And grasping for this vision has cut him off from the very relationships that might otherwise have sustained him. Striving for autonomy has led to the experience of alienation (see thesis 26). As he concludes, "I know better than to claim any completeness for my picture. I am a fragment, and this is a fragment of me."[54] The self as fragment—alienated, lonely, orphaned—is the dark side of Emerson's Idealistic vision of the panoptic, tyrannical self. In striving to become "part or particle of God," the composing eye has become instead a broken bit of type, a solitary letter abstracted from any context in which it might find meaning.

2

Men of Adamant

In 1937, the year after Emerson published *Nature*, Nathaniel Hawthorne published a brief "apologue" or moral fable titled "The Man of Adamant." The interpretive posture of Richard Digby, the protagonist of this story, shares certain affinities with that of Emerson's transparent eyeball. Digby in fact enacts Emerson's fantasy—he cuts off "communion" with everyone and "shake[s] off the dust of his feet" as he leaves his village. Taking his axe, sword, gun, and Bible, he journeys through the wilderness to impose his egotistical vision on a blank landscape. Hawthorne's description of Digby's mode of travel makes his solipsism clear:

> He talked to himself, as he strode onward; he read his Bible to himself, as he sat beneath the trees; and, as the gloom of the forest hid the blessed sky, I had almost added, that, at morning, noon, and eventide, he prayed to himself. So congenial was this mode of life to his disposition, that he often laughed to himself, but was displeased when an echo tossed him back the long, loud roar.[1]

After traveling for three days, Digby finds a cave, a "tomb-like den," and decides to stay there: "Here my soul will be at peace; for the wicked will not find me. Here I can read the Scriptures, and be no more provoked with lying interpretations. Here I can offer up acceptable prayers, because my voice will not be mingled with the sinful supplications of the multitude. Of a truth, the only way to Heaven leadeth through the entrance of this cave—and I alone have found it!"[2] Digby has found a place where no other voice will disturb his own reading of the Bible. His rendering can be perfectly univocal here, and the Bible's meaning will be perspicuous and certain.

What could possibly go wrong? Plenty, of course, as Hawthorne intends his readers to recognize. Digby's optimism never wavers, but Hawthorne undermines his triumphalism throughout the story. The clarity and certainty he attains come at the cost of both truth and any human community. As the narrator's comment about praying to himself implies, it may even come at the cost of a relationship with God. In case readers miss these hints, Hawthorne's conclusion makes the dangers of this interpretive posture obvious: Digby dies abruptly and the minerals in the cave turn his corpse into a stone statue. He becomes a literal man of adamant.

A generation earlier, Thomas Jefferson adopted Digby's hermeneutic posture in his own approach to the Bible, although he escaped the allegorical demise that Digby suffered. Jefferson famously cut sections out of six different printed Bibles—in Greek, Latin, French, and English—and then arranged and pasted them onto pages that he had bound into a book. He titled his volume *The Life and Morals of Jesus of Nazareth*, and it represented his preferred version of Jesus' teachings.[3] He used this book for nightly devotional reading, which he intended to support his religious and moral edification. Yet the voice that emerges from Jefferson's Bible is, as one would expect, Jefferson's own voice; this book is the material product of his conviction "that each individual's belief was a matter of concern only for the individual and for God." As he himself declared, "I am of a sect by myself."[4] Albert Schweitzer aptly remarks about this genre, of which Jefferson's book is just one example, "There is no historical task which so reveals a man's true self as the writing of a Life of Jesus," for "each individual create[s] Him in accordance with his own character."[5] This genre, and particularly Jefferson's idiosyncratic contribution to it, is only imaginable in an era of print; a sacred, communal narrative has become an individual commodity tailored to an audience of one.

While Jefferson's particular project was unique, his impulse was not. It is reflected as well in the 1807 Bible whose audience is made explicit in its title, *Parts of the Holy Bible, selected for the use of the Negro Slaves, in the British West-India Islands*. This Bible was greatly truncated, with "about 90 percent of the Old Testament" and half of the New Testament excluded.[6] During the early nineteenth century, even when the biblical text was reproduced in whole, it was increasingly marketed as a consumer product, one tailored to different denominations, tastes, and classes. The result is that the Bible came to be seen as a commodity rather than a holy, unifying, divine word. Paul Gutjahr summarizes the effect of the proliferation of editions in the mid-nineteenth century:

> Episcopal Bishop Arthur Cleveland Coxe led a crusade against the diversification of bible editions before the Civil War arguing, among other things, that different editions of the Bible would erode faith in the

Bible's sacred and unchanging nature. . . . Fulfilling Coxe's worst fears, the image—accurate or not—that the Bible was a cohesive, unchanging text began to disintegrate in the minds of Americans as nearly 2,000 editions of the English Bible poured into the American marketplace. These different editions, with their varying translations, illustrations, commentaries, formats, and bindings contributed to a notion that the Bible—far from being an unmediated, unchanging text produced by the hand of God—was a human production, open to the failings inherent in any work wrought by human hands.[7]

Hence even when readers did not go to the extremes Jefferson did, their experiences of the Bible became more individualized.

Today, publishers have perfected the ability to rearrange and represent the Bible to accommodate individual preferences. As befits our therapeutic and consumerist age, Amazon has over fifty thousand products listed in its "Christian Bibles" category. You might be drawn to the *Busy Dad's Bible: Daily Inspiration Even If You Only Have One Minute* or to the *Duck Commander Faith and Family Bible*, containing "stories and testimonials" from the stars of the Duck Dynasty television show. If you want a politically flavored version, you could try the *1599 Geneva Bible: Patriot's Edition*, which adds texts such as the Mayflower Compact and the United States Constitution, or you could get *The Green Bible*, which helpfully highlights environmental passages and includes "inspirational essays."[8] If you are looking for a Bible app, you have even more options, and many such apps offer customized reading plans tailored to your interests or Enneagram type. Each individual can have his or her personalized Bible to scroll and tap and skim.

This proliferation of editions is the natural culmination of the commodification of the Bible that began in earnest with the advent of industrialized printing technologies in antebellum America. David Jeffrey rightly observes that these "niche editions seem . . . to be packaged in such a way as to justify, in some measure, current fashions and practices of the sub-groups to which they are directed."[9] Such niche Bibles transform a strange and unsettling book into a therapeutic consumable: the Bible becomes another fashion accessory, an indicator of the social club to which I belong, just one more object I purchase to shape and express my individual identity. This perception of the Bible as a private text that individual readers should handle and read and interpret on their own is the logical outworking of mass print and digital technologies and of a consumer capitalism that stokes individual appetites (see thesis 9).[10]

To be fair to Digby and his real-life counterparts, a printed Bible that an individual can own and read by himself was a welcome antidote to a serious problem: the cacophony of competing religious authorities. Interpretive disagreements, particularly those centered on the Bible, caused great emotional, intellectual, and civic upheaval in antebellum America. Even as the spread of cheap printed books and pamphlets inflamed these conflicts, printed books continued to be seen as a solution to them. Many, like Digby, doubled down on the authority of individual interpreters as the solution to interpretative disagreements. When the noise of competing voices grew too confusing and chaotic, these men of adamant shook the dust off their feet, retreated with their Bibles, and insisted ever more firmly on their own rendering of the text. They remained unable to imagine a harmonious polyphony, and so they gave up on—or actively suppressed—interpretive conversation. Instead of cultivating practices oriented to the relational telos of language, they clung to print as a truth-bearing commodity.

Transforming the Bible into a Portable—and Divisive—Commodity

In his provocative and often incisive book *The Gutenberg Galaxy: The Making of Typographic Man*, Marshall McLuhan claims that "print is the technology of individualism."[11] As print spread, the ideal reader shifted from an educated person reading aloud for the benefit of a broader audience to a solitary reader silently scanning the text for his or her own benefit (see thesis 11).[12] The result, as Walter Ong explains, is that reading contributed to the erosion of community: "Reading itself fosters divisiveness to the extent that it isolates the individual from communal structures. . . . When it became silent reading, as it appears to have become by the time of print more commonly than it earlier was, it forced the individual into himself and out of the tribe."[13] These silent, individual readers found themselves confronted with stark evidence of their disagreements with other members of their communities. Instead of hearing texts read aloud or learning in conversation with teachers, they now had access to black-and-white statements from across vast stretches of time and space. Contradictions that previously could be avoided now had to be confronted. As McLuhan notes, "print presents arrested moments of mental posture." As a result, print "translated the dialogue of shared discourse into packaged information, a portable commodity."[14] This gradual shift away from reading as an aid to embodied dialogue and toward reading as a commodity chosen and enjoyed by the individual had far-reaching consequences.

One of these was the intensification of theological differences. In charting the course of religious conflicts in early modern Europe, Elizabeth Eisenstein points out the ironic role that print played in exacerbating preexisting disagreements: "Heralded on all sides as a 'peaceful art,' Gutenberg's invention probably contributed more to destroying Christian concord and inflaming religious warfare than any of the so-called arts of war ever did. . . . As a heritage that was transmitted by texts and that involved the 'spreading of glad tidings,' Christianity was peculiarly vulnerable to the revolutionary effects of typography."[15] In particular, Eisenstein describes how the spread of print heightened latent tensions and contradictions in Christian thought: "Doctrines that could co-exist more or less peacefully because full implementation was lacking, thus came into sharp conflict after printers had set to work. With typographical fixity, moreover, positions once taken were more difficult to reverse."[16] She cites Eugene Rice on this point, who observes, "The medieval Church was more ecumenical, more genially encompassing, more permissive doctrinally than the . . . sixteenth century . . . churches . . . . All the bits and pieces that were to make up the sixteenth-century theologies of Protestantism and Catholicism were in solution in medieval thought. What so dramatically happened during the age of Reformation is that they crystallized into two distinct and opposed systems, each more exclusive, more consistent, and more rigid than the medieval tradition from which they both derived."[17] Ong notes similarly that Protestant modes of reading inevitably led to doctrinal divisions: "The Protestant stress on the primacy of the written word of the Scriptures—*sola scriptura*—reflects quite patently the growing confidence in the word-in-space, whatever its foundations in the Christian tradition itself. . . . Protestant defenders of the practice have [not] commonly been aware of how far reading itself fosters divisiveness to the extent that it isolates the individual from communal structures."[18] Print's ability to order and systematize information contributed to this hardening and fragmentation; people came to see contrasting claims in stark relief, and then they had to choose between them. When words are heard within an auditory sensorium, their differences can be harmonized more easily: different notes or contrasting voices can be heard simultaneously. When words exist within a primarily visual space, however, they appear one at a time, as discrete phenomena that must be seen and understood sequentially (see thesis 12).

Not just words, but persons also came to be understood in increasingly visual terms, and the differences between individuals likewise became more pronounced. I discussed this briefly in relation to Emerson's obsession with sight, but Ong develops a multifaceted narrative of how shifts in communications technologies contributed to a shift from an aural understanding of persons to a predominately visual one. On Ong's account, the auditory self is more porous and communal, vulnerable to other voices; the visual self is more buffered and individuated (see thesis 25).[19] Whereas "acoustic space is in a way a vast interior in the center of which the listener finds himself together with his interlocutors," visual space is silent, and the viewer retains control over where he looks.[20] These shifts contributed to a reconfiguration of social relations: "Because it consists of silent words, writing introduces . . . communication which lacks the normal social aspect of communication, encounter with one who is not present, participation in the thought of others without commitment or involvement."[21] With writing and, even more so, print, ideas are taken out of their social context and made available to individual readers.

Hence a third consequence was a shift in the way readers understood truth itself (see thesis 5). Ong traces the way in which Ramist logic combined with the spread of print to make knowledge appear more spatial and visual, attributes which make truth seem discrete, manipulable, and controllable.[22] Following these developments, "an epistemology based on the notion of truth as 'content' begins to appear. Out of the twin notions of content and analysis is bred the vast idea-, system-, and method-literature of the seventeenth and eighteenth centuries. [These] conceived of . . . box-like units laid hold of by the mind in such a way that they are fully and adequately treated by being 'opened' in an analysis."[23] As Chad Wellmon aptly summarizes, "the technology of print made knowledge manageable, accessible, and available."[24] Ong and Wellmon both emphasize that print technology led people to imagine truth as graspable content—in other words, as a portable commodity.

These developments climaxed in antebellum America due to the technological and cultural conditions I narrated in the introduction. American Protestants in the early national period took the Reformation credo of *sola Scriptura* more seriously than its European adherents ever did. As Mark Noll explains in describing the shift from the religion of the revolutionary period to that of the antebellum era, "divine revelation was equated more simply with the Bible alone than with Scripture embedded in a self-conscious ecclesiastical tradition. . . . Theological method came to rely less on instinctive deference to inherited confessions and more on self-evident propositions organized by scientific method."[25] Whereas the original European Reformers such as Luther and Calvin maintained the need for ecclesiastically sanctioned biblical interpretation, by the late eighteenth century many Americans embraced a more democratic view of interpretation, claiming any individual could examine the scriptures and determine their meaning.[26]

One example of the confidence theologians had in the ability of individuals to read the Bible and inductively determine its clear meaning can be found in the works of Charles Hodge, who became the principal of Princeton Theological Seminary in 1851. In the introduction to his *Systematic Theology*, Hodge declares, "The Bible is to the theologian what nature is to the man of science. It is his store-house of facts; and his method of ascertaining what the Bible teaches, is the same as that which the natural philosopher adopts to ascertain what nature teaches."[27] Hodge's view of the Bible as a "store-house" parallels Ong's observation that print encourages readers to imagine knowledge in spatial metaphors and then to access and manipulate it via proper analysis. Later, Hodge asserts under the heading "Perspicuity of the Scriptures. The Right of Private Judgment" that the "Bible is a plain book. It is intelligible by the people. And they have the right, and are bound to read and interpret it for themselves; so that their faith may rest on the testimony of the Scriptures, and not on that of the Church."[28] Hodge recognizes the dangers of such a position: "If every man is at liberty to exalt his own intuitions, as men are accustomed to call their strong convictions, we should have as many theologies in the world as there are thinkers." Yet he quickly asserts this will not be a problem because the Bible is so obviously perspicuous: "What is self-evidently true, must be proved to be so, and is always recognized in the Bible as true."[29] The passive construction of this sentence indicates the flaw in Hodge's logic; his sentence leaves out the subject, the interpreter who must do this "recognizing." The ability of different interpreting subjects to "recognize" vastly different truths in the Bible led to the welter of competing sects and denominations in early nineteenth-century America.

When Hawthorne wrote "The Man of Adamant," these political and religious divisions were becoming unignorable. By threatening the confidence readers had in printed texts, these divisions led many authors in the antebellum period to question the authority and perspicuity of print. In the religious sphere, the Second Great Awakening contributed to the proliferation of Christian sects.[30] As Brian Yothers observes, "an often-overlooked source of the epistemological uncertainties that pervade the gothic works of Poe, Hawthorne, and Melville is the frequently chaotic religious pluralism of nineteenth-century America. Nineteenth-century Americans faced a bewildering variety of religious options that offered widely disparate ontological, ethical, and epistemological bases for understanding their world."[31] For many people, the increasingly shrill political and religious disagreements made it impossible to believe in the perspicuity of texts, printed or otherwise.

And yet some, like Hodge, held on to this conviction. In the face of the chaotic proliferation of viewpoints, readers were tempted to choose meanings that suited their private interests and then simply ignore competing interpretations. Digby's efforts to withdraw from society and establish a perfectly univocal religious authority—himself—stand as a prime example of this approach. One Baptist preacher in the late eighteenth century resolved "theological perplexity" with a similar method: "locking the door and coming to grips with Scripture for himself."[32] Such an approach led some outside the bounds of orthodox Christianity altogether, as was the case with Jefferson. In *The Age of Reason* Thomas Paine confesses, "I do not believe in the creed professed by the Jewish Church, by the Roman Church, by the Greek Church, by the Turkish Church, by the Protestant Church, nor by any church that I know of. My mind is my own church."[33] Paine's blunt declaration is the outworking of the dynamic that George Marsden explores in his aptly titled essay "Everyone One's Own Interpreter?" The actual result of making the Bible the highest authority was to give its interpreter the last word: "In antebellum Protestant America there was no higher court of appeal [than the Bible]. Two judges, however, sat in this court and the one never spoke without the other. The authoritative pronouncements of the ancient Scriptures always needed to be understood by the modern interpreter."[34]

Mass-produced texts put reliable, identical versions of a set of words in front of any reader who held a copy of the Bible. This material reality—one paralleled in today's digital texts—encourages hermeneutic confidence: because the words are frictionlessly present, readers tend to think their meaning is also frictionlessly transparent. A belief in a perspicuous text leads readers to undervalue or even reject mediating institutions, and when interpretive disagreements persist, this belief can even lead to violence as the only remaining means of adjudication. One American theologian asked the obvious question in the 1840s: "'If the Bible be at once so clear and full as a formulary of Christian doctrine and practice, how does it come to pass that where men are left most free to use it in this way . . . they are flung asunder so perpetually . . . instead of being brought together?'"[35] The most egregious example of such division is the war that resulted, in part, over disagreements about whether or not the Bible condoned slavery. Ultimately, as Noll points out, the Civil War revealed the unsustainable nature of each individual insisting on his private interpretation of the Bible: "The obvious crisis that bore directly on the fate of the nation was that 'simple' readings of the Bible yielded violently incommensurate understandings of Scripture, with no means, short of warfare, to adjudicate the differences."[36]

What Hast Thou to Do with My Bible?

Hawthorne's story displays keen insight into these paradoxical and troubling dynamics. He represents Digby's Bible as a tool to gain and secure individual power and as a replacement for mediating institutions. And because Digby uses his Bible in this fashion, he cuts himself off from the possibility of redemptive community and hardens his sectarian, partisan commitments. To put it in the terms of Hawthorne's metaphor, he becomes a lifeless man of stone.

The details Hawthorne provides about the objects that Digby brings with him into the wilderness portray his Bible as a tool or weapon of control. Hawthorne's story is obviously not realistic—there is no mention of how Digby plans to grow food or secure other necessities—so the practical details he does include convey heavy symbolic import. In addition to the Bible that he reads to himself, Digby carries only three other objects: "an axe, to hew space enough for a tabernacle in the wilderness, and some few other necessaries, especially a sword and a gun, to smite and slay any intruder upon his hallowed seclusion."[37] In the company of these three implements, Digby's Bible appears as a tool to build his own church and a weapon to defend this church from any who might pollute it. Figuring the Bible as a tool or weapon may seem odd—it's just a book!—but Stephen Greenblatt argues that Protestant reformers came to see their printed Bibles in precisely this manner: "The printed English New Testament is, above all, *a form of power*. It is invested with the ability to control, guide, discipline, console, exalt, and punish that the church had arrogated to itself for centuries."[38] In seeking to wield the power of this book on his own behalf, Digby becomes a paradigmatic example of a curious reader, one who, as Griffiths puts it, seeks to "control, dominate, or make a private possession of" knowledge.[39] Unlike a studious reader, Digby does not use his Bible to deepen his relationships with God or fellow humans but to ward off anyone who might impinge on his own knowledge.

Although Digby plans to build a tabernacle, then, he does not plan to found or participate in some institution. His journey is an explicit repudiation of human institutions. In the introduction to this chapter, I quoted the passage where Hawthorne describes Digby talking to himself, reading to himself, and perhaps even praying to himself. After he finds his "congenial" cave, he spends his days enjoying its peaceful solitude and reading his Bible without any "lying interpretations" to disturb him. One evening, he deigns to read "the Bible aloud, because no other ear could profit by it," yet as he does so, he reads "it amiss, because the rays of the setting sun did not penetrate the dismal depth of shadow roundabout him, nor fall upon the sacred page."[40] The irony, which Hawthorne certainly intends readers to recognize, is that Digby mistakes the literal words of the Bible because he insists on reading it in his private cave. In a reversal of Plato's Allegory of the Cave, Digby turns away from those whom he believes are in error only to plunge further into his own darkness.

And yet at this moment, a strange light shines on his page, and he looks up to find Mary Goffe, a young woman whom his preaching in England had converted. She looks at him with an expression that "might beam from an angel's eyes" and greets him. Digby, however, rebuffs her, "keeping his finger between the leaves of his half closed Bible." Goffe offers him medicine to cure the "grievous distemper" that afflicts his heart, and she pleads with him to return to a life-giving community: "Come back to thy fellow-men; for they need thee, Richard, and thou hast tenfold need of them."[41] It is significant that Goffe tells Digby his fellow-men need him. To most readers, Digby's need of others is painfully apparent: he needs his misreadings corrected by a friend, and he needs to hear the Bible's gracious and merciful words along with its words of judgment. But when Digby withdraws from his village, the other inhabitants are also deprived of his presence and his insight, flawed though they may be.

Digby, however, refuses Goffe's offer and returns to his private reading. Yet the shadows have deepened, and he now makes "continual mistakes in what he read[s], converting all that was gracious and merciful, to denunciations of vengeance and unutterable woe, on every created being but himself." Goffe brings him a drink of water, one perfumed with her tears, and pleads with him to take the drink from her hand and let her read with him: "Make room for me by thy side, and let us read together one page of that blessed volume—and, lastly, kneel down with me and pray!

Do this; and thy stony heart shall become softer than a babe's, and all be well." Digby is so offended at her request that he "cast[s] the Bible at his feet" before declaiming, "Tempt me no more, accursed woman . . . Lest I smite thee down also! What hast thou to do with my Bible?—what with my prayers?—what with my heaven?"[42] It is at this moment that Digby's heart stops and the form of Goffe melts away (she has been dead several months, and is apparently an apparition offering him one final chance at redemption).

Hawthorne's apologue demonstrates the way in which everyone suffers when some individuals withdraw from the messy work of institutional life to set themselves up as solitary, adamantine authorities. Healthy institutions—whether ecclesiastical or civic, scientific or educational—find ways to orchestrate competing voices into a harmonious whole. When institutions weaken and fail to do this, the temptation is for powerful individuals to squelch the voices they do not like and insist on their own interpretation to the exclusion of the interpretation of others. And Digby's final gesture, in which he throws his Bible upon the ground, testifies to the accuracy of Marsden's assessment: the modern interpreter who insists on the perspicuity of the Bible is in fact setting himself up as the ultimate arbiter of its meaning. A belief in textual perspicuity means the only reason that others would disagree with *my* interpretation is willful blindness. Hence the reason why those who insist on textual perspicuity are prone to resort to violence when hermeneutic disagreement persists: Digby had his sword and gun ready for just such an occasion.

Instead of understanding the Bible as a book whose ultimate telos is to transform human lives and bring them into right relation with God, other humans, and creation, Digby clings to the inviolability of the self: "What hast thou to do with my Bible?" Saint Augustine would remind Digby that his interpretive stance misses the point badly. Augustine's standard for judging the validity of a biblical interpretation was whether or not it promoted love: "Anyone who thinks that he has understood the divine scriptures or any part of them, but cannot by his understanding build up this double love of God and neighbour, has not yet succeeded in understanding them."[43] In refusing to let Mary sit beside him and read and pray with him, Digby demonstrates that he is willing to give up love and friendship in order to prevent his interpretation from being questioned or qualified in any way. In his concern to prevent anyone from meddling with his reading, he loses sight of the fundamentally relational purpose of all words, and most especially the words of Scripture (see thesis 1).

Because he views the printed Bible as a portable commodity, Digby reads it for individual ends rather than communal ones, and the predictable result is the fragmentation of community. This individualistic orientation can take many forms: we have seen the way it led Jefferson to literally cut out the parts of the Bible that did not serve his religious views. This retreat from disagreeing voices can also lead people to read the Bible on an app or in a digital echo chamber that provides therapeutic confirmation of their biases. Digital texts with their fluidity and malleability facilitate this approach. Truth appears less fixed than it does in a culture dominated by printed texts; instead, truth is infinitely customizable. You can select and curate the truth that suits your identity (see thesis 14). Such reading practices succumb to the temptation to withdraw from a contested, common discussion of the biblical text—or of truth itself—and retreat to a more comfortable monologue. Even those who do not impose a pure interpretive monologue—as Digby does—may seek to tightly circumscribe the conversation by finding ways to silence or exclude or cancel those voices they find unsettling. And as Hawthorne's fable suggests, textual technologies can enable this monologue, inviting us into echo chambers or providing commodified versions of the Bible tailored to our personal tastes. Tragically, such readers, like Digby, fail to recognize that the goods enabled by reading—and particularly reading the Bible—are intrinsically common goods: they can only be enjoyed when they are shared.

Those who are protected by their commodified texts may be optimistic about their ability to grasp and control truth. They may mourn the benighted state of those who are less enlightened, and they may shake their heads ruefully at the people who have succumbed to fake news or false teaching, but they are firm in their conviction that they possess the truth. It is this conviction that is the basis for their optimism. The conclusion of Hawthorne's story, of course, undermines the ground of Digby's optimism. Digby may be the protagonist of this apologue, but he is not the hero. Nevertheless, Digby's fears have a legitimate basis—conflicting biblical interpretations can spread chaos and doubt. They can even foment civil war. In a later novel, *The Scarlet Letter*, Hawthorne would take up this problem again and suggest a more productive response to the very real challenges of interpretive disagreements. This will be the subject of chapter 12. For now, however, it is sufficient to recognize the problem Digby identifies, the further problems his adamantine approach causes, and his own confidence in his rectitude, a confidence that remains unshaken until his heart suddenly stops beating.

3
Encyclopedists and Map-Plotters

Moby-Dick's famous opening sentence is not, in fact, the book's opening sentence.[1] Before we are told, "Call me Ishmael," we have to wade through two prefatory chapters: "Etymology" and "Extracts." These bookish endeavors to define and describe whales set the tone for one of the novel's central themes: whether print technologies can enable individuals to "attai[n] the truth" about life's most profound mysteries.[2] And if these bumbling efforts by a "Late Consumptive Usher to a Grammar School" and a "Sub-Sub-Librarian" are clearly tongue-in-cheek, they are but prolegomena to the two more serious attempts in the novel to use print-derived methods to define and apprehend the enigmatic Moby Dick.[3] For Ishmael, encyclopedic methods of categorization offer his best chance to organize and make sense of all the cetological information he has acquired. And for Ahab, it is printed charts that he thinks will give him the power to plot the whale's location and track him down.

As printing matured, all sorts of organizational methods developed to enable readers to navigate the vast amount of information that was now available to them. Tables of contents, indices, more readable page layouts, dictionaries, encyclopedias, and atlases were all created or took new forms in the wake of movable type. These various tools encouraged new ways of relating to words and ideas. As the authors of *Interacting with Print* conclude, "the vision of systematization embodied in indexical forms presumes a knowable world, one in which knowledge can be compiled, organized, and synthesized textually."[4] Developments in cartography had a parallel effect, altering readers' default orientation toward space: "Only after print and the extensive experience with maps that print implemented would human beings, when they thought about the cosmos or universe or 'world', think primarily of something laid out before their eyes, as in a modern printed atlas, a vast surface or assemblage of surfaces (vision presents surfaces) ready to be 'explored.'"[5] As readers became accustomed to such tools, they imagined themselves navigating a visual, spatial habitat of printed words as they tracked down whatever truth they sought (see theses 12, 13, and 15).

The digital era has, of course, led to a proliferation of new organizational tools. As we find ourselves at sea amid the Internet's vast swells, we turn to increasingly powerful tools to make sense of all this information. The most prominent creator of these tools is Google, whose mission "is to organize the world's information and make it universally accessible and useful."[6] Besides their popular search engine, they have developed products like Google Earth and Google Maps to put the entire surface of the globe at our fingertips. As one theorist notes, Google Earth aims to render the planet "into a searchable and zoomable database."[7] In a related endeavor, Wikipedia has taken the ambitions of Enlightenment-era encyclopedias to a previously unthinkable scope: as of 2020 it has more than 55 million articles in over three hundred languages.[8]

The truly remarkable power of these digital tools can generate a wild optimism regarding the possibility of organizing all knowledge and wielding it to achieve our desires. The renowned scientist E. O. Wilson, for instance, traces the roots of his interest in science to his childhood discovery of the Linnaean system for classifying all living creatures. Building on such print-enabled projects in the digital age should enable us, Wilson claims, to achieve "the unification of knowledge. When we have unified enough certain knowledge, we will understand who we are and why we are here."[9] These are quite grand claims. Such ambitions lie behind his work on the digital Encyclopedia of Life, which aims to provide "global access to knowledge about life on Earth."[10] Wilson's confidence that humans will soon achieve what he calls "consilience," or the integration of all knowledge, may not be widely held, but the power of these digital tools to access and organize oceans of data leads many to believe that mystery and uncertainty are temporary, solvable problems.[11] Wilson's ambitions are the contemporary manifestation of the seventeenth-century quest for a *mathesis universalis*, a universal science that would enable certain, perfect knowledge.

Melville probes these tendencies in his rich 1851 novel. Ishmael uses encyclopedic methods to further his cetological endeavors, but he remains aware that no tool can make these mysterious inhabitants of the depths fully intelligible. Whales—like all truth—ultimately elude the grasp of human intellect. While Ishmael comes to terms, albeit reluctantly, with these limitations, Ahab rages against them. Early in the voyage, he attempts to use charts and navigational instruments to track down and kill the White Whale. When these tools fall short, he flings them down in desperate rage and blindly continues his doomed quest. The tools we've developed to organize print and digital texts can be useful aids, but Melville warns against the dangers of optimistic confidence regarding their ability to enable us to access final truth.

Encyclopedias and the Organization of Knowledge

As printing developed and texts proliferated, readers came up with various methods to navigate and systematize this new abundance of information.[12] The indices, encyclopedias, and reference works of the eighteenth and nineteenth centuries were the precursors to the search algorithms, crowdsourced wikis, and artificial intelligence we rely on today to make sense of digitized information. The underlying problem of chaotic, overwhelming information regularly provokes new methods for accessing, organizing, and using this newly available data. Yet these methods are always marked by failure; they are helpful coping mechanisms, but no matter how powerful they may be, they cannot keep pace with the flood of new information, nor can they enable finite beings to master reality. Such tools can make "knowledge [more] manageable, accessible, and available," but they do not necessarily help us relate to the world in a proper, harmonious, and just manner (see thesis 6).[13]

Nonetheless, many Enlightenment thinkers were smitten with the various tools that promised to bring order to the welter of new knowledge. During the eighteenth and nineteenth centuries, ambitious new publishing projects sought to manage vast amounts of information. The most famous such project is the eighteenth-century French *Encyclopédie* edited by Denis Diderot and Jean le Rond d'Alembert. Its subtitle, translated to English, indicates the scope to which it aspired: *A Systematic Dictionary of the Sciences, Arts, and Crafts*. While this project became a monument to Enlightenment thinking, many of the publishing endeavors it inspired were less successful. Chad Wellmon surveys some of the German failures. Friedrich Martini, for instance, began his *Universal History of Nature in Alphabetic Order* in 1774; he abandoned the series in 1793 after publishing eleven volumes that covered the first three letters of the alphabet. Another group of academics made more progress on their project, titled *German Encyclopedia, or Universal Dictionary of All Arts and Sciences*: they made it all the way to the letter K.[14] Even more successful—and somewhat more manageable—dictionary projects soon grew obsolete. Samuel Johnson's definitive eighteenth-century dictionary was superseded, particularly in the American context, by Noah Webster's 1806 *A Compendious Dictionary of the English Language*. Continued frustrations with "incomplete and deficient" English dictionaries led to the mammoth undertaking in the mid-nineteenth century to create the *Oxford English Dictionary*, which was first published in a ten-volume set and now lives in a regularly updated online version.[15]

Beyond such encyclopedias and dictionaries, this age of systemization also altered the form of printed books. Page layouts became more readable, and various kinds of indices became more common and more sophisticated. As the authors of *Interacting with Print* argue, indices in particular exemplify this period's underlying quest to make newly abundant information more orderly and useful:

> Spurred by the proliferation of print, the Enlightenment index also partakes of some of the same concepts that motivate other compendiary forms of the era. Alongside dictionaries, concordances, digests, lexica, almanacs, catalogues, and encyclopedias, the index was driven by the widespread interest in indexical comprehensiveness . . . and the emerging emphasis on 'systemization' during the period . . . . Taken as a whole, such genres are part of the era's attempt to manage the large bodies of information circulating in print by making them more accessible. But beyond their utility, these textual forms embody a specific epistemological position: they attempt to enact a comprehensive, synoptic, and systematic vision.[16]

This systematic vision has much in common with Emerson's transparent eyeball: both aspire to a panoptic perspective from which they can survey and control the chaotic welter of information. When you navigate a book with an index, you do not have to wade through the whole argument from beginning to end; rather, you can choose which parts to access and skip over the rest. Information can be more easily abstracted from its fuller context and deployed in whatever way is most useful to the individual reader.[17]

Indices and encyclopedias and dictionaries are the physical manifestations of the inductive hermeneutic I discussed in the introduction. As Marsden explains, many Americans believed that if you could just get the facts laid out clearly in front of you, the facts would speak for themselves: truth could be discovered by "looking carefully at the evidence, determining what were 'the facts,' and carefully classifying these facts."[18] This is the method advanced by Carl Linnaeus' 1735 *Systema Naturae*, in which he put forth his famous system of taxonomy. Many other disciplines adapted his method; hence, as we have seen, Charles Hodge could call the Bible a "store-house of facts" to be cataloged in the same way that natural philosophers categorize objects in nature.[19] The underlying premise is that if you can delineate clear and defined facts, you will be able to perceive how they fit together and so advance knowledge and gain new control over a bewilderingly complex reality.

This inductive method and its accompanying forms of organizing printed information shape Ishmael's efforts to understand whales and the deeper truths that they seem to signify. The novel opens with older methods of textual organizations, ones relatively discredited by the mid-nineteenth century. As readers would expect, these methods fail to render the mysterious whale intelligible. The first brief chapter offers an etymology of "whale" and a list of words other languages use to name this animal. In the following chapter, "Extracts," Ishmael relies on a *"Sub-Sub-Librarian,"* a print expert, to compile a series of quotations about whales.[20] This commonplace book genre had been a standard feature of medieval pedagogy, derived from Aristotle's *Topics*, in which students write passages under logical topoi or loci to guide them as they construct their own dialectical arguments. By the late seventeenth century, however, commonplace books were no longer instruments to facilitate argument but were merely personal collections of interesting quotations or sayings. As Ann Moss explains, a commonplace book's "open-ended acceptance of variety and self-contradiction in its assembled quotations was a potential irritant to a political culture centred on uniformity."[21] The "Extracts" provided in *Moby-Dick* certainly embody these features of abundance and self-contradiction. Ishmael mocks the poor librarian's futile efforts to collate all the "higgledy-piggledy whale statements" he can find in the vast "street-stalls of the earth." On the one hand, these extracts promise to afford a "bird's eye view" of all that has been said about the whale, but Ishmael qualifies this panoptic perspective with the adjective "glancing," and indeed the contradictions between the various extracts cast doubt on their reliability.[22] Some of the gathered quotes are not even really about whales, for example, "'Spain—a great whale stranded on the shores of Europe.' *Edmund Burke. (somewhere.)*."[23] The process of locating all these bookish citations does not shed light on the whale itself but rather overwhelms and confuses readers; while the Sub-Sub's exhaustive efforts are commendable, they fail to render the whale perspicuous and instead induce the very experience of information abundance that threatened to overwhelm readers in the age of industrialized print.[24]

Perhaps, however, the "sallow" Sub-Sub fails to grasp the truth of whales not because he uses print technology, but because he does not use the proper *method* to organize and read his printed texts. Following these two prefatory chapters, Ishmael employs the inductive method preferred by Hodge and other Americans who followed the empirical science of Bacon. The idea is that if individuals just see the relevant facts laid out in front of them, the logical relations and overall meaning will become apparent. Enumeration and classification promise to reveal deeper significance. Ishmael draws on these methods in his attempt to interpret the attraction people feel for water. He presents a long list of relevant facts, spanning observed human behavior, the composition of landscape painting, and Greek deities. He concludes by trying to induce a general purpose that would unite this disparate evidence, yet while he asserts there must be meaning in these facts, Ishmael's inductive method does not help him articulate this elusive meaning: "Surely all this is not without meaning. And still deeper the meaning of that story of Narcissus, who because he could not grasp the tormenting, mild image he saw in the fountain, plunged into it and was drowned. But that same image, we ourselves see in all rivers and oceans. It is the image of the ungraspable phantom of life; and this is the key to it all."[25] All these facts are not without meaning, Ishmael insists, but what exactly their meaning is remains unclear. Ishmael's grammar here is ambiguous and, dare I say, ungraspable. What is the "It" that is the image of the ungraspable phantom of life? What is the "this" that is the "key to it all"? Is it the meaning of water's pull upon humans, which remains unstated, the still deeper meaning of Narcissus, which also remains unstated, or the image that we see—perhaps our own image reflected?—in bodies of water? Ishmael's grammar, like the list of facts he piles up, ultimately remains ambiguous and open to conflicting interpretations.[26] This same interpretive failure marks other catalogs of facts throughout the novel: the most notable such instance occurs when Ishmael strings together—in one sprawling sentence—eighteen examples of the positive connotations of the color white only to conclude that "there yet lurks an elusive something in the innermost idea of this hue, which strikes more of panic to the soul than that redness which affrights in blood."[27] He draws this conclusion *despite* all the facts he has listed to the contrary: induction does not seem an infallible method of discerning truth.

Given the failures of both printed texts and inductive methods to provide Ishmael with clearly graspable truth, it is not surprising that his most ambitious effort to use induction and book technologies to make sense of whales similarly fails. In his "Cetology" chapter, Ishmael presents a Linnaean taxonomy of whales under the guise of variously sized books. He begins by promising "some systematized exhibition of the whale in his broad genera," but he immediately undercuts such ambitions by acknowledging that he is attempting nothing less than "the classification of the constituents of a chaos."[28] In fact, he remarks a few paragraphs later, this chapter comprises merely a "draught of a systematization of cetology." Even though he has "swam through libraries" and has practical experience with whales themselves, he can but sketch the mysterious branches of the leviathan family. Lacking a panoptic view of the whale, Ishmael can only "grope . . . among the unspeakable foundations, ribs, and very pelvis of the world," bringing up what individual species he can to place in their respective volumes.[29] Ishmael groups the whales into three "BOOKS": "I. THE FOLIO WHALE; II. the OCTAVO WHALE; III. the DUODECIMO WHALE."[30] These titles refer to various sizes of books that correspond to the magnitude of the whales each contains. Each book is then divided into chapters that contain one species. But Ishmael cannot cram all the species of whales into his three books: at the conclusion of this taxonomy, he lists a variety of other sea creatures that may also be whales, although he does not have the knowledge necessary to classify them. Thus he leaves his three-volume library unbound, as it were, waiting for future authors to add chapters or reclassify species as more knowledge is discovered. Indeed, Ishmael extends this lack of completion to *Moby-Dick* itself: "God keep me from ever completing anything. This whole book is but a draught—nay, but the draught of a draught."[31] Although *Moby-Dick* is printed and published, Ishmael insists that it is also an incomplete, a never-to-be-completed, draft. In this respect, at least, it is like Wikipedia.

As Ishmael continues to write about the whale, he turns to ever more extravagant textual technologies to describe the impossibility of rendering truth from the whale's thick blubber: "Would you, you could not compress him. By good rights he should only be treated of in imperial folio" (a folio book printed on extra-large sheets). Ishmael apologizes for his "grandiloquent" language, but "when Leviathan is the text," only such large words will do. He even draws his vocabulary from a "huge quarto edition of Johnson, expressly purchased for that purpose; because that famous lexicographer's uncommon personal bulk more fitted him to compile a lexicon to be used by a whale author like me."[32] Building on these textual figures, he imagines himself as a biblical author—either Paul who wrote with large letters or Moses who needed others to support his arms—as he strives to inscribe his tale: "Unconsciously my choreography expands into placard capitals. Give me a condor's quill! Give me Vesuvius' crater for an inkstand! Friends, hold my arms!"[33] As Ishmael's exaggerated language indicates, no dictionary, no matter how massive, no scripture, even, contains the words that could contain leviathan truth.

Given these failures, it makes sense that as *Moby-Dick* continues, Ishmael's voice recedes into the background, exerting less control over the narrative. Some chapters are even presented as scenes in a drama with no organizing consciousness at all. This lack of narrative unity has attracted much critical commentary that offers competing explanations, but at least one effect of this shift is to decenter Ishmael, giving him less control of his story's meaning and forcing readers to interpret and reconcile the conflicting voices on the *Pequod* for themselves.[34] The book becomes increasingly polyphonic.

Maps and the Control of Space

Captain Ahab does not relinquish his desire for print-enabled mastery so easily, however. From the outset of the *Pequod*'s voyage, Ahab is fixated on locating, accessing, and conquering the White Whale. Melville knows that readers may think it "an absurdly hopeless task thus to seek out one solitary creature in the unhooped oceans of this planet." He explains, however, that Ahab has at his disposal "elaborate migratory charts of the sperm whale."[35] The kinds of printed charts on which Ahab relies serve a similar purpose to the indices and encyclopedias that developed during roughly the same time period: they alter the way that travelers (or readers) imagine and navigate the space of the world (or the text). In particular, such tools give the illusion of far greater control over our movements than we actually have.

Prior to the development of modern cartography, travelers relied on oral accounts and itinerary or tour maps, which represent a traveler's-eye perspective on space rather than the God's-eye perspective offered by modern maps. Modern maps, in Donna Haraway's apt phrase, perform "the god-trick of seeing everywhere from nowhere."[36] This panoptic spatial perspective shares much in common with other tools that print culture developed to organize and control information. Earlier in this chapter I cited Ong's claim that "print and the extensive experience with maps that print implemented" led people to imagine the "cosmos or universe or 'world', . . . [as] a vast surface . . . ready to be 'explored.'"[37] Ivan Illich makes a similar point in describing the way that medieval students were trained to navigate "memory mazes" and texts in a tour-like fashion. He contrasts this with the modern way of relating to texts and information in a maplike way: "Reference work before the table of contents and the index" involved laboriously traveling through entire books. "The book for the monastic reader was a discourse which you could follow, but into which you could not easily dip at a point of your choosing," Illich explains. It is only after the development of these reference tools that individual readers can easily navigate to particular points in a given text according to their interests and desires.[38] Such print tools, like modern maps, enable readers to imagine that they can stand outside and above the play of meaning in order to navigate and manipulate words on a spatial plane. This panoptic, divine perspective offers the illusion that they will be able to manage and grasp the truth about a complex reality (see theses 13 and 15).

Many scholars have considered the manifold ways in which print, and its ability to reproduce accurate copies of charts and images, gradually contributed to a reimagination of space and cartography. Modern maps, for instance, played a key role in the work of exploration and discovery, and they reflected and shaped national identities.[39] They also influenced how individuals imagined themselves moving through space. William Cavanaugh follows the work of Michel de Certeau in drawing out the significance of the shift from itinerary maps to panoptic, grid maps:

> Pre-modern representations of space marked out itineraries which told "spatial stories," . . . Rather than surveying them as a whole, the pilgrim moves through particular spaces, tracing a narrative through space and time by his or her movements and practices. A fifteenth-century Aztec representation of the exodus of the Totomihuacas, for example, displays what amounts to a log of their travels: footprints accompanied by pictures of successive events from the journey, such as river crossings, meals, and battles. By contrast, modernity gave rise to the mapping of space on a grid, a "formal ensemble of abstract places" from which the itinerant was erased. . . . Space itself is rationalized as homogeneous and divided into identical units. . . . The point of view of the map users is detached and universal, allowing the entire space to be seen simultaneously.[40]

To go on a tour entails relinquishing control regarding your destination. It entails adapting your desires to the purpose and end that your tradition or community sets before you—often some site of religious pilgrimage such as Jerusalem. It entails traversing the route set before you step-by-step. In sum, it entails giving up the freedom to choose where you want to go and how you want to get there. By contrast, readers of modern maps—like Emerson's transparent eyeball—appear freed from their bodily limits and traditions: the world is laid bare before them. It is this stance, of course, that appeals to Captain Ahab, who refuses the economic ends that the ship's owners prescribe. He likewise does not share Ishmael's philosophical and religious ends, and in the novel's final chapters, he refuses the humane ends that the captain of the *Rachel* begs him to pursue. Throughout, Ahab insists on his personal mission of vengeance, and the charts in his possession—unlike itinerary-style maps—grant him the freedom to choose his own end and set his course accordingly.[41]

Yet in the early American republic, these two basic methods for mapping space competed with one another. Christopher Colles planned an ambitious project—*A Survey of the Roads of the United States of America* (1789)—to map all the roads in the new nation so that travelers could more easily navigate across state lines. His series of maps would trace the routes or itineraries between major cities (see fig. 3-1). As Loughran describes, "In disavowing conventional orientation, the maps resolutely banish the familiar bird's-eye viewer (whose head is always assumed to be pointed north) and construct instead an embodied traveler who is projected into the actual landscape as if holding the map in hand and looking down at it while standing on the road in question (without knowing, as travelers often do not know, in what direction that road runs)."[42] Loughran rightly notes that Colles' design draws on medieval antecedents, and despite the title, ironically, these maps do not survey the United States—they trace its arterial roads.[43] Yet Colles' method was caught between two times: it borrowed the itinerary form from medieval tour maps, but it aspired to the completeness and systematization prized by Enlightenment readers, and unlike older maps, it allowed travelers to choose where they wanted to go. Given these internal conflicts, it is not very surprising that he never secured the funding needed to complete his project.

Colles' maps share the older perspective of the "metes and bounds" system for describing territory, in which property is described from the view of someone walking its perimeter. But this method was being displaced by the Public Land Survey System, which the Continental Congress established in 1785 to survey American land. Thomas Jefferson was one of the chief architects of this system, and indeed he played a

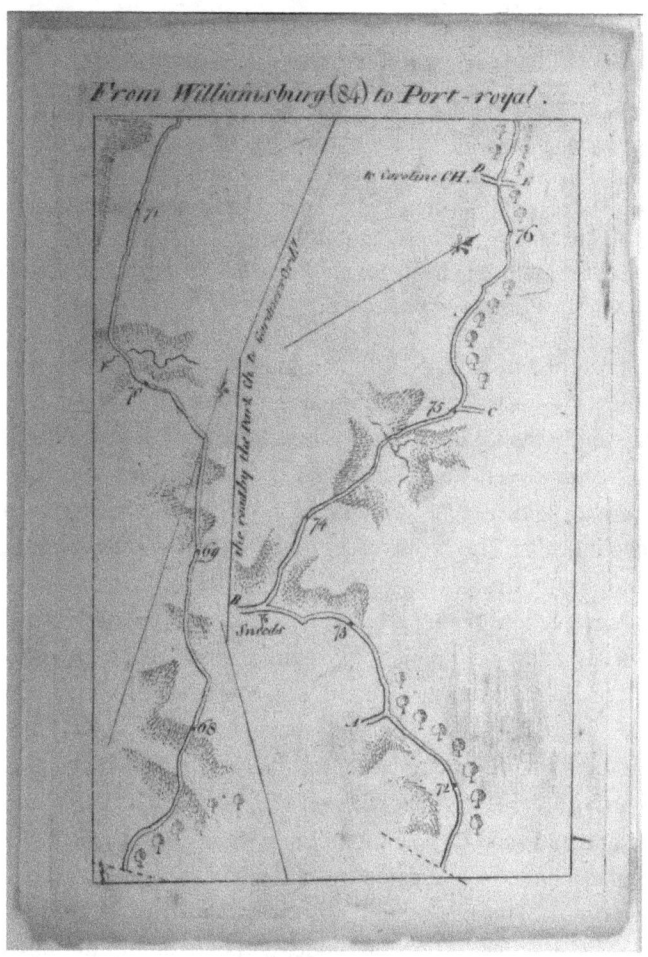

FIGURE 3-1. "Proposals For Publishing – A Survey of the Roads of the United States of America Copy 1." Christopher Colles, 1738–1816. Cornelius Tiebout, 1777–1832. [New York]: Christopher Colles, 1789.

prominent role in mapping the new nation. As president, he created the post of "surveyor general of the United States"; he authorized the U.S. Coast Survey, which was charged with mapping the country's coasts; and he involved himself in the design of the new city of Washington, D.C.[44] His most influential action, though, took place when he was the governor of Virginia and led efforts to cede western lands from the original colonies to the new federal government so that it could raise funds and create new states. He wanted these new lands to be surveyed on a strict, rectilinear grid.[45] Loughran's description of this plan highlights its imposition of an abstract ideal onto a more complex reality:

> Jefferson's plans for the 1785 Ordinance . . . projected onto the land-scape a geometrically exact grid of endlessly replicable boxes (each box, called a township, being six miles square and subdivided into thirty-six smaller boxes). The result was a Pythagorean fantasy of pure order and equanimity laid over a materially resistant, uneven landscape—a uto-pian but futile effort to harmonize and equalize the everyday disequiva-lences inherent in nature's nation.[46]

This plan resulted in the U.S. Public Land Survey System, which has left a permanent footprint on the American landscape, visible in the section line roads and street grids crisscrossing the country. The often striking juxtaposition between the landscape's natural features and the straight road or property lines of the survey grid forms the inspiration for an Insta-gram account titled The Jefferson Grid that featured satellite images that chronicle the enduring legacy of Jefferson's vision.[47]

This same vision of mapping was extended to the sea, and the U.S. Coast Survey and Navy undertook many expeditions to create detailed ocean charts. In describing Ahab's charts, Melville drew from work done by the explorer Charles Wilkes, who spent several years working in Ant-arctica and the Pacific and argued "for the links between ocean currents, paths along which food was borne, and seasons when and locations where whales could be found."[48] In a footnote in *Moby-Dick*, Melville explicitly cites another chart—one created by "Lieutenant Maury, of the National Observatory. . . . 'This chart divides the ocean into districts of five degrees of latitude by five degrees of longitude; perpendicularly through each of which districts are twelve columns for the twelve months; and horizon-tally through each of which districts are three lines; one to show the num-ber of days that have been spent in each month in every district, and the two others to show the number of days in which whales, sperm or right, have been seen.'"[49] Melville quotes here from a circular announc-ing the imminent publication of this chart, and Matthew Maury's "Whale Chart," published later in 1851, followed through on this promise (see fig. 3-2). Maury worked from the U.S. Navy's library of ship's logs. By imposing an abstract grid on the sea and then collating individual whale sightings recorded by many ships, he was able to make these disparate experiences easily accessible to future ship captains. As he wrote to John Quincy Adams, he hoped "to generalize the experience of navigators in such a manner that each may have before him, at a glance, the experience of all."[50] Maury's charts of sea currents and seasonal winds enabled ships to navigate across the oceans much more rapidly and efficiently, and his whaling chart applied this same method to clearly display the likelihood of finding a particular species of whale in any given place or time.[51]

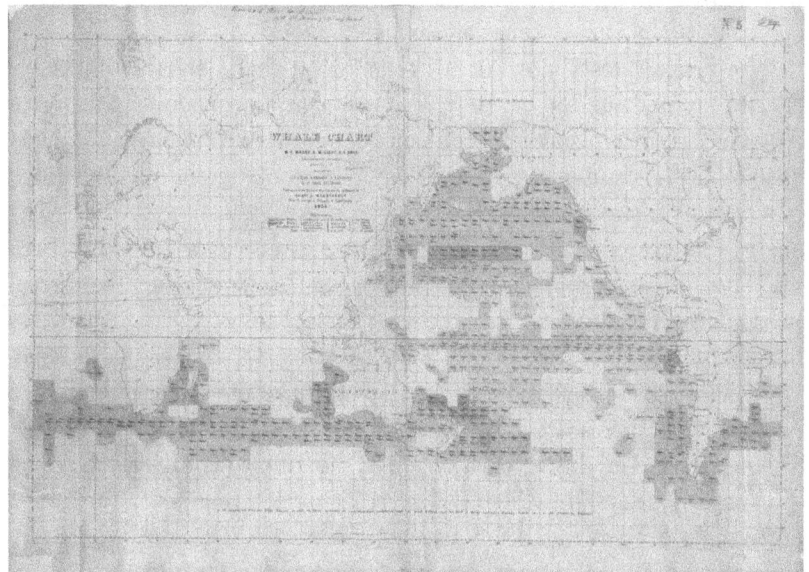

FIGURE 3-2. "Whale Chart." M.F. Maury; constructed by Lts. Leigh. Herndon & Fleming & Pd. Midn. Jackson. 1851.

This is the kind of whaling chart that makes Ahab optimistic he will be able to track down and capture the elusive Moby Dick. "Almost every night" Ahab retired to "the solitude of his cabin [and] pondered over his charts."[52] He does this in a quest for certitude: "with the charts of all four oceans before him, Ahab was threading a maze of currents and eddies, with a view to the more certain accomplishment of that monomaniac thought of his soul." Armed with his charts and his knowledge of leviathan migratory patterns, Ahab has confidence he can master these chaotic "unhooped oceans."[53] This mastery, of course, will result in him tracking down the elusive White Whale, in finding the "particular set time or place . . . when all possibilities would become probabilities, and, as Ahab fondly thought, every possibility the next thing to a certainty."[54] Ahab strives to turn the possibilities of Moby Dick's location into probabilities and then certainties, and he relies on his charts to achieve this mastery of space. Ahab even figures his technical ability in textual images: "And have I not tallied the whale, Ahab would mutter to himself, as after poring over his charts till long after midnight he would throw himself back in reveries—tallied him, and shall he escape?"[55] "Tallied" is a textual mark, a mark made over a word to cross it off, to control it. Ahab tries to control Moby Dick via his charts and tallies, yet as the novel's ending makes apparent, Moby Dick escapes all textual confines.

The chapter describing Ahab's reliance on charts ends with a reference to Prometheus and his eternal punishment, foreshadowing the price Ahab will pay for his attempts at technical mastery. While Ahab's charts enable him to stand in the place of the gods, looking out over the globe and plotting his movements, they cannot make his hunt successful. The charts, like Prometheus' fire, bring only a pyrrhic victory. Ahab realizes this later in the narrative when the *Pequod* finally reaches the fateful Season-on-the-Line where he expects to locate Moby Dick. As Ahab uses his quadrant to calculate the ship's latitude, he complains to the sun that, while he can use his charts and quadrant to make the sun tell him where he is, he cannot extract information about where he or others will be: "Thou high and mighty Pilot! thou tellest me truly where I *am*—but canst thou cast the least hint where I *shall* be? Or canst thou tell where some other thing besides me is this moment living? Where is Moby Dick?" Even the navigation systems of today's ships, fitted with the latest GPS technology, could not provide Ahab with the knowledge he desires. In the absence of certain predictive information, Ahab grows disillusioned with the advanced navigational tools at his disposal: after these haunting questions, he throws his quadrant to the deck and stomps on it, determining to be guided only by horizontal instruments like "the level ship's compass, and the level dead-reckoning."[56] Ahab desperately desires to occupy the panoptic, divine position to which charts promise to elevate the viewer, and when he realizes this status is an illusion, and that his charts will not tell him where his prey is or where he will be or where he should go—in other words, that they will not make him godlike—he prefers to travel without vertical guidance rather than cede this place of authority to the sun or to God.

Ironically, it was the earlier medieval itinerary maps that provided the kind of information Ahab now longs for. Such maps did not pretend to offer individuals a godlike perspective or the freedom to choose their own ends: they simply pointed pilgrims toward Jerusalem or other holy sites. In this way, medieval maps told pilgrims where they *should* go. In the absence of such prescriptive, hierarchical guidance, Ahab is given the freedom to chart his own course, and the course he chooses proves to be self-destructive. Medieval itinerary maps made no pretension of offering realistic, up-to-date information about the destination toward which they directed travelers. Rather, they set readers and pilgrims on a journey with spiritual ends; they ultimately pointed beyond any particular, physical place. In this way, they recognized the truth of Ishmael's remark about the location of Queequeg's island home: "It is not down on any map; true places never are."[57] Contrary to E. O. Wilson's ambitions, no map or encyclopedia, no search engine or database, will finally reveal "who we are and why we are here."[58] Instead, as we will see in chapter 13, the work of "attaining truth" remains an "art" to be cultivated over a lifelong pilgrimage as we journey in hope of a given epiphany.[59]

4

Celebrities

In the 1855 edition of *Leaves of Grass*, Walt Whitman begins the second untitled poem with a frank declaration of his desire for intimacy with all his readers. Paradoxically, the medium of the printed book is at once essential to this prospective intimacy and an impediment to it:

> Come closer to me,
>
> Push close my lovers and take the best I possess,
> Yield closer and closer and give me the best you possess.
>
> This is unfinished business with me . . . . how is it with you?
> I was chilled with the cold types and cylinder and wet paper between us.
>
> I pass so poorly with paper and types . . . . I must pass with the contact of
>   bodies and souls.
> I do not thank you for liking me as I am, and liking the touch of me I
>   know that it is good for you to do so.[1]

The cold types and cylinder press enable Whitman to at least imagine that he can create a personal, intimate relationship with innumerable individuals throughout the nation, but these bookish technologies also frustrate him. He wants to "contact" the bodies and souls of all his readers, yet the very technology that promises to extend his body so that each reader can finger the tangible form of his words also "chill[s]" and inhibits him. Imagining his readers as lovers may be rather odd, but Whitman hoped that his poetry could fulfill the emotional and affectional needs of the American people at a time when social fragmentation, geographic mobility, and political polarization made many individuals feel lonely and in need of community. Read in this context, Whitman's invitation to "come closer" sounds like an early iteration of the asymmetric intimacy performed by Instagram influencers and TikTok celebrities.

Twenty-first-century warnings about social fragmentation—and the resulting isolation and loneliness—recapitulate concerns that were aired in the antebellum years.[2] In that era, improved mail service, inexpensive periodicals, and the rise of sentimental fiction all promised to mitigate these problems by connecting disparate individuals and fulfilling their needs for emotional connection and community. Digital technologies such as social media have proved popular for similar reasons: they promise to ameliorate the isolation caused by geographic and social mobility and to restore communal connections. The tragic irony is that the very technologies that promise to connect us tend instead to exacerbate our loneliness.[3] Researchers report that teens who visit social networking sites on a daily basis are more likely to report feeling unhappy and lonely than those who spend less time on such platforms.[4] And studies of older adults warn that the "loneliness epidemic," which entails serious health consequences, is worsening despite new communications technologies.[5] These realities, however, have done little to slow the adoption of technologies that promise social and emotional intimacy to isolated individuals.

One twenty-first-century phenomenon that might help us understand Whitman's aspirations for a universal, promiscuous intimacy with his readers is the rise of what some have dubbed the "Insta-poets." Rupi Kaur is perhaps the most famous of these, but many others also use Instagram and other social media platforms to create the kind of intimacy with their readers that Whitman sought.[6] Whitman's use of various print technologies—particularly author photographs, autograph facsimiles, and organic-looking typography—prefigure some of the methods that these digital platforms facilitate. Many of Whitman's poems feature a sexualized persona that also marks the work of popular Insta-poets. The latter tend to intersperse selfies with their poems and often post pictures of their poems written out by hand or typed on a manual typewriter. Such methods allow them to "conjure feelings of intimacy with their many followers." As Seth Perlow concludes about their use of this platform, "Instagram encourages a visual rhetoric of personal authenticity."[7] But the intimacy offered by both Whitman and the Insta-poets remains asymmetric: individual readers may feel a powerful emotional connection to the poet who seems to be baring his or her soul. The poets themselves, however, remain detached and aloof from the emotional lives of their readers or fans. Even the simulacrum of reciprocity offered by comment features or fan mail maintains this emotional imbalance. Insta-poets engage comments on their accounts in different ways, but Whitman used the many fan letters he received to feed his wood stove.[8] Whitman can urge his readers to "give me the best you possess," but in reality *Leaves of Grass* and most Insta-poetry relies on publishing technologies to perform intimacy rather than to foster the authentic give-and-take that convivial relationships require.

Insta-poets, of course, are not unique in this regard. Contemporary celebrities and influencers of all stripes cultivate a peculiar, asymmetric intimacy with their fans through Instagram photos, TikTok videos, and other forms of digitally mediated access to their private lives and emotions.[9] The emotional dramas of celebrities play a significant role in the daily lives of millions of people. Whitman would have been jealous of the tools available to today's celebrities, but he mastered the technologies available to him in his performance of this peculiar mode of intimacy as he sought to fulfill and profit from readers' social and emotional needs.

Literacy and Affective Bonds in a Fragmenting Society

Social and economic shifts in the antebellum years uprooted many individuals from their families and communities. New immigrants from various European countries are perhaps the most obvious example of this reality, but internal migration within the United States also contributed to the fragmentation of community life: "Population persistence rates for any number of towns and cities could be as low as 40 or 50 percent for but a decade. By 1860 more than a third of free Americans resided outside the state of their birth; probably an equal or greater proportion relocated within their home states. . . . This swarming, migratory population hardly broke down into neat, intact family units, but instead to a great extent consisted of individuals thrust away from kin and other loved ones by the shifting tides of economic misfortune."[10] Newly available farmland in the West attracted many of these economic migrants. With the gradual closing of the frontier, in Frederick Jackson Turner's famous formulation, mobility declined up until the end of World War II, at which point it rose sharply as Americans moved from the countryside to homes in the new suburbs or to find work in urban, industrial areas; this latter population shift included the Great Migration, in which black Americans from the South moved to northern cities.[11] Since the postwar period in the 1950s, geographic mobility has steadily declined; twenty-first-century Americans move much less frequently than their counterparts in the middle of the twentieth century or the middle of the nineteenth.[12]

As Ronald Zboray observes in his book *A Fictive People: Antebellum Economic Development and the American Reading Public*, the geographic mobility of individuals in nineteenth-century America bore significant "emotional costs."[13] One result was that literacy played an increasingly important role in maintaining family and community bonds and in meeting individuals' emotional needs. Zboray notes that "as long as Americans remained in fairly stable regional communities, literacy would be acquired and exercised mostly for religious and only secondarily for social or economic reasons."[14] This changed, however, as people became more mobile, and Zboray traces some of the resulting shifts in literacy instruction and reading practices. He outlines a "continuum of literary expression of emotion, from the concrete grounded in community and family life to the ideal portrayed in literature. That spectrum of options began in the intense, face-to-face, affectional lives of preindustrial communities that shaped the emotional needs and expectations of individuals. As the whirlwind of economic development scattered these people all over America they struggled vainly to preserve the former affectional networks through correspondence."[15] One mark of the growing importance of correspondence is simple volume: Between 1840 and 1860, the volume of mail in the United States increased "from 1.61 pieces yearly per capita to 5.15."[16] As canals and (especially) the railroad made people more mobile, they also made words mobile, enabling more people to maintain long-distance relationships.

Mail did not just carry personal correspondence; it also carried newly affordable periodicals and books, including sentimental novels and other fiction meant to fill the void felt by individuals living far from their families and homes. These shifts contributed to a new sense of the self as constituted within a national "imagined community," to use Benedict Anderson's resonant phrase.[17] As Zboray argues, antebellum fiction became a partial replacement for or a "competitor to traditional community life."[18] As authors, publishers, and booksellers sought to meet this growing demand for sentimental fiction and fireside poetry, the "printed word" became "a primary tool of community building":

> The massive expansion of the printing industry made it certain that information would indeed flood down the rail lines, with little regard for the needs, hopes, or the very ways of life of local communities. But the destruction of the traditional relationship between the self and the community tells only half the story. The railroad and the printed word laid the foundation for an entirely different sense of identity, one writ on a national scale and within what would become an increasingly integrated and rationalized economic system. The self and the local community would not only have to make peace with this larger structure but, indeed, redefine themselves in relation to it. In this way, economic

development provoked the problem [the breakdown of local, embodied community] and proffered the solution, in the form of illusory, print-oriented connectedness that could pose as community. Certainly, that a text appeared in print meant that other copies existed, that someone intended this to be so, and that other readers shared the experience.[19]

If the industrializing economic system of antebellum America forced many people to leave their communities in search of gainful employment, it also provided printed products that these uprooted individuals could then purchase and consume to cultivate a new sense of themselves as members of a national community. Zboray concludes that "the world of print itself bec[a]me a surrogate for community on a national scale. The desire to maintain a traditional community existence that so strongly motivated people to become literate ultimately contributed to the destruction of that very way of life."[20] Literacy, geographic mobility, and the economic breakdown of local communities fed a shift in how people lived their "affectional lives": from face-to-face to letters to fiction—and, Whitman hoped, to poetry as well (see thesis 20). As Zboray remarks, however, "the chill in human relations that attended national economic expansion too often left readers little comfort but cold type."[21] This is precisely the tension that Whitman articulates in the poem with which I opened this chapter: he wants "the cold types and cylinder and wet paper" to convey his presence and even touch to each of his many readers, but he also fears these technologies will be inadequate substitutes for embodied relationships.

More a Person than a Book

I should begin this discussion of Whitman's poetic, book-mediated persona with an important caveat: what follows is not a summative assessment of Whitman's poetry. As is the case with Emerson's essays, there is much I admire in Whitman's poems: "When Lilacs Last By the Dooryard Bloomed" is a marvelous elegy. So my criticism of this particular strand in his poetry should not be taken as the full or final word about his work. What makes him so illuminating for the themes I am tracing in this book, however, is his ambition to exploit the new affordances of print technology to forge a kind of pseudo-intimacy with a vast mass of readers. Whitman was remarkably optimistic regarding the ability of books to mediate his presence to far-flung individuals and thereby bring together the citizens of the young American nation.

While Whitman is at times frustrated with the limitations of print technologies—"I pass so poorly with paper and types"—but for the most part he remained optimistic that his books could substitute for his person.[22] Perhaps the clearest articulation of this ideal is found in the special edition of his poems that Whitman had prepared for his seventieth birthday (see fig. 4-1). Only three hundred copies were printed, and they were priced at $5.[23] Whitman personally signed each copy underneath this notice to the reader: "Today, after finishing my 70th year, the fancy comes for celebrating it by a special complete, final utterance, in one handy volume of L. of G. with their Annex, and Backward Glance—and for stamping and sprinkling all with portraits and facial photos, such as they actually were, taken from life, different stages. Doubtless, anyhow, the volume is more A PERSON than a book. And for testimony to all (and good measure) I here with pen and ink append my name."[24] The author portraits, the signature, even the organic feel of the title sloping across the top of the page personalize the book and make it seem—Whitman hopes—a physical token of his person and friendship.

A similar note marks the close of several other editions. "Now Lift Me Close" originally appeared at the end of the "Leaves of Grass" cluster and invites readers to treat the book they hold in their hands as a person rather than an inert clump of pages:

> Now lift me close to your face till I whisper
> What you are holding is in reality no book, nor part of a book;
> It is a man, flush'd and full-blooded—it is I—*So long*!
> —We must separate awhile—Here! Take from my lips this kiss;
> Whoever you are, I give it especially to you;
> *So Long*!—And I hope we shall meet again.[25]

Whitman literally imagines his readers lifting their copy of *Leaves of Grass* to their faces and then pressing their lips to the pages. The book, he hopes, will stand in for his face and will return their kiss "especially." When he expands on this theme in "So Long!" he asserts the book's personhood explicitly:

> Comerado, this is no book,
> Who touches this touches a man
> (Is it night? are we here together alone?)
> It is I you hold and who holds you,
> I spring from the pages into your arms.[26]

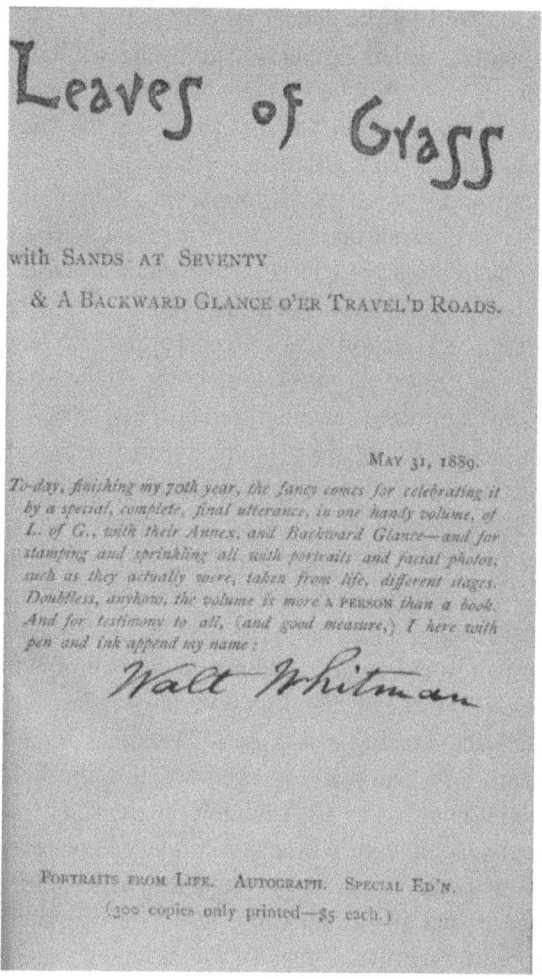

FIGURE 4-1. *Leaves of Grass with Sands at Seventy & a Backward Glance o'er Travel'd Roads. May 31, 1889 . . . Portraits from Life. Autograph. Special Ed'n.* Camden, New Jersey, 1889.

The same hope can be seen in "As I Lay with My Head in Your Lap Comerado," where Whitman imagines the book as his head, resting in a reader's lap and confessing his inmost thoughts in a confidential manner.[27]

In keeping with this aspiration for his books to convey his presence, Whitman experimented with different methods for making his books appear to grant intimate access not just to his words but to his very self. In the first editions of *Leaves of Grass*, Whitman left his name off the title page and instead let the engraving of his portrait stand in for his presence. He wanted readers to associate his poems not with a mere name but rather with his body. As Charles Eliot Norton commented at the time, such a decision followed from the conviction that the "name is merely accidental; while the portrait affords an idea of the essential being from whom these utterances proceed."[28] Whitman was not unique in including a picture of himself; author portraits were increasingly common features of printed books in the eighteenth and nineteenth centuries and became an "essential element of authorial self-fashioning in the burgeoning marketplace for print."[29] Such portraits were part of the broader trend, particularly among the Romantics, to foreground the author's persona and to see publishing as a means of gaining "personal celebrity."[30] Like today's Insta-poets, however, Whitman was innovative in experimenting with different portraits and using the nineteenth-century version of Photoshop to enhance his appearance. For instance, the famous image of Whitman with his head cocked and his hand on his hip that opens the first edition of *Leaves of Grass* actually appears in several variations. In analyzing these, Ted Genoways concludes that "all these changes are made with one obvious goal in mind: to emphasize and enlarge the size of Whitman's concealed manhood."[31] It seems that if he were alive today, Whitman would have no qualms about taking advantage of Instagram filters.

In later years, Whitman worked to contextualize this bold, rather sexualized authorial image. The 1881 edition opens with a more dignified portrait, one in keeping with Whitman's cultivated image as the respectable "Good Gray Poet." He wanted to retain the cachet of the edgy, youthful poet, however, and placed the original 1855 image later in the book, opposite "Song of Myself." David Reynolds notes that Whitman also edited this poem's opening section to read "I, now thirty-seven years old in perfect health begin." Yet "in 1881, readers knew well enough that Walt Whitman was neither thirty-seven nor in perfect health."[32] Whitman's careful distancing act serves his public persona; he wants to be associated with his youthful, sexualized figure but not identified solely with this persona. Like the Insta-poets and their posed selfies, he worked to curate a multifaceted public image.

Whitman's attention to the size and appearance of his books likewise shows his concern to make them serve, as much as possible, as a kind of friend readers could take with them throughout the day. If Whitman could not hope for a book the size of a smartphone, he nonetheless worked with some of his printers to make his books portable. Whitman tried to appeal to various markets, so some of his books were more substantial, but in 1881 he worked with James R. Osgood, who was known for producing elaborate, decorative volumes, on an edition that readers could keep in their pockets.[33] Whitman specifies the kind of simple book he has in mind: "The press-work (which I hope will be *very carefully done*, & with good ink)—& the binding, color, style, (strong, plain, unexpensive, is my notion, nothing fancy) are now about to be prepared for immediately. . . . I am in favor of its being trimmed & bound that will be as eligible as possible for the pocket, & to be carried about—& I am *not* in favor of wide margins."[34] As he had explained in an earlier letter, he wanted the book to be "handy," which meant it needed to be "markedly plain & simple even to Quakerness." The reason for all these requests was Whitman's hope that it would be "a well made book for honest wear & use & carrying with you."[35] If the book were to function as a person, it should be one available for frequent conversation and caresses.

The possibility of such a portable book permitted Whitman to indulge in flights of fancy about widespread, familiar readership. Take, for example, this passage in "Song of Myself":

The young mechanic is closest to me, he knows me well,
The woodman that takes his axe and jug with him shall take me with him all day,
The farm-boy ploughing in the field feels good at the sound of my voice,
In vessels that sail my words sail, I go with fishermen and seamen and love them.

The soldier camp'd or upon the march is mine,
On the night ere the pending battle many seek me, and I do not fail them,
On that solemn night (it may be their last) those that know me seek me.

My face rubs to the hunter's face when he lies down alone in his blanket,
The driver thinking of me does not mind the jolt of his wagon,
The young mother and old mother comprehend me,
The girl and the wife rest the needle a moment and forget where they are,
They and all would resume what I have told them.[36]

The technological capacity to print his book in a format that allowed people to carry it with them as they went about their lives and work enabled Whitman to imagine not just his words but his *self* traveling with all these prospective comrades.

If Whitman had had his way, his book would have occupied many thousands of pockets. He obsessed over his readership during his entire career, and he was mostly frustrated that his books did not gain the popularity he thought they merited. Whitman's most famous, or infamous, publicity stunt was his use of Emerson's private letter to advertise his book. He had the most laudatory phrase from this letter—"I greet you at the beginning of a great career"—stamped in gold on the spine of the 1856 second edition of *Leaves of Grass*. Whitman thus invented the now common practice of including blurbs on the cover of a book, though most authors and publishers who do so today get permission from the person supplying the endorsement.[37] This was by no means Whitman's only attempt to drum up sales for his books. At one point, he considered becoming an unofficial presidential candidate, thinking that would at least garner publicity; fortunately, unlike many publicity hounds today, he thought better of this idea. He also considered taking to the lecture circuit as a "wander-speaker."[38] He desperately wanted to tap into the new forms of fame that public intellectuals in the nineteenth century had available to them. Lawrence Buell notes the remarkable success that authors like Emerson, Charles Dickens, and others enjoyed on the lyceum circuit and writes, "This was part of a broader proliferation of media in the nineteenth-century in Britain and the United States that allowed the intelligentsia of both countries to speak to wider publics."[39] It was this wider public that Whitman was after.

While he never launched a presidential campaign and really only gave popular lectures in his later years, Whitman did experiment with less traditional means of reaching his imagined public. One method he employed was writing anonymous "self-reviews" of *Leaves of Grass* and leveraging the friends he had in the publishing world to place these in various periodicals. He then included some of these reviews and Emerson's entire letter to him in the 1856 edition.[40] In today's publishing world, Whitman would have perhaps employed "burner accounts" or some kind of native advertising to drum up sales.

Many contemporary reviewers found his self-promotion, and particularly his use of Emerson's private letter, distasteful, but Whitman seemed to see such methods as licit means to reach the readership that he deserved and that his country needed.[41] As Reynolds notes, Whitman's public reply to Emerson claims his book will sell "ten or twenty thousand copies" a year, which would make it orders of magnitude more popular than the best-selling antebellum book of poetry, Longfellow's *Hiawatha*, which averaged four thousand copies a year over the first thirteen years of publication. "Whitman was not in the realm of reality," Reynolds concludes. "He was fantasizing again about being absorbed by his country."[42] Whitman's popularity never reached the heights of his fantasy, but in his later years he did enjoy a significant measure of fame. In his retrospective essay "A Backward Glance O'er Travel'd Roads," Whitman reflects on his legacy and concludes, "I consider the point that I have positively gain'd a hearing, to far more than make up for any and all other lacks and withholdings. Essentially, *that* was from the first, and has remain'd throughout, the main object."[43] This desire to gain a hearing, which might be heard as a euphemism for personal fame and celebrity, was key to Whitman's aspiration to be "absorbed" by his nation. As he writes, "(The proof of a poet shall be sternly deferr'd till his country absorbs him as affectionately as he has absorb'd it.)"[44] This dream of being absorbed by his country was part of his aspiration to serve American democracy; perhaps he could unite disparate citizens through their shared identification with himself.

The Master Myself

Yet if celebrity fandom can forge a kind of emotional community, it cannot really substitute for the give-and-take of more embodied, rooted communities. I will point to two substantial, irresolvable tensions that haunt Whitman's efforts to unite the nation through Americans' shared intimacy with his poetic persona. These tensions continue to mark the attempts made by today's celebrities to create intimate emotional relationships through digital technologies. The first tension, which I have already alluded to, is that Whitman's desired intimacy with his readers remained asymmetric: they could kiss his bookish face and have access to his inmost thoughts, but he could not reciprocate this intimacy with a mass readership. The bathing scene of *Leaves of Grass* portrays these rather voyeuristic dynamics. In "Song of Myself," Whitman describes twenty-eight young men bathing together while a single woman gazes down at them from behind the blinds of a window. While the passage is notoriously ambiguous, it seems that without leaving her window, the woman becomes an imagined, invisible participant in the men's comradeship. As the narrator says, "You splash in the water there, yet stay stock still in your room."[45] This is the kind of intimacy to which Whitman invites his readers; the poet's exhibitionist performance provokes the reader to fantasize about intimate emotional or physical relations while remaining shielded behind the pages of the book. Later in this poem, in the midst of one of his catalogs, Whitman parenthetically remarks of a wagon driver, "(I love him, though I do not know him;)."[46] Is it possible to love someone who remains unknown and anonymous? Whitman's poetic project depends on readers answering this question in the affirmative, but such unreciprocated, irresponsible "love" is a far cry from the profound experience of being known and loved in a marriage or family or other forms of embodied community.

Even more insidiously, the promiscuous, anonymous intimacy proffered by the Whitmanian "I" carries with it a creepy self-assertion: you do not get any say in the relationship. As the famed opening lines of "Song of Myself" put it, "I celebrate myself, and sing myself / And what I assume you shall assume, / For every atom belonging to me as good belongs to you."[47] The "you" in these lines does not get any say in the matter. The second tension, then, that haunts Whitman's efforts to forge a social body through his poetic persona is that his imagined community is ruled by a totalitarian "I." In responding to the opening lines of "Song of Myself," David Reynolds concurs with Pablo Neruda's claim that Whitman is "the first totalitarian poet": "Indeed, there is a despotic force in Whitman's theory and practice of poetry: 'What I assume you shall assume.' 'The presence of the greatest poet conquers.' 'He does not stop for any regulation . . . He is the president of regulations.' In these and other passages Whitman controls, almost bullies, us, just as elsewhere he proclaims himself our friend and equal."[48] It is one thing to assert that I am "a Southerner soon as a Northerner," or "of every hue and caste am I, of every rank and religion," but such assertions do little to bridge the real divides between those regions and groups.[49] Instead, they rely on "poetic fiat" to paper over deep differences.[50]

Whitman believed, however, that such dictatorial edicts were needed to hold together his fragmenting nation.[51] As he writes in "By Blue Ontario's Shore," a poetic manifesto adapted in part from the preface to the 1855 edition of *Leaves of Grass*,

> I listened to the Phantom by Ontario's shore,
> I heard the voice arising demanding bards,
> By them all native and grand, by them alone can these States be fused into
>   the compact organism of a Nation.
>
> To hold men together by paper and seal or by compulsion is no account,
> That only holds men together which aggregates all in a living principle, as
>   the hold of the limbs of the body or the fibres of plants.[52]

Mere legal documents like the Constitution cannot hold a nation together. But perhaps a bard, singing a unifying song, could form a body out of the many members of the union. And Whitman aspired to be that bard. This tyrannical tendency emerges clearly near the end of the poem where he positions himself—the "I"—as the "master" of America's diverse geography and inhabitants:

I match my spirit against yours you orbs, growths, mountains, brutes,
Copious as you are I absorb you all in myself, and become the master
   myself,
America isolated yet embodying all, what is it finally except myself?
These States, what are they except myself?[53]

Much like Emerson's assertions about the poet's vision, Whitman's democratic sentiments could all too easily take on totalitarian forms. Emerson himself seems to acknowledge this in his famous letter to Whitman, declaring, "I am very happy in reading [*Leaves of Grass*], as great power makes us happy."[54] Whitman's assertive declarations of intimacy with his readers claimed the power to unite disparate Americans by fiat. If Emerson's print-enabled, panoptic posture led him to fantasize about being "part or particle of God" and ruling America with a "tyrannous eye," Whitman's print-enabled gestures of intimacy led him in similarly tyrannical directions.

A Rimless Wheel

Yet despite Whitman's optimism that his books could convey his person to a multitude of readers and thereby forge a unifying, emotional community, the results were decidedly mixed. His poems obviously did not do much to prevent or impede the Civil War, though it is absurdly unfair to judge a poet by such a standard. More to the point, the print-based emotional and social intimacy that Whitman offered could not supply the "characteristics of moral community," which Bill McClay argues "include genuine sources of moral authority and moral obligation." McClay situates Whitman as a key figure in nineteenth-century American debates over the ideal shape of community, debates he characterizes as riven by "contradictory desires to feel both autonomous and connected."[55] Whitman largely concurred with Emerson's transcendental approach to this tension, one that envisioned society, in McClay's terms, "as a rimless wheel, whose spokes were united only through their shared connection to the numinous hub."[56] This transcendental mode of community, which unites individuals through their shared participation in the Oversoul or Universal Being, shares an affinity with the literary, print-mediated national communities that Zboray describes. As communities mediated through networks of local, embodied relations weakened, print-mediated communities that connected autonomous individuals to national conversations and figures strengthened. As the "rim" faded, the spokes connecting individuals to the center became more important.

While these spokes may play a significant role in the "affectional lives" of individuals, they cannot sustain the reciprocal obligations that convivial, moral communities provide. McClay rightly notes that "every way of life" entails particular benefits and particular costs. And one of the costs of a society arranged as a rimless wheel, "it seems, may be some version of the tension that Whitman exemplified in extremis: a reflexive, unvanquished individualism accompanied by a perpetual yearning for unrealizable forms of community—a dream of being both autonomous and connected, which in the end often settles for being merely lonely or crowded."[57] Elsewhere, McClay describes this tension as the "quintessentially Tocquevillean polarization inherent in Whitman's social philosophy. . . . It seemed to posit an immense social gulf between the only two things that were certain: the sprawling abstraction of the En-Masse and the simple separate person in whom the theory of the universe supposedly converged. Where, one might well ask, were the other quotidian and mediating forms of relatedness that might, like Burke's 'little platoons,' bridge the giant chasm yawning between the individual and the mass?"[58] McClay's question here points to the flaw at the heart of Whitman's emotional and political poetic efforts. Whitman might be tempted to blame the limitations of the media technologies he had at his disposal—"I pass so poorly with paper and types . . . . I must pass with the contact of bodies and souls"—but no technology can forge a moral community between a solitary poet and a mass fandom. Indeed, the early decades of the digital revolution have only reaffirmed the limitations of communities shaped by asymmetric intimacy between a crowd of fans and a celebrity poet or entertainer or influencer. As Sherry Turkle has argued, our digital communities all too often leave us "connected but alone."[59] This is not a recipe for genuine intimacy or healthy democracy.

5

Benevolent Bosses

The narrator of Mark Twain's *A Connecticut Yankee in King Arthur's Court* sounds an awful lot like a twenty-first-century Silicon Valley technocrat. Enamored of the glories of industrial manufacturing—telephones and newspapers, revolvers and Gatling guns, trains and fireworks—the Yankee firmly believes these products can spread enlightened civilization to the benighted sixth-century British world in which he finds himself. Of course, things do not work out quite how he plans.

The Yankee reserves his supreme adoration for the newspaper. When he prints and disseminates the first issue, he announces the newsboy's arrival by claiming, "One greater than kings had arrived—the newsboy. But I was the only person in all that throng who knew the meaning of this mighty birth, and what this imperial magician was come into the world to do."[1] Despite their illiteracy, the people around him are suitably impressed by the product this imperial magician offers them. Hank explains to his eager listeners that a man and a boy produced one thousand identical copies of these paper sheets in just a day. Upon hearing of this inconceivable feat, "they crossed themselves, and whiffed out a protective prayer or two. 'Ah-h—a miracle, a wonder! Dark work of enchantment.'" As the Yankee passes the paper around to the astonished throng, the recipients treat it accordingly: "They took it, handling it as cautiously and devoutly as if it had been some holy thing come from some supernatural region; and gently felt of its texture, caressed its pleasant smooth surface with lingering touch, and scanned the mysterious characters with fascinated eyes."[2] The mechanically printed paper is a kind of cult object, a talisman, and it is surely significant that the narrator's name—Hank Morgan—appears in full only once in Twain's novel: when it is reproduced in a clipping from one of the Yankee's sixth-century newspapers.[3]

While Hank does not think his printed newspaper is a literal miracle, he does expect it to have miraculous results. Hank operates on the assumption that if you have newspapers and factories and railroads, then equality, democracy, and material progress will inevitably follow. He would concur with Frank, Melville's con man, that the printing press deserves the title of "Advancer of Knowledge:—the iron Paul! Paul, I say; for not only does the press advance knowledge, but righteousness."[4] In the early euphoria of iPhones and Twitter, many political activists were similarly under the false impression that the Internet would almost magically bring about just, democratic societies. In the introduction, I pointed to Wael Ghonim's about-face during the Arab Spring as an example of the disorienting effect of crossing Illich's second watershed. Ghonim and many of his allies believed that social media would inevitably serve the cause of democracy, assuming that "if you want to liberate a society, all you need is the Internet."[5] As he discovered, matters are considerably more messy. Zeynep Tufekci pours cold water on overwrought claims for the magical power of digital technology, concluding in her analysis of the Internet's role in the Arab Spring that "technology influences and structures possible outcomes of human action, but it does so in complex ways and never as a single, omnipotent actor."[6] Such claims may be more qualified in the 2020s than they were in the early years of the twenty-first century, but plenty of people—including those in positions of authority in Silicon Valley and Washington D.C.—still share Hank Morgan's assumption that new information technologies can solve intractable human problems.

One of the best analyses of twenty-first-century techno-optimism is Kentaro Toyama's book *Geek Heresy*. He chronicles his work with Microsoft in India, where he was involved in a number of projects intended to use digital technologies to address social and economic problems. In some respects, Toyama's book reads like a real-life version of Twain's fantasy: What happens when you drop "advanced" technology into a relatively poor country, one where eight hundred million people live on less than two dollars per day?[7] It turns out the results are less than miraculous. Many of Microsoft's initiatives sought to make computers accessible to schoolchildren, and they were joined in this effort by other groups, such as MIT's One Laptop Per Child program. Toyama sums up their ambitions: "By inventing and disseminating new, low-cost devices for learning, we believed we were improving education for the world's less privileged children."[8] Yet as he worked on these projects, he came to realize that they failed to deliver on this promise and instead tended to amplify already existing inequalities. Well-run, well-funded schools had the physical infrastructure and the personnel to take advantage of new computers; at poorer schools, however, power surges fried devices, no one knew how to maintain them, and teachers lacked the resources to incorporate computers into their curricula. Time and again Toyama found that "new technology never made up for a lack of good teachers or good principals. . . . If anything, [existing] problems were exacerbated by the technology, which brought its own burdens."[9] Other studies confirm his observations: schools around the world that receive laptops do not report any improvement in student learning.[10] While Toyama learned from Microsoft's mistakes, Hank does not realize the failures of his enchanting newspapers and educational "man-factories" until he and his civilizational agenda have wreaked havoc and destruction on the society he intended to enlighten.[11]

As the bloody ending of Twain's novel gruesomely portrays, industrial technologies can shed blood even more easily than they can spread democracy. Much like Luther, Hank never recants his firm faith in the printing press and its power, but he increasingly combines democratic rhetoric with authoritarian tactics. If the printed word fails to magically persuade people of the transparent rightness of his enlightened rule, Hank will use Gatling guns and explosives to coercively persuade. And while Hank is in some respects a caricatured version of a techno-optimist, industrially minded, nineteenth-century Yankee, Twain based his narrator on a genuine American type and on his own personal proclivities. Furthermore, Twain constructs his novel in a way that provokes readers to question their own unexamined technological assumptions and to critique Hank's simplistic optimism. Readers of *A Connecticut Yankee* should never raise their glasses to toast the printing press as an "iron Paul." But despite its pessimistic conclusion, Twain's novel also offers glimpses of a genuinely convivial practice: friendship.

Wielding the "Dark Work of Enchantment"

Twain's Yankee is convinced that newspapers and their attendant institutions can magically produce an enlightened populace and a thriving republic. In keeping with this conviction, his first act upon being named "the second personage in the Kingdom" was to establish a patent office.[12] As Hank explains, "the very first official thing I did, in my administration—and it was on the very first day of it, too—was to start a patent office; for I knew that a country without a patent office and good patent laws was just a crab, and couldn't travel any way but sideways or backways."[13] Hank elaborates on the other ingredients in his theory of nation building: "The first thing you want in a new country, is a patent office; then work up your school system; and after that, out with your paper. A newspaper has its faults, and plenty of them, but no matter, it's hark from the tomb for a dead nation, and don't you forget it. You can't resurrect a dead nation without it; there isn't any way."[14] Hank may seem to have a rather simplistic view of the work required to found and sustain a liberal republic, but he gives voice to a significant tradition within American political discourse, a tradition by which Mark Twain himself was often seduced. In essence, this tradition holds that if the right institutions and technologies are put in place, liberal values and republican government will inevitably flourish.

One prominent American spokesman for this tradition was Benjamin Rush, a Pennsylvanian physician and politician who served as a delegate to the Continental Congress and signed the Declaration of Independence. Rush argued that widespread publication and reading of newspapers could have nearly magical results for the young nation: "Henry the IVth of France, used to say, he hoped to live to see the time, when every peasant in his kingdom would dine on a turkey every Sundays. I have not a wish for the extension of literature in the state, that would not be gratified, by living to see a weekly news paper in every farm house in Pennsylvania. Part of the effects of this universal diffusion of knowledge, would probably be, to produce turkies and poultry of all kinds on the tables of our farmers, not only on Sundays, but on every day of the week."[15] As Michael Warner remarks about this bold claim, Rush believed that "print metonymically produces poultry because of its relation to the political economy of the nation. Given the conditions of representational polity, letters can be seen as the medium not just of utterance but of regular civilization."[16] In a similar vein, Noah Webster draws on Montesquieu to argue that "information is fatal to despotism."[17] In the ensuing decades, this simple formula—the spread of print and industry will lead to the spread of virtue and republican values—remained popular. William Henry Seward declared, for instance, that "popular government follows in the track of the steam-engine and the telegraph."[18] Such claims ring hollow, however, in a digital era where the proliferation of information abets despotism at least as often as it undermines it.

Indeed, an incipient despotic tendency is already present in Rush's view of print's effects. The only qualification that Rush offers to his otherwise straightforward, causative link between the spread of print and the spread of civilization is that print may need to be accompanied by proper education. As he puts it, "I consider it as possible to convert men into republican machines. This must be done if we expect them to perform their parts properly in the great machine of the government of the state. That republic is sophisticated with monarchy or aristocracy that does not revolve upon the ills of the people, and these must be fitted to each other by means of education before they can be made to produce regularity and unison in government."[19] His essentially mechanistic formula—print + education = civilized republic—reduces people to manipulable parts in a vast machine.

Yet, treating people as cogs seems antithetical to the project of republican self-government. Warner identifies the irony implicit in Rush's vision: "Here the same rhetoric that claims to base government on 'the wills of the people' is the rhetoric that conceives itself as mechanically fitting those wills together. The people appear active with respect to the public sphere, but passive with respect to the institutions of letters."[20] And this same irony marks Hank's efforts to spread republican sentiments throughout King Arthur's realm by means of newspapers and "man-factories" or "civilization-factories."[21] The notion that free-thinking, virtuous persons can be mass-produced in a mechanistic process seems self-contradictory, yet we have seen similar pairings of print technologies and despotic tendencies in Emerson's tyrannous eye, Richard Digby's solipsistic hermeneutic, Ahab's totalizing charts, and Whitman's totalitarian self-assertion. Such despotic uses of verbal technologies result when optimistic users have a naive belief in the magical effects of these technologies. These optimistic wielders of words concur with Melville's Frank, who proclaimed the printing press to be "an iron Paul" that not only "advance[s] knowledge, but righteousness."[22] If we have the technology to mass-produce and widely disseminate words, the Franks of the world assume, it must be a straightforward task to use these tools to spread ideas and sentiments and values throughout a community.

This deep-seated optimism about the power of technological short-cuts is the underlying attitude that results in the absurd conviction that weekly newspapers can produce turkeys or that man-factories can produce republican citizens. Such techno-optimism is deeply ingrained in American culture, and if it was widespread in the early republic period, it reached fever pitch in the late nineteenth century as Thomas Alva Edison performed miracle after miracle from Menlo Park. Inventors, it seemed, could do anything they set their minds to. What had once been the domain of magic now seemed achievable.

Twain himself was infected by this enthusiasm for technological inventions, particularly those related to writing and publication. Twain "was probably the first author to turn in a typed manuscript," and he even "dictated part of one of his books into a phonograph."[23] The most notorious result of this enthusiasm was his massive investment in James Paige's Compositor, a machine that promised to mechanize the laborious task of setting type. After he achieved success as an author, Twain often invested in various newfangled inventions, but the Paige Compositor in particular captivated his fancy. Twain was fascinated by Paige and his machine, which had more than eighteen thousand parts. As someone who had set type by hand beginning in his early teens, Twain knew the immense labor such a machine could save (see fig. 5-1). And while other stages of the printing process were successfully mechanized during the nineteenth century, typesetting remained a stubbornly slow and painstaking process.

FIGURE 5-1. "Sam: portrait of Samuel Clemens as a youth holding a printer's composing stick with letters SAM." G. H. Jones, 1850.

The full saga of Twain's involvement in the Paige Compositor is a long and sad one, but the brief version is that he began investing in Paige's machine in the early 1880s, and over the next decade, kept throwing good money after bad until he had sunk more than $200,000 into the machine.[24] As Twain became more and more dependent on realizing a profit from this massive investment, he desperately sought financial backing from others, including an (unsuccessful) pitch to Edison, "the Wizard of Menlo Park."[25] At times, the Compositor performed wonderfully, and Twain kept believing it would make him fabulously wealthy. During one of its few working moments, the machine even set the type for one of Twain's sequels to *Tom Sawyer*.[26] As one scholar explains, "the fiendishly complicated machine . . . left him convinced time and again that it was perfected or on the brink" (see fig. 5-2).[27] Paige, however, ultimately failed to produce a reliable and easily manufactured machine, and Ottmar Merganthaler's Linotype machine—which simply cast hot metal into whole lines of type that could be used and then recast—proved much more effective. The loss of his investments and the mismanagement of his publishing house forced Twain to declare bankruptcy in 1894, and it took him years of public lectures (which he had come to dislike) to eventually pay back his creditors.

FIGURE 5-2. The Paige Compositor, an automated typesetting machine from the late nineteenth century. 1901.

Mark Twain had placed his hopes and his financial security in the magical promises of information technology. Those hopes were utterly dashed. He knew what it was like to optimistically wager all and then experience the whiplash of pessimism when his dreams went up in smoke. Like Wael Ghonim and Kentaro Toyama, Twain felt the gut punch of having his techno-optimism shattered by intractable reality.

This experience certainly shaped the plot of *A Connecticut Yankee*, which he began writing in 1884 and completed in 1889. The most overt connection is that Paige worked on his Compositor out of the Colt Arms factory in Hartford, the same shop in which Hank worked as a head superintendent.[28] Both Hank Morgan and Samuel Colt are showmen who used their mechanical aptitude for arms manufacture, communications technologies, and explosive special effects.[29] More broadly, Twain gives Hank his own admiration for other mechanically minded inventors. Early on in their acquaintance, Twain called James Paige "the Shakespeare of mechanical invention" and even called him "a divine magician."[30] Hank goes even further in praising men such as "Gutenburg, Watt, Arkwright, Whitney, Morse, Stephenson, [and] Bell" as the "creators of this world—after God."[31] Yet while Hank's belief in the magical results of industrial technologies has an analog in Twain's experience, Twain became increasingly self-aware regarding his—and his culture's—misguided tendency to invest such technologies with magical powers.

Although reality finally punctured Twain's faith in textual technologies, Hank remains a true believer to the bitter end, and his indefatigable optimism has deadly consequences. Despite the claims of some literary critics, then, and despite his real sympathies for Hank's point of view, Twain should not be conflated with Hank.[32] Twain became all too well aware of the limitations of industrial technologies, and he uses his fictional protagonist to dramatize the consequences of naive faith in technology's magical powers. When a culture's disease entails unexamined faith in technology's magical powers, "the diagnosis *is* the treatment," or at least the first step of the treatment.[33] Twain offers his readers precisely this prescription. Hank, however, makes the fatal mistake of clinging to his belief in his own magic.

No Magician Can Thrive Who Believes in His Own Magic

It is Hank's magical view of technology that sets him up for inevitable disappointment and leads to the novel's tragic outcome. His fundamental error is to collapse the distinction between, on the one hand, inventing technologies that can manipulate and mass-produce and transmit words and, on the other, the much more difficult, manifold task of shaping culture and hearts and minds. Those who hold a magical view of technology—people like Wael Ghonim at the outset of the Arab Spring or a young Kentaro Toyama or Hank Morgan—think that solving the technical challenges related to the former task are sufficient to accomplish the latter. And for those who persist in believing that print and other information technologies can cause people to change their minds, the natural response to frustration and failure is to increase the technological power: print more papers, invest more capital, design better algorithms, and, at least in Hank's case, use force to coerce those who are not persuaded by your technologically disseminated words. Hank's weakness is his utter confidence in the magical powers of his industrial technology. But as the author of the story, Twain does not let this optimism go unexamined. Perceptive readers, then, gradually discover that perhaps Hank's printing press is more akin to a Colt's revolver than to an iron Paul.

Twain sets us up for this revelation by structuring *A Connecticut Yankee* as itself a kind of con. Twain, in his guise as the narrator for the novel's frame narrative, purports to describe an experience he has while visiting Warwick Castle. The tour guide remarks on a bullet hole in some armor on display, speculating that one of Cromwell's soldiers shot it, but a fellow tourist leans over and tells Twain that he, in fact, shot the bullet himself. Twain experiences an "electric surprise," but the man disappears without further explanation.[34] That evening, Twain settles down to read a passage from Malory in which Sir Lancelot and Sir Kay spend the night in the same house. In the morning, Sir Lancelot takes Sir Kay's armor, shield, and horse. When Sir Kay awakes and realizes what has happened, he remarks, "Now by my faith I know well that he will grieve some of the court of King Arthur: for on him knights will be bold, and deem that it is I, and that will beguile them: and because of his armour and shield I am sure I shall ride in peace."[35] While Twain is reading Malory, the tourist who claimed to have put a bullet hole in the armor knocks on his door. Twain gets him to relate his story, but after beginning his tale, the man grows tired and hands him his journal. Twain describes the strange sheaf of papers: "The first part of it—the great bulk of it—was parchment, and yellow with age. I scanned a leaf particularly and saw that it was a palimpsest. Under the old dim writing of the Yankee historian appeared traces of a penmanship which was older and dimmer still—Latin words and sentences: fragments from old monkish legends, evidently."[36] This unique textual artifact makes the Yankee's account appear genuine and allows him to speak in his own voice, thus able to portray himself sympathetically. In the same way that Lancelot's disguise as Sir Kay tricks unsuspecting knights into jousting with him, so Hank's appearance as a benevolent, democratic Yankee tricks readers into sympathizing with him. Only gradually does Twain reveal that under this disguise lies a would-be magician, an autocrat, and a tyrant.[37] Aside from this brief introduction and Twain's two-page "P.S." at the conclusion, the rest of the book purports to reproduce the Yankee's palimpsestic journal.[38] In an age of mechanical reproduction, the handwritten manuscript makes Hank's story seem authentic; it makes the literary fiction more convincing. If we trust its veracity, however, the joke is on us.

More subtly, the fact that Hank's journal is a palimpsest conveys his attitude toward sixth-century Britain: he writes over preexisting voices without bothering to listen to them. He fails to attend to or learn from this culture. Hank takes great pleasure, for instance, in blowing up Merlin's tower with gun powder and lightning rods. He acknowledges the Roman-era tower is "handsome" but justifies its dramatic destruction as a way of proving his superiority over Merlin.[39] When the lightning strikes and ignites the gun powder, "that old tower leaped into the sky in chunks, along with a vast volcanic fountain of fire that turned night to noonday, and showed a thousand acres of human beings groveling on the ground in a general collapse of consternation. Well, it rained mortar and masonry the rest of the week. This was the report; but I reckon they added on a couple of days. It was an effective miracle."[40] Hank believes that he has to erase Merlin's tower and utterly discredit his magic in order to secure his own power and project his new authority. The colonial erasure symbolized by his palimpsest journal is a fitting image of his inability to imagine multiple voices or cultures harmonizing—the old must be erased to make way for the new.

One of the results of this erasure is that Hank never realizes the profound similarities between himself and his rival magician Merlin. When he first encounters him, Hank mocks Merlin for the soporific effect of his tales, but, ironically, it is Merlin who performs the only actual magic in the book (aside from the blow that somehow sends Hank back to sixth-century Britain).[41] All of Hank's "miracles," no matter how "effective" they may be, are rationally explainable scientific feats, but at the end of the book, Merlin casts the spell that puts

Hank to sleep for centuries. Aside from this significant difference, both men have a flair for theatrical effects that razzle-dazzle their audiences. Merlin burns "smoke-powders" and speaks incomprehensible words when attempting to work his magic.[42] Hank, of course, cloaks his technological "miracles" in all manner of special effects—smoke billowing from his helmet, multicolored fireworks, and incomprehensible German words (with hysterically irrelevant meanings).[43] More to the point, both men are also true believers in their own powers. Hank recognizes this flaw in Merlin: "He was an old numskull, a magician who believed in his own magic; and no magician can thrive who is handicapped with a superstition like that."[44] Yet Hank fails to recognize that he believes in the powers of industrial technology as fervently as Merlin believes in his magical powers.

And it is because he believes in his own magic that he fails to recognize the many clues that his technologies are not in fact magical. Twain provides several humorous examples of this reality. For example, Hank is overjoyed when he unexpectedly happens across a telephone operator on the outskirts of the Valley of Holiness. The operator had found an empty cave, recently vacated by a hermit, and had established a telephone office. Hank is delighted: "The home of the bogus miracle become the home of a real one, the den of a medieval hermit turned into a telephone office!"[45] The operator has not yet made inquiries about his surroundings, and when Hank tells him he is in the Valley of Holiness, the operator does not recognize that place. Hank is confused because news of his recent miracle in this valley—repairing a well that had gone dry—had spread far and wide. The operator confirms he has heard about that feat,

> "But the name of *this* valley doth woundily differ from the name of *that* one; indeed to differ wider were not pos—"
> "What was that name, then?"
> "The Valley of Hellishness."
> "*That* explains it. Confound a telephone, anyway. It is the very demon for conveying similarities of sound that are miracles of divergence from similarity of sense."[46]

Hank's conclusion here indicts his own technology. It turns out that telephones—along with other communication technologies—can spread words without spreading understanding.

Twain offers another subtle critique of Hank's technological marvels through the way in which the novel reproduces his various newspaper clippings (see fig. 5-3). As we have seen, Hank is very impressed by the first edition of his printed newspaper, the "Camelot *Weekly Hosannah and Literary Volcano.*"[47] Its title indicates both the religious fervor with which Hank invests it and its explosive potential: each issue is termed an "irruption." Hank admits the tone of the writing is in poor taste: "It was good Arkansas journalism, but this was not Arkansas."[48] More significantly, the paper's poor quality becomes apparent whenever clippings from it are reproduced: misspellings, poorly set type, and foreign debris mar the page. Again, Hank acknowledges the poor production value: "Little crudities of a mechanical sort were observable here and there, but there were not enough of them to amount to anything, and it was good enough Arkansas proof-reading, anyhow, and better than was needed in Arthur's day and realm. As a rule, the grammar was leaky and the construction more or less lame; but I did not much mind these things."[49] The authors of *Interacting with Print* describe the larger tradition in which Twain participates by reproducing these badly printed newspapers: "The very notion that print was a transparent, reliable vehicle for conveying ideas was sufficiently widespread . . . that it inspired satirical or ironic commentaries, which themselves appeared in printed texts and images. Several writers, printers, and artists used print to draw attention to its own materiality and fallibility, and thus to disrupt the impression that print was a transparent vehicle for ideas."[50] Twain's "typographic play" is his way of highlighting the gap between the Yankee's high view of his paper, which he calls his "imperial magician," and the reality of the printed newspaper itself. Twain thus prompts readers to doubt the magic of telephones and newspapers and patent offices. These tools may be useful, but if they do not even function reliably, they certainly will not magically produce just, democratic societies.

That sad reality becomes clearer and clearer over the course of the novel. For although Hank repeatedly claims his technologies and mode of rule promote democracy and justice, the evidence suggests otherwise. For instance, he takes great pride in the currency that he manufactures and forces the kingdom to adopt. But the first object that he uses his new money to accomplish is gutting the closest thing King Arthur's government has to a welfare system. At allotted times, sick people could come to be touched by the king for healing. They would also receive a small gold coin worth a third of a dollar. Hank substitutes his new nickels for these

FIGURE 5-3. Mark Twain, *A Connecticut Yankee in King Arthur's Court*. Edited by Bernard L. Stein, 1979, 340–41.

coins and thereby saves the king's treasury considerable expense, and he justifies his lack of charity by stating that "of course you can water a gift as much as you want to; and I generally do."[51] Hank may express outrage at the economic inequality that prevails in the kingdom, but he squelches the primary mode of economic redistribution.

As Hank consolidates power, his coercive, tyrannical mode of rule becomes apparent, even as he continues to give lip service to democracy. When he is first given his title, "The Boss," he takes great satisfaction that it was adopted by popular acclaim and asserts that he was thereby "elected by the nation." Yet in that same paragraph, he calls himself "a giant among pigmies, a man among children, a master intelligence among intellectual moles."[52] He sets himself the task of educating these intellectual moles so that they will come to appreciate his benevolent rule more fully. Hank notes that would-be revolutionaries, including Jack Cade, "get left" if they do not "first educat[e their] materials up to revolution-grade."[53] Elsewhere he admits that "Arthur's people were of course poor material for a republic."[54] The methods Hank turns to are his newspapers and civilization factories. Yet as Kaplan observes, "The very names the Yankee gives to his institutions—'civilization factories' and, a dehumanizing pun, 'man factories'—suggest not the fervent brotherhood of Whitman's utopian democracy but instead a bleak, industrial collectivism, the nightmare society of a monolithic state ruled by the Boss."[55] This is the danger inherent in Rush's faith that it is "possible to convert men into republican machines." In Hank's defense, he recognizes that democracy and religious pluralism require citizens to be formed in certain virtues and practices. His failure lies in thinking that this formative work can be accomplished through purely technical means—newspapers and telephones and boarding schools.

Hank's deep-seated optimism prevents him from recognizing this failure, and he turns to increasingly coercive means to enforce his economic and political rule. When the products of his "vast factories, the iron and steel missionaries of [his] future civilization" do not find ready customers, Hank enlists a formidable sales force, one that excels at the "force" aspect of their job in particular.[56] He dresses knights in rude sandwich boards advertising various manufactured goods such as stove-pipe hats, Persimmon's Soap, and stove polish. Hank describes these travelers as "the most effective spreaders of civilization we had. They went clothed in steel and equipped with sword and lance and battle-axe, and if they couldn't persuade a person to try a sewing-machine on the installment plan, or a melodeon, or a barbed-wire fence, or a prohibition journal, or any of the other thousand and one things they canvassed for, they removed him and passed on."[57] Unsurprisingly, these particular products do not seem to be in high demand in sixth-century Britain, yet Hank finds a way to coercively manufacture demand and keep his factories humming.

Hank even violates his vaunted principles of free speech. He had first taken offense at Sir Dinadan for telling a bad joke, one he considered worn out and overtold.[58] This grudge comes to fruition when Hank finally defeats knight errantry (by means of lasso and revolver) and sets his industrial civilization to work in earnest. He describes the effects with great pride:

> Consider the three years sped. Now look around on England. A happy and prosperous country, and strangely altered. Schools everywhere, and several colleges; a number of pretty good newspapers.

Even authorship was taking a start; Sir Dinadan the Humorist was first in the field, with a volume of gray-headed jokes which I had been familiar with during thirteen centuries. If he had left out that old rancid one about the lecturer I wouldn't have said anything; but I couldn't stand that one. I suppressed the book and hanged the author.

Slavery was dead and gone; all men were equal before the law; taxation had been equalized.[59]

Hank is remarkably un-self-aware here. In the same breath as he claims that "all men were equal before the law," he also admits that, in his role as "the Boss," he censors a book he personally dislikes and kills the author. When the effects of the printing press do not suit Hank's predilections, he turns to coercion to produce his ideal society. This is a natural response for one who believes that textual technologies ought to magically realize our desires, but it is not particularly democratic or just.

The dangers of Hank's optimistic faith in his industrial technologies become horrifically apparent in the final pages of the novel. Through some political intrigue, Hank is out of the country when war breaks out and the church turns against him. Upon his return, he seems more interested in the battle photographs and the newspaper reports produced by his war correspondents than he is the death of his many friends and the dissolution of King Arthur's kingdom. Hank's response to the war is to issue a proclamation declaring that Britain is a republic and appointing himself the "executive authority" over the purported republic. He has great faith in the "piece of paper" bearing this proclamation, but he takes care to back up this paper with industrial military technologies.[60] And at the Battle of the Sand-Belt, Hank massacres thirty thousand knights with his mines, electrical wires, and Gatling guns. When his handpicked boys complain to him that "*All England is marching against us!*"[61] Hank justifies the impending massacre by promising that only the knights and gentry in the vanguard will be killed. Nevertheless, the only democratic thing about this destruction is the grim equality with which all participants were vaporized: "Of course, we could not count the dead, because they did not exist as individuals, but merely as homogeneous protoplasm, with alloys of iron and buttons."[62] Hank's republic is the perfect emblem of a tyrant who cloaks his reign in the language of democracy. There is no vote. He is not persuading the populace to support democracy and freedom of religion: he is brutally enforcing a tyrannical regime. The result is that he kills the country in order to save it, to paraphrase a twentieth-century U.S. military commander.[63]

The Temptations of Optimistic Readers

I do not want to be unduly hard on Twain's Yankee. In the context of Illich's understanding of technological change as crossing two watersheds, Hank occupies a position not too far past the second watershed of industrial printing technologies, a watershed he fails to recognize. He sees all the ways in which these technologies might ameliorate real weaknesses in sixth-century Britain (or at least the somewhat caricatured version of sixth-century Britain in which Twain places him): newspapers and improved literacy might hold the upper classes to account for their excesses, they might expose and punish corruption, and they might remedy ignorance regarding agricultural or medical or scientific matters. But because of his entrenched optimism about these technologies, he fails to consider their very real dangers and drawbacks. And his naive optimism leads to tragic consequences.

A Connecticut Yankee in King Arthur's Court ends in a dystopic massacre. This pessimism has plenty of warrant, as my next four chapters will confirm. When techno-optimism proves to be ill-founded, the usual result seems to be a swing toward bitter pessimism. Twain experienced such bitter pessimism in the years following his bankruptcy and the untimely deaths of his wife and two of his daughters. Indeed, with the possible exception of Whitman, all the figures we've considered in this first section end up as lonely, isolated, sad men: Emerson's transparent eyeball, Digby's adamantine stance, Ahab's monomaniacal charting, Whitman's aspiration to asymmetric intimacy, and Hank's benevolent tyranny lead not to conviviality but to loneliness. Thinking they can wield the powers of industrial print to master the world, these literary figures end up being isolated. And as we have discovered, their aspirations often damage those around them.

But though Twain eviscerates Hank's techno-optimism, he also offers a note of genuine hope in the final "P.S." that he affixes at the conclusion of Hank's palimpsestic journal. When Twain finishes reading this manuscript, he walks into Hank's room and finds the Yankee on his deathbed. Twain speaks to him, and Hank mistakes him for Sandy, the sixth-century British woman whom Hank initially finds exasperating yet eventually marries and comes to love:

> His glassy eyes and his ashy face were alight in an instant with pleasure, gratitude, gladness, welcome:
> "Oh, Sandy, you are come at last—how I have longed for you! Sit by me—do not leave me—never leave me again, Sandy, never again.

Where is your hand?—give it me, dear, let me hold it—there—now all is well, all is peace, and I am happy again—we are happy again, isn't it so, Sandy? . . . I lost myself a moment, and I thought you were gone. . . . Have I been sick long? It must be so; it seems months to me. And such dreams! such strange and awful dreams, Sandy! Dreams that were as real as reality—delirium, of course, but so real! . . . I seemed to be a creature out of a remote unborn age, centuries hence, and even that was as real as the rest! Yes, I seemed to have flown back out of that age into this of ours, and then forward to it again, and was set down, a stranger and forlorn in that strange England, with an abyss of thirteen centuries yawning between me and you! between me and my home and my friends! between me and all that is dear to me, all that could make life worth the living! It was awful—awfuler than you can ever imagine, Sandy. Ah, watch by me, Sandy—stay by me every moment—don't let me go out of my mind again; death is nothing, let it come, but not with those dreams, not with the torture of those hideous dreams—I cannot endure that again. . . . Sandy? . . ."[64]

His affection for Sandy brings out an uncharacteristic tenderness in Hank. He even identifies himself as an inhabitant of sixth-century England rather than nineteenth-century America, an identification he makes nowhere else in the book. His love for Sandy and his friendship with many of those people whom he initially took to be "pigmies" and "intellectual moles" have changed him in profound ways. Genuine friendship—even across the barriers of centuries and cultures—manifests as an unexpected possibility. And friendship can effect more actual change than all the printed words or Gatling guns Hank might manufacture. On his deathbed, Hank has finally discovered that printed words do not have magical effects, but he also experiences friendship as a miraculous and unpredictable gift, one that can have lasting, transformative results in our hearts and minds. We will return to this convivial practice in the book's final section.

II
Dystopia
Or, What does industrial print lead its victims to fear
they will become?

6

Loose Fish

In part 1 of this book, we heard five representative answers to the question, "What powers do optimistic readers with access to industrial printing technologies imagine themselves wielding?" Now, in part 2, we turn to those who find themselves on the receiving end of such powers. Their concerns lead them to pose answers to a rather different question: What fate do the victims of these print-enabled powers fear they will suffer? In terms of the macabre metaphor Frank uses to describe industrial print, if someone is pulling the trigger of a Colt's revolver, others are liable to receive the bullets. In both cases, literary authors offer perceptive testimony regarding these experiences. As Elizabeth Eisenstein observes, "The literary artist, whether poet, fiction-writer or historical romancer, not only exploited the new media most fully and deliberately. Like the early printer, he also registered most forcefully the consequences of access to proliferating printed materials."[1] To begin elucidating these consequences, we will turn again to Melville, who warns that if powerful textual technologies enable some to be more effective predators, they render far more of us vulnerable prey.

His most telling commentary on these dynamics comes in a brief chapter of *Moby-Dick* in which Ishmael delineates the legal code that guides whalers in the vicissitudes of their chase. The code contains two laws:

I. A Fast-Fish belongs to the party fast to it.

II. A Loose-Fish is fair game for anybody who can soonest catch it.[2]

Ishmael immediately notes, however, that "what plays the mischief with this masterly code is the admirable brevity of it, which necessitates a vast volume of commentaries to expound it."[3] In his ensuing description of particular cases that depend on esoteric legal interpretation, it becomes clear that this twofold law governs not just whaling disputes but human societies more broadly. Ishmael claims these laws contain "the fundamentals of all human jurisprudence," for all too often experience testifies that "possession is the whole of the law." Ishmael's legal theory can be summarized by simply stating that "to be a [Fast-Fish] is to be possessed . . . , whereas to be a Loose-Fish is to be liable to possession."[4] Such a law makes sense of European colonialism, American slavery, economic oppression, and—perhaps somewhat surprisingly—religious belief and verbal persuasion:

> What are the sinews and souls of Russian serfs and Republican slaves but Fast-Fish, whereof possession is the whole of the law? What to the rapacious landlord is the widow's last mite but a Fast-Fish? What is yonder undetected villain's marble mansion with a door-plate for a waif; what is that but a Fast-Fish? . . .
>
> But if the doctrine of Fast-Fish be pretty generally applicable, the kindred doctrine of Loose-Fish is still more widely so. That is internationally and universally applicable.
>
> What was America in 1492 but a Loose-Fish, in which Columbus struck the Spanish standard by way of waifing it for his royal master and mistress? What was Poland to the Czar? What Greece to the Turk? What India to England? What at last will Mexico be to the United States? All Loose-Fish.
>
> What are the Rights of Man and the Liberties of the World but Loose-Fish? What all men's minds and opinions but Loose-Fish? What is the principle of religious belief in them but a Loose-Fish? What to the ostentatious smuggling verbalists are the thoughts of thinkers but Loose-Fish? What is the great globe itself but a Loose-Fish? And what are you, reader, but a Loose-Fish and a Fast-Fish, too?[5]

In this final paragraph, the ambitious scope of Ishmael's commentary comes into view. It is not only slaves, impoverished widows, and non-European countries that are vulnerable Loose-Fish: all readers are in danger of being harpooned by "ostentatious smuggling verbalists." Even that part of us which seems most free from exterior coercion—our religious convictions—is at the mercy, Ishmael claims, of roaming predators. Readers may imagine themselves as liberated individuals and free thinkers, but Ishmael suggests that they are in fact Loose-Fish, always vulnerable to being harpooned by manipulative verbalists and so becoming, perhaps unknowingly, Fast-Fish.

Significantly, the economic, political, social, and ideological dynamics that Ishmael's whaling code describes can be understood by analogy to the mechanics of movable type. Movable type, like other advances in textual technologies (the alphabet, punctuation, spaces between words, and digital pixels), breaks language into smaller bits—it frees bits of words from their broader context—in order to rearrange them more easily (see thesis 11). When preexisting relationships are dissolved, the discrete parts that remain can be reordered freely. A similar process occurs when individuals are detached from thick communities and local civic bonds; they may be freed from unjust power structures, but they also become vulnerable to predatory authorities who can more easily manipulate them (see theses 18 and 20). In both cases, detachment precedes seizure. This analogy between the literal mechanics of textual technologies and their social effects may seem arbitrary, but it plays out with remarkable consistency.

For instance, consider a contemporary illustration of the dynamics Ishmael has in mind: the microtargeted ads that proliferate on digital platforms. Siva Vaidhyanathan shows how Facebook's massive troves of data enable companies and politicians to tailor targeted ads to specific segments of the population. As Facebook and similar corporations become more and more fully the "operating system of our lives," power becomes "more concentrated" and "manipulation [becomes] constant."[6] In her book *Weapons of Math Destruction: How Big Data Increases Inequality and Threatens Democracy*, Cathy O'Neil traces the ways in which corporations aim their digital harpoons at individuals made vulnerable by isolation and weakened mediating institutions. We have become like whales swimming around with tracking chips that alert the lurking Ahabs to our precise location. As an example O'Neil highlights Corinthian College and other for-profit colleges that have marketed to prospective students who they knew had low odds of successfully completing a degree program: "Corinthian College targeted 'isolated,' 'impatient' individuals with 'low self-esteem' who have 'few people in their lives who care about them' and who are 'stuck' and 'unable to see and plan well for future.' . . . . Why, specifically, were they targeting these folks? Vulnerability is worth gold. It always has been."[7] And someone's vulnerability, their status as a Loose-Fish, is revealed by the data trails they leave as they navigate the digital web: "As we turned from paper to e-mail and social networks, machines could study our words, compare them to others, and gather something about their context."[8] Thus O'Neil concludes that "when it comes to WMDs [Weapons of Math Destruction], predatory ads practically define the genre. They zero in on the most desperate among us at enormous scale."[9] Digitally enabled personalization promises to treat us as individuals rather than members of a herd or group. It seems to free us to be autonomous selves. But more nefariously it enables big corporations and political groups to target us with ever more refined ads.[10] As we come to rely more and more on digital networks, we are becoming increasingly enticing and vulnerable prey.

O'Neil's analysis demonstrates the underlying irony: the very technologies that promise to free us from oppressive authorities and institutions end up rendering us vulnerable to more cunning predators. It is this same irony that Melville refers to in *The Confidence-Man* when he observes, "Where the wolves are killed off, the foxes increase."[11] Melville recognizes the injustices and frustrations that lead people to seek freedom from oppressive systems and institutions, but he also worries that atomized freedom—whether economic, political, religious, or hermeneutic—will not in fact liberate people but will instead render them vulnerable to populist strongmen and profit-seeking hucksters (see thesis 18). Individuals floating along in what Zygmunt Bauman terms "liquid modernity" may feel incredibly free, but they are in fact Loose-Fish susceptible to micro-targeted ads and political propaganda.[12] When mediating groups and institutions are stripped away, the individuals that remain are left adrift and vulnerable.[13] As Bauman observes, "The dismembering and disabling of the orthodox, supra-individual, tightly structured, and powerfully structuring centers seem to run parallel with the emergent centrality of the orphaned self."[14] Striving to become masterless, we discover we are orphans.[15] Indeed at the conclusion of *Moby-Dick*, Ishmael calls himself "another orphan," and those who feel themselves to be Loose-Fish might identify with this self-description.[16]

As Ishmael's commentary on the brief laws that govern whalers indicates, these dynamics play out in a multitude of spheres. This chapter will follow Ishmael in briefly considering colonial, political, economic, and religious spheres before focusing on how Melville develops the hermeneutic experience—and the unpleasant consequences—of being a Loose-Fish in the famous "Doubloon" chapter. As abundant and accessible texts disrupt preexisting communities and mediating institutions, many of the individuals caught up in the ensuing liquidity find their new-found freedom to be double-edged.

Fair Game for Anybody

Ishmael's reference to Columbus seizing the Loose-Fish of America has clear historical warrant. The 1493 papal bull titled *Inter Caetera* declared that Spain had a right to acquire and govern the lands discovered by Columbus. In essence, this legal doctrine authorized European nations to claim property rights to any land they discovered before other Europeans possessed and secured it: as long as the land was not yet fast to another European nation, it was fair game. Underpinning this reasoning was the notion of *terra nullius* or *vacuum domicilium*, the belief that because non-European people did not actually possess land in ways Europeans were accustomed to, it was, basically, a Loose-Fish. This "Doctrine of Discovery" was reasserted in the U.S. context in the 1823 Supreme Court case *Johnson v. M'Intosh*, the case that affirmed the legal warrant for dispossessing Native American tribes of their claims to land rights.[17] The documentary legal system refused to recognize oral or communal claims to land that were less legible to a culture in which property ownership—along with constitutional rights and religious truth—was authorized by printed texts.[18] Thus, by textual fiat, the U.S. government declared the land a Loose-Fish so that it could justify making it a Fast-Fish over which it had total authority.

This court case was one particularly egregious example of broader developments occurring in the antebellum years. As the national government strengthened, ties that had bound colonists to their colonies and then their new states were eroded and replaced by ties to the federal government. What took place in the American context was one particular iteration of the broader trend that William Cavanaugh traces through which nation-states gain power: "Above all, the state contributes . . . to the creation of 'possessive individualism,' the invention of the universal human subject liberated from local ties and free to exchange his or her property and labor with any other individual."[19] In the U.S. context, this occurred through several means. The Northwest Ordinance of 1787 made it possible for someone to be a U.S. citizen without being a citizen of any particular state. And the U.S. Constitution, through the structure of the U.S. House of Representatives and its appeals to "the people," further served to accomplish "the reallocation of federal identity from the state to the individual." This question—whether the Union was comprised of states or individual citizens—was, of course, hotly debated during the secession crisis. But as Trish Loughran outlines, the Constitution explicitly appeals to individuals, to "the people":

> Despite the word "federalism," the Constitution was not merely a compact between states (as the Articles of Confederation had been) but sought instead to extract consent from (and ultimately to exert power

over) individual citizens, each alone in their body in the realm of the everyday. As Publius plainly put it, the new state will "carry its agency to the persons of the citizens," and there was little dissimulation about why this might be useful. As Madison knew, it is easier to compel individuals to pay their taxes than it is to get states to do so.[20]

The federal government frees individuals from the states only in order to tie them tightly to itself. It makes them Loose-Fish to make them Fast-Fish.

These political developments were mirrored in the economic system that developed around the ideal of "free labor." The Free Soil Party, which later merged with other groups to form the Republican Party, summarized its platform as "Free Soil, Free Speech, Free Labor, and Free Men." The core assumption linking these freedoms was that a free laborer could expect to save enough money to acquire land or capital: "The successful laborer was one who achieved self-employment, and owned his own capital—a business, farm, or shop."[21] And if opportunities to do so proved scarce in eastern urban centers, workers could move West and acquire free soil. But the 1850s proved to be a key inflection point between small-scale manufacturing and farming—an economic environment in which laborers could reasonably hope to acquire productive property of their own—and the consolidation of capital, which led to the rise of wage labor.[22] Melville perceptively recognized this incipient shift, which undercut the Republican ideology that labor was merely a step along the path toward ownership. In *Moby-Dick*, as Ian McGuire argues, Melville responded to a growing sense that free labor might not be a viable path toward economic freedom: "The great anxiety felt by almost all its advocates from the 1830s onward was that free labor was under threat from both chattel slavery in the South and 'wage slavery' in the North. 'Wage slavery,' [was] a term popularly used to suggest a permanent condition of wage labor from which there was no chance of rising to economic independence."[23] Such wage slavery is the fate that awaits many Loose-Fish workers in a free labor economy.

The key point to grasp is that this vision of "free labor" stood in contrast not only to Southern slavery—or, in Ishmael's biting phrase, "Republican slaves"—but also to Jefferson's vision of the yeoman farmer, whose labor was tied to his land. Despite the promise of freedom offered by the free labor ideology, laborers often discovered that the ties of land ownership, apprentice systems, or small-scale capital—a mill, an anvil, a shop—had protected them from being Loose-Fish.[24] And while the fate of wage slav-ery is certainly preferable to that of chattel slavery, that does not mean it represents genuine freedom (see thesis 18).[25] If this state of affairs was incipient in the 1850s, it has become fully realized in our era of liquid modernity. As Bauman observes about contemporary economic freedom,

> Bosses prefer to employ unburdened, free-floating individuals who are ready to break all bonds at a moment's notice and who never think twice when "ethical demands" must be sacrificed to the "demands of the job." We live today in a global society of consumers, and the pat-terns of consumer behavior cannot but affect all other aspects of our life, including work and family life. We are all now pressed to consume more, and on the way, we become ourselves commodities on the con-sumer and labor markets.[26]

Ishmael's whaling codes warn that the laborer who is free to sell his labor in the marketplace to the highest bidder is at risk of such commodification and exploitation, and the fewer limitations or regulations there are, the greater the danger faced by the laborer. In other words, as McGuire con-cludes, "the desire for masterlessness may only reconfigure rather than eradicate hierarchies of race and class."[27]

Ishmael goes on to astutely observe that these dangers mark not only political and economic interactions; the "religious beliefs" and "the thoughts of thinkers" are also susceptible to being speared by predatory hunters. Religious historians such as Mark Noll and Nathan Hatch have shown that as religious institutions weakened in the antebellum years, "charismatic, self-selected leaders" gained greater authority.[28] "These populist religious leaders," Hatch observes, "were intoxicated with the potential of print. . . . In this moment of democratic aspiration, religious leaders could not foresee that their assault upon mediating structures could produce a society in which grasping entrepreneurs could erect new forms of tyranny in religious, political, and economic institutions."[29] And so the same paradox that marked antebellum politics also marked the religious sphere: "The conjunction of democratic aspiration and authoritarian style is a characteristic pattern of populist cultures, religious and political, both in the North and the South."[30] A few religious leaders did worry about these dangers. Hatch cites one Pennsylvania pastor, writing in the 1840s, who identified "the dichotomy between the rhetoric of people going to the Bible for themselves and the reality of a few strong figures imposing their own will." Such "liberty," John W. Nevin wrote, consists "in thinking its particular notions, shouting its shibboleths and passwords, dancing its religious hornpipes, and reading the Bible only through its theological goggles. These restrictions, at the same time, are so many wires, that lead back at last into the hands of a few leading spirits, enabling them to wield a true hierarchical despotism over all who are thus brought within their power."[31] The lines holding fast these purportedly free thinkers might be informal and hidden, but they are binding, nonetheless. When the mediating structures of formal church institutions are weakened, religious beliefs become more prone to such subtle forms of manipulation.

More broadly, the vulnerability of Loose-Fish believers and thinkers is exploited via various forms of propaganda, slogans, and advertising. In an age characterized by the twin conditions of weak communities and abundant information, these methods of hunting readers become potent. The twentieth-century social critic Jacques Ellul describes this process in terms that are eerily reminiscent of Ishmael's whaling code:

> In individualist *theory* the individual has eminent value, man himself is the master of his life; in individualist *reality* each human being is subject to innumerable forces and influences, and is not at all master of his own life. As long as solidly constituted groups exist, those who are integrated into them are subject to them. But at the same time they are protected by them against such external influences as propaganda. An individual can be influenced by forces such as propaganda only when he is cut off from membership in local groups. Because such groups are organic and have a well-structured material, spiritual, and emotional life, they are not easily penetrated by propaganda.[32]

Ellul recognizes the same tragic paradox here that Ishmael does. So even while he sympathizes with members of solidly constituted groups who find those communities constricting or even oppressive, he warns that liberation may prove elusive, particularly in a mass, technological society:

> In theory this [desire for individual freedom] is admirable. But in practice, what actually happens? The individual is placed in a minority position and burdened at the same time with a total, crushing responsibility. Such conditions make an individualist society fertile ground for modern propaganda. The permanent uncertainty, the social mobility, the absence of sociological protection and of traditional frames of reference—all these inevitably provide propaganda with a malleable environment that can be fed information from the outside and conditioned at will.[33]

Ellul's point is that Loose-Fish have great difficulty in maintaining positive freedom. It is, ironically, their negative freedom that makes them particularly vulnerable to those "smuggling verbalists" who seek to make fast "the thoughts of thinkers" and direct them to profitable ends.

Orphaned Readers

Ishmael articulates these dynamics only briefly at the conclusion of the "Fast-Fish and Loose-Fish" chapter, but they play a significant role in the novel's narrative. The *Pequod*'s crew is composed of *"isolatoes,"* Loose-Fish who sign up for the harsh and dangerous rigors of a whaling voyage because they lack social bonds and the opportunities and obligations those bonds entail. Ishmael describes the crew as a motley set of lonely individuals: "They were nearly all Islanders in the Pequod, *Isolatoes* too, I call such, not acknowledging the common continent of men, but each *Isolato* living on a separate continent of his own."[34] Hence the conditions on the *Pequod* are precisely those that Ellul identified as offering a fertile ground for propaganda: "the permanent uncertainty, the social mobility, the absence of sociological protection and of traditional frames of reference."[35] These Loose-Fish are vulnerable to the wiles of a charismatic "strong figure," in John W. Nevin's words, who would impose a despotic authority.[36]

Such an authority is present, of course, in the person of Captain Ahab. Ahab easily turns the crew toward his unauthorized, personal vendetta against the White Whale because of their vulnerabilities. He is one of those "smuggling verbalists" Ishmael warns about, and he uses twisted religious ceremonies and self-serving political arguments to generate enthusiasm among the *isolatoes* for his goal.[37] As Starbuck bitterly observes, Ahab "would be a democrat to all above" while at the same time "lord[ing] it over all below."[38] His success in this endeavor means that by the time Ahab does battle with Moby Dick, the individual crew members are totally submissive to his will: "Ahab's purpose now fixedly gleamed down upon the constant midnight of the gloomy crew. It domineered above them so, that all their bodings, doubts, misgivings, fears, were fain to hide beneath their souls, and not sprout forth a single spear or leaf." In fact, during the chase itself, Ahab describes these men as incorporated members of his body: "Ye are not other men, but my arms and my legs; and so obey me."[39] It is because Ahab has effectually conscripted his crew members' minds and bodies that he can pursue his doomed quest for the White Whale. And the reason these sailors are so easily welded fast to

Ahab's insane hunt—even against their economic interests and personal well-being—is that they are Loose-Fish, orphaned individuals susceptible to being harpooned by this foxy captain.

The famous "Doubloon" chapter dramatizes the way in which the orphaned *isolatoes*, whose reading is characterized by interpretive indeterminacy and hypersubjective hermeneutics, do not enjoy authentic freedom but, instead, suffer from confusion and vulnerability. Ahab has nailed a doubloon to the *Pequod*'s mast and promised that whoever first sights Moby Dick will receive the gold piece as a reward. The "strange figures and inscriptions stamped on" the coin intrigue Ahab as he passes by one morning, and he pauses to ponder their meaning and see if they might hold some clue to the outcome of his quest.[40] Ahab, unsurprisingly, sees his own egotistical obsessions mirrored back to him: "There's something ever egotistical in mountain-tops and towers, and all other grand and lofty things; look here,—three peaks as proud as Lucifer. The firm tower, that is Ahab; the volcano, that is Ahab; the courageous, the undaunted, and victorious fowl, that, too, is Ahab; all are Ahab; and this round gold is but the image of the rounder globe, which, like a magician's glass, to each and every man in turn but mirrors back his own mysterious self."[41] And others besides Ahab see their desires mirrored back by this enigmatic text. Intrigued by Ahab's long contemplation of the coin, several individuals parade by it and offer their own renderings of its symbols.

As Starbuck, Stubb, Flask, the Manxman, and finally Pip offer their interpretations, the only consensus that emerges is that there is no consensus. As we've seen earlier, particularly in the discussion of Hawthorne's "Man of Adamant," eliminating all interpretive authorities does not lead to vibrant dialogue or mutual understanding: it leads to confusion and loneliness and violence. Stubb articulates the problem with characteristic forthrightness when he exclaims in frustration, "Book! You lie there; the fact is, you books must know your places. You'll do to give us the bare words and facts, but we come in to supply the thoughts."[42] For Stubb, this despair of ever finding a common meaning justifies his might-makes-right subjectivity. He can render whatever interpretation suits his appetites and interests. The black cook Fleece's earlier judgment, delivered after he endured merciless teasing and tormenting from Stubb, seems accurate: "'Wish, by gor! whale eat him, 'stead of him eat whale. I'm bressed if he ain't more of shark dan Massa Shark hisself.'"[43] The fact that the Doubloon, like the world itself, bears no clear, agreed-upon meaning to which he is accountable means that Stubb can "supply the thoughts" he chooses and then violently enact them.

Pip names this radically subjective state of affairs when, while standing in front of the coin, he conjugates the verb *to look*: "I look, you look, he looks; we look, ye look, they look."[44] What matters now is not so much the text on which readers look, but the desires and strength of the individual reader doing the looking. Readers may have gained the freedom to supply their own thoughts in making sense of a text, but when taken to its extreme, this freedom becomes the negative freedom of Loose-Fish rather than the positive freedom that leads to genuine understanding and conviviality. Such negative freedom and the interpretive chaos that results leaves "minds and opinions" exposed to the "ostentatious smuggling verbalists."

It is in light of this danger that Pip offers a telling warning: "Here's the ship's navel, this doubloon here, and they are all on fire to unscrew it. But, unscrew your navel, and what's the consequence? Then again, if it stays here, that is ugly, too, for when aught's nailed to the mast it's a sign that things grow desperate. Ha, ha! old Ahab! the White Whale; he'll nail ye!"[45] The navel, of course, is the physical mark of a mammal's dependence on its mother. Pip warns that unscrewing our navels—in other words, aspiring to become parentless and masterless—renders us orphans susceptible to strongmen who assert and enforce their will. As McGuire argues, "the desire for masterlessness" does not eliminate hierarchies; it reconfigures them.[46] Ahab is no exception to this rule. In his rebellion against God and against his legal and economic obligations to the ship's owners, he has asserted his own vindictive purpose for the ship's voyage. Yet while he manages to convince his crew of *isolatoes* to submit to his will, the White Whale will indeed "nail" Ahab.

The literary critic Roger Lundin draws attention to this trope of orphanhood in *Moby-Dick* and situates it within the broader political, cultural, and theological contexts I have considered in this chapter. "Given the cultural dynamics prevailing in the early modern West," Lundin observes, "it is not surprising that orphans came to figure so prominently in the fiction of the nineteenth and twentieth centuries." *Moby-Dick* in particular "uses orphaning as a metaphor for the human condition in a world enduring the absence and silence of God."[47] People may think that by killing God, to borrow Nietzsche's metaphor, and rendering his judgment nugatory, they will gain the freedom of self-determination. Yet even Ahab, in one of his moments of haunting self-doubt, confesses his sense of orphaned confusion: "Where is the foundling's father hidden? Our souls are like those orphans whose unwedded mothers die in bearing them: the secret of our paternity lies in their grave, and we must there to learn it."[48] Lundin sees this sense of orphaned confusion as testifying to the way in which the initial joy of liberated freedom eventually gives way "to the terror of abandonment."[49]

At the conclusion of the book, Ishmael experiences this abandonment literally when he is cast adrift and becomes the *Pequod*'s sole survivor. In fact, he explicitly calls himself an "orphan" in the final sentence of the book.[50] This conclusion forms an apt bookend to his famous opening declaration: "Call me Ishmael." Ishmael, of course, is the name of a biblical character who grew up believing himself to be the heir of God's promise to Abram. When Isaac is unexpectedly born, however, Ishmael finds himself a de facto orphan, cast away by Abraham and Sarah and denied the divine inheritance he had anticipated. This sense of divine and familial abandonment marks Melville's narrator, so it is fitting that at the book's conclusion he floats on Queequeg's coffin-turned-life-buoy alone in the vacant ocean. He is like an atomized, orphaned bit of type that has lost its place in any context that would endow its fragment of signification with meaning and purpose. And yet Ishmael's abandonment does not end in death; the ship *Rachel*, searching for her captain's boys who have apparently been killed in their hunt for Moby Dick, picks up Ishmael and returns him home. Despite their vulnerability, as we will see more fully in the final chapter, even Loose-Fish may be spared from a cunning harpoon and instead find themselves mercifully rescued and restored.

7
Macadamized Minds

While Melville is worried that the "thoughts of thinkers" who have been cut adrift from thick local or religious communities are vulnerable to manipulation, Thoreau harbors an even more fundamental concern: the very ability of thinkers to think thoughts may be jeopardized by industrial print. In the lecture he developed as a sequel to *Walden*, "Life without Principle," Thoreau proposes a striking metaphor to describe the effects of paying attention to the steady stream of trivia produced by industrial printing and the news media.[1] He claims that such trivial bits of information can *macadamize* our intellects, a term that may require a bit of explanation. *Macadam* refers to a kind of road construction named after its inventor, Scottish engineer John McAdam. While the best engineering methods of that era called for road beds to be built on a foundation of large stones, McAdam determined that small, hand-broken stones would better withstand the freeze-thaw cycle. He had supervisors carefully measure hand-broken stones to be sure that no large ones slipped through. The angular edges of these rocks would bind together and form a smooth, long-lasting surface for traffic. McAdam's name lives on today in the word tarmac, which refers to macadam roads that were sprayed with tar to cut the dust (see fig. 7-1).

Given this context, here is Thoreau's account of how patterns of attention can alter our minds:

> I believe that the mind can be permanently profaned by the habit of attending to trivial things, so that all our thoughts shall be tinged with triviality. Our very intellect shall be macadamized, as it were—its foundation broken into fragments for the wheels of travel to roll over; and if you would know what will make the most durable pavement, surpassing rolled stones, spruce blocks, and asphaltum, you have only to look into some of our minds which have been subjected to this treatment so long.[2]

FIGURE 7-1. *First American Macadam Road.* Carl Rakeman, 1823.

Thoreau weaves together several key terms and metaphors in these two sentences. To begin with, "profaned" compares our minds to temples. *Fane* is the Latin word for temple, so *profane* literally means before or outside the temple. When we attend too closely to temporal affairs, we "desecrate" our minds. Hence Thoreau goes on to say in the following sentence that we should "make once more a fane of the mind." What we give attention to has lasting consequences, and Thoreau appeals to his audience to consecrate their intellects by excluding unworthy objects.

Habit emphasizes the repetitive, formative nature of attention. When readers become accustomed to consuming a continuous array of ephemera—a habit encouraged by the infinite scroll feature of social media feeds—they become passive recipients of a stream of information. By warning about information habits, Thoreau is not advocating that we hole ourselves up and ignore everything going on around us; on the contrary, his own life and writings demonstrate his active participation in contemporary events. While Thoreau is sometimes accused of withdrawing from society, Laura Dassow Walls' masterful biography demonstrates this is an unfair caricature.[3] After all, Thoreau helped people fleeing slavery, participated in abolitionist movements, and spent a night in jail over his refusal to pay a tax that helped fund the Mexican-American War.

Indeed, his speech passionately defending John Brown after the failed Harpers Ferry raid changed the tide of public sentiment and galvanized support for abolition, and his essay "On the Duty of Civil Disobedience" inspired and informed subsequent generations of protesters, including Gandhi and Martin Luther King Jr.[4] Such social engagement flowed not from an obsession with the news of the day, however, but from his habits of attending to natural phenomena and classic books. Such habits, he worried, were threatened by the proliferation of titillating printed materials. In Thoreau's view, the quality of our social engagement is inversely proportional to the quantity of our informational intake.

Finally, *trivia* is more than merely an indictment of the frivolous affairs that populate the news; this word also continues Thoreau's road metaphor. *Trivia* comes from a Latin word meaning an intersection of three roads, so by implication it refers to a place that is well-traveled. In English, it came to refer to things that are common, well-known, and hence insignificant. Thoreau nods to these roots when he writes earlier in this paragraph, "If I am to be a thoroughfare, I prefer that it be of the mountain-brooks, the Parnassian streams, and not the town-sewers."[5] Thoreau imagines our minds as conduits or roadways for ideas, and we are shaped by what we allow to travel down our intellectual thoroughfares. If we habitually attend to trivial things, our minds turn into finely crushed gravel and become susceptible to whatever ads or slogans or memes other people send spinning down our macadamized intellects.

Even though Thoreau did not have twenty-first-century research about the brain to support his claims that our habits of attention have long-lasting effects, recent scholarship backs up his metaphor. As we become increasingly embedded in an "ecosystem of interruption technologies" that fosters a state of "continuous partial attention," our neural networks are actually being restructured.[6] Books like Susan Greenfield's *Mind Change: How Digital Technologies Are Leaving Their Mark on Our Brains* and Nicholas Carr's *The Shallows: How the Internet Is Changing the Way We Think, Read and Remember* chart the work of neuroscientists who are discovering the incredible plasticity of our brains.[7] As Carr explains, "The tools man has used to support or extend his nervous system—all those technologies that through history have influenced how we find, store, and interpret information, how we direct our attention and engage our senses, how we remember and how we forget—have shaped the physical structure and workings of the human mind.... Neuroplasticity provides the missing link to our understanding of how informational media and other intellectual technologies have exerted their influence over the development of civilization and helped to guide, at a biological level, the history of human consciousness."[8] The synaptic networks in our brains shift depending on how we exercise them, so it turns out that Thoreau's metaphor names a biological reality: you can quite literally "look into . . . minds" that have habitually attended to trivial ephemera and see the resulting damages.[9]

Due to this increasingly common experience, there is now a whole genre of essays and books in which authors describe how smartphone use, social media, or simply the Internet in general have diminished their ability to engage in sustained reading. Caitlin Flanagan, for instance, recounts how Twitter wormed its way into her consciousness and sapped her ability to complete a book: "For the past few years, I've felt a strange restlessness as I read, and the desk in my bedroom is piled with wonderful books I gave up on long before the halfway mark. I had started to wonder if we were in a post-reading age, or if reading loses its pleasure as we age—but I knew that wasn't really true. . . . I had suspected for a while that my reading problems had something to do with Twitter, and several times I'd tried leaving the phone in another room—but it was no good. Twitter didn't live in the phone. It lived in me."[10] Judging from the corroborating testimonies of other readers and writers, Flanagan's experience is not unique; many people swimming in a sea of digitally abundant words feel similarly disoriented as their patterns of attention and thought shift.

Many people treat these shifts as unprecedented features of a digital era, and by so doing they project a rather naive vision of focused reading and deep thinking on earlier print cultures. Maryanne Wolf, in her book *Reader, Come Home: The Reading Brain in a Digital World*, exemplifies this attitude in a series of questions: "Will the quality of our attention change as we read on mediums that advantage immediacy, dart-quick task switching, and continuous monitoring of distraction, as opposed to the more deliberative focusing of our attention? . . . Will our quality of attention in reading—the basis of the quality of our thought—change inexorably as our culture transitions away from a print-based culture toward a digital one?"[11] These are important questions, but they overstate the newness of digital temptations.

Similarly, while Neil Postman acknowledges that "every new technology for thinking involves a tradeoff," he also claims that during the first century of the American republic "what reading would have been done was done seriously, intensely, and with steadfast purpose."[12] Yet distraction is an age-old temptation. New technologies have produced more sophisticated means for preying on human curiosity, but humans have always been tempted by the easy pleasures of titillation and amusement, and textual technologies have long been used to exploit these temptations. From the beginning of the age of print, pornographic books spread widely, and superficial news and stories, from the obscene to the sensational, drove a booming business in antebellum America.[13] In response, many nineteenth-century Americans expressed concerns that closely parallel Wolf's. As I described in the introduction to this book, Samuel Griswold Goodrich observed that "amusements" such as "books and newspapers" had become "toys and pastimes, taken up every day, and by everybody, in the short intervals of labor, and then hastily dismissed, like waste paper."[14] Even expert readers have long been tempted by the pleasures of mass-produced "easy reading," to use Thoreau's term of opprobrium.

The perennial nature of this problem does not mean that it is insignificant, however, and Thoreau makes a strong case that engaging in easy reading is not merely a harmless diversion: there are serious personal and social consequences when our minds become macadamized by the habit of attending to trivial things. Nineteenth-century advances in communications technologies, the telegraph in particular, networked individuals in newly intimate ways. Disturbing news and sensational stories competed for individuals' attention and impeded their ability to sustain focused thought. Thoreau warns that readers who fail to discipline their intellectual appetites in this context will experience intellectual and emotional disorders and will lack the ability to contribute responsibly to the needs of their communities.

Networked by Iron Nerves and Iron Muscles

Thoreau's choice of vehicle for his metaphor—a macadam road—is particularly apt because nineteenth-century transportation technologies served as a key factor in fragmenting Americans' attention and chipping away at their ability to think deliberately and independently. The 1792 Postal Service Act authorized the establishment of postal routes and heavily subsidized newspaper delivery. Congress believed the health of the democracy depended on cheap and reliable transportation of information, and this act was the culmination of their efforts to ensure this, efforts that began when the Continental Congress chartered a postal service in 1775 and named Benjamin Franklin postmaster general.

This legal and economic framework made possible a truly incredible level of news consumption in antebellum America. Newspapers were already taking on an increasingly prominent place in cultural life throughout the Atlantic world. German philosopher G. W. F. Hegel boldly claimed that "reading the morning newspaper is the realist's morning prayer," and his understanding of historical progression lent great importance to the day's news: one could see the development of human civilization unfolding in the pages of the daily paper.[15] Yet the American appetite for newspapers far surpassed that of any other country. In 1810 "Americans bought 24 million copies of newspapers annually, the largest aggregate circulation of any country of the world, regardless of size. The early part of the century also measured the largest increase of newspaper copies per capita, from 3.4 in 1810 to 5.1 in 1820. This was a remarkable figure considering that of the 8 million Americans, half were under the age of sixteen and a fifth enslaved and forbidden to read."[16] To put these numbers in perspective, consider that there were "thirty times as many newspapers [in America] per head of the population in 1835 as in England."[17] Americans were uniquely fixated on the events of the day.[18]

It was into this news-hungry environment that the telegraph entered with great fanfare in 1844. The following year, an essay in Horace Greeley's *Tribune* lauded this technology with almost messianic fervor: "The Magnetic Telegraph, which is literally material thought, and flies as swift, absolutely annihilating space and running in advance of time, will be so extended to all the great cities in the Union—so that a net-work of nerves of iron wire, strung with lightning, will ramify from the brain, New York, to the distant limbs and members—to the Atlantic seaboard towns, to Pittsburgh, Cincinnati, Louisville, Nashville, St. Louis and New Orleans." The result of this new nervous system was to be the spread of truth and enlightenment: "The infallible Telegraph will contradict [newspapers'] falsehoods as fast as they can publish them . . . so that fraud and deception will be next to impossible." Hence "the deeper thoughts and capacities of the world" will be expressed and so "lift the public mind" to new heights.[19] Such messianic rhetoric recurred regularly; in particular there was another burst when the first transatlantic cable was laid in 1858. This feat was greeted with exuberant claims, and "a popular slogan suggested that the effect of the electric telegraph would be to 'make muskets into candlesticks.'" One enthusiastic report concluded breathlessly, "It is impossible that old prejudices and hostilities should longer exist, while such an instrument has been created for the exchange of thought between all the nations of the earth."[20] The fact that the cable failed after only three weeks and would not be replaced until 1866 barely dimmed the encomiums. According to such optimistic accounts, the telegraph becomes the network that stitches together disparate individuals into a unified, harmonious body politic—even knitting their minds into one neural network.[21]

Oliver Wendell Holmes Sr. further developed this imagery of networked public consciousness, though he recognized the dark side of such collective thought and feeling. Writing in the early months of the Civil War, he differentiated the way Americans were experiencing the Civil War from their experience of previous conflicts such as the Revolution. In particular, he figured the telegraph and the railroad as iron nerves and iron muscles which unite the nation's minds and bodies:

> The first and obvious difference [from the Revolutionary era] consists in the fact that the whole nation is now penetrated by the ramifications of a network of iron nerves which flash sensation and volition backward and forward to and from towns and provinces as if they were organs and limbs of a single living body. The second is the vast system of iron muscles which, as it were, move the limbs of the mighty organism one upon another. . . . This perpetual intercommunication, joined to the power of instantaneous action, keeps us always alive with excitement.

The people receive "almost hourly paragraphs, laden with truth or falsehood as the case may be, making us restless always for the last fact or rumor they are telling."[22] Holmes sees some good in the unity effected by these technologies, but he also notes the negative symptoms, the "nervous restlessness" that prevents people from focusing on any task; in particular, he cites people who find themselves unable to write or even read a book and who instead re-read newspaper reports of the latest war news. And like Thoreau, Holmes is concerned about the effect this has on a person's ability to sustain independent or deliberate thought: "When any startling piece of war news comes, it keeps repeating itself in our minds in spite of all we can do. The same trains of thought go tramping round in a circle through the brain like the supernumeraries that make up the grand Army of the stage show. Now, if a thought goes round the brain a thousand times in a day, it will have worn as deep a track as one which has passed through it once a week for 20 years."[23] Yet even while he shares Thoreau's concerns that this media and transportation infrastructure turns individuals into passive nodes within a vast nervous system, Holmes also perceives its benefits in unifying and mobilizing the nation to wage war, and his essay remains ambivalent about the overall consequences of a networked public.

One of the most notable consequences of this network of iron nerves and iron muscles is the intimate experience of a common feeling or *consensus*. The word *consensus*, in fact, first enters English in the mid-nineteenth century, and it refers to the organs in an individual body feeling and working together as well as to a nation or other group of people sharing the same sensations and opinions.[24] Yet as people come to think and feel in unison, the dangers of groupthink become more pronounced. Political slogans and sentimental appeals pulse through these networks and speed along the macadamized thoroughfares of the individual minds plugged into them. And when there is an exception, when a limb or organ of this "single living body" encounters a sensation that it finds revolting, the experience is more intimate and hence more disconcerting. To give the most obvious nineteenth-century example of this, when Northerners read pro-slavery essays or Southerners received abolitionist pamphlets in the mail, their deeply divergent sentiments became unignorable.[25] The networking technologies that make public consensus possible also make the divisions that persist more apparent and galling.

Holmes' reservations about the damaging effects of war news may seem distinct from Thoreau's concerns about the effects of habitually attending to trivia. War news, after all, seems the polar opposite of trivia—it involves matters of life and death, and it reports on events that will determine the fate of the union and the cause of freedom. Yet even deadly serious events—and perhaps *especially* such events—can be trivialized by the manner of their communication and reception. The narrator of Nathaniel Hawthorne's 1862 essay "Chiefly about War Matters" wrestles with this tension. On the one hand, he feels that "there is a kind of treason in insulating one's self" from news about the war, but the alternative—giving himself "up to reading newspapers and listening to the click of the telegraph"—proved "abominably irksome" and left him susceptible to war propaganda.[26] When we become passive feelers of intense emotions—fear, outrage, horror—and have little means of acting upon these emotions, our perspectives become distorted, and we are more likely to neglect mundane and local responsibilities. When we are plugged into this iron network, distant news colonizes our attention and our priorities and perspective become distorted. The result, in Thoreau's terms, is "a stagnation of the vital circulations, and a general deliquium and sloughing off of all the intellectual faculties."[27] In this macadamized and passive state, we lack the freedom to shape our emotional and rational responses to particular events.

Confirmed Dyspepsia

While the optimistic article published in Greeley's *Tribune* proclaims that the "infallible Telegraph" will spread "deeper thoughts" to the nation, Thoreau is concerned that the opposite is in fact happening: abundant information does not spread wisdom and deep thinking so much as it spreads trivia and sensational gossip. The Internet age has borne out Thoreau's worries: we all have access to those books which "are the treasured wealth of the world," but it is cat videos and superficial memes that go viral.[28] While his claim that this state of affairs macadamizes our intellects may be his most striking metaphor, it is not the only comparison he uses to describe the damages caused by distracted consumption of abundant information. In both *Walden* and "Life without Principle," Thoreau develops his concerns through a dietetic metaphor: if we attend to the informational equivalent of junk food, we—as both individuals and communities—will get indigestion and lose the mental and emotional energy we need to understand complex issues and respond rightly to them.

His fullest statement of this metaphor comes near the end of "Life without Principle":

> Those things which now most engage the attention of men, as politics and the daily routine, are, it is true, vital functions of human society, but should be unconsciously performed, like the corresponding functions of the physical body. . . . Not only individuals, but States, have thus a confirmed dyspepsia, which expresses itself, you can imagine by what sort of eloquence. Thus our life is not altogether a forgetting, but also, alas! to a great extent, a remembering, of that which we should never have been conscious of, certainly not in our waking hours.[29]

Thoreau's vivid imagery—or perhaps I should say his pungent olfactory description—conveys the dangers of indiscriminate consumption of the products of industrial print. An unhealthy mental diet results in a kind of intellectual bloating and discomfort, and the problem is further compounded because such a diet intensifies our craving for mental junk food. This is not just an individual problem: Thoreau points out that states too can suffer the dyspeptic effects of fragmented attention. Politics in the age of social media bears out his warnings.

Thoreau calls this disordered intellectual appetite *curiosity*, which, as I described in the introduction, is the same word Augustine uses for this vice. This mental craving for some "new" tidbit of information is anal-ogous to a craving for snacks that are salty or sweet but that lack real nutrition.[30] The more we give into this craving, the less we are able to resist it: "In proportion as our inward life fails, we go more constantly and desperately to the post-office. . . . In health we have not the least curiosity about such events. We do not live for idle amusement. I would not run round a corner to see the world blow up."[31] Attending to titillating ephemera creates a vicious cycle as our "inward life fails" and we become further enslaved to the whims of our curiosity.

This is an old problem; humans have always been prone to rubber-necking and gossip. But just as junk food poses new threats when food engineers find ways to make it maximally addictive, so the publishing and news industries prey on our inherent disposition to curiosity by ever more sophisticated techniques. In antebellum America, the penny press and sensational novels proved very profitable. Today, TikTok and other social media sites tweak their algorithms to be maximally addic-tive.[32] Advanced analytics enable website editors to identify the traits that are likely to make a story go viral, and they use this information to choose what news to cover and to hone clickbait headlines that will entice more revenue-generating clicks.[33] We cannot simply blame journalists for these developments—existential economic pressures lead newsrooms to adopt such tactics, and they would not be effective if readers demanded more substantive, nuanced fare. But *BuzzFeed* quizzes will always be more enticing than longform essays in the *Atlantic*.[34] It is always more tempting to eat candy and fast food instead of fresh vegetables from the garden. It is easier to get an emotional "hit" from shallow, sensational news than it is to spend the mental energy required to engage with more serious matters; watching the world blow up is more exciting than studying its treasured wealth.

The irony is that when we succumb to these temptations, we are not satiated. Instead, we get that bloated feeling that has led people to talk about "binging" on Netflix. Thoreau did not have streaming TV to cri-tique, so his targets are the "profane and stale revelation of the bar-room and the police court" and the wildly popular sentimental novels.[35] In *Walden*, he upbraids his neighbors who "with saucer eyes, and erect and primitive curiosity, and with unwearied gizzard" gorge themselves on the latest installment from the pen of their favored novelist.[36] "To read well," Thoreau writes, "is a noble exercise, and one that will task the reader more than any exercise which the customs of the day esteem."[37] Hence he urges his neighbors to feed their minds on a more robust diet than can be found in "the columns of the daily paper."[38]

Thoreau's rigorous standards can make him seem like a tiresome scold. After all, is there not something to be said for unwinding after a long day with some light, mindless reading? Perhaps, but Thoreau's dietary metaphor contains an important insight. Some modes of relaxation—much like "comfort food"—actually keep us in a state of bloated exhaustion. The ennui that leads us to, as Holmes reports, "read the same telegraphic dispatches over and over again in different papers" or binge-watch Netflix or mindlessly scroll through a social media feed looking for easy tidbits of emotional excitement is a result of overstimulation and indiscriminate news consumption.[39] Paradoxically we may be less tired and have more mental energy if we shut up the doors of our fane and discipline our attention. In an environment where we are constantly bombarded with enticing distractions, such discipline is essential: "By all kinds of traps and signboards, threatening the extreme penalty of the divine law, exclude such trespassers from the only ground which can be sacred to you. It is so hard to forget what it is worse than useless to remember!"[40] Other scholars have noted that in the age of industrialized print, "ensuring this equation between modern print culture and progress was possible only through the formation of particular types of readers. In the new world of print saturation, readers who lacked self-restraint and discrimination might easily fritter away their lives on the lowliest productions of the press."[41] Thoreau's injunction to exercise readerly discipline partakes of this broader cultural conversation about how to develop readers who could prudently navigate this new information abundance.[42]

Thoreau's diagnosis of personal and public dyspepsia leads him to focus on two particular consequences of this disorder. The first is that a restless curiosity, a craving for some new bit of entertainment, makes us incredibly vulnerable to the wiles of advertisers and politicians and ideologues. We become susceptible to the latest groupthink because our thoughts are dictated by slogans, trending jargon, or viral hashtags. To return to Thoreau's core metaphor, a macadamized mind, an intellect ground to bits and made into a highway, offers no resistance to whatever thought or emotion is driven down it. If our intellects are macadamized, we will lack the vocabulary or categories to see the world truthfully. We'll simply take in the events around us through the prepackaged categories provided by the mass media. Hashtags and slogans lack the precision and nuance required to do justice to the complexity of our world and time.

Hence we become passive thoroughfares, the objects of our attention determined by whatever headlines or memes happen to be going viral. And Thoreau reminds us that what is popular is unlikely to be very edifying: "If I am to be a thoroughfare, I prefer that it be of the mountain brooks, the Parnassian streams, and not the town sewers."

The second consequence is that our emotional, affective responses become disproportionate; we come to care deeply about issues or events that we have little opportunity to respond to, while we can neglect matters for which we are directly responsible. In *Walden* Thoreau describes this problem by critiquing the recent boom in philanthropic activity: "There are a thousand hacking at the branches of evil to one who is striking at the root, and it may be that he who bestows the largest amount of time and money on the needy is doing the most by his mode of life to produce that misery which he strives in vain to relieve."[43] Thoreau's polemic against the "drastic philanthropy [that] seeks out the Esquimaux and the Patagonian" is famously echoed in fictional form by Charles Dickens' character Mrs. Jellyby. A minor character in *Bleak House*, Mrs. Jellyby is a "telescopic philanthropist" fixated on helping people in Africa while blithely neglecting her own children.[44] The twenty-first-century digital media ecosystem puts all of us in danger of becoming Mrs. Jellybys: making today's news the primary lens through which we view the world magnifies the significance of distant, shocking events and obscures the important events happening at hand.

The temptations to telescopic or misdirected attention, and the disordered emotions that follow, become more acute as communications technologies improve. Thoreau fingered the telegraph as part of the problem in his day, and he quipped that once the transatlantic telegraph cable was finally laid, "perchance the first news that will leak through into the broad, flapping American ear will be that the Princess Adelaide has the whooping cough."[45] Neil Postman agrees with Thoreau that this technology inaugurated many of the problematic dynamics associated with the modern news industry: "Only four years after Morse opened the nation's first telegraph line on May 24, 1844, the Associated Press was founded, and news from nowhere, addressed to no one in particular, began to crisscross the nation. Wars, crimes, crashes, fires, floods—much of it the social and political equivalent of Adelaide's whooping cough—became the content of what people called 'the news of the day.'" Thus Postman claims that the telegraph "dramatically altered what may be called the 'information-action ratio.'"[46] By flooding us with information to which we can have no meaningful response, these technologies threaten to malform our affective sensibilities and keep us—on both a personal and public level—in a state of confirmed dyspepsia.

Near the end of "Life without Principle" Thoreau stubbornly declares, "I have not got to answer for having read a single President's Message."[47] If we find our attention fragmented and our emotional lives disordered, Thoreau would recommend that we be "tied to the mast like Ulysses."[48] Perhaps an equivalent to the rope that bound Ulysses would be getting rid of our smartphones or at least establishing device-free times and spaces. Such practical, physical measures are required if we want to unplug ourselves from the digital networks that impinge on our freedom to exercise sustained attention and think carefully. Hence Thoreau's two-part remedy for those whose minds have been macadamized: "If we have thus desecrated ourselves,—as who has not?—the remedy will be by wariness and devotion to reconsecrate ourselves, and make once more a fane of the mind. We should treat our minds, that is, ourselves, as innocent and ingenuous children, whose guardians we are, and be careful what objects and what subjects we thrust on their attention. Read not the Times. Read the Eternities."[49] As Thoreau acknowledges, we have all, to one degree or another, desecrated our minds by habitual attention to trivia, but he hopes that by (1) wariness and (2) devotion we can reconsecrate our minds and preserve their status as temples or fanes. If the problem is habitual attention to things outside the temple, the solution is habitual attention to things inside the temple. This is a two-part movement: it's a movement away from—of wariness toward—the gossip and trivia of the Times and a movement toward—of devotion to—the good, beautiful, complex truth of the Eternities. I will have more to say about all this in chapter 11, which considers the methods Thoreau develops to wrestle with complex truths and tune himself to discern deeper harmonies that are otherwise drowned out by the noise of the day's news. At this juncture, the important point is that being plugged in to iron or fiberoptic nerves can damage our ability to exercise sustained attention and think freely and deliberately. Thoreau warns that our intellectual and emotional health depends on detaching ourselves—at least to some extent—from the information network.

8

Commodities

Thoreau was concerned that mass media would fragment our attention and damage the health of our personal and public thought. Emily Dickinson shared Thoreau's concerns, and, like him, she recommended that individuals protect their minds and souls by shutting out the noisy clamor of mass media:

> The Soul selects her own Society—
> Then—shuts the Door—
> To her divine Majority—
> Present no more—[1]

By making once more a fane of herself or, as Dickinson puts it in the last stanza of this poem, by closing "the Valves of her attention—/ Like Stone—," the Soul preserves her integrity. The words we allow to infiltrate our minds inevitably shape the quality and content of our thoughts, hence the need to discipline the valves of our attention.

Dickinson's greater concern, however, was not that industrialized print would macadamize her mind but that it would commodify her mind. By addressing her as a generic part of a homogeneous mass audience—as a voter, as a woman, as a potential consumer—such media reduced the "Human Spirit / To Disgrace of Price—." Publishing her poetry in this media ecosystem would make her complicit in its damaging commodification of human persons. Dickinson thus refused this bargain even if it meant her poems would go unread. In "Publication—is the Auction" she lays out these concerns in her distinctive fashion:

> Publication—is the Auction
> Of the Mind of Man—
> Poverty—be justifying
> For so foul a thing

Possibly—but We—would rather
From Our Garret go
White—unto the White Creator—
Than invest—Our Snow—

Thought belong to Him who gave it—
Then—to Him Who bear
Its Corporeal illustration—sell
The Royal Air—

In the Parcel—Be the Merchant
Of the Heavenly Grace—
But reduce no Human Spirit
To Disgrace of Price—[2]

Dickinson admits that poverty "possibly" justifies selling one's words, but otherwise there is no excuse for reducing the priceless gift of a human spirit to a base commodity. Shaping our thoughts into a product that can be marketed and sold defiles their divine origin.

Dickinson's poem does not, of course, condemn all forms of sharing our ideas and words with others. Her particular concerns stem from the increasing commercialization of the print market in midcentury America. As she wrote to T. W. Higginson in her second letter to him, "Two Editors of Journals came to my Father's House, this winter—and asked me for my Mind—and when I asked them 'Why,' they said I was penurious—and they, would use it for the World."[3] As her few efforts to publish poems quickly taught her, editors insisted on standardizing her poems to fit the market of the day and make them palatable to readers. One of her biographers thus clarifies that "at the time she wrote Higginson she does not seem to be trying to avoid publication as such; she is inquiring how one can publish and at the same time preserve the integrity of one's art."[4] If the only way to share her poems is to have them bowdlerized, to have their syntax and rhymes smoothed to appeal to the expectations of the reading public, then Dickinson would prefer to go from her garret white and unpublished.

Media developments in recent decades have only exacerbated this tendency to commodify the human spirit. By now, thanks to marketing algorithms and social media, we are all invited to imagine ourselves as the sum of a narrow set of factors or choices: Identify your race, gender, class, age, education level, favorite TV show, political party, hobby, and favorite color. Now that you have articulated and constructed this identity, you can perform it. Given your chosen set of identity markers, you know what clothes to buy, what music to stream, what political party to support, what opinions

to express. In a radio interview he gave in the late 1990s, Ivan Illich critiqued this constant invitation to "intensive self-algorithmization" as both
disembodying and depersonalizing. He even verbalizes—in an aside that
Dickinson would approve of—his constant awareness "of the mercenary
side of the relationship between the two of us. I am being used for a show,
by a good madame."[5] Even in a conversation with a trusted friend and inter-
viewer, Illich could not shake the awareness that the result would be a verbal commodity to be sold to a mass audience.

Social media in particular amplifies this reductive view of the human
person by rendering people as legible and profitable trails of data. Justin
E. H. Smith articulates how this reductive interpretation colors our interpersonal relationships and even shapes how we view ourselves:

> human subjects are vanishingly small beneath the tsunami of likes,
> views, clicks and other metrics that is currently transforming selves
> into financialized vectors of data. This financialization is complete, one
> might suppose, when the algorithms make the leap from machines orig-
> inally meant only to assist human subjects, into the way these human
> subjects constitute themselves and think about themselves, their tastes
> and values, and their relations with others.[6]

Publishers, movie producers, marketers, and politicians increasingly treat
people as commodities that can be known and manipulated by their data
trails. As a result, "the tech companies' transformation of individuals
into data sets has effectively moneyballed the entirety of human social
reality."[7] It is not merely that we are caught in systems that treat us as digital representations of our analog selves; it is that we now are formed and
habituated to relate to digital approximations of our fellow citizens, our
friends and family members, and even ourselves. This is the culmination
of a process that began with various governmental and corporate methods to make citizens and consumers "legible," in the parlance of political
scientist James C. Scott. States develop many techniques "to reduce an
infinite array of detail to a set of categories" to facilitate "appropriation,
control, and manipulation."[8] This is the same model of legibility on which
Netflix, Amazon, and Google build their algorithms, and various social
media platforms democratize this perspective, predisposing us to imagine
ourselves and others as legible commodities.

Algorithms and social media platforms do not have access to actual
persons; they manipulate and display the data trails left behind by people
and their interactions. As we participate in these forums, we become habituated to relate to others—and ourselves—based on digital approximations

rather than real-world interactions. As inhabitants of a digitally mediated world, we all find ourselves playing the role of data scientists, trying to make sense of and interact with our "followers" or "friends" based on scraps of data gleaned from what they post on Facegramitterok.[9]

Thus if Whitman would have been an Instagram power user, Dickinson would have been a dumb phone–toting abstainer from all social media. She opts out of a media ecosystem that threatens to damage her expansive and irreducible self. The poem cited above valorizes the blank page by comparing it to snow; the white of the page is polluted, like dirty snow, when invested with type's black marks. And Dickinson is of course punning on the meaning of "invest." On one level, she means simply that words clothe the blank of the given self to make it legible to the public, but the word's financial meaning is also present. She is refusing to treat her self as capital that might be invested in search of profit. Doing so would be to transform the invaluable self, given by a Heavenly Grace, into "a financialized vector."

Situating Dickinson in the context of a burgeoning mass-media market clarifies the significance of her refusal to sell her poems. Her poetry often gestures to her sense of an expansive, mysteriously irreducible self, and she explored various forms of relating to other persons in ways that might honor this view of the self: hymns, marginalia, and personal correspondence. These more personal, relational forms of address offered the possibility of mutual sharing between Human Spirits while avoiding the public sphere's distorting effects.

Buy—Here!

The national census, mass media, newspaper advertisements—all of these were increasingly significant realities in antebellum America, and all lump individual persons into a limited set of categories in order to count, control, or profit. The census was the grand national effort to make the new nation's inhabitants legible to the fledgling federal bureaucracy. Yet the act of making full-orbed persons legible invariably reduces and distorts them. As Paul Schor argues, the census became "a locus for assigning collective identities to individuals in a national context," and his analysis demonstrates how these collective identities flatten the particular complexities of individuals.[10] Scholars of the census have particularly emphasized the racial aspects of this distortion.[11] The Constitution's language tortuously avoids mentioning slavery: it specifies that free persons (including indentured persons) should be counted; Indians should be excluded; and "three fifths of all other Persons" should be added to the number of free persons. Over the ensuing decades, the census tried to categorize race in all sorts of flawed and bizarre ways. Efforts to represent people more accurately generally faltered. For instance, political tensions in the late 1840s led to hot debates about the structure of the 1850 census, and the result was that free individuals were listed by name for the first time, but enslaved people were still enumerated rather than named.[12] When it was politically expedient or profitable to do so, persons could be counted but not given even the minimal dignity of a name.

The census took place only every decade and was not on the top of most Americans' minds. But a much more pervasive and potent institution had a parallel effect: the newspaper. Newspapers did not literally reduce persons to numbers in the same fashion as the census did, but over the course of the nineteenth century, newspaper publishers shifted from political partisans to business investors, and readers were viewed less as potential voters than as possible consumers. At the beginning of the nineteenth century, most papers were run by a political party or faction, but as the industry professionalized, papers became profitable businesses rather than party organs, and successful ones broadened their appeal in an effort to reach as many consumers as possible. Instead of viewing the news primarily as "political information or persuasion," the news became seen as "a commodity to be shaped and marketed with an eye for profit."[13]

This transition helped diffuse the shrill rhetoric of the Jacksonian era, but it was not an unmixed improvement. One danger with such commercialization is that it "imposes the imperative that newspapers must entertain their readers" in order to grow their circulation numbers. But as Gerald Baldasty asks, "Will a vision of news as a money-making commodity always square with broader societal interests and needs? . . . When commercial considerations dictate the general news process, the press will serve democracy only when such service is financially profitable."[14] Beyond such prioritization of the entertaining and sensational, commercial newspapers also commodified their readers, treating them as products to be sold to potential advertisers. They increasingly imagined readers not as persons to persuade or inform but as quantifiable sets of consumers whose value derived from the likelihood that they would purchase a particular product.

Advertising agencies figured prominently in this shift. They developed during the middle decades of the nineteenth century to help businesses craft and place their ads for maximum effectiveness, and newspapers in turn became financially dependent on these agencies for their revenue. Advertising agents worked to define "the quality of a newspaper . . . based not on its ability to produce news but on such things as the size of its circulation, the demographic profile of its readers, and its willingness to accommodate advertising interests."[15] Advertisers pushed editors to "view readers not as a monolithic mass but as differentiated by class, location, purchasing power, religion, or even race."[16] These advertising agents could not hope to attain the specific audience targeting made possible by Google, Facebook, or X (formerly Twitter), but already by the mid-nineteenth century this trajectory toward viewing persons as "financialized vectors of data" had been set, and different ads were run in different papers to better target certain demographics. At the prodding of these agencies, some papers even experimented with "reading notices" or "puffs," which masked ads in the form of news stories and prefigured today's "native advertising."[17] Thus neither political parties nor advertisers proved to be disinterested patrons of the news: both, in their own ways, treated readers as pawns and sought to manipulate them for power or profit.

Because of the distortions mass communication wrought upon interpersonal relations, and the resulting threats to the integrity of the "Human Spirit," Emily Dickinson was leery of the whole publishing ecosystem. She mostly evaded it, choosing instead to stitch her poems in hand-bound fascicles or to enclose them in personal letters. Her poetry remained illegible to a mass audience. A telling symbol of this illegibility is the way her artistic work escaped the narrow categories of the U.S. census: the 1870 census lists her as "without occupation" (see fig. 8-1). Clearly "private poet" was not a recognized "Profession, Occupation, or Trade."

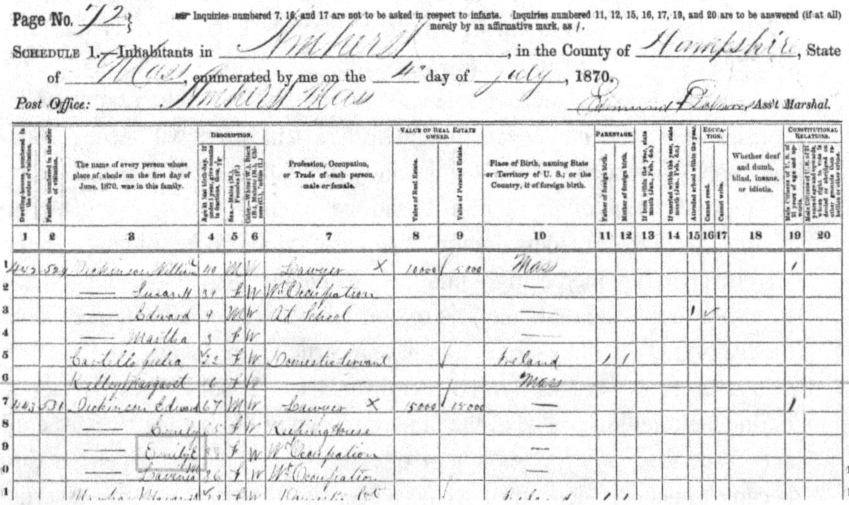

FIGURE 8-1. Amherst, Mass. census, displaying the occupational status of Emily Dickinson. 1870.

In one of her rare poems responding directly to the problems endemic to mass media, Dickinson diagnoses the corrupting address of advertising jargon. She encloses this humorous poem in a letter to her friend Samuel Bowles, the very successful editor of the local *Springfield Republican*. Her poem mimics the way in which newspaper ads refer to readers as a discrete set of possible desires with their accompanying commercial fulfillment. If you are X, you will want to buy Y:

> Would you like summer? Taste of ours—
> Spices? Buy—here!
> Ill! We have berries, for the parching!
> Weary! Furloughs of Down!
> Perplexed! Estates of Violet—Trouble ne'er looked on!
> Captive! We bring Reprieve of Roses!
> Fainting! Flasks of Air!
> Even for Death—a Fairy medicine.
> But, which is it—sir?[18]

The poem follows an if-then marketing formula: depending on the identity of my prospective customer, I will sell him the appropriate commodity. The reader, Bowles, must fit one of the enumerated conditions: Ill? Weary? Perplexed? Captive? Whatever the case may be, I have a product for you! None of the above is not an option: "Which is it—sir?"

As Shannon Thomas demonstrates, Dickinson's language here parodies ads that Bowles regularly ran in his newspaper.[19] Advertisements for patent medicines in particular made outlandish promises. Often, they were marketed as cure-alls, so regardless of your ailment, you were instructed to purchase one and the same product. Dickinson at least offers different remedies for different ailments, and significantly all the remedies she proposes are free and so resist commodification: no business can bottle summer and put it up for sale. Further, Dickinson's poem appears only in this personal letter to Bowles. As Thomas notes, "Dickinson implicitly contrasts her preferred form of interpersonal communication, the letter, with a form of mass communication, the mass media advertisement."[20] Friendship and personal dialogue serve as possible antidotes to the reductive effects of an industrial media ecosystem, one fueled by advertising dollars. Hence Dickinson's poem gently ribs the newspaper editor: while he may address his readers as potential customers, she will not reciprocate.

A Reduceless Mine

Dickinson's resistance to the commodifying tendencies within advertising-driven mass media flowed from her view of the ungraspable, endlessly complex nature of the human soul. The human person could never be reduced to a discrete set of categories or desires or needs without doing violence to that person's full self. She returns to this view of the infinite soul in many poems. "To own the Art within the Soul" includes several of her richest metaphors that gesture to this view of the human person:

> To own the Art within the Soul
> The Soul to entertain
> With Silence as a Company
> And Festival maintain
>
> In an unfurnished Circumstance
> Possession is to One
> As an Estate perpetual
> Or a reduceless Mine.[21]

The opening stanza figures the soul's art as something that is best enjoyed in a kind of continuous, silent festival within the self. As in "Publication—is the Auction," Dickinson seems worried that displaying this art to others will truncate its enjoyment. Making the soul's art public fixes it in its current form, but as the soul is in a state of continuous growth and development, so its art can only be owned properly by its creator. Because the Soul remains "an unfurnished Circumstance," because it continues to revise its interior architecture and design, the one who inhabits his or her own soul owns "an Estate perpetual / Or a reduceless Mine." Dickinson's closing two images describe the inexhaustibility of the soul. It is an estate whose yearly proceeds provide sufficiently for life. It is a mine whose riches can never be fully extracted. Dickinson's concluding pun emphasizes both that the soul is a "reduceless" resource that will never run dry and that it cannot be possessed by any other—it is "Mine."

The distinctive stylistic features of her poetry fittingly address the kind of contemplative, expansive soul she celebrates. She refuses to cater to readers who might want to draw a single, simple meaning from a poem. Instead, as she famously declares, "I dwell in Possibility." She inhabits possibility most blatantly through the gaps and ambivalences of her poems. She keeps readers nimble, unsettling them wherever they may be tempted to land on one single interpretation.[22] Readers of her poems learn to attend to the multiple meanings of each word, to watch for the way a dash or line break swerves the poem's meaning, to listen for surprising rhymes and aural echoes. In other words, Dickinson writes for the contemplative and developing soul, which she celebrates in "To own the Art within the Soul." Her poems are tightly built edifices with uncanny passageways and surprising windows; they are buildings that, like the soul itself, are larger on the inside than the outside.

Indeed in both these poems and in many others, Dickinson relies on architectural figures to describe this illegible, uncommodifiable self and declare its independence from those who might seek to own or commandeer it. She elaborates the possibilities she inhabits in terms of a house with many portals:

I dwell in Possibility–
A fairer House than Prose–
More numerous of Windows–
Superior—for Doors—[23]

And she names her "Occupation" in this poem as "The spreading wide my narrow Hands / To gather Paradise—." The interior of this house opens onto heaven itself; the soul is not a narrow enclosure but a mysterious interior from which she can access the infinite. In this respect, Dickinson's view of the soul parallels the account Augustine gives in book 10 of *Confessions*. The vast treasuries and storehouses he finds while trying to map his memory lead him to God. Marissa Grunes shows how Augustine's images inspired Dickinson's poetic figures of an architectural self: "Rather than protective enclosures, the structures in her poems are porous, prone to invasion, flooding, destruction, ghosts, and madness." These metaphors allow Dickinson "to understand her mind or soul as composed of dissonant parts, some of which remain obscure."[24] As such, the process of self-exploration is endless and leads not toward solipsism but toward unsettling encounters with hitherto unknown aspects of the soul and, indeed, with God.

In other poems, Dickinson elaborates on the uncanny encounters she has within her unexpectedly expansive self:

One need not be a Chamber—to be Haunted—
One need not be a House—
The Brain—has Corridors surpassing
Material Place—

It is safer to meet a ghost or an assassin, Dickinson writes near the end of this poem, than to encounter ourselves: "Ourself—behind ourself—Concealed— / Should startle—most—."[25] If we are startled by an uncanny encounter with even our own selves, then how much more will advertisers or census takers be flummoxed in their efforts to pin down such a soul? The face we show to others thus conceals far more than it reveals: "The Cellars of the Soul" remain hidden behind the "Countenance" that walks the public street:

> The Subterranean Freight
> The Cellars of the Soul—
> Thank God the loudest Place he made
> Is license to be still.[26]

Dickinson's concluding reference to God's creation of a place within us where we can be still responds to the instruction recorded by the psalmist: "Be still, and know that I am God."[27] Thus Dickinson thought that representing this self for public consumption within the mass print culture would misrepresent the soul and distort its true depths. If she allowed herself to be commodified, she might find the soul's doors and windows no longer opening, she might no longer encounter a startling self within her self, she might no longer find the silence where the divine can be encountered. Like Tolkien's one ring, some tools are inevitably exploitative and cannot be wielded well. Not wanting to become a transparent eyeball or adamantine self or—God forbid!—a Whitmanian celebrity, Dickinson opts to be still within the reduceless, subterranean cellars of her soul.

Celebrity and its attendant forms of self-consciousness reach into the soul and remodel its delightful and surprising depths. In the process of fashioning a persona to be consumed by the masses, one subtly and inevitably deforms a soul that might otherwise be convocated in personal relationships or local, embodied communities.[28] To avoid this, Dickinson celebrates un-self-conscious forms of life:

> Aurora is the effort
> Of the Celestial Face
> Unconsciousness of Perfectness
> To simulate, to Us.[29]

The sky's beauty is not intended for us; it is unconscious of its own perfectness, and that lends its beauty a serene power. Similarly, Dickinson praises the "North" that is "So preconcerted with itself— / So distant—to alarms—."[30] The public poet cannot be distant to alarms. Such a poet must cater to market pressures, readerly expectations, and contemporary controversies. And in Bartleby-esque fashion, Dickinson preferred not to.

So when others endeavored to capture her countenance or commodify the art within her soul, she demurred. When Higginson, for instance, requested that she mail him her "portrait," she replied, "Could you believe me—without? I . . . am small, like the Wren, and my Hair is bold, like the Chestnut Bur—and my eyes, like the Sherry in the Glass, that the Guest leaves—Would this do just as well?" She offers this series of lively similes instead of an image because "I noticed the Quick wore off those things, in a few days, and forestall the dishonor."[31] For Dickinson, "to be fixed in a daguerreotype is to lose this liveliness and is dishonorable to human nature."[32] What Dickinson sought instead was a kind of unselfconscious life, a life that refuses to "disgrace" the "Heavenly Grace" she has been given with even the slightest taint of price.

I'll Tell It You

I have emphasized Dickinson's "no" to industrial print culture in this chapter, but to conclude on this note would not be fair to her work. For of course she spoke this "no" firmly in order to affirm and pursue alternative modes of writing, publication, and relationship. To borrow a phrase from Michel de Certeau, Dickinson found ways to "make do" along the margins of a profit-oriented media ecosystem.[33] She shares her soul's art in these marginal human and relational contexts because she saw the end of language as well-tended relationships rather than fame or profits (see theses 1 and 8). Her aspiration, then, is not simply to privacy but to conviviality, to relationships that escape the distortions of mass media and an impersonal public.

It is crucial to recognize this move as both a resolute "no" and, at the same time, an act of faith in the incalculable value of a human spirit. Justin E. H. Smith concludes that some respond to environments that reduce humans to "financialized vectors of data" by "going off the grid." Thoreau describes this mode of responding in *Walden* via a parable about an Indian who wove beautiful baskets only to discover no one wanted to buy them. Many readers have noted Thoreau's reference here to his first book, *A Week on the Concord and Merrimack Rivers*, which sold very poorly: "Yet not the less, in my case, did I think it worth my while to weave them, and instead of studying how to make it worth men's while to buy my baskets, I studied rather how to avoid the necessity of selling them."[34] This parallels Dickinson's approach. As Smith notes, such "creative work" takes on "a mystical character, where it is carried out not from any belief in its power to influence the world as it is at present, as it may remain for the next millennia, but as a simple act of faith, as something that must be done, to misquote Tertullian, because it is absurd."[35] Dickinson valued her poetry not for any income or recognition it might bring her but because it came from the reduceless mine of her expansive soul.

Thus Dickinson sought ways to evade the distortions of mass media and to employ her poems in cultivating personal relationships. In "The only news I know," she avows her rejection of commercial or political news and her attention to the "bulletins" that come from "Immortality." If she receives anything to report from this source or from her meetings with "God," she promises to "tell it you." Such personal testimony to eternal news—an "I" speaking to a "you" (or a Thou, in Martin Buber's formulation)—is Dickinson's goal.[36]

Perhaps most significantly, Dickinson regularly adapted hymnic forms to accomplish this goal. She draws on this tradition in part because it provides a context—an economy of sorts—in which an author's words are offered to the broader community as a deeply personal gift, a gift given in the hope of voicing another soul's deep, inchoate spiritual yearnings and so providing others a longed for, yet elusive, expression of these longings. For some readers, at least, these poems might grant the satisfactions of articulation. In one letter to Higginson, Dickinson writes that she was asked to give some poems for a mission fundraiser: "I have promised three Hymns to a charity, but without your approval could not give them—They are short and I could write them quite plainly, and if you felt it convenient to tell me if they were faithful, I should be very grateful."[37] Christopher Phillips parses Dickinson's phrasing here as wrestling with the tension between her view of these poems as hymnic gifts and the prospect of their being sold, albeit for a good cause:

> Dickinson was concerned that her poems did not fit their new context, or might be judged so because she offered them as commodities; they were gifts, but meant to fetch a price. These poems were destined for the market, however local, and by referring to them as "hymns," Dickinson claimed a very particular kind of social life for what critics have generally considered her private poetry. The connections to God and to others must hold in order to keep these poems faithful, even as they moved out of old contexts and into something the poet could not foresee.[38]

Dickinson worried that if these poems were sold—even for charity—their gift nature might be distorted. The gift nature of a hymn, on this account, depends on its faithful articulation of the muddled mysteries found in the dark labyrinth of another's soul. Some souls will not be able to profess or unreservedly sing the hymn. It will not be suitable for all potential readers. But some readers can find comfort in the midst of spiritual or emotional angst through a hymnic poem's articulation of spiritual experience. In this context, a hymn is not something sold but is a gift offered to a soul in need.[39] It supplies the wings—or what Dickinson calls in one poem the "Thews of hymn— / And Sinew from within"—that sustain us in "ways I knew not that I knew—till then."[40]

Dickinson employed other methods in search of such convivial modes of language. She copied out hundreds of her poems and enclosed them in letters to friends. Sometimes she included a pressed flower as well.[41] As a reader, she imagined old books as friends, "Kinsmen of the Shelf" with whom she could "banquet."[42] It is a "privilege," she writes, to take the "venerable Hand" of an "Antique Book" and cultivate its acquaintance, "warming" the book's hand "in our own."[43] Her treatment of books follows from this view of them: she dog-eared pages, marked in the margins, and even pressed flowers between leaves.[44] These were all ways of personalizing books and interacting with them as one would converse with a friend. And these book friendships could play a meaningful role in her human friendships. In one poem, she describes how she cherished a book whose pages had been annotated by a friend before his death:

> A Book I have—a friend gave—
> Whose Pencil—here and there—
> Had notched the place that pleased Him—[45]

The pencil marks tracing the record of his thoughts had converted this fungible market commodity into a personal, known, and loved object.

These poetic and reading practices were Dickinson's ways of making do along the margins of her industrial print culture. But she was pessimistic about the possibility of participating fully in this media ecosystem without distorting or reducing her soul and its art. Instead, she imagined her handwritten, hand-bound fascicles as a one-way correspondence with an unresponsive readership: "This is my letter to the World / That never wrote to Me—."[46] If her letter never reaches its intended recipient or never receives a response, such is the cost of preserving her "reduceless mine" in a media ecosystem designed to commodify and profit from souls.

9

Slaves

Dickinson could afford to withdraw from the print-mediated public sphere because her social and financial security were such that she was not under pressure to auction her mind. Frederick Douglass and other African Americans who endured enslavement did not have that luxury. Douglass and his peers sought means by which they might enjoy the freedoms mass print affords while remaining cognizant of the dangers it unleashes. Douglass navigated the media technologies of his day shrewdly, keenly aware of both their possibilities and perils. In this regard, he exemplifies the hopeful posture I will turn to in the next section. He is a transitional figure from the pessimists who emphasize various forms of withdrawal to the hopeful users who are alert to the dangers of industrial print culture but nonetheless remain committed to finding convivial ways of using these tools. And his awareness of the enslaving potential in textually mediated relationships sheds light on the continuing dangers posed by the digital systems that identify and control people today.

Douglass wrestled with the tensions inherent in creating a public persona during his early years on the abolitionist speaking circuit. Like many prominent African Americans in the antebellum years, Douglass' very intelligence risked making him a pawn in the dispute over the humanity of black people.[1] As his biographer David Blight explains, "His power rested in part on his sheer talent with words on the platform. But it also emanated from his role, one he could almost never avoid, as symbol, as an exhibit of the black man, the slave with a stunningly informed, active, and brilliant mind."[2] Douglass articulates his frustrations with this role in his 1855 autobiography. He describes the way he was introduced on the lecture circuit organized by white abolitionists to drum up new subscribers for their abolitionist papers: "Many came, no doubt, from curiosity to hear what a Negro could say in his own cause. I was generally introduced as a 'chattel'—a '*thing*'—a piece of southern '*property*'—the chairman assuring the audience that *it* could speak."[3] While intended to generate support (and revenue) for the abolitionist cause, the way in which William Lloyd Garrison, John Collins, and others exhibited Douglass "was also of a piece with the exhibition culture of freaks, missing links, and other human oddities put on view in circus and carnival shows."[4] Douglass felt demeaned by this situation, and he confesses that some of his "colored friends in New Bedford thought very badly of my wisdom for thus exposing and degrading myself."[5]

This tokenizing effect was exacerbated by the abolitionists' insistence that Douglass confine his speeches to a simple recital of the abuses he'd endured during his years of enslavement. "Give us the facts," one told him, and "we will take care of the philosophy." But Douglass records that this "was a task altogether too mechanical for my nature. . . . I could not always obey, for I was now reading and thinking."[6] And in these oral settings, he began trying out his own philosophy, his own arguments for abolition. When his friends urged him to perform the role his audience was expecting, Douglass insisted on breaking out of this mold: "It was said to me, 'Better have a *little* of the plantation manner of speech than not; 'tis not best that you seem too learned.' These excellent friends were actuated by the best of motives, and were not altogether wrong in their advice; and still I must speak just the word that seemed to *me* the word to be spoken *by* me."[7] The embodied, oral setting of these events, a setting that made Douglass' presence and humanity palpable and persuasive to his audience, provided him the opportunity to push beyond the expectations of those who came to hear "a 'chattel'—a '*thing*'" speak.

Yet as Douglass took advantage of media technologies to spread his message and presence to a broader audience, he had to take great care to resist being "thingified," to borrow a term that Martin Luther King Jr. often used, echoing the label employed by Douglass' abolitionist friends.[8] Take, for example, Douglass' use of new photographic technologies. He quickly recognized that this technology was too powerful *not* to use in his efforts to advance the cause of abolition and racial justice. At the same time, it was too dangerous to embrace fully. Douglass was the most photographed nineteenth-century American, but his photographs construct a careful portrayal of an "inscrutable" human.[9] In his writings about photographic technology, Douglass explains its great potential, and he lionizes Louis Daguerre for his potent invention, which "by the simple but all-abounding sunlight, has converted the planet into a picture gallery."[10] These photographs hold great power in "reaching and swaying the heart."[11] Douglass showed great caution, however, in his poses for the camera. He mostly eschewed props, with the occasional exception of books or newspapers.[12] As Zoe Trodd argues, the effect of his poses was to "make him as unavailable as possible. [His portraits] offer the viewer no clues, symbolic objects, or accessible messages to help 'read' him. . . . In this way, by refusing to offer accessible smiles, readable props, and expressive backdrops, Douglass countered the visual culture of exposure that made black bodies *available*. His photographs transformed the black body from an emblem of passive suffering to one of stoic, inscrutable manhood."[13] His fierce eyes, staring back at the camera, testify to his determination to resist tokenization or appropriation.

Douglass knew all too well that moving from local, embodied networks to far-flung, document-based networks was not a linear, inevitable movement toward freedom. Despite the breathless claims of their boosters, powerful communication tools and networks are not intrinsically liberatory. The potential such documentary networks had to serve the cause of justice was conditioned upon whether their participants were motivated by personal affection and a deep commitment to justice. Even as he mediated his identity through print and photography to further his political and moral goals, Douglass knew that he remained vulnerable to forms of reenslavement, to technologies and institutions and practices that threatened to "thingify" him.

The digital era has shifted and intensified causes for concern over the thingifying potential of document-based self-representation. In our era of biopolitics and surveillance capitalism, the very tools we rely on to share words and images, to verify our identities, and to participate in social and economic life render us vulnerable to manipulation and control. In more authoritarian countries, such as China, this takes the form of explicit governmental coercion. Particularly in regions such as Xinjiang, China uses a mixture of tools—"including but not limited to DNA samples, iris scans, voice samples, applications installed on phones, and records of power consumption"—to track members of the Uighur Muslim minority. Infamously, China also confines many Uighurs in "reeducation" camps.[14] China's broader "Social Credit System" aims to roll out a softer version of such digital surveillance to the whole country.[15]

While Western democracies look askance at such methods of control, many employ their own tracking systems. In the United States, the Patriot Act, which was passed to support the so-called war on terror, authorized widespread surveillance of citizens. In the wake of COVID-19, many countries passed laws to monitor and discipline individuals. If people wanted to enter particular public spaces or cross a political boundary, they had to download an app and consent to the authority of this system to police their movements.[16] As Justin E. H. Smith notes about COVID tracking, "What is occurring in both cases, the liberal-democratic and the overtly authoritarian alike, is the same: a transition to digitally and algorithmically calculated social credit, and the demise of most forms of community life outside the lens of the state and its corporate subcontractors."[17] And COVID measures are themselves just one offshoot of what Shoshana Zuboff, in her definitive book on the subject, terms "surveillance capitalism," a multifaceted phenomenon that uses data trails in the service of "instrumentarian power" that "knows and shapes human behavior toward others' ends."[18] This power typically operates not through physical or legal coercion but through the "smart" devices that we rely on to navigate more and more aspects of our lives.

With the possible exception of China's treatment of the Uighur people, none of these examples come close to matching the totalizing control and horror of the racial chattel slavery in antebellum America that Frederick Douglass experienced. But as Douglass himself articulates about his experiences on the abolitionist speaking circuit, well-intentioned systems can still reduce persons to things and thereby dangerously degrade their humanity. His efforts to teach his enslaved friends how to read, his method for selecting a new name, and his commitment to embodied community all stemmed from a keen awareness that the tools that could free him from legal slavery's oppression might also enthrall him in their own networks of oppression. Douglass, like many other people who suffered the indignities and arbitrary injustices of slavery, wanted to be free from documentary reduction of the self entirely. Douglass did not want to exchange one mode of documentary life for another; he wanted to be freed *for* moral community and convivial relations.

Documentary Identity and Biopolitics

From its invention, writing has been a tool used by those in power to count, tax, and control the population of a state. In his book discussing these dynamics, James C. Scott opens with Claude Lévi-Strauss' grim observation that "writing . . . seems to favor rather the exploitation than the enlightenment of mankind."[19] This claim appears difficult to reconcile with the many testimonies of those who have found literacy to be liberating and empowering—figures from Olaudah Equiano and Frederick

Douglass, to more recent authors such as Helen Keller, Lamin Sanneh, and Malala Yousafzai.[20] Putting these individual testimonies within the broader context of writing's development and use, however, provides a more nuanced assessment of the effects of textual technologies and also draws attention to the complexity within the testimonies of enslaved persons like Equiano and Douglass.

James Scott traces the way early states employed the first forms of writing to centralize power and improve communication and tax collection: writing flourished in Mesopotamia in the service of bookkeeping "for more than half a millennium before it even began to reflect the civilizational glories we associate with writing: literature, mythology, praise hymns, kings lists and genealogies, chronicles, and religious texts."[21] There was a reason that "barbarians" outside the bounds of these states saw writing as a threat to their existence and a technology to be rejected entirely.[22] Crucial to the success of these states was their efficiency in controlling and profiting from the work of their inhabitants, many of whom endured some form of slavery. It is not surprising, then, that among the earliest cuneiform tablets are lists of slaves.[23] As Scott concludes, "Early states surely did not invent the institution of slavery, but they did codify and organize it as a state project."[24] From its beginning, then, writing served purposes of accounting and control that enabled those in power to profit from the labor of others more effectively.[25]

Writing and various kinds of legal and financial documentation played a crucial role in sustaining racial chattel slavery in the British colonies and antebellum America. Caitlin Rosenthal's *Accounting for Slavery* provides chilling descriptions of the ways that Southern planters used innovative accounting methods to track the productivity of their enslaved workers so they could monitor the effectiveness of various incentive structures and labor practices. These account books helped estates maximize their productivity and profitability.[26] And they represent just one part of the far-flung network of financial and legal documentation that legitimated and governed a system by which some humans could "own" and profit from other humans. Auction advertisements, bills of sale, fugitive slave notices, and other documents helped to make human persons appear as mobile capital, as transferable commodities.

Forms of printed documentation and identification offered ways of understanding people as fungible and quantifiable resources rather than as embedded in particular places and families and communities. Document-based representations became increasingly important throughout the colonial era as people left—or were forcibly taken from—intergenerational communities. More and more people were known not by their family relations or tribal identity but by the papers they carried. As Benedict Anderson argues, the "standardized language-of-state" that developed in the colonial empires fostered "documentary interchangeability, which reinforced human interchangeability."[27] Others, most notably Willie Jennings, have traced the ways in which this new and often violent mobility created modern forms of racial identity. The color of one's skin becomes more significant in the relative absence of other distinguishing relationships: "Racial agency and especially whiteness rendered unintelligible and unpersuasive any narratives of the collective self that bound identity to geography, to earth, to water, trees, and animals. People would henceforth (and forever) carry their identities on their bodies, without remainder. . . . Without place as the articulator of identity, human skin is asked to fly solo and speak for itself."[28] If Jennings overstates the reality, it is by neglecting the role of various printed documents in identifying and policing these racialized and mobile bodies.

This tension between a "geographic, or place-based" identity and a more mobile documentary, "racial, or body-based" understanding of identity played out in antebellum America. And as Trish Loughran chronicles, the latter understanding gradually won out: "Under the compressing pressures of national consolidation . . . place became a bygone mode of political and affective affiliation, as individual actors and the federal state itself became more invested in locating identity not in places but in persons."[29] The Fugitive Slave Law of 1850 serves as a telling instance of this shift. This law created a new legal category of individuals, persons subject first of all to the nation rather than to a particular state: "The fugitive becomes a special and spectacular kind of federal subject, one whose case, because it crosses and confuses local jurisdictions, must finally be determined by a national (and nationally visible) arbiter: the federal government."[30] This status as a new kind of atomized, federal citizen deprived fugitives of whatever protections state and local jurisdictions might provide. Prior to the passage of this law, fugitives such as Douglass sought protection and help by becoming members of local places and communities. After 1850, however, this became more dangerous, as Loughran explains: "Before the passage of the Fugitive Slave Law, newly arrived fugitives were primarily seeking ways to establish local credibility in ways that might foster roots in the community and help establish new geographic identities as free New Yorkers, Philadelphians, Bostonians, and so on. . . . After the passage of the Fugitive Slave Law, however, the route to a secure and free identity grew trickier, for the more established one's identity after 1850, the more easily one might be retrieved under the auspices of the law."[31] By cutting fugitives off from the protections of their new communities, the law made them—as well as legally free blacks—vulnerable to forged affidavits that enabled slave hunters to profit from kidnapping. This trans-local, document-based form of identifying and controlling people was not liberating but served to maintain the control of "owners" over those people they considered to be property. The shadow side of organizing society as a "rimless wheel," with individuals defined by their connection to a powerful center, now becomes painfully apparent.[32]

Geographic identities often get critiqued as provincial, prejudicial, and oppressive, yet as this example makes painfully clear, the reality is more complicated. Loughran summarizes the irony by which "geograph-ically conceived identity politics" may not in fact be more confining than the "far more mobile and highly individualized kind of identity politics in which the only border that matters is the biological border of each indi-vidual body. Of the two, geo-identity (as we might call it) would appear to be the more regressive model, rooted in the climatological theories of the Enlightenment and the social structures of a less mobile, more agrarian society. Bio-identity, on the other hand (based in the individual body), is far more suited to capitalism's mobile networks."[33] Those who control capital can reap greater profits when people are uprooted from the local communities where they are known and redefined as racialized commodities to be bought and sold. Nevertheless, representing all peo-ple as "fungibl[e]" seemed to be the only "solution to the essentializing fixities of antebellum identity categories," and the post–Civil War con-stitutional amendments followed this logic to protect the rights of newly freed African Americans.[34] This legal framework "mark[s] the permanent rejection of place (and place collectivity—such as statehood and section-alism) as the keys to American identity, which is rewritten instead in the form of the more mobile, individualized identities."[35] This rejection of geographic identity may have been a tragic necessity in light of postbel-lum conditions—it is unfortunately hard to imagine another way that the entrenched system of chattel slavery could have been dismantled—but it resulted in a fragile and partial solution at best, and many African Amer-icans recognized that mobile, individualized identities left them vulnera-ble to other forms of injustice (see thesis 18).[36]

This kind of portable identity has now become the norm for most Americans, and it paves the way for today's digitally enabled surveillance capitalism and biopolitics. When identity becomes document-based rather than relationship-based, it can be more comprehensively disciplined. Hence there is a throughline that connects the many forms of mobility-enabling documentary ID: from the passports, slave passes, and freedom papers of the nineteenth century, to the later development of birth certificates, Social Security cards, and draft cards, to today's social credit systems or COVID vaccine passports or the more banal digital networks we rely on to participate in public and economic life. These free us to participate in society but only at the cost of reaffirming that our identities are defined by and dependent on these corporate and legal systems to control our lives, police our speech, and dictate our movements. Thus they reinforce what Willie Jennings describes as the "less helpful freedom, freedom from the ground, the dirt, landscapes, and animals, . . . and from the possibilities of imagining a joining to other peoples exactly in and through joining their lives on the ground."[37] In the terms of Melville's analogy, this is the freedom of Loose-Fish, a freedom for vulnerability rather than for conviviality.

In Search of Moral Community

Those subjected to the harsh realities of chattel slavery learned to appreciate both the power and limitations of documentary forms of identification and representation; such legal or social systems offered only fragile protections and remained in need of constant buttressing with embodied communal support. These dynamics play a key role in the narrative of Olaudah Equiano, for instance, an eighteenth-century African who is kidnapped and sold into slavery. He is eventually purchased by an officer in the British navy and fights in several engagements during the Seven Years' War. After being sold again, Equiano purchases his freedom and leads a remarkable life traveling throughout the British Atlantic and even journeying to the Arctic.

Even after gaining his legal freedom, however, Equiano has to guard it jealously. One evening, while he is visiting with a black friend in Savannah, the town patrol stops by. They drink some punch together, ask Equiano if he'll give them some limes (which he does), and then tell him that he is under arrest because "all negroes who had light in their houses after nine o'clock were to be taken into custody, and either pay some dollars or be flogged." Equiano's friend could escape this vigilante punishment because he is enslaved, and the patrol knows that his "master [would] protect him." But because Equiano is legally free, he has no one who would defend him and is vulnerable to this band of "imposing ruffians." He barely escapes being flogged by convincing one member of the patrol that his status as a freeman offers him legal protection, and this gives Equiano the opportunity to appeal to a white friend who comes to the jail and vouches for him. Equiano goes on to recount another experience in Savannah where he is almost kidnapped by two white men who plan to sell him fraudulently and pocket the profits, but Equiano's fluent English and "revengeful stick" make them reconsider their scheme and let him escape.[38] In the slave state of Georgia, Equiano's legal freedom is in constant doubt. All it takes is a forged bill of sale, and Equiano becomes just one more fungible black body to be sold and put to work. Even white people were not immune from such dangers: Equiano recounts meeting two men from the West Indies who "confessed they had made at one time a false bill of sale, and sold two Portuguese white men among a lot of slaves."[39]

Equiano had similar experiences in England, learning through bitter experience that legal protections are not worth the paper they're printed on without communities committed to enforcing them. After the 1772 Mansfield decision, it was supposedly illegal for a black person on English soil to be forcibly removed from England, and many understood the ruling to essentially free enslaved persons who were in England.[40] But Equiano had to watch his friend John Annis be kidnapped from a ship by a former master; despite Equiano's efforts to seek legal redress, Annis was taken back to the Caribbean island of St. Kitts, where he was beaten and eventually died.[41] The lawyer Equiano hired to help Annis took his money but "proved unfaithful" and did not pursue the case. As Equiano's biographer Vincent Carretta concludes, "Despite the Mansfield decision, blacks remained in jeopardy . . . as long as an owner was willing to risk arrest for illegally taking a black from England to the Americas."[42] Much like Douglass would do in the following decades, Equiano learned to compensate in part for his vulnerability by wielding the power of print culture in his own defense: "A genius at self-representation and self-promotion, Equiano defied convention by writing his autobiography and then publishing, marketing, and distributing it himself. . . . By retaining the copyright to his book he maintained control over his 'round unvarnished tale' and could make changes in every one of the nine editions he published of his autobiography."[43] Many of these changes were in response to slanders that pro-slavery advocates printed in newspapers to undermine his credibility. Equiano managed to use his autobiography and his network of powerful abolitionist friends to maintain his own freedom and to advocate for the end of slavery.[44] He was keenly aware, however, that without a supportive community, legal documents and published self-representations were insufficient to sustain true freedom.

This same awareness haunts Frederick Douglass' *Narrative*. Scholars tend to emphasize—for good reason—the liberating effect that literacy has in Douglass' life. Indeed, he describes learning how to read as having almost salvific results. As Douglass recalls, Mr. Auld forbade his wife to continue her lessons with Douglass, warning her that "if you teach that nigger (speaking of myself) how to read, there would be no keeping him. It would forever unfit him to be a slave." Douglass receives this news as "a new and special revelation," one that unlocks "the white man's power to enslave the black man."[45] Hearing literacy described in this fashion motivates him to go to extreme lengths in learning how to read and write.

As he gains these skills and, through books like *The Columbian Orator*, gains an awareness of the arguments for and against slavery, Douglass begins to doubt the benefits of literacy. Reading deepens his awareness of his plight without delivering him from it: "I would at times feel that learning to read had been a curse rather than a blessing. It had given me a view of my wretched condition, without the remedy. It opened my eyes to the horrible pit, but to no ladder upon which to get out. In moments of agony, I envied my fellow-slaves for their stupidity."[46] Further, as some critics have pointed out, by learning to read and thereby acquiring the rhetoric and language of literate culture and the white abolitionist movement, Douglass risked estranging himself from his community of origin and its oral culture.[47]

Eventually, however, Douglass finds ways to use his book learning to strengthen his communal ties rather than dissolve them. For instance, he helps his enslaved friends by participating in a Sabbath school "for the instruction of such slaves as might be disposed to learn to read the New Testament," but after meeting only three times, this group was violently broken up.[48] Later, at the urging of others, he agrees to try again "and accordingly devoted my Sundays to teaching these my loved fellow-slaves how to read. Neither of them knew his letters when I went there. Some of the slaves of the neighboring farms found what was going on, and also availed themselves of this little opportunity to learn to read." Douglass cherishes this memory because it represents a rare moment when he and his enslaved friends found a way to behave "like intellectual, moral, and accountable beings."[49] Douglass recalls that "over forty scholars, and those of the right sort, ardently desiring to learn" attended these gatherings, many of them learning how to read and at least one eventually gaining his freedom. In the words of Daniel Royer, this was one of the ways that Douglass used his literacy to foster "intersubjective community."[50] Such community, rather than simply individual freedom from slavery, was Douglass' ultimate goal.

The convivial education and discussion experienced in these Sabbath schools provided a glimpse of the joys that freedom could enable. Douglass laments that all too often the slave masters corrupted his community's fleeting experiences of leisure. He describes how drunken revelry often marked the Christmas holidays: "Thus, when the slave asks for virtuous freedom, the cunning slaveholder, knowing his ignorance, cheats him with a dose of vicious dissipation, artfully labelled with the name of liberty." The tragic result was that "when the holidays ended, we staggered up from the filth of our wallowing, took a long breath, and marched to the field,—feeling, upon the whole, rather glad to go, from what our master had deceived us into a belief was freedom, back to the arms of slavery."[51] By inviting his companions to participate in the kind of communal activities proper to their condition as "intellectual, moral, and accountable beings," Douglass sought to use his hard-won literacy to benefit his friends rather than to divide himself from them.

Such communal solidarity was essential if he hoped to survive under the harsh conditions of slavery, much less escape from them. Douglass' friends save him when he fights one master, and when he makes plans to escape with several friends, they are betrayed, but because they all trust one another, they surreptitiously eat their passes and refuse to cooperate with the authorities.[52] Without loyal, committed friends, the forged passes he could write would only have made Douglass more vulnerable to oppression.

When he finally makes it to the north and freedom, Douglass remains committed to cultivating embodied community, and his later participation in the abolitionist network and print culture remains dependent on these thick communities. He describes how, upon his arrival in New York, he was

> seized with a feeling of great insecurity and loneliness. I was yet liable to be taken back, and subjected to all the tortures of slavery. . . . The loneliness overcame me. There I was in the midst of thousands, and yet

a perfect stranger; without home and without friends, in the midst of thousands of my own brethren—children of a common Father, and yet I dared not to unfold to any one of them my sad condition.[53]

Douglass expresses his gratitude to a friend, Mr. David Ruggles, who came to his aid, helped him reunite with his fiancée, and found a preacher to marry them. Mr. Ruggles also provided Douglass with contacts in New Bedford, and members of the community there helped the newly married couple find housing and work. As an isolated fugitive, Douglass is particularly vulnerable to being recommodified. It is because he is atomized that he is exposed. This does not mean, of course, that he wants to return to slavery and the "protection" of his master. It means, though, that he is skeptical of purely negative freedom or an individualistic, "body-based" identity and instead seeks to join himself to a new community, one that will help him flourish. Douglass is in search of a new "geo-identity," a new community that will help him thrive as an intellectual, moral, and accountable being. Hence, when he discovers upon his arrival in New Bedford that there are already several people here with the name of "Johnson," he asks a friend to select a new name for him. He does not want his name imposed upon him by an owner or other oppressive authority, but neither does he want to name himself. He wants his identity and name to come from a loving community.

Douglass particularly admires the solidarity exhibited by the black community here in New Bedford. When one black man threatens to reveal a fugitive's whereabouts to his enslaver, a general meeting is called under other auspices. After the black community gathers, a respected religious elder stands up and declares, "'*Friends, we have got him here, and I would recommend that you young men just take him outside the door, and kill him!*' With this, a number of them bolted at him; but they were intercepted by some more timid than themselves, and the betrayer escaped their vengeance, and has not been seen in New Bedford since. I believe there have been no more such threats, and should there be hereafter, I doubt not that death would be the consequence."[54] This community models for Douglass the kind of commitment and solidarity required to sustain freedom. While in New Bedford, he joined the African Methodist Episcopal Zion Church and became very involved, regularly preaching. This formative experience shaped his lifelong endeavors to forge a moral community through his speeches and newspapers: "In a letter near the end of his life, written in December 1894, Douglass reminisced with joy about how the little AMEZ Church in New Bedford had offered his first chance to 'exercise my gifts' and launched him in his 'new vocation.'"⁵⁵

This experience contributed to his enthusiasm for the power that newspapers and print culture possess to shape public consciousness and form a community committed to justice. Once he could afford it, he subscribed to Garrison's *Liberator* and read it enthusiastically: "The paper became my meat and my drink. My soul was set all on fire. Its sympathy for my brethren in bonds—its scathing denunciations of slaveholders—its faithful exposures of slavery—and its powerful attacks upon the upholders of the institution—sent a thrill of joy through my soul, such as I had never felt before!"⁵⁶ Such periodicals and other forms of printed discourse—like *The Columbian Orator* that Douglass read while still enslaved—can form a "public hope," and Douglass became very involved with the *Liberator* and other abolitionist media.⁵⁷ Yet as his fallout with Garrison demonstrates, print publications could fragment community rather than strengthen it.⁵⁸ Hence Douglass sought to keep his newspaper work subordinate to his broader community-building work. Significantly, when he looks back on his time editing the *North Star*, he cites its local influence in the Rochester region as among the newspaper's primary benefits. In addition to his printed editorials, he gave a lecture each Sunday evening in town and would often travel to neighboring cities: "If in these lectures I did not make abolitionists, I did succeed in making tolerant the moral atmosphere in Rochester; so much so, indeed, that I came to feel as much at home there as I had ever done in the most friendly parts of New England. I had been at work there with my paper but a few years before colored travelers told me that they felt the influence of my labors when they came within fifty miles."⁵⁹ Douglass saw his newspaper work and his public lectures as ways to raise public consciousness about moral causes such as abolition and women's suffrage; the measure of their efficacy was not whether they made him famous or empowered him personally but whether they contributed to the formation of moral community.

From Pessimism to Hope

Douglass is not a simple pessimist regarding the effects of industrial print, as demonstrated by his efforts to use his newspapers and books to foster public hope. In fact, he often expressed a millennialist view of history that looked confidently toward a coming era of justice and peace.⁶⁰ Such optimism regarding human progress was reinforced by his own biography: he was born into slavery, but in his later years he worked for the government

that once legalized his oppression. Hence he could assert stunningly optimistic or even naive claims about moral progress:

> Material progress may for a time be separated from moral progress. But
> the two cannot be permanently divorced. . . . Steam and lightning and
> all manner of labor-saving machinery have come up to the help of moral
> truth as well as physical welfare. The increased facilities of locomotion,
> the growing inter-communication of distant nations, the rapid trans-
> mission of intelligence over the globe—the worldwide ramifications of
> commerce—bringing together the knowledge, the skill, and the mental
> power of the world, cannot but dispel prejudice, dissolve the granite
> barriers of arbitrary power, bring the world into peace and unity, and
> at last crown the world with just[ice], liberty, and brotherly kindness.[61]

In passages such as this, Douglass sounds like a techno-optimist assert-
ing the power of mass communication to bring about consensus and
moral progress. His sentiments here are sympathetic with Horace Greeley's claims about the "infallible telegraph" lifting "the public mind" and
spreading truth.[62]

What makes Douglass such a fascinating writer and thinker, however,
is his simultaneous awareness, particularly in the decades immediately
following his escape from slavery, that these media technologies have a
shadow side. His experience of the oppressive ends to which textual technologies could be turned led him to rightly fear the ways that identification
documents and self-representations in the mass media might commodify
and enslave human persons. He did not want mere legal freedom while,
at the same time, being represented "as a 'chattel'—a '*thing*'—a piece of
southern '*property*.'" So while in later years he sometimes indulged in
paeans to newspapers and photographs and the telegraph, his use of such
tools was marked by his keen awareness of their dangers.

In the same way that tech executives and programmers who work in
Silicon Valley adjust the settings on their phones carefully, cover their laptop cameras when not in use, and send their children to Waldorf schools,
so Douglass grasps the dangerous potential of technologies that identify
and represent human persons through photographs, identity papers, and
mass media.[63] So while he embraced these new technologies, he sought
to surround these products of industrial print culture with institutions
and practices that would strengthen embodied communities and foster
the moral commitments and cultural habits necessary to use them in the
service of freedom and justice.

Shifting our lives from geographic, embodied communities to mobile, documentary representations will not inevitably liberate us. On the contrary, when we conduct our lives within such print or digital networks, we open ourselves up to being manipulated or coerced by those who control these systems. Again, with the exception of extreme cases such as China's oppression of the Uighurs, these digital systems do not sustain the kind of formalized, legal enslavement that Equiano and Douglass and other black people experienced during the antebellum years. We should be grateful for this and recognize the asymmetries in the analogy between Douglass' context and those of us who navigate today's Western digital networks. Nevertheless, we can still recognize that these digital modes of mobile identity and self-representation need to be used carefully if they are to serve the kinds of communal ends that people like Equiano and Douglass longed for and that Douglass glimpsed in his Sabbath schools, in the black community at New Bedford, and in the Rochester region. In this regard, Douglass stands as an exemplar of the hopeful posture to which we will now turn; he sought to make do with the textual technologies of his day and turn them—despite their negative affordances—toward convivial ends.

III
Hope

Or, What alternative metaphors might orient more convivial reading?

10

Walkers

In this final section I turn to others who took up the tools of industrial print with the same sort of wary yet hopeful attitude that guided Douglass' use of photography and newspapers. In doing so, they imagined metaphors and practices that could orient their engagement toward *convivial* ends rather than coercive ones—they sought to use verbal technologies in the service of friendship and conversation rather than profit or power (see thesis 8).

My use of the word *convivial* is indebted to Ivan Illich and his book *Tools for Conviviality*. Illich argues that while technologies developed in an industrial context tend to concentrate power, reduce personal freedom, and amplify inequalities, alternative technological and social arrangements remain possible. In particular, it is possible to use even advanced, powerful tools to enlarge "the range of each person's competence, control, and initiative." He names this "modern society of responsibly limited tools" a convivial one. In doing so, Illich gestures to the word's Latin root, referring not just to feasting together but also to living together. Such a society requires its members to discipline their use of tools in order to foster "personal relatedness," "friendship," and "joyfulness."[1] These are some of the marks of a convivial society, and over the course of the next four chapters, we will see how Henry David Thoreau, Margaret Fuller, Nathaniel Hawthorne, and Herman Melville imagined practices that might help us read and write in ways that foster this kind of interdependent, participatory society.

Using powerful verbal tools in a convivial manner requires shifting away the industrial mode or the device paradigm and taking up verbal work in the more disciplined manner of those who engage in focal practices. This distinction between a device paradigm and focal things or practices comes from Albert Borgmann (who in turn draws on Martin Heidegger) and parallels Illich's contrast between industrially structured technologies and convivially organized tools.[2] Under the industrial device paradigm, users value tools and techniques that make accomplishing tasks easy and frictionless. By contrast, focal things and practices reward disciplined, skillful, and responsible engagement. Think, for example, of the difference between streaming music on Spotify and playing a violin. Or the difference between prompting ChatGPT and actually writing an essay. Or the difference between consuming a TED talk and wrestling with a Socratic dialogue. Or the difference between following someone on social media and conversing with that person over a meal. The distinction is not between "advanced" and "primitive" technologies: violins are incredibly sophisticated instruments, and digital composing and publishing technologies can facilitate genuine conversation. As Illich makes clear,

> Convivial reconstruction . . . . impl[ies] the adoption of labor-intensive tools, but not the regression to inefficient tools. . . . Its dynamics depend on wide distribution of the power to make effective change. . . . Continued convivial reconstruction depends on the degree to which society protects the power of individuals and of communities to choose their own styles of life through effective, small-scale renewal.[3]

Hence while the device paradigm situates persons as passive consumers who simply have to learn a technique or purchase a machine to achieve their desired outcome, convivial modes of engagement require disciplined, skillful persons and, in turn, enable these people to exercise freedom and responsibility as they deepen their relationships with one another and the world.

The path toward convivial reconstruction is not easy or inevitable, but neither is it impossible. Hence, this work of hopefully making do diverges sharply from the more deterministic attitude of those who survey the technological landscape and perceive utopia or dystopia on the horizon.[4] Our verbal tools are not necessarily some kind of iron Paul bringing the gospel of enlightenment, nor are they a Colt's revolver indiscriminately spewing harm and confusion. The first step toward a more convivial path lies in dispelling the aura of inevitability that so often surrounds powerful new technologies.

This is why Neil Postman insists on the need to question the unexamined metaphors through which our dominant communications media frame our experience: "This is an instance in which the asking of the questions is sufficient. To ask is to break the spell.[5]" And as Lakoff and Johnson argue, the best way to question metaphors that are deeply rooted in our cultural imagination is through trying out alternative ones.[6] The metaphors I explore in the first two sections of this book are largely diagnostic: they seek to name and reveal the kinds of relationships that powerful verbal technologies—whether print-based or pixel-based—invite us to inhabit. In this third section, I turn to prescriptive, aspirational metaphors that entail more convivial practices by which we might relate with each other, our world, and perhaps even God. These convivial practices may always be marginal to a technocratic society, but they enable us to imagine the possibility of "mak[ing] do" within the world in which we find ourselves.[7]

To wield verbal tools in convivial ways, however, requires disciplined and skilled persons. Rather than trusting the technology itself to spread truth or to exert power, convivial readers and writers have to cultivate a range of studious virtues in order to wisely discharge the responsibility these tools grant them. Anyone can stream music on Spotify, but it takes practice to play the piano. Anyone can respond to the prompt on X (formerly Twitter)—"What's happening?"—but it takes practice to contribute to a public conversation in ways that deepen relationships among the participants and lead them toward a richer participation in truth. The metaphors and practices in this final section can reveal the shortcomings of seeing reading and writing as techniques, where we just need better tools to ensure a more successful and efficient outcome. These metaphors might help us instead practice reading and writing as arts by which—if we cultivate them lovingly and skillfully—we can seek the truth alongside our fellow pilgrims.

Sauntering

The first of these metaphors is *walking*, which Henry David Thoreau employs both as a literal practice and as a metaphor for reading and sensemaking. In his lecture "Walking," which he first delivered in April 1851, he gives an implicit description of how this practice might form us to read and write well—an account that applies whether we inhabit a world of trains and telegraphs or a world of AI-driven cars and AI-generated messages. Thoreau begins by proposing an etymology for *saunter* (an etymology that is almost certainly false but nonetheless delightful) that indicates the spiritual aims of this activity: "I have met with but one or two persons in the course of my life who understood the art of Walking, that is, of taking walks—who had a genius, so to speak, for *sauntering*, which word is beautifully derived 'from idle people who roved about the country, in the middle ages, and asked charity, under pretense of going *à la sainte terre,*' to the holy land, till the children exclaimed, 'There goes a *sainte-terrer,*' a saunterer, a holy-lander."[8] As Thoreau expounds on this art of walking toward the Holy Land, and as he develops these ideas in *Walden*, three key features of this practice emerge.

The first is that walking provides an opportunity to think in a different mode than conscious, focused, and sedentary cognition. In his lecture Thoreau specifies that "you must walk like a camel, which is said to be the only beast which ruminates when walking."[9] Something about the action of walking, of moving your body at a leisurely pace, prompts deliberation. A pedestrian can digest ideas in the same way that a ruminant animal chews the cud, extracting more nutrients from the food—or ideas—already consumed. Thoreau expounds on the symbiotic relationship between walking and writing later that year in his journal: "How vain it is to sit down to write when you have not stood up to live! Methinks that the moment my legs begin to move, my thoughts begin to flow—as if I had given vent to the stream at the lower end & consequently new fountains flowed into it at the upper. . . . Only while we are in action is the circulation perfect. The writing which consists with habitual sitting is mechanical, wooden, dull to read."[10] The goal of walking, for Thoreau, is not so much to arrive at a particular destination as it is to enter into a more participatory and deliberate mode of relating to the world. Adopting this mode of relation may not seem a very significant outcome, but one of the salubrious fruits of such rumination is that it can move us beyond the stereotyped conventions on which more superficial thinking relies and, in this way, serve as an antidote to the macadamized mind that results from attending to trivial ephemera.

The second benefit that Thoreau ascribes to walking is that it exposes us to unexpected perspectives and voices: in a word, it puts us in contact with the *wild*. He testifies that he generally finds his daily walks extend in a westward direction, away from civilization and toward the forests and fields. He imbues this compass direction with symbolic significance: "The West of which I speak is but another name for the Wild; and what I have been preparing to say is, that in Wildness is the preservation of the world."[11] By "wild" Thoreau does not simply mean uninhabited or untainted by humans; rather, he means something more elemental: "Life consists with wildness. The most alive is the wildest."[12] By encountering this wild life, Thoreau hopes also to learn how to articulate and represent it in his writing. He names this "wild and dusky knowledge" by the

Spanish phrase *gramatica parda*, which means "tawny grammar" or "a kind of mother-wit."[13] His lecture and, as we will see, *Walden*, follows this tawny grammar by casting ideas in their most extreme forms. As the opening line of "Walking" declares, "I wish to make an extreme statement, if so I may make an emphatic one."[14] His extravagant declarations may offend or confuse some readers; instead of building a straightforward, linear argument, Thoreau's prose proceeds by contraries. He does this, however, to replicate the rhythm of walking itself, a way of moving ahead by going side to side: left, right, left, right, left, right. Reading Thoreau is thus a kind of vicarious wild saunter, a meander that might wake readers to a more vigorous mode of life.

Indeed this back-and-forth method is crucial to the third feature of Thoreau's practice of walking as a way of sense-making: he aims at a different kind of understanding or knowledge than that sought by more utilitarian, linear modes of thought. Rather than leading him to a single, discrete proposition about the benefits of walking or, in the case of *Walden*, the true end of life, Thoreau's dramatic, extravagant declarations develop a kind of harmonious or resonant truth (see theses 4, 5, and 6). In the same way that the individual notes of a musical chord sound individually *and* resonate together in harmony, so Thoreau's wild statements form a kind of interpenetrating, harmonious truth.[15] Thoreau articulates this distinction in terms of the contrast between "knowledge" and "sympathy": "The highest that we can attain to is not Knowledge, but Sympathy with Intelligence. I do not know that this higher knowledge amounts to anything more definite than a novel and grand surprise on a sudden revelation of the insufficiency of all that we called Knowledge before—a discovery that there are more things in heaven and earth than are dreamed of in our philosophy. It is the lighting up of the mist by the sun."[16] Walking may get a traveler from point A to point B more slowly than a train or car would (though Thoreau famously challenges this critique of his preferred mode of travel), but Thoreau is not simply trying to arrive at point B.[17] He is after a transformational, sympathetic participation with truth rather than a detached, noetic, propositional account.

Thoreau is hardly the first person to associate walking with a certain kind of transformative understanding, and contemporary advocates of the practice of walking abound. The idea that walking might open up modes of understanding that are not accessible to the disembodied intellect has deep roots. The Hebrew word for law, *halakhah*, is related to the word for walk, *halak*, because the only way to genuinely know the law is to enact it. Similarly, the Latin phrase *solvitur ambulando*, or "it is solved by walking," refers to philosophical questions that are best addressed not by some propositional answer but by motion or practice.[18] By extension, some types of existential questions cannot be explicitly and fully articulated: rather, they need to be lived out.

Walking as a metaphor for certain kinds of understanding has its corollary in many thinkers who testify to the phenomenological benefits of walking. Whether it is wild walkers such as John Muir or Wendell Berry or urban flaneurs such as Chris Arnade or Garnette Cadogan, these acolytes find that the practice of walking enables them to participate more deeply in the world around them.[19] In her book on this theme, *Wanderlust: A History of Walking*, Rebecca Solnit concludes that "walking shares with making and working that crucial element of engagement of the body and the mind with the world, of knowing the world through the body and the body through the world."[20] Such accounts confirm Thoreau's claims that walking can be a way of engaging the world in conversation, of practicing convivial understanding.

Walk like a Camel

Thoreau's injunction to "walk like a camel" names a more deliberate mode of thinking and reading than he thought his neighbors commonly practiced. Slow reading is just as rare in a digital age that encourages the endless consumption of video clips, snippets of text, and emotionally charged memes. In both these contexts Thoreau's ruminant method of digesting our reading material functions as a kind of counterformation—and indeed "counterfriction"—that disrupts the conventional or "stereotyped" sentiments we might otherwise unthinkingly adopt.[21] Rather than a pragmatic approach to reading that aims to access information or amusement, Thoreau imagines reading as an *exercise*, an activity intended to strengthen intellectual muscles. He is not interested in reading to find out the ending of a mystery plot or fend off boredom or learn how to accomplish a discrete task. These may have their place, but they are not the convivial and invigorating practice he is most interested in cultivating.

In *Walden* he similarly describes such reading by analogy to athletic training. After confessing his desire "to live deliberately," Thoreau considers what it would look like to read deliberately: "To read well, that is, to read true books in a true spirit, is a noble exercise, and one that will task the reader more than any exercise which the customs of the day esteem. It requires a training such as the athletes underwent, the steady intention almost of the whole life to this object. Books must be read as deliberately and reservedly as they were written."[22] This is a tall order; *Walden* took Thoreau nearly nine years to write, and the book you're holding in your hands is the result of more than a decade of thinking and writing. I am sure even Thoreau would recommend reading more than one book per decade, but his point is that slow reading can be a way of stretching our intellects and imaginations and so forming us into better thinkers and neighbors. Chewing on the metaphors and insights of a rich book can exercise our minds in a way analogous to taking a long walk in order to strengthen our legs and foster a healthy body.

In particular, such mental exercise might counteract the intellectual atrophy caused by what Thoreau derisively terms "Little Reading." Popular reading material—whether it be sensational news or potboiler fiction—caters to readers' expectations and desires rather than challenging them. The result, Thoreau thinks, is not mental improvement but rather stagnation: "All this they read with saucer eyes, and erect and primitive curiosity, and with unwearied gizzard, whose corrugations even yet need no sharpening, just as some little four-year-old bencher his two-cent gilt-covered edition of Cinderella,—without any improvement, that I can see, in the pronunciation, or accent, or emphasis, or any more skill in extracting or inserting the moral. The result is dulness of sight, a stagnation of the vital circulations, and a general deliquium and sloughing off of all the intellectual faculties."[23] The problem lies in part with the reading material itself, but yellow journalism, clickbait, and formulaic novels are profitable precisely because of the appetite readers have for easy, titillating content. Those who exercise their minds by perambulatory rumination, however, will gradually lose interest in ephemeral trivia and seek out the kind of books that reward deliberate reading—that, at least, is Thoreau's hope.

Such books would not be conventional or formulaic. They would perplex, intrigue, or confound readers, prompting a deep reassessment of the opinions and feelings we often take for granted. In *Walden*, Thoreau develops this idea through a metaphor derived from a relatively new printing technology: stereotype plates. To create these plates, printers take a page of locked type and create a mold of the whole page. This mold is then used to cast a metal plate that can print the entire page or an imposition containing eight or sixteen individual pages. Printers experimented with various stereotype methods throughout the eighteenth century, and in the early nineteenth century the practice became widespread. At first, only popular books such as the Bible and other "steady sellers" were printed from stereotype plates, but as the technology improved, most books were printed from stereotype plates, and publishers would store the plates so that they could easily run off additional print runs without having to reset the pages.[24] Hawthorne's publisher for *The Scarlet Letter* underestimated its popularity and had to pay for the book to be typeset three times in order to print more copies before finally creating stereotype plates to have on hand for future printings.[25] This technology has obvious benefits for book and newspaper printing, but for Thoreau it also functioned as an image of the way that industrial publishing technologies and a more central-ized media market might reinforce conventional sentiments and inhibit the exploration and independent thought needed for learning and growth. By the twentieth century, *stereotype* named set forms of thought such as prejudice, but already Thoreau presents this technology as a metaphor for ways that common sentiments about individuals or groups or life might become fixed in individuals' minds.[26]

In the opening pages of *Walden*, Thoreau famously declares that "the mass of men lead lives of quiet desperation." He elaborates by way of analogy to this printing technology: "A stereotyped but unconscious despair is concealed even under what are called the games and amuse-ments of mankind."[27] This background despair is particularly danger-ous because of its conventional nature; a widespread feeling or attitude gets set in stereotype plates, as it were, and then imposed on a whole society. Thoreau argues that most people unthinkingly accept preformed answers regarding the proper ends and means of life instead of earnestly questioning them and exploring alternative possibilities. In the same way that stereotype plates enable books to be mass-produced, Thoreau thinks the centralizing mass media market of his day promoted a nar-rowing set of possibilities for living, which in turn elicited a paralyzing anxiety and despair. In response, Thoreau sought to provoke the rumi-nation and reassessment that might lead readers to new possibilities and the grounds for hope.

Near the end of "Spring," in what is perhaps the most famous para-graph of *Walden*, Thoreau returns to the dangers of stereotyped senti-ments. He begins the paragraph by extolling the virtues of wildness, a theme I will expound on below: "Our village life would stagnate if it were not for the unexplored forests and meadows which surround it. We need the tonic of wildness." This tonic of wildness, Thoreau thinks, cures by way of opening our imaginations to other lives and possibilities: "We need to witness our own limits transgressed, and some life pasturing freely where we never wander." In part, this entails being humbled by having our ability to easily comprehend a text frustrated. He describes how encounters with vultures and carrion and predation transgress his limits and so expand his sense of compassion. Rather than pitying individual victims of predation—tadpoles eaten by herons, say—he has learned to take a broader view: "Compassion is a very untenable ground. It must be expeditious. Its pleadings will not bear to be stereotyped."[28] Stereotype plates threaten to lock readers into fixed forms of thinking and feeling, but Thoreau hopes that we might learn to set these down, take a long walk, and tune our thinking and feeling to a more variegated and complex reality. If our minds have atrophied by the passive acceptance of preformed sentiments promulgated through the mass media, we can strengthen them through deliberate rumination on challenging, wild words.

Speak without Bounds

It was with precisely this goal in mind that Thoreau crafted *Walden*. Over the course of several years of revision and rewriting, he shaped a wild or extravagant book that follows the "tawny grammar" he praises in "Walking." *Walden* is structured around extreme and often conflicting statements, statements that can confuse or offend readers expecting a more linear style of exposition. In a world of stereotyped thought, where convention and common sense lock our thinking into predetermined ruts, Thoreau invites his readers to strike out cross-country and grapple with reality in all its complexity and contradictions.

He articulates his reasons for employing this wild grammar in the book's final chapter. His prose leads readers on a kind of wild saunter, and the work required to keep up with him does not give readers some definable content so much as it promotes their intellectual growth: "It is a ridiculous demand which England and America make, that you shall speak so that they can understand you. Neither men nor toad-stools grow so."[29] Thoreau is not after a kind of superficial intelligibility. Rather, he wants readers to encounter in his prose the variegated reality he himself has experienced. In seeking to articulate this aim, he plays on the etymology of *extravagance*, which means to wander outside or beyond limits:

> I fear chiefly lest my expression may not be extra-vagant enough, may not wander far enough beyond the narrow limits of my daily experience, so as to be adequate to the truth of which I have been convinced. . . .

> I desire to speak somewhere without bounds; like a man in a waking moment, to men in their waking moments; for I am convinced that I cannot exaggerate enough even to lay the foundation of a true expression.... The volatile truth of our words should continually betray the inadequacy of the residual statement.[30]

This effort to convey a volatile truth, to trespasses the bounds of convention in order to gesture toward a revelation that lies beyond language itself, leads Thoreau to make contradictory and startling claims. He does not intend any single claim be taken as the final word. Rather, readers have to proceed from one wild statement to the next, experiencing their "volatile" truth without coming to rest on any individual or isolated assertion.[31]

Thoreau knows this method of composition risks confusing readers. As he declares in "Economy," after explaining his intentions to jettison all clutter and pursue the essence of life: "There is a certain class of unbelievers who sometimes ask me such questions as, if I think that I can live on vegetable food alone; and to strike at the root of the matter at once,— for the root is faith,—I am accustomed to answer such, that I can live on board nails. If they cannot understand that, they cannot understand much that I have to say."[32] This is indeed an extravagant statement, but Thoreau's point is not that he can literally digest board nails. Rather, he wants to discover a mode of life that fulfills "the chief end of man" and does not merely keep body and soul together. Readers looking for a kind of literal, superficial sense may be confounded by this, but Thoreau is inviting them to journey through *Walden* in the pursuit of a more volatile and wild kind of truth.

In pursuing this goal, he follows a thesis-antithesis structure that parallels the bipedal, left-right-left-right motion of walking itself. Instead of seeking a middle ground or compromise between contrasting points, Thoreau tends to embrace one extreme and then another. By doing so, he follows William Blake's adage that "without Contraries is no progression."[33] Thoreau wants plenty of visitors *and* seasons of solitude. He wants to read old books *and* listen to contemporary voices. He wants bitter cold *and* summer's heat. He wants to eat a woodchuck raw *and* to be a vegetarian. He feels that he "could spit a Mexican with a good relish" *and* he went to jail rather than pay a tax to a state prosecuting a war against Mexico in the furtherance of slavery. Some readers—perhaps even many readers—may discern no coherent organizing pattern that makes sense of the book as a whole. Other critics have perceived a seasonal progression through summer, fall, winter, and spring as the cyclical organizing principle that Thoreau imposes on the two years and two months that he lived at the pond.[34]

Portions of the book violate this seasonal cycle, however, and the more fundamental structure consists of a binary, back and forth, bipedal progression in which pairs of chapters present alternating points of view. A cursory glance at the book's table of contents indicates the general pattern. Two opening chapters present complementary accounts of Thoreau's reasons for moving to Walden Pond and his practical mode of providing food and shelter while living there. The chapters then explore various contrasts that mark his sojourn at the pond and his efforts to suck out all the marrow of life. Some of the pairings are complementary: the agrarian work of "The Bean-Field" and the more urban life of "The Village"; "Winter Animals" and "The Pond in Winter"; "Spring" and "Conclusion." Whereas "Reading" considers the value of reading old books slowly, "Sounds" attends to ephemeral and contemporary voices. Other pairs are more explicitly contrasting: "Solitude" and "Visitors," "Higher Laws" and "Brute Neighbors." The shifts between some of these chapters can be jarring. He opens "Visitors" with a declaration that seems to contradict everything he has just argued about the goods of solitude: "I think that I love society as much as most, and am ready enough to fasten myself like a bloodsucker for the time to any full-blooded man that comes in my way. I am naturally no hermit, but might possibly sit out the sturdiest frequenter of the bar-room, if my business called me thither."[35] Thoreau aims to give due weight to all sides of a complex and wild reality, and a good life includes both solitude and human society.

In addition to creating a back-and-forth, to-and-fro rhythm to the book's pedestrian progression, one effect of these turns is to undercut readers' first impressions of Thoreau's persona as a brash know-it-all. His sweeping declarations—"I have lived some thirty years on this planet, and I have yet to hear the first syllable of valuable or even earnest advice from my seniors"—do not represent the final word on any subject but chart his attempts to state the extremities of a volatile truth.[36] The dialogue that opens "Brute Neighbors" puts Thoreau in the guise of the "Hermit" and his friend Ellery Channing in the persona of the "Poet," and readers are invited to laugh heartily at the pretensions of the Hermit. His deepest meditations do not seem too deep: as he confesses, "I know not whether it was the dumps or a budding ecstasy." And it turns out his claims to be on the verge of a profound revelation are, in fact, a cover to avoid the work of digging worms. So he is quite happy to leave off meditating and go fishing.[37] Similarly, after praising the virtues of voluntary poverty and asceticism in "Economy," he inserts Thomas Carew's poem "The Pretensions of Poverty." The poem lambasts the arrogant "wretch" who claims "a station in the firmament" due to his material poverty. Being poor is not a sign of virtue or godliness, the poem argues, and poverty prevents one from exercising a whole set of heroic virtues such as generosity and magnanimity. It is a harsh rebuke to Thoreau's claims that material simplicity enables him to pursue the true ends of life, and this "complemental" verse suggests that Thoreau wants readers to grapple with a double-edged, volatile truth about the possible connections between material possessions and spiritual aspirations.[38]

Thoreau's goal in crafting a book that speaks without bounds is to offer readers a vicarious experience of a long, cross-country ramble. Instead of taking readers on the shortest route to some discrete conclusion, *Walden* confronts readers with those aspects of reality from which conventional and stereotyped forms of thought have insulated them. The encounter with such truth can be a discomfiting experience: "If you stand right fronting and face to face to a fact, you will see the sun glimmer on both its surfaces, as if it were a cimeter, and feel its sweet edge dividing you through the heart and marrow, and so you will happily conclude your mortal career. Be it life or death, we crave only reality."[39] By showing us both sides of a given fact, *Walden* wields its wild truth as a sword that cuts through habitual ways of thinking and feeling.

Cultivate a Discriminating Ear

Such truth is quite obviously not some discrete idea to grasp but an experience that transforms the knower. This is a different type of truth than Thoreau—or his readers—may have been searching for at the outset, but even if Thoreau does not develop a five-point checklist for living the good life, he concludes that his experience at Walden was a success. For as he goes back and forth throughout the book, he also goes forward toward a truth that is not so much a destination to arrive at but an exercise or encounter to undergo. Success lies in the transformation that happens in Thoreau—and perhaps in his readers: his intellect and imagination become able to perceive harmonies or patterns that before seemed meaninglessly chaotic (see thesis 15).

Near the end of the book Thoreau records an exchange he witnessed that portrays this possibility of a transformed perception. One evening in early winter he hears geese flying over the pond, their leader "honking all the while" as they speed south:

> Suddenly an unmistakable cat-owl from very near me, with the most harsh and tremendous voice I ever heard from any inhabitant of the woods, responded at regular intervals to the goose, as if determined to expose and disgrace this intruder from Hudson's Bay by exhibiting a greater compass and volume of voice in a native, and *boo-hoo* him out of Concord horizon. . . . *Boo-hoo, boo-hoo, boo-hoo!* It was one of the most thrilling discords I ever heard. And yet, if you had a discriminating ear, there were in it the elements of a concord such as these plains never saw nor heard.[40]

This scene exemplifies the typical back-and-forth contrast that defines *Walden*'s structure. The owl and the goose, the native and the foreigner, the bird of night and the bird of day, the solitary bird and the social bird sound their distinct notes. Yet as Thoreau listens to this wild discord, he imagines the possibility that by undergoing a change himself, by cultivating a more discriminating ear, he could gain the ability to hear the harmony (or, in a pun on his town's name, *concord*) produced by this intense avian clangor. The point of his sojourn at Walden—and the book he crafts to convey this experience to readers—is to cultivate ears able to hear the concord amid a complex and wild world. Readers with such ears will be capable of conviviality, of friendship. They would listen deeply to what others say and meditate slowly on it. They would attend to a full range of divergent perspectives. And they would listen in hopes of hearing harmonies or resonances arise in unexpected ways.[41]

Perhaps the best index to this change in Thoreau's perception lies in the way his attitude toward the railroad shifts over the course of the book. In "Sounds," his enjoyment of the noises coming from the pond and its creatures is threatened by the whistle of the passing locomotive. The newly built train tracks run right next to the pond, and Thoreau walks to and from Concord along them as they offer the most direct route to town. But over the course of several pages, Thoreau employs a myriad of metaphors and images to try to relate the train—and the industrial, globalizing economy it signifies—to the pond's community: the train is a flushed partridge, or a predatory hawk, or a comet, or a planet, or some new mythic creature, or William Tell's arrow shooting toward us. But all his efforts to perceive some concord between the railroad and his life at Walden fail, so he turns his back on the train: "I will not have my eyes put out and my ears spoiled by its smoke and steam and hissing."[42]

Despite this failure, and the strident critiques Thoreau directs at the technological system the railroad represents, the imaginative climax of *Walden* happens on the train tracks.[43] On his way to Concord through the railroad cutting, Thoreau witnesses the warm spring sun melting the frozen water within the sandbanks and producing beautiful patterns as the wet sand flows down. In these designs, Thoreau discerns the prototype of all animal and vegetable life and of human language, and he is "affected as if in a peculiar sense I stood in the laboratory of the Artist who made the world and me,— had come to where he was still at work." He thus concludes that "there is nothing inorganic" and all human "institutions" and technology remain malleable "clay in the hands of the potter."[44] The railroad is not a foreign imposition upon the organic, natural lives of Walden's inhabitants; Thoreau now sees it too as part of the Creator's work and so ultimately reconcilable to a well-lived life.[45] He has gained the discriminating ears to hear harmony where he once heard only discord.

One way to name this shift that Thoreau undergoes over the course of *Walden* is to say that he moves from a state of alienation to one of resonance. These terms come from Hartmut Rosa's sociological analysis, which defines modernity as an experience of disorienting acceleration, of dynamic change that ruptures prior modes of relationship. The solution to alienation is not to learn some new life hack or acquire some set of facts; neither is it to accrue more resources or wealth. Instead, Rosa parallels Thoreau in arguing that the proper response to alienation is to cultivate a different way of relating to the world, one defined by what he calls resonance.[46] As one reviewer defines Rosa's term, "resonance with the world means that we are open to being transformed by the world, and transformed in ways that we cannot predict."[47] This experience of resonance brings us back to Thoreau's emphasis on walking as both a practice and as a metaphor for reading and sense-making: walking seems like an inefficient way to arrive at a destination or a conclusion. It is slow. It takes work. Travel by horse or train (or car or plane) seems more optimal. But if the goal is to change one's relationship with the world, then a slow, embodied encounter with the world in all its wild variety is essential. *Solvitur ambulando*.

It is hard to articulate this shift in character and perceptual faculties, and Thoreau never distills his ruminations about the end of life, the proper role of technology, and the right relationship between humans and nature into a set of easy answers. Instead he articulates the success of his sojourn at Walden in terms of his changed state of being. At the outset of "The Pond in Winter" he states, "After a still winter night I awoke with the impression that some question had been put to me, which I had been endeavoring in vain to answer in my sleep, as what—how—when—where? But there was dawning Nature, in whom all creatures live, looking in at my broad windows with serene and satisfied face, and no question on her lips. I awoke to an answered question, to Nature and daylight."[48] It is then that he can proceed to his morning work. His sojourn at Walden Pond, like his daily walks, does not result in a set of talking points or actionable revelations, but it changes his disposition and character, thereby enabling him to do good work.[49]

In this chapter, one of the tasks he undertakes is to survey the bottom of the pond in order to discover its deepest point. He finds that this point lies at the intersection of the pond's greatest width and greatest length, and this observation of literal profundity at the juncture of extremes leads him to posit a set of analogies between the physical shape of the pond and immaterial realities such as the shape of a human soul. The conclusion of these ruminations is an affirmation of harmony existing beyond our usual facilities of perception: "Our notions of law and harmony are commonly confined to those instances which we detect; but the harmony which results from a far greater number of seemingly conflicting, but really concurring, laws, which we have not detected, is still more wonderful."[50] If readers have listened well to the seemingly conflicting but really, perhaps, concurring statements Thoreau has made over the course of his book, they may be ready to hear the volatile truth he wonders at here. Such harmonious truths can only be perceived when we have cultivated the ears to hear them, which is why the ultimate goal of Thoreau's experiment at Walden is, in Walter Ong's phrase, "the proper attunement of man to actuality" (see thesis 1).[51] Such attunement, not a noetic apprehension of a proposition, is the highest expression of truth (see theses 4, 5, and 6). There is certainly a place for conceptual clarity, particularly in judging and testing one's sense of attunement, and Thoreau's careful survey of Walden Pond employs such quantitative tools, but these are only means to his ultimate end: a resonant mode of living.

Thoreau crafts *Walden* to provide a readerly experience that might parallel his experiences living in the woods and taking wild walks. He hopes to form readers who can recognize analogies between various extremes and so discern the concord that might arise from seemingly discordant voices. Such people can experience the dissonance of a wild world or a pluralistic society and have the patience, humility, and aesthetic sensibilities to keep listening for deeper harmonies, to slow down enough to turn back and forth with an interlocutor in pursuit of deeper understanding. And these are precisely the kind of people who might use words in the service of friendly conviviality rather than personal profit or power (see thesis 8). Thoreau's metaphor of walking as a way of sense-making, then, invites us to read not merely to acquire information but more profoundly to cultivate a different mode of being in the world, one that makes us capable of conversation and friendship.

11

Conversationalists

Thoreau's neighbors attested to his prickly personality, and he himself admits that he had a "stiff neck."[1] So although he offers one account of bending industrially published texts to convivial ends, he himself was not the best practitioner of reading-for-friendship—though he was a famous conversationalist with his close friends. In contrast, Margaret Fuller practiced her vision for conversational reading in both her published writings and in her life. She found it most natural to facilitate conversation in embodied contexts. Nevertheless, she approached her role as the editor of the transcendentalist journal the *Dial* with an eye to staging a discussion on its pages, and she also sought to structure her essays as a kind of conversation with readers. As she explains about her preference for conversational literary forms, "There is something very propitious to good writing in the form of dialogue. The regular build of an Essay (maugre the unpretending name) is dangerous. It tempts to round the piece into a whole by filling up the gaps between the thoughts with—words—words—words."[2] While Fuller's efforts to translate an oral exchange from its embodied life to the inert page annoyed some readers—Orestes Brownson panned *Summer on the Lakes, in 1843* and criticized its "slipshod style"—they mark her determination to push against the tendencies of her print culture and form readers capable of participating magnanimously in rigorous intellectual discourse.[3]

We can get a sense of Fuller's approach from the method she uses to review *The Seeress of Prevorst*.[4] She read this book while in Milwaukee and offers a "conversational account of the work" in chapter 5 of *Summer on the Lakes, in 1843*—a book that combines travelogue and responses to various books into a meditation on the ideal American pioneer and the best means to form such people.[5] *The Seeress of Prevorst* is a case study of a mystic woman, whose visions and clairvoyant utterances elicit spiritualist explanations from the medical doctor who authored the book.

Fuller seems drawn to the way this account intertwines natural and super-natural, medical and "magnetic" explanations. She asserts that "my own mental position on these subjects . . . may be briefly expressed by a dia-logue between several persons who honor me with a portion of friendly confidence and of criticism, and myself expressed as *Free Hope*. The oth-ers may be styled *Old Church*, *Good Sense*, and *Self-Poise*."[6] *Old Church* voices a conservative theological response, *Good Sense* speaks for a "Wordsworthian" position, and *Self-Poise*'s contributions contain quota-tions from Emerson.[7] Significantly, Fuller claims both that *Free Hope* will voice her views *and* that her position is expressed by the dialogue as a whole. In other words, while she takes a particular position, it can only be articulated in dialectical form.

The dialogue that Fuller proceeds to stage exhibits real disagreements, but all the personae make plausible cases for their perspectives. Fuller resists the temptation to strawman any of them, and she displays the patience necessary to learn from even those perspectives that she thinks are erroneous. *Good Sense* begins by recommending that we "be com-pletely natural" and not "trouble ourselves with the supernatural." *Free Hope* replies that it is impossible to understand a phenomenon in iso-lation. In order to rightly interpret the evidence for spiritual forces—or "magnetic influences"—we must patiently consider all the phenomena that we can: "For [investigation] is tampering unless done in a patient spirit and with severe truth. . . . And some there are who work in the true temper patient and accurate in trial, not rushing to conclusions, feeling there is a mystery, not eager to call it by name, till they can know it as a reality: such may learn, such may teach."[8] This patient approach is neces-sarily slow and uncertain, but it seeks to learn from mysteries we do not understand rather than preemptively exclude them from consideration.

Yet *Old Church* criticizes *Free Hope* for being too curious about mat-ters that are not proper for humans, and *Self-Poise* likewise urges that the spirit of the universe can be found in the most mundane things, so there is no need to search the "infatuations and illusions of this world of emotion." She rejects the warnings of *Old Church* and *Self-Poise* against chasing after mystical ideals, but *Free Hope* recognizes the validity of their advice by acknowledging the potential dangers of her explorations. She concludes, "I dare to trust to the interpreting spirit to bring me out all right at last—to establish truth through error." Fuller expresses her conviction that difference and disagreement are to be welcomed because a patient and careful dialectic process enables us to discern truth through errors. At the conclusion of this imagined dialogue, *Free Hope* has a word of praise for each of her three interlocutors even while she reiterates her disagreements with them. Fuller's method here demonstrates why she values differing perspectives: by testing her ideas in conversation with other perspectives, she recognizes the weaknesses of her positions and journeys toward a fuller understanding of truth.[9] Fuller continues to model this patient interpreting spirit in the discussion of the book that follows this dialogue, and she tries to balance credulity and skepticism as she seeks to discern the truth regarding this woman's mystical experiences.

This passage from *Summer on the Lakes, in 1843* displays Fuller's commitment to the conversational form. Rather than simply state her assessment of *The Seeress of Prevorst*, she performs the kind of vigorous discussion that she hopes readers will engage in. Fuller's example stands as a rebuke to those who would prefer to be spoon-fed by some guru spouting best practices from a TED talk stage. Easily digestible content may be more palatable to lazy readers, but convivial participation in seeking complex, multifaceted truth will require more work on our part. It will require a generosity of spirit, a magnanimity, to recognize the truth articulated by our interlocutors. Such virtuous effort enables us to participate in the drama of truth. As Josef Pieper insists, "The natural *habitat* of truth is found in interpersonal communication. Truth lives in dialogue, in discussion, in conversation."[10] Interpersonal communication is not a simple matter of "connecting" with others via some social media app; it demands the careful, patient engagement of virtuous interlocutors (see theses 5 and 6).

Despite the prevalence today—and in Fuller's day—of experts who disseminate prepackaged content to passive recipients, there remains a deep hunger for convivial forms of discussion. In fact, several of the forums for conversation that flourished in the nineteenth century are experiencing a renaissance today; I will briefly mention three examples. The lyceum phenomenon swept across America in the early nineteenth century, and people from all classes gathered to hear public lectures and debate key questions.[11] In 2021 a new lyceum movement started in Des Moines, Iowa, in response to a growing desire "for an alternative to the alienating experience of life online; [people are] hungry for a substantive conversation with a neighbor."[12] Other venues for public lectures and discussions abound—college lecture series, library events, local historical societies, and more. In our era of digital social media, there is a real hunger for such embodied social media.

Fuller frequented lyceum lectures in her day, but women were mostly excluded from speaking in these venues, and she invested her intellectual energies in the conversations she organized for Boston women beginning in 1839.[13] These conversations looked something like a cross between a book club and a college seminar discussion and involved in-depth debates about a wide range of philosophical and literary topics.[14] There are many groups today, ranging from formal institutions to informal neighborhood gatherings, that foster such opportunities for adult education, but one notable example is the Catherine Project.[15] In the wake of the post-COVID videoconference boom, Zena Hitz started organizing small reading groups to tackle authors such as Aristophanes, Homer, and Kafka. She quickly discovered more people were interested in participating than she had the capacity to organize, and so she launched the Catherine Project to try to serve this appetite. Hitz describes the vision of rich discussion that she is aiming to facilitate: "The pinnacle of intellectual life, so far as I am concerned, is to sit around a table talking about the deep questions, inspired by an excellent book. We are drawn to that table from a desire to understand and to learn, with and from one another."[16]

Finally, before her years as a writer and editor for Horace Greeley's *New-York Tribune*, Fuller served as the inaugural editor of the small transcendentalist periodical the *Dial*. This magazine had around three hundred subscribers; even so, it was likely the "most widely read intellectual journal in the country" for the few years it was published.[17] Such journals play a key role in sustaining serious conversations when the mass media chases large circulation numbers and the accompanying advertising dollars. Staking out a position on the margins of this commercialized mainstream serves as a precondition for important intellectual debates; as one scholar notes, "Exile, in fact, is the keynote of little-magazine literature."[18] From this position on the outskirts of the mainstream discourse, little magazines can invigorate a moribund public sphere: they offer opportunities for young writers to hone their craft (Fuller's editorial hand improved Henry David Thoreau's prose considerably); they test out ideas that could not gain a mainstream hearing; and they prod their readers to think more deeply than the twenty-four-seven demands of the news cycle permit.[19] Peter Mommsen, the editor of *Plough*, offhandedly lists a dozen small print journals in a 2023 essay articulating the vital goods served by such publications. He concludes, "The aim of small magazines like *Plough* is not simply to inform or entertain but to offer fresh perspectives that help readers think differently and equip them to live their lives more intentionally."[20] As these examples demonstrate, all three venues for convivial conversation were valuable in the nineteenth century and remain viable in our digital era. Fuller's efforts to foster genuine dialogue in her various roles as editor, conversation leader, and writer can inspire and guide our participation in such conversations today.

Fostering a Culture of Conversation

Fuller emphasizes the value of conversation as a counterpoint to the print ideal of a complete, polished, linear monologue. And as we have already glimpsed, she found ways to structure her printed prose in conversational forms. The name *essay*, as she alludes to in her comment about the benefits of writing in the form of a dialogue, comes from a Latin word meaning to weigh or test; essays are meant to try out an idea rather than to promulgate some totalizing system of thought. Conversation thus becomes a model for a responsive mode of thought and, indeed, being. In this regard, Fuller's various efforts to promote conversational forms align with Hartmut Rosa's observation that human flourishing depends not on enforcing total control on our surroundings but on the possibility of responding meaningfully: "The basic mode of vibrant human existence consists not in exerting *control* over things but in resonating with them, making them respond to us—thus experiencing *self-efficacy*—and responding to them in turn."[21] This is precisely the goal Fuller aimed at when facilitating conversations.

A healthy conversation requires authentic give-and-take. Superficial affirmation of preexisting opinions and patting members of one's tribe on the back does not constitute genuine conversation. We need to learn from other groups and have our thinking sharpened by testing it against the ideas of others, but this process backfires when we confer within a group that shares too many predispositions. In fact, when members of such a group talk together, the evidence suggests that their thinking becomes more polarized and narrow-minded. In this context, as Cass Sunstein demonstrates, the law of "group polarization" will take over, according to which "members of a deliberating group move toward a more extreme point in whatever direction is indicated by the members' predeliberation tendency."[22] As David French summarizes this phenomenon, "When people of like mind gather, they tend to become more extreme."[23] Unfortunately, many of the venues that might support genuine conversation tend instead to gather likeminded groups to affirm their preexisting opinions and mock those who might offer a different perspective. Social media algorithms, for instance, exacerbate our human tendencies to listen to people with whom we already agree. Siva Vaidhyanathan points out that "homophily—a sociological term used to describe our urge to cavort with those similar to ourselves" was present long before Facebook, but Facebook, and the broader media landscape shaped by that platform, amplifies and reinforces this tendency.[24]

In contrast to such centripetal, ingrown affirmation of one's preexisting ideas, conversation entails attending to different voices and testing these contrasting perspectives against one another. The path and outcome of a conversation can never be predetermined. This unpredictable character defines its ability to sustain hope, hope that we might learn and grow in our understanding. As Ivan Illich remarks, "Our hope of salvation lies in our being surprised by the Other."[25] Yet it takes practice to veer away from predetermined scripts and enter into a genuine conversation. This is why Fuller sought to develop her abilities as a facilitator, as a guide to the art of conversation: she aimed to prevent participants from settling for easy confirmation, and she pushed them to consider contrasting ideas and opinions.[26] Insofar as people accept such an invitation, they gain the opportunity to take ownership of and responsibility for ideas with all their complexity and ramifications. Rather than being mere passive recipients of prepackaged content, members of a conversation actively participate in a living form of truth (see theses 3 and 6).

Healthy conversation depends on the presence of both some common ground and some substantive disagreements. For instance, Fuller would pause her conversations to define terms and forestall fruitless confusion. But she'd also push participants to broaden the perspectives under consideration when the conversation threatened to move in a centripetal direction. And while she had strong opinions herself, she did not want to impose those on her interlocutors.[27] In making a similar argument for the attitude that characterizes healthy disagreement, Wendell Berry quotes his friend the theologian William E. Hull, who "said that the way to prevent disagreement from becoming destructive is to seek 'clarity rather than victory.' Clarity is what we owe, in honesty and goodwill, to one another. . . . But if we hope to have clarity we will have to submit to complexity."[28] It was out of a similar conviction—the conviction that clarity requires us to grapple with the complexity of different voices—that Fuller refused to let her listeners or readers settle for the easy, but almost certainly false, presumption that they had a final grasp on any matter. Whether in her capacity as editor of the *Dial* or as leader of in-person conversations or as author of essays and books, Fuller challenged others to listen patiently to different voices and so shape their own thoughts in response to other perspectives.

In seeking to strike the right balance between common commitments and clarifying disagreements, a tension necessary for productive conversation, Fuller discovered that scale is essential. Her in-person conversations and the relatively small readership of the *Dial* provided spaces in which people could come to know and trust one another. When she experimented with other formats, such as opening up her conversations to paying participants of both genders, she struggled to facilitate genuine dialogue. Too many different perspectives and competing religious and philosophical commitments among the attendees hindered the flow of conversation and the possibility of real learning.[29] Productive conversation does not really scale up; as Dunbar's number suggests, there are limits on how many people (approximately 150) we can know and trust and learn from.[30] This issue of scale explains why, for instance, the Catherine Project is qualitatively different from (and far superior to) MOOCs (Massive Open Online Courses). Ten or fifteen people discussing a common text in an online video chat offers possibilities for real dialogue that dissipate as the scale increases (unless it increases fractally). In smaller settings, Fuller excelled at guiding participants through productive disagreements and toward a deeper understanding of the issues at hand.

In this work, Fuller drew on a rich lineage of dialogical forms of thought. Plato's Socratic dialogues are the fountainhead of this tradition. Fuller wrote to Emerson while preparing for one of her conversations, "I have been reading Plato all the week, because I could not write. I hoped to be tuned up thereby."[31] Closer to hand, the European salon culture also served as an inspiration to Fuller, but she provided more structure and had a clearer pedagogical telos for her conversations.[32] In this regard, she followed the example of her friend Bronson Alcott, who cultivated his version of conversation as the preferred transcendentalist mode of education.[33] While Alcott generally led children in conversations, Fuller typically gathered two or three dozen women (though sometimes men would join in as well) in Elizabeth Peabody's fashionable Boston home for two hours of conversation. The Peabody home served as a center for international culture; one could find books and periodicals from around the world, and the leading intellectuals of the region would regularly pass through.[34] One scholar reconstructs the character of a typical Fuller-led conversation in this home: "Fuller would eloquently introduce the topic for the day, outlining it and suggesting points for discussion, and then invite questions and discussion from the participants. There was no assigned reading, and as Fuller indicates in the first conversation, she defined her role not as teacher but facilitator—she would be 'one' among, not over, the 'class' in their mutual exploration of the topics she proposed."[35] Fuller was not interested in rote learning or in ornamental knowledge; she modeled thinking as an activity, a practice that required attendees' full engagement. One participant recalled "the skill, the tact, with which she threw back the ball of conversation, so as to start this listener or that, and the success with which she made him speak and say his best."[36] Her conversations thus modeled "a pedagogy that encouraged participation, not passivity."[37]

A similar vision shaped her approach to editing the *Dial*. Biographer Charles Capper explains why Fuller turned out to be the ideal editor for this periodical: "she had two qualities indispensable for an editor of a new intellectual journal. One was her widely acknowledged talent as a conversationalist and social mediator. The other was her superior experience and shrewdness in publishing in magazines beyond the usual Unitarian fold."[38] Yet in seeking to expand the transcendentalist conversation and include a broad range of topics and contributors, Fuller knew she would struggle to find a receptive audience. Capper surveys her worries about whether there was an audience who would appreciate the kind of writings she wanted to write and publish in the *Dial*, but Fuller's efforts as editor aimed—much like her efforts in leading the conversations—to *cultivate* the audience she envisioned.[39] Like Thoreau, she recognized that most readers prefer "Easy Reading" that appeals to their "erect and primitive curiosity."[40] Her response to this reality was to invite them into more challenging and rewarding forms of thinking and hope that the rewards they experienced thereby would encourage them to continue making the needful effort. She describes this goal in an essay published in the initial issue of the *Dial*:

> [This] has been the greatest mistake in the conduct of these journals. A smooth monotony has been attained, an uniformity of tone, so that from the title of a journal you can infer the tenor of all its chapters. But nature is ever various, ever new, and so should be her daughters, art and literature. We do not want merely a polite response to what we thought before, but by the freshness of thought in other minds to have new thought awakened in our own. We do not want stores of information only, but to be roused to digest these into knowledge. Able and

experienced men write for us, and we would know what they think, as they think it not for us but for themselves. We would live with them, rather than be taught by them how to live; we would catch the contagion of their mental activity, rather than have them direct us how to regulate our own. . . . We would converse with him, secure that he will tell us all his thought, and speak as man to man.[41]

By actively engaging in the dialectical modes of thought Fuller offered, readers might "catch" Fuller's patterns of thought and cultivate a taste for more substantive intellectual fare.

This gambit carried real risks; readers might choose to shun the effort required to follow the intellectual demands of such prose and seek out easy reading. And indeed the *Dial* tended to elicit "alternating ridicule and disgust" from reviewers over the course of its brief four year run.[42] In fact, in all three modes I have considered—in-person conversations, the *Dial*, and her own prose—Fuller's listeners and readers were not always eager to rise to her demands for intense participation. Listeners wanted to sit passively and hear her speak. Readers wanted the *Dial* to confirm their views rather than challenge them and to espouse a more confined and predictable range of perspectives rather than publish such a wide variety. And contemporary reviewers of *Summer on the Lakes, in 1843* found its mishmash of genres and texts confusing and hard to follow. Capper cites one participant in the Boston conversations who found that Fuller exhibited an "extraordinary capacity for associating 'far divergent links, in the chain of thought.'" He goes on to comment that "one can also see this in her writing, but there she seems to have had less control over it."[43] Most critics concur with Capper's assessment of her prose, particularly regarding her first book. I have already mentioned that Brownson critiqued the "slipshod style" of *Summer on the Lakes, in 1843*, and Perry Miller calls it "a potpourri" in which "reports on scenes alternate with random associations or with insertions of brazenly extraneous matter, especially with ad hoc poetic flights."[44] My contention is that these reactions say less about the coherence of the book itself and more about the demands its form makes on readers, demands many of them are not prepared to meet.

Staging a Conversation in Print

The first sentence of *Summer on the Lakes, in 1843* alerts readers to the digressive form the book will follow. Fuller labels her work a series of "foot-notes as may be made on the pages of my life during this summer's wanderings."[45] Her pun links her descriptions of her pedestrian travels with her notes on her wide-ranging reading. While readers might find this combination awkward and confusing, they cannot claim they were not warned. And if they give careful attention to Fuller's varied footnotes, they might find that a surprising harmony emerges. While the whole book rewards such attention to the effects of its dialogical form, I will focus here on the fourth chapter, which incorporates a poem, two letters (one of which includes a dialogue), a long sketch that purports to tell the story of one of Fuller's youthful classmates (and includes another poem), a brief note on the scenery around her, and an account of an early settler taken from a guidebook. Because Fuller does not explicitly explain the connections between these stories, many readers have been perplexed by the apparently digressive structure. Attending to the tensions that each episode probes, however, reveals Fuller's purpose in this chapter and, indeed, her whole book. As it turns out, her heterogeneous style plays an integral role in forming readers who are able to patiently listen to disparate voices and lovingly relate them in an effort to participate more fully in a complex and polyphonic truth. Such readers were particularly necessary in the American West, with its diversity of landscapes and its combination of Native Americans and settlers from many European countries. And they may be equally necessary today, in a digital era where disagreements tend to prompt shrill partisan posturing rather than earnest conversation.

Chapter 4 begins with "Triformis," an unattributed poem whose three parts chronicle three different stages in a romantic relationship.[46] In the first section, the speaker is enraptured by the beauty of his beloved, but he remains "far off." By the second section, however, they have met and come to know one another, so much so that the lover incorporates her beauty into himself: "I breathed her beauty as we talked." By the final section, their romance is over; even when they do meet by chance, "miles of polar ice" remain between them. The two have moved from distance, to identification, to distance once again. In each section, the stages of their romance are likened to the cycles of the moon, figuring the changes in human affections as analogous to the moon's natural waxing and waning. For the speaker, this relationship was the "music of my boyhood's hour" that shed "light on manhood's way." And the particular nature of his maturation is characterized as a more open-handed posture toward the one whose beauty he values: "all thy love has waned, and so / I gladly let thy beauty go."[47] To be mature, the poem suggests, means to accept and release the beloved rather than trying to consume her; it entails holding beauty at an understanding distance rather than wanting to possess and control it. Such a posture is a precondition for genuine conversation.

Immediately following this poem, Fuller inserts a letter she received that exemplifies the consequences of not loving beauty in this selfless manner. The letter opens by describing the beautiful prairies and forests of the West. Yet after two paragraphs of lush, romantic description, the writer confesses, "I was a prisoner where you glide, the summer's pensioned guest, and my chains were the past and the future." These chains prevented the writer from being the poet whom these beauties deserved, and so the letter concludes with a hope that in the future, some poet "whose lyre had never lost a string . . .—that to him these plains might enter, and flow forth in airy song."[48] The soul of the letter writer, bound by foreign cultural commitments, prevents him from properly sympathizing with and interpreting these natural beauties; his chains restrict his ability to fully enter into the beautiful life of this wild place and give it the voice it merits. A selfless artist is required, one who can perceive beauty without allowing his distracted vision to warp his understanding of the land.

Again, Fuller abruptly shifts to a transcription of a letter sent three years previously from a painter traveling through this same country. The painter's description of the country is self-consciously filtered through his experiences. Because the prairie looks like a carefully maintained pasture, he writes, "the whole country reminds me perpetually of one that has been carefully cultivated by a civilized people, who had been suddenly removed from the earth, with all the works of their hands, and the land given again into nature's keeping." Because of its appearance, he feels that the country is "inviting" and "accessible."[49] Yet he admits that his perception differs manifestly from the uninhabited reality of the prairie: "All looks like the work of man's hand, but you see no vestige of man." The letter writer then dramatizes the unreliability of individual perception by including a conversation "between the solitary old man and the young traveller." The young traveler is an idealist, "driven by insatiable desire" for the "source" of all reality and beauty. The old man cautions him that all his intimations of higher truth are only dreams: "even so I dreamed, / And even so was thwarted."[50] The young man remains hopeful, however, wondering if in fact the material world is more dreamlike than the eternal forms he seeks. Their conversation ends without any assessment by Fuller or the letter writer, leaving readers to consider for themselves to what extent either the young traveler or the old man is right. The only certainty is that individual perception is shaped by personal experience, whether the landscapes familiar to the painter, the disappointed dreams of the old man, or the romantic visions of the young traveler; for all three, the outside world mirrors the expectations and desires carried within the self. Thus perception and interpretation are inevitably, at least to some extent, a function of the viewer's eyes. Such subjectivity means that if we want to encounter the reality of the world around us, we must test our perceptions against the perceptions of others.

After this letter, it appears that Fuller will return to her travel narrative as she begins describing Chicago and the diverse ethnicities of the inhabitants of the young town. But then she tells of meeting an acquaintance who informs her that one of Fuller's schoolmates has died, and this news results in a long episode—nearly six thousand words—describing the life and death of her classmate, Mariana. This story seems like the most egregious digression yet from her travels as it has nothing to do with Illinois or the West, but upon closer examination, Fuller's story testifies to the need for the same kind of patient, dialogical perception that the preceding poem and letters did.

Mariana's story is long and intricate, but the focus throughout remains on her passionate personality and the self-centered love she expressed: "She was very loving, even infatuated in her own affections, and exacted from those who had professed any love for her, the devotion she was willing to bestow." Mariana only loves those who will love her in return. Over time, most of the other girls at school come to dislike Mariana, and when she is shamed by a prank her classmates play on her, Mariana responds by becoming a "genius of discord among them," spreading gossip to get revenge. As a young girl, however, Fuller admired Mariana and practiced the same sort of conditional love, this love-for-the-sake-of-being-loved.[51] Fuller tried to make herself agreeable to Mariana, but after failing to gain the attention of the older girl, she flung herself on her knees and begged, "O Mariana, do let me love you, and try to love me a little."[52] Mariana makes light of Fuller's plea and leaves her deeply hurt. The core problem with the way that both Mariana and the youthful Fuller practice "love" is that they twist love into a demand for another's affection. Much like the immature lover in "Triformis," they seek to identify with the beloved rather than relating dialogically. And in the effort to satisfy their own egos, they resort to guilt trips that alienate others and leave themselves hurt.

When Mariana is disgraced as a result of her gossip, she grows sick and wretched, no longer desiring to live. One of her teachers, however, tends to her and shares a story from her own past. While Fuller does not give us the details of this story, she describes it as a tale "of pain, of shame, borne, not for herself, but for one near and dear as herself."[53] In other words, it is a story of other-centered love, of an individual serving another's good without personal benefit. This story restores Mariana's desire to live and leads her to seek reconciliation with her classmates.

After she leaves school, Mariana quickly falls in love and gets married, but, unfortunately, her husband views love as a means of satisfying his own desires. He does not so much love her as he loves "hav[ing] her near him"; he likes having her as an attractive accessory. Because he does not seek to meet her needs, he does not love her in a way that unfolds her character. Fuller mourns this unequal marriage, but she warns her readers not to blame the youthful, immature Mariana for marrying an unworthy man. Mariana simply had not yet learned to properly judge love. Fuller echoes the lunar metaphors from "Triformis" when she writes, "blame no children who thought at arm's length to find the moon."[54] Like a child who thinks the moon is so close that she can reach out and grasp it, Mariana has not yet learned the painful lesson dramatized in "Triformis": she attempts to possess and benefit from the beloved rather than engaging the other in dialogue across their differences.

The failure of both spouses to seek patiently and lovingly to understand one another results in a marriage that is a tragic failure. Without the attention of her husband, Mariana gradually weakens, falls sick, and then dies. Mariana's tragedy, according to Fuller, is twofold. On the one hand, she did not know "more of God and the universe," a knowledge that would have enabled her to weather the vicissitudes of love. On the other hand, her husband did not truly love her, and given the place of women in society, a woman like Mariana is unfortunately dependent on finding a man who can "revere her rare nature."[55] Such selfless love would not seek to gratify its own needs but rather strive to enable the other to flourish. Yet this kind of love remains sadly lacking throughout Mariana's story.

Fuller concludes her chapter, then, by longing for the arrival of people who are capable of such patient, other-oriented love, love that is attuned to the actual voice and needs of the beloved: "When will this country have such a man? It is what she needs; no thin Idealist, no coarse Realist, but a man whose eye reads the heavens while his feet step firmly on the ground." This plea functions as the transition from the kind of lover Mariana needed to the kind of man that Illinois and the rest of the frontier needs to come and serve "the best interests of the land" in establishing a harmonious society, one that puts human interests in right relationship to the land's inherent limits and beauty.[56] Such a settler would put his desires and aspirations in conversation with the reality of the place as it is.

Thus all of the texts that form this heterogeneous chapter speak in different ways about the need for patient, loving perception and interpretation. Humans are plagued by the temptation to co-opt other voices, to exploit the land and other people in ways that we think will benefit ourselves. According to Fuller's diagnosis, individuals can all too easily collapse the space between their perspective and another's and so (often violently) silence other voices. Alternatively, they might just ignore those voices they find difficult to respond to. Yet genuine conversation requires that we remain in relationship with those who have different opinions and then patiently and lovingly seek the truth alongside them.

Fuller's method in this chapter—and indeed the whole book—is to offer readers a taste of this difficult process. Rather than providing some propositional, easily digested "content," she composes a symphonic meditation on the patience and love required to engage in a dialogical search for truth. She juxtaposes different voices, none of which is complete in isolation, and invites readers to discern the implicit connections or harmonies that unify them. Through the unusual form of her book, she frustrates readers' expectations for a straightforward narrative and challenges them to set aside their predispositions and enter into the book on its own terms, learning to attend closely to the conversation she curates between her various episodes. Practicing such attentive, patient reading of a variegated text may shape readers in the dispositions and virtues necessary to seek the truth in conversation with others.

As we have seen, Fuller's efforts met with mixed success, and her greatest influence likely came through the in-person conversations she led in Boston. But her writing on a range of topics—her cultural criticism, her advocacy for greater opportunities for women, her efforts to imagine more just ways of settling the West—exhibits this commitment to think in a conversational mode. Whereas industrial print culture caters to passive readers, whether those seeking easy reading for superficial amusement or those looking for intellectual gurus whose conclusions they can parrot, Fuller provided a different kind of fare in her writing, editing, and pedagogy. And even in our digital age, opportunities still abound to gather with friends or neighbors for lively, structured, sustained conversation.

12

Friends

The kind of conversation that Fuller aspires to orchestrate, conversation that leads its participants toward the truth about themselves and the world, only thrives in the context of friendship. Such friendship—and, more prominently, the absence and distortion of friendship—lies at the heart of Nathaniel Hawthorne's *The Scarlet Letter*. Hawthorne dramatizes the way that we so often use words either to shame and control others or to escape from those we find distasteful, but he also points to the possibility that friends might share words and stories with one another in order to provoke the internal change and repentance necessary to journey toward truth.

These themes come to the fore in the narrator's account of the rooms shared by the Reverend Arthur Dimmesdale, the town's respected minister as well as the secret lover of Hester, and Roger Chillingworth who, unbeknown to anyone else in town, is Hester's husband:

> The new abode of the two friends was with a pious widow, of good social rank. . . . The motherly care of the good widow assigned to Mr. Dimmesdale a front apartment, with a sunny exposure, and heavy window-curtains, to create a noontide shadow, when desirable. The walls were hung round with tapestry, said to be from the Gobelin looms, and, at all events, representing the Scriptural story of David and Bathsheba, and Nathan the Prophet, in colors still unfaded, but which made the fair woman of the scene almost as grimly picturesque as the woe-denouncing seer. Here the pale clergyman piled up his library, rich with parchment-bound folios of the Fathers, and the lore of Rabbis, and monkish erudition, of which the Protestant divines, even while they vilified and decried that class of writers, were yet constrained often to avail themselves. On the other side of the house old Roger Chillingworth arranged his study and laboratory; not such as a modern man of science would reckon even tolerably complete, but provided with a distilling

apparatus, and the means of compounding drugs and chemicals, which the practised alchemist knew well how to turn to purpose.[1]

The description begins by calling these two men "friends," and yet as the narrative soon makes clear, Chillingworth has cultivated an intimacy with Dimmesdale not because he loves him or desires to serve his best interests but because he wants to exact a painful revenge on the man who committed adultery with his wife.

The subject of the tapestries hanging in Dimmesdale's room, then, offers a stark contrast to the guilt-ridden pastor's own situation. King David's adultery with Bathsheba, and his subsequent murder of her husband in an attempt to cover up the evidence of his sin, would seem to merit his death. These are grievous sins indeed. Yet Samuel records that instead of immediately punishing David, the Lord sends Nathan to him, and Nathan proceeds to tell his friend the king a remarkable story. Nathan relates a parable about a rich man with many flocks and a poor man who had one lamb that the family treated as a pet. When a guest comes to the rich man, he steals his neighbor's beloved lamb and slaughters it to feed his visitor. Upon hearing this story, David responds with the appropriate judgment: "As the Lord liveth, the man that hath done this thing shall surely die." Nathan then turns the tables on David by pronouncing, "Thou art the man."[2] Nathan's story provokes David to sincere and humble repentance. He and his family still suffer serious consequences for his sins, but through the ministrations of a true friend, David repents of his sin, receives forgiveness, and lives as a changed man.[3]

When Nathan confronts David, he imagines his friend not only as an adulterer and murderer but also as a king who loves justice and a poet who longs for God. No single act defines his life. Instead, David's character is ambiguous; he is polysemous. Hence he is convertible. As a prophetic friend, Nathan does not identify David with any single facet of his character; he wisely appeals to those commitments of David's that might enable him to recognize and repent of his reprehensible acts. We all need friends like Nathan who will tell us the stories we need to hear to be made whole. Unfortunately for Dimmesdale, he does not have a true friend to proclaim his woe and so is slowly tormented by his sworn enemy posing as a friend (see thesis 26).

In this passage, the narrator also establishes a set of analogies between Nathan's imaginative and friendly posture toward David and the attitudes that Dimmesdale and Chillingworth take toward their respective subjects of study. Dimmesdale cherishes his library of church fathers and Jewish rabbis. As a committed Puritan, he does not agree with everything they write: such indiscriminate assent would be impossible as Jewish commentators dispute the meaning of biblical passages as virulently as Christian theologians do. But the fact that he has an extensive library of valuable folios indicates he studies them, and the narrator's syntax absolves Dimmesdale himself of his peers' worst tendencies to vilify and decry these writers even as they rely on them. Disagreement with authors from the past should not lead readers to dismiss them but rather to engage them in careful, discerning study, discarding the dross and treasuring the wisdom they might share with our contemporary age.[4]

In contrast to Dimmesdale's study of books whose value he finds ambivalent—sometimes worth learning from, sometimes necessary to correct—Chillingworth sets up his laboratory to transform natural substances into drugs that will serve his purposes. Rather than enter into a dialogue with nature, Chillingworth aims to transform its raw materials into forms he can profit from. Now, a good physician may do something that appears very similar, but as readers discover, Chillingworth's aim is not to serve the health of his "friend" Dimmesdale but to exact revenge. At the end of the book, the narrator reports that some even attribute the "A" many observed on Dimmesdale's chest to "the agency of magic and poisonous drugs" given him by Chillingworth. The narrator alerts us to Chillingworth's coercive approach to nature by terming him a "practised alchemist." By comparing his mastery of the "processes by which weeds were converted into drugs of potency" to alchemy, Hawthorne situates Chillingworth in this tradition's magical quest for knowledge as coercive power.[5] For the alchemist, the potential ambiguity in the nature of a substance can be exploited to transform it. The standard for such transformation lies not in the good of the substance nor in some common good; rather, it lies in the personal wealth or selfish benefit that could come from converting base materials to gold or to the elixir of life. As such an alchemist, one motivated by curiosity rather than studiousness, Chillingworth leverages his intimacy with Dimmesdale and with the material world not to serve their respective goods but to further his selfish vengeance.

Hawthorne's narrative thus turns on a set of contrasting responses to the "mesh of good and evil" that makes up every human soul.[6] Cultural and technological upheavals exacerbate the perennial human tendency to impose a singular, self-serving meaning on others and so bring order to a confusing social reality. In Hawthorne's Salem, this manifests most clearly in the fabric "A" that Hester is required to wear. She becomes typed and defined by her one act of adultery. In the early years of digital social media, this tendency has manifested as "cancel culture," and indeed many commentators have noted the parallels between the dynamics of cancel culture and Hawthorne's romance. As Anne Applebaum explains, digital mobs or swarms seize on "incidents that are interpreted, described, or remembered by different people in different ways" and gives these acts a single, damning interpretation. Real differences exist between the intimate, embodied shaming of Hester and the anonymous, digital denouncing that occurs online, but the underlying dynamics bear striking similarities. When established orthodoxies and institutions and mores are unsettled, people reach for simplistic, univocal labels they can impose on others in order to make sense of a chaotic and confusing context. Online mobs may not sew a literal letter on individuals deemed guilty, but they can still reduce a person's entire life to a single act or statement. Applebaum's warning is apt: "Nobody is perfect; nobody is pure; and once people set out to interpret ambiguous incidents in a particular way, it's not hard to find new evidence."[7]

Denizens of Hawthorne's seventeenth-century Salem and our twenty-first-century digital culture seem pulled toward one of two interpretive stances, both of which are marked by distrust and antagonism rather than the imaginative friendship portrayed by the prophet Nathan. Online culture tends toward the mirrored pairs of total publicity and total privacy. Digital denizens shame people via cancel culture and then crawl the dark web for nefarious business or appetitive lust. Hawthorne's Salem offers an analogous mirrored pair: the scaffold and the woods. These settings invite their inhabitants to respond to fraught ambiguities with either coercive and reductive literalism or escapist and nihilistic relativism. The action of Hawthorne's romance turns on Hester and the narrator both learning to avoid both these temptations and instead commit to the difficult work of imaginative friendship. Ambiguity in a context of distrust and antagonism becomes weaponized for the interpreter's benefit. But ambiguity in a context of friendship becomes an opportunity for needed correction, clarification, and mutual growth.

We might understand these three postures—escapist relativism, imaginative friendship, and coercive literalism—by reference to the three chairs (and their distortions) that Thoreau describes in his house by Walden Pond. Thoreau writes that he had "three chairs—one for solitude, two for friendship, and three for society."[8] In her book *Reclaiming Conversation*,

Sherry Turkle cites Thoreau's furniture as a model for healthy human community, arguing that these three chairs can form a "virtuous circle," but that the introduction of powerful new communication technologies tends to disrupt such an arrangement. Turkle documents how the forms that our digital culture has taken encourages solitude to become solipsistic and escapist and public society to become dominated by reductive memes and slogans. These tendencies are exacerbated because the middle space of friendship—the third places, the front porches, the mediating institutions wherein we can cultivate human-scale community and lasting friendships—gets hollowed out.[9] Yet these middle spaces, where we can know one another as full-orbed persons with plenty of faults *and* virtues, provide the context necessary to hold individuals accountable for their failures while also giving them opportunities to repent, be forgiven, and pursue reconciliation with their communities.[10]

In the previous chapters of this final section I have pointed to walking and conversation as two practices that can cultivate the disciplines by which we might wield even industrial and digital textual technologies in the service of convivial ends. In this chapter I explore how friendship with others, even our enemies, might enable our words to provoke repentance and redemption and so help our communities truly flourish. The paradigmatic example for Hawthorne, as I suggested, is Nathan's prophetic encounter with David. But imaginative friendship with one's intellectual or moral enemies takes many forms. The common denominator is that this work is by definition not public, not scalable, not prominent.[11] This is because it requires the patient, particular work of imagining others as ambiguous, multifaceted persons whose growth and redemption might be served by our words.

Sometimes, however, the work of friendship spills over into various public forms and reveals a hint of the quiet, ongoing efforts necessary to sustain such relationships.[12] One might think, for instance, of the friendship between professors Robbie George and Cornel West, whose political views could not be more different but who nonetheless find real common ground to work from.[13] Or the friendship between professor Molly Worthen and Southern Baptist pastor J. D. Greer. Worthen recounts how this unlikely friendship eventually led to her unexpected religious conversion.[14] Or the remarkable Daryl Davis, a black musician who befriends members of the Ku Klux Klan and through these relationships has convinced over two hundred Klansmen to give up their robes.[15] Or the friendly relationship that developed between bell hooks and Wendell Berry as two

Kentucky authors thinking from opposite sides of a deep racial divide. hooks records a conversation between them in her book *Belonging* and reflects on what she appreciates about Berry, despite their real disagreements.[16] In his own book on how we might heal the festering wounds of racism, Berry likewise praises hooks and points to examples of those who reached out in friendship even to their bitter enemies. Among others, he commends Will Campbell, a white, Baptist pastor who included black people in his ministry and participated in the civil rights movement, "but then, realizing that they might not after all be 'the least,' or if the least not the only ones, Brother Campbell felt that his own work was incomplete. He then troubled to get to know members of the Ku Klux Klan, whom he had considered his enemies." In a nod to John Lewis, Berry concludes that Campbell "was an embarrassment and a troublemaker, no doubt an actual follower of Jesus."[17]

In all these cases, individuals divided by gender or race or politics or religion turn aside from the easy paths: they refuse to reductively label and shame their enemies in an effort to coercively change them and to score points with their fellow partisans, and they refuse to ignore their enemies and so abandon them to their errors. Instead, they befriend them. In doing so, they begin with the advice offered by the poet Richard Wilbur to a group of student strikers: "Go talk with those who are rumored to be unlike you."[18] Through the resulting conversations, they discover that cultivating relationships with ambiguous persons, that imagining others as full-orbed humans rather than avatars, creates opportunities to speak words of correction and comfort that can lead to repentance, reconciliation, and redemption.

The Scaffold

The red fabric "A" that Hester wears sewn to her bosom represents the most obvious example of textual control in Hawthorne's romance. As Hester stands with her baby on the scaffold at the center of town, the single letter on her breast stands for an entire life. This alphabetic magic, analogous to Chillingworth's alchemy, aims to cast a spell to transmute the ambiguity of a whole life into a single significance. Hester's punishment is only conceivable in an alphabetic, literalistic culture, one that relies on letters to impose clarity on an ambiguous and chaotic reality.

The Protestant rejection of medieval, allegorical interpretations of the Bible underlies the literalistic Puritan hermeneutic that Hawthorne critiques in his story. Taken to its extremes, such a hermeneutic eschews ambiguity and portrays meaning as singular and controllable. Many scholars have noted the tendency in various Protestant cultures not only to develop widespread visual literacy but also to assume a more univocal literal meaning than prevailed under earlier media and theological cultures.[19] As Walter Ong explains, the pedagogy designed to inculcate visual literacy fosters the impression "that literal meanings, meanings according to the letter, are all fixed and neatly segmented too. Since letters are so clear and distinct, literal meaning must be the same."[20] Ong goes on to describe how alphabetic education can incubate a sense that meaning is as arbitrary and manipulable as letters are: "The alphabet, useful and indispensable as it has certainly proved to be, itself entails to some extent delusional systematization if not necessarily schizophrenia so called. The alphabet, after all, is a careful pretense. Letters are simply not sounds, do not have the properties of sounds. . . . With alphabetic writing, a kind of pretense, a remoteness from actuality, becomes institutionalized."[21] In her masterful study of early alphabetic reader primers, Patricia Crain makes a parallel case that "alphabetization renders not merely texts but the world itself legible."[22] These tendencies became particularly pronounced in New England, where literacy was remarkably widespread. Through texts such as *The New England Primer*, which Hawthorne specifies was used to instruct Pearl, students were taught that letters can stand for and even manipulate bodies and creatures. Describing the implications of this "poetics of alphabetization," Crain concludes that "whether objects, animals, or body parts, this alphabet represents, in words or images, the world at large, arrayed through the arbitrary but powerful order of the ABCs, forcefully producing a world that is knowable, graspable, and, most strikingly, obtainable."[23] In its extreme and distorted form, then, Protestant alphabetic instruction could produce readers who are impatient with ambiguity and accustomed to using language to impose clarity (see thesis 15).

Hawthorne portrays this attitude in the Puritan magistrates' punishment of Hester. And he offers a subtle critique of its shortcomings through their use of the catechism to surveil and discipline the wayward Pearl, herself a symbol of her parents' sin. When Hester hears that the colony's leaders were discussing whether to take Pearl away from her and ensure Pearl received a properly Christian upbringing, she goes to the governor's house to plead that she be allowed to keep her daughter. Mother and daughter wait in the entrance of his mansion, standing in front of his suit of armor, and Pearl exclaims to her mother that she sees Hester reflected in the breastplate. The narrator explains the appearance of

Hester reflected in this defensive armor: "Owing to the peculiar effect of this convex mirror, the scarlet letter was represented in exaggerated and gigantic proportions, so as to be greatly the most prominent feature of her appearance."[24] Seen from the governor's harsh, militaristic perspective, Hester's sin entirely defines her and her daughter. The implications of this lens become clear in the subsequent interview as the governor cross-examines the three-year-old girl to determine the effectiveness of her mother's training: "Dost know thy catechism? Or art thou one of those naughty elfs or fairies, whom we thought to have left behind us, with other relics of Papistry, in merry old England?"[25] The governor assumes that Pearl must fit into his binary framework: either she can recite the catechism's answers to prove that she is "a Christian child," or she is some kind of demonic or inhuman creature. Ong's claim that the catechism as a genre derives from print culture and the "feeling for exact textual control encouraged by alphabetic typography" defines the governor's approach precisely.[26] It is only through the Reverend Dimmesdale's personal intercession that the governor is persuaded to allow Hester to keep Pearl. The Puritans' alphabetic and catechismal assumptions about the nature of language give them a distorted view of Hester and lead them to misapprehend the full complexity of her character.

The Wood

Through their punishment of Hester and their examination of Pearl, Hawthorne's Puritan leaders demonstrate their use of textual technologies to label and control people. When she stands on the scaffold with a red "A" sewn on her dress, the fraught ambiguities of Hester's life and actions receive a harsh, univocal meaning. She has been more effectively "canceled" than any twenty-first-century online mob could hope to accomplish. In reacting against this reductive, unforgiving environment, Dimmesdale, Hester, and others seek refuge in the dark secrecy afforded by the surrounding woods. But if unrelenting publicity cannot provide the context necessary for the exchange of redemptive words, neither can unrelieved privacy.

Readers can certainly understand why Dimmesdale lacks the courage to confess his adultery to his superiors and his congregation, given the strict punishment that Hester receives at their hands. But Dimmesdale's cowardly secrecy nonetheless destroys his soul from the inside out. When his partner in adultery stands exposed on the scaffold, Dimmesdale enjoins her—in words laced with agonized irony—to name the father of her child: "Be not silent from any mistaken pity and tenderness for him; for, believe me, Hester, though he were to step down from a high place, and stand there beside thee, on thy pedestal of shame, yet better were it so, than to hide a guilty heart through life. What can thy silence do for him, except it tempt him—yea, compel him, as it were—to add hypocrisy to sin?" Dimmesdale prophecies his own fate accurately, yet Hester refuses to name her preacher as her fellow sinner, and Dimmesdale is right to tell her that Pearl's father "hath not the courage" to step forward himself.[27]

Dimmesdale may be wise to shun the harsh, reductive light of public exposure, but he also refuses to confess his sin to a friend or superior. "Trusting no man as his friend," Dimmesdale renders himself vulnerable to Chillingworth's torments.[28] As he tells Hester, "Had I one friend,—or were it my worst enemy!—to whom, when sickened with the praises of all other men, I could daily betake myself, and be known as the vilest of all sinners, methinks my soul might keep itself alive thereby. Even thus much of truth would save me! But, now, it is all falsehood!—all emptiness!—all death!"[29] Despite this assertion, he never seeks out such a friend, and his refusal to be accountable, to confess his sin, to make what restitution he can, and to live with the consequences of his error leads him into mazes of hypocrisy and psychological torture. Hawthorne brilliantly portrays the devilish logic by which Dimmesdale convinces himself that hiding his sin enables him to glorify God and makes him a more effective preacher.[30]

The fruit of Dimmesdale's isolation becomes apparent when he and Hester meet in "the dim wood."[31] As she walks with Pearl into the wood, Hester lies to her daughter about the meaning of her scarlet letter, and in doing so allows "some new evil" to creep into her own heart.[32] In this moment, she responds to the merciless judgment of her community by indulging in self-exculpatory relativism and dreaming of an escape from the consequences of what she herself acknowledges was a sin. During this tryst, Hester urges Dimmesdale to flee with her into the trackless forests or voyage across the sea and escape from this place where they can never be free of their sin: "Leave this wreck and ruin here where it hath happened," Hester declares. "Begin all anew!"[33] This impulse lies near the core of the American identity: when Americans can no longer imagine how to live amid the frustrations and challenges of their community, they can always go west. Huck Finn's attitude is paradigmatic: if ever a time comes when he cannot handle Aunt Sally's civilizing rules, he will "light out for the Territory."[34]

In accepting Hester's invitation to join her in "a moral wilderness," Dimmesdale does not find freedom or redemption. Instead, he becomes a "lost and desperate man," wandering in a moral "maze" where he loses all sense of self and all control over his words and actions.[35] In reacting against the Puritans' literalistic alphabetic coercion, this poor couple falls prey to the opposite extreme: they respond to the ambiguous circumstances in which they find themselves by giving up any effort to discern and enact their moral responsibilities. Needless to say, such an escapist use of imagination does not improve their situation. Hester and Dimmesdale turn from a merciless public to an unaccountable private refuge when what they really need are friends who would love them enough to offer words of correction and forgiveness.

A Cottage of Comfort

While waiting for Dimmesdale to ascend to the pulpit and deliver his Election Sermon, Hester receives the news that Chillingworth has discovered their plot and reserved a place for himself on the ship that was to be their means of escape. No matter where they go, their past choices and acts will follow. Dimmesdale recognizes the futility of their escapist dream as well, and after his sermon, he proceeds to the scaffold where Hester was publicly shamed at the book's outset. Standing there with his lover and their child, he finally takes responsibility for his sin, only thereby escaping the clutches of Chillingworth and asking Hester—as they stand together on display—"Is not this better . . . than what we dreamed of in the forest?"[36] In the moment, Hester is unsure of her answer, but her actions during the previous seven years and in the years following Dimmesdale's confession and death demonstrate a commitment to using her imagination not to escape her plight but to serve and befriend others, even those who shame her.

From the outset of the story, Hester uses her artistic skill and sympathetic heart to serve others and, as an unforeseen result, redeem the significance of the "A" she wears. Through "her delicate and imaginative skill" in needlework, Hester beautifies the letter that is her punishment and lavishly adorns Pearl's clothes.[37] Her ability soon makes her a sought-after seamstress in the colony, and Hester supports herself and her daughter by this labor. Yet while she makes lavish clothes for occasions of state and men and women of degree, she likewise uses her art to serve the poor members of the town in making them serviceable garments.[38] Though she lives as a single mother, she sacrifices her time and pride to befriend others who are in physical or emotional distress:

> It had been her habit . . . to go about the country as a kind of volun-
> tary nurse, and doing whatever miscellaneous good she might; taking
> upon herself, likewise, to give advice in all matters, especially those
> of the heart; by which means, as a person of such propensities inevita-
> bly must, she gained from many people the reverence due to an angel,
> but, I should imagine, was looked upon by others as an intruder and a
> nuisance.[39]

As this description indicates, one of the results of her charitable service is that the significance of the letter on her breast begins to change. She remains ambiguous: some find her a nuisance, and she continues to be seen and known as a shamed sinner. But in befriending those in need, the "A" comes to signify not only "adulterer" but also "angel." Another description of her "self-devoted" service further expands the multivalent meaning of her badge:

> None so ready as she to give of her little substance to every demand
> of poverty; even though the bitter-hearted pauper threw back a gibe
> in requital of the food brought regularly to his door, or the garments
> wrought for him by the fingers that could have embroidered a mon-
> arch's robe. None so self-devoted as Hester, when pestilence stalked
> through the town. In all seasons of calamity, indeed, whether general
> or of individuals, the outcast of society at once found her place. She
> came, not as a guest, but as a rightful inmate, into the household that
> was darkened by trouble; as if its gloomy twilight were a medium in
> which she was entitled to hold intercourse with her fellow-creatures.
> There glimmered the embroidered letter, with comfort in its unearthly
> ray. Elsewhere the token of sin, it was the taper of the sick-chamber. . . .
> The letter was the symbol of her calling. Such helpfulness was found in
> her,—so much power to do, and power to sympathize,—that many peo-
> ple refused to interpret the scarlet A by its original signification. They
> said that it meant Able; so strong was Hester Prynne.[40]

She does not erase her scarlet letter's previous meaning; she does not attempt to escape from or deny her sin. In fact, when the magistrates consider letting her remove the letter, she refuses to consider this possi-bility, expressing instead her hope that she might live in such a way that the letter's meaning would shift: "Were I worthy to be quit of it, it would fall away of its own nature, or be transformed into something that should speak a different purport."[41] And indeed, by giving her life in service to other sufferers, she accomplishes such a transformation: the ambiguity inherent in the single letter "A" becomes an opportunity for Hester to broaden and redeem the meaning of her life. The Puritan leaders attempt to define her entire life through their reductive label, but rather than seeking to escape from this verdict, Hester undertakes the far more difficult work of placing her act of sin into the context of a life that might renarrate and redeem its ultimate significance.

After Dimmesdale's death, Hester and Pearl leave Salem for several years, and Pearl apparently marries an English noble and settles in England. But Hester eventually returns to the site of her sin and punishment in order to spend her final years befriending and serving those who once had shamed her:

> There was a more real life for Hester Prynne here, in New England, than in that unknown region where Pearl had found a home. Here had been her sin; here, her sorrow; and here was yet to be her penitence. She had returned, therefore, and resumed,—of her own free will, for not the sternest magistrate of that iron period would have imposed it,—resumed the symbol of which we have related so dark a tale. Never afterwards did it quit her bosom. But, in the lapse of the toilsome, thoughtful, and self-devoted years that made up Hester's life, the scarlet letter ceased to be a stigma which attracted the world's scorn and bitterness, and became a type of something to be sorrowed over, and looked upon with awe, yet with reverence too. And, as Hester Prynne had no selfish ends, nor lived in any measure for her own profit and enjoyment, people brought all their sorrows and perplexities, and besought her counsel, as one who had herself gone through a mighty trouble. Women, more especially,—in the continually recurring trials of wounded, wasted, wronged, misplaced, or erring and sinful passion,—or with the dreary burden of a heart unyielded, because unvalued and unsought,—came to Hester's cottage, demanding why they were so wretched, and what the remedy! Hester comforted and counselled them as best she might.[42]

Hester lives out her days befriending her erstwhile enemies. She seeks neither public revenge nor private escape. Instead, she imaginatively applies her own suffering and experience to comfort and guide others in their distress. This is an arduous task that brings little glory, but her faithful, loving labors transform her place of exile into a cottage of comfort.

Through her faithful and imaginative friendship, Hester becomes the moral heroine of Hawthorne's tale. And she serves as a model not only to readers but also to the narrator of her story. In remarkably deft fashion,

Hawthorne implicates himself in both of the destructive tendencies we have explored in this chapter. He succumbs to the temptation first to wield his verbal abilities to reductively label and shame people he dislikes and then to indulge in escapist fantasies. But when he finds Hester's embroidered "A" and a brief outline of her story tucked away in a corner of the Custom House, her example inspires him to use his imaginative art for redemptive ends. Even if he fails to write the "better book" that an artist such as Hester might compose, the book he gives us praises her sympathetic and redemptive mode of imaginative friendship.

In "The Custom-House," which serves as a preface and backstory to Hester's tale, Hawthorne cruelly mocks his business colleagues. Much like the Puritans do to Hester, Hawthorne dismissively reduces them to a single attribute and then exaggerates this trait in order to create a caricature. On Hawthorne's telling, they care only for their income and are lazy, corrupt, and practically on death's doorstep. They are "a set of wearisome old souls, who had gathered nothing worth preservation from their varied experience of life" and fritter away the time exchanging "frozen witticisms of past generations."[43] Hawthorne reserves particular vitriol for the Inspector, declaring that he has "no soul, no heart, no mind" and spends his life recalling delicious meals he had eaten.[44] In similar fashion, Hawthorne condemns his own Puritan ancestors with the same sort of totalizing finality that they employed in condemning and punishing women they considered to be of dubious or heterodox character.[45]

When he first returns to Salem, the town of his distinguished Puritan forebears, Hawthorne fancies these stern and practically minded men turning their judgmental eye upon him and condemning him as a mere "idler." "A writer of story-books!" one of them might say, "Why, the degenerate fellow might as well have been a fiddler!"[46] Writing fiction does not seem to be a very useful endeavor, and Hawthorne confirms, in part, this assessment after he finds Hester's embroidered letter and strives to weave a fantasy from this artifact to escape from the humdrum monotony of Custom House business. His efforts to accomplish this task are frustrated—his employment has "tarnished" his imagination and he cannot write her story no matter how hard he tries.[47] This failure provokes him to formulate a more redemptive mode of imaginative writing, one that would be in keeping with Hester's faithful, sympathetic service of her neighbors. "A better book than I shall ever write," Hawthorne confesses, would flow from a "wiser effort" that, instead of trying to escape from his workaday world, would strive "to diffuse thought and imagination through the opaque substance of to-day." This sympathetic imagination would "seek, resolutely, the true and indestructible value that lay hidden in the petty and wearisome incidents, and ordinary characters, with which I was now conversant. The fault was mine," he concludes, for not composing such a book.[48]

Yet Hawthorne's efforts are not entirely in vain. He is brought to this conviction of his own shortcomings by meditating on Hester's remarkable example, and in lieu of crafting the better book he fails to write, he offers a narrative that praises Hester's faithful, imaginative friendship and in turn models a friendly interpretation of Hester's letter and life. After a presidential transition causes him to lose his job—after, in other words, he suffers a pale shadow of the public condemnation that Hester experiences—Hawthorne devotes himself to a sympathetic reading of Hester's embroidered letter "A." While the magistrates who ordered Hester to wear this letter thought it was unambiguously perspicuous—it is a single letter that stands for a single act—Hawthorne discovers that to read it aright, he must "imagin[e] the motives and modes of passion that influenced" the woman who wore the letter and the other members of her community.[49] As Hawthorne, who positions himself as the editor and interpreter of Hester's story, imagines the meaning of this mysterious and ambiguous text, so his readers might apply the interpretive virtues and practices that Hawthorne models in their own reading of his romance.[50] This is why Hawthorne continually foregrounds the conflicting interpretations of the events he relates. At the dramatic denouement, when Dimmesdale uncovers the alleged mark on his chest, Hawthorne refuses to fix its origin and thus its meaning: he enumerates several possible explanations and concludes that "the reader may choose among these theories."[51] In leaving this work to his readers, he invites them likewise to respond to ambiguity with the attitude of a friend, one who seeks to read with a loving, sympathetic imagination.

By grappling with ambiguity in the spirit of sympathetic friendship, Hawthorne offers an alternative to hermeneutics characterized by either coercive and reductive literalism or escapist and nihilistic relativism. In pointing to Hawthorne's approach as a counterpoint to the cancel culture dynamics that prevail on social media, Anne Applebaum notes the importance of the narrative genre he chooses: "There is a reason . . . that Hawthorne dedicated an entire novel to the complex motivations of Hester Pryne, her lover, and her husband. Nuance and ambiguity are essential to good fiction."[52] An acceptance of the multifaceted reality of human persons is also essential to lasting and redemptive friendship. By modeling this acceptance, Hawthorne's book shows readers how we might likewise welcome the sorrowful and perplexed whom we encounter and extend the remedy of sympathetic comfort and counsel.

And to the extent that Nathaniel Hawthorne narrates Hester's life with friendly sympathy, perhaps he becomes a worthy heir of the prophet whose name he shares. Like the Nathan who used a story to confront David about his sins, Hawthorne strives to be a prophetic friend who provokes readers to repent of our tendencies to label people and to seek instead to imagine them in all their complexity. Befriending others—especially if, like Hester, these others include our enemies—is an act of remarkable hope, hope that those we believe to be wrong in some significant respects might yet be redeemable. Only in such friendship can we learn to use words convivially, to wield words for the correction and restoration of the erring members of our communities.

13

Cross-Bearers

The Scarlet Letter ends with a description of the heraldic emblem on Hester's tomb: "On a field, sable, the letter A, gules."[1] On the cover of Herman Melville's lengthy narrative poem *Clarel* is a more intricate figure, which readers eventually encounter tattooed in red and blue on Agath, one of several pilgrims journeying through the Holy Land (see fig. 13-1). Melville's journal from his own trip to the Levant cites the source where he learned about this mark, which pilgrims to Jerusalem would have tattooed on their bodies: "five crosses gules, in form of that which is at this day called the *Ierusalem* crosse; representing thereby the five wounds that violated the body of our Saviour."[2] These two red signs—one a cloth letter worn as a punishment for sin, and one a tattoo signifying hope in a sacrifice that atones for sin—indicate sharply contrasting ways of imagining and using texts. Hester's letter, at least as imagined by the Puritan magistrates who imposed it on her, serves as a fixed and final representation of her character. The pilgrim's tattoo, however, is a way of bearing in one's flesh the promise of a hoped-for redemption. The instrument of torture worn as an emblem of redemption defines the pilgrim's posture toward the confusions and failures and pains of life: a pilgrim lives in the hope that a Word to come may transform the meaning of all that is endured along life's arduous way.

Clarel's subtitle, *A Poem and Pilgrimage in the Holy Land*, names both its subject and its form. Over the course of four lengthy parts totaling nearly eighteen-thousand lines, readers follow Clarel on a circular pilgrimage through key sites in Palestine, beginning and ending in Jerusalem. Published in 1876, *Clarel* is admittedly a difficult poem, and it has a mixed reputation even among Melville's admirers. Andrew Delbanco calls it "a hopelessly talky poem" that does "not rise to the level of the great effort Melville put into it."[3] Yet for those readers who are willing to endure its rigors, the poem provides substantive fare. In this way, its readers enact a kind of vicarious pilgrimage, which, as Christopher Phillips notes, is precisely what the subtitle promises: "Melville's terse, jagged, often barely readable tetrameters are to deliver not beauty but earnest striving in which the reader must participate to continue. *Clarel* is, after all, both a poem *and* a pilgrimage" (see thesis 7).[4] The journey is not an easy one for either readers or Clarel as he travels alongside, and engages in lengthy dialogues with, a motley cast of fellow pilgrims who give voice to the religious, scientific, and political views current in the late nineteenth century. Although Clarel begins his journey on the Vigil of Epiphany, the Bible has become a dead book to him: listening to a group of earnest worshipers, he fears he has become a "pilgrim-infidel" whose doubts "pollute" these "sites of Faith."[5] Despite his despair, however, he follows the steps of Christ in the hope that he can recover a sense of the living Word.

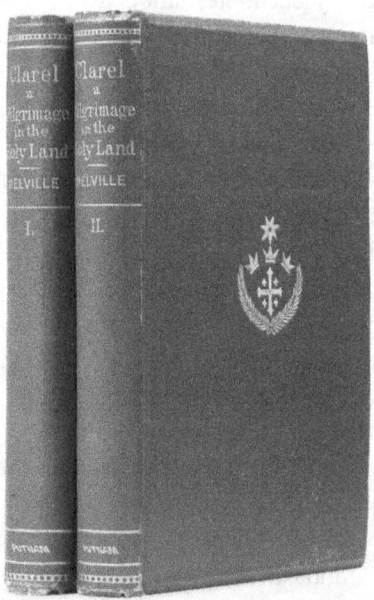

FIGURE 13-1. Herman Melville (1819–1891), *Clarel: A Poem and Pilgrimage in the Holy Land.* New York: G.P. Putnam's Sons, 1876.

Clarel's resigned sense that he will himself never experience a divine epiphany surely has its origins in Melville's own experience of loss and futility. Melville began work on the poem in earnest around 1867, the year his son Malcolm died from a self-inflicted gunshot, and Melville worked on the poem in the shadow of this death and the deaths of many close friends and family members that occurred in close succession.[6] His failed writing career, the erosion of religious faith in the wake of Darwinian science and the rise of rationalism, the nation's brutal civil war and the bumbling of Reconstruction all compounded his sense of despair and the closing in of possibility.

Clarel picks up, then, where *The Confidence-Man* leaves off. Indeed, *Clarel*'s origins lie in the trip Melville took to Europe and the Holy Land upon the completion of *The Confidence-Man* in 1856, though he did not begin drafting the book until ten years later. And the poem grapples with the same set of questions as does Melville's final published novel: How might we live on after a personal and collective loss of faith? Are we doomed to confusion and fear as we make our way among the half-truths promulgated by tricksters seeking to take advantage of any remaining scrap of trust? In a digital landscape beset by deepfakes, would-be thought-leader-influencers, and an endless barrage of targeted advertisements, Melville's pilgrimage poem remains all too relevant. Given that the introduction of this book began with the dueling metaphors proposed by the con men of his last novel, it seems fitting to conclude with Melville's poetic response to the wasteland of meaning that results from such deception and trickery.

While Frank believes the printing press is an iron Paul and an infallible spreader of righteousness, and while Charlie holds that the press is more like an erratic Colt's revolver that spreads discord and confusion, both view print and its attendant communications technologies as determinative. As such, they exhibit symptoms of what L. M. Sacasas terms the "Borg Complex," a condition that causes people to "explicitly assert or implicitly assume that resistance to technology is futile."[7] As Sacasas points out, whether one is cheerful or embittered about this prospect matters less than the underlying determinism both perspectives share. This determinism risks obscuring the opportunity and indeed the responsibility we have, regardless of our technological milieu, to respond faithfully to the words we do hear. As Melville comes to believe, the fundamental question is not which new technology or institution will spread truth or untruth, but rather what posture we are called to take in order to follow the echoes of truth we encounter within even a bleak verbal landscape.

For instance, if we follow Frank and insist that digital technologies are a silicon Paul, as it were, we will see the Internet and social media as means of sharing facts and knowledge that will lead to agreement and universal harmony. And we will be frustrated and surprised when these outcomes do not appear. We will yell at people who spread what we see as misinformation, and we will cling to the facts and explainers that promise to provide certainty and clarity. If, on the other hand, we insist that digital media are more like a Colt's revolver, amplifying the barrel but not consecrating the aim, we may give up on truth entirely and indulge in endless self-promotion, watch whatever amusing videos we can find to dull our boredom, or, even worse, get our kicks by spreading snark and insults. Borat or Bronze Age Pervert are extreme examples of this meta-ironic attitude that surfs the chaos looking for kicks.[8] Such dark, cynical humor finds no point in searching after truth or seeking to act faithfully in response to the glimpses of truth we can perceive.

In *Clarel*, however, Melville invites us to imagine ourselves as "cross-bearers," as pilgrims who are journeying toward an epiphany we have not yet experienced but for which we nonetheless hope.[9] If we take up this convivial posture, we will look for ways to use social media and other digital tools to bear witness to our fellow pilgrims of the truths we have glimpsed and to listen in turn to the meaning that their lives bear. As cross-bearers, we will seek to embody sacrificial love rather than to maximize our own power or prominence or pleasure. And as pilgrims, we will prioritize friendships with our fellow travelers. Further, we will recognize that the ultimate goal of information is not some kind of gnosis—intellectual knowledge—but metanoia—repentance—so that our lives conform ever more fully to the truth our words falteringly participate in.[10] Melville's image of cross-bearing pilgrims reminds us that flashy new verbal technologies do not change the fundamental purpose of speaking and listening, writing and reading. The point of these activities is not merely to spread ideas but to transform persons and foster proper relationships with our world, with one another, and ultimately with God (see theses 1 and 26). If we imagine ourselves as pilgrims exchanging testimonies on our way to an encounter with the incarnate Word of God, perhaps we will be in a better position to navigate a chaotic media landscape graciously and redemptively.

There are several contemporary examples of this posture that I could point to. Literal religious pilgrimages continue to be popular: every year hundreds of thousands of people walk portions of the Camino de Santiago. But I want to follow Peter Moe in linking Melvillian tattoos with the act of memorizing and pondering a religious text. In both cases, persons invest themselves with words they do not fully comprehend and yet nonetheless want to be guided by. In Agath's case, he avers that he does not know the meaning of the emblem tattooed on his arm; he had it inked one Christmas day at sea, copied from the body of a fellow sailor with no explanation of its significance. One of the other pilgrims proceeds to interpret it for him and explains that in addition to the five crosses that correspond to the five wounds of Christ, there is a star to represent the sign that the Magi followed to find Jesus in Bethlehem.[11] Agath, like the Magi and like all the pilgrims in *Clarel*, follows a sign that is only partially intelligible to him, and yet perhaps those who wear a word they do not fully understand may still be granted an epiphany.

Agath's tattoo in *Clarel* recalls the two tattoos described in *Moby-Dick*. The first is a set of "hieroglyphic marks" that cover Queequeg's body, inscribed by a prophet from his island in some script that no one can decipher. These marks comprise "a mystical treatise on the art of attaining truth; so that Queequeg in his own proper person was a riddle to unfold; a wondrous work in one volume; but whose mysteries not even himself could read, though his own live heart beat against them."[12] Queequeg may not be able to interpret this "treatise on the art of attaining truth," but as we will see, this art nonetheless guides his life and proves redemptive. In an intimate memoir that reflects on whales, *Moby-Dick*, and his faith journey, Peter Moe recounts his experience memorizing the biblical book of Jonah. Moe compares this act to the other tattoo mentioned in *Moby-Dick*, the whale dimensions that Ishmael inks on his arm so as not to lose them: "Ishmael becomes a Jonah here, his arm inside this whale." Ishmael says he saves the rest of his body for "a poem I was then composing," and Moe confesses that he likes "to think that poem is *Moby-Dick*, and I picture Ishmael's body—his arm covered in numbers, his chest, back, and thighs covered in words. . . . He is inside those sentences, his body wrapped in letters, the whale athwart him."[13] While Moe does not get a literal tattoo, the process of memorizing Jonah and meditating on those ancient words results in a similar experience:

> I spend time inside these sentences, inside these ancient phrases translated from another language—another experience—to my own, inside these words handed down. I read them, I reread them, I speak them, I hear them. I hoist myself up on them, move about and within them. For if I can learn to inhabit these inherited sentences, dwell inside these words I do not get to choose, maybe even incarnate them somehow—perhaps then I might learn to bide my time within the belly of the whale.[14]

Like the Jews who bind the Shema on their bodies in obedience to the command in Deuteronomy 6, Moe seeks to inhabit these words so that they might guide him, even as he does not fully know where they will lead him.[15] His experience testifies that the words we learn by heart may in turn transform our hearts.

Memorization is thus an act of hope, hope that as we digest and ruminate on a profound religious or even literary text, its meaning will resonate and grow. The temporal movement of a pilgrimage evokes this temporal dimension of language, in which words, rather than static signs that transfer meaning from one location to another, are present promises of future fulfillments. The pilgrim who gets a tattooed sign and the believer who memorizes a sacred text are not interested in merely accessing information. Rather, they long for a transformative intimacy with a verbal deposit of some hoped-for epiphany.

An Immensity of Waiting

This attitude toward words makes little sense if we understand language primarily in structuralist terms, according to which words signify some absent concept or reality. While such a view of language has real explanatory power—as demonstrated by theorists from Plato to Saussure to Derrida—it does not exhaust language's possibilities. In particular, a pilgrim who journeys under the sign of the cross comes to understand words as promises of some hoped-for fulfillment. The conversations and debates that occupy Clarel's pilgrimage are opportunities for him—and for readers—to gradually, asymptotically approach a fuller understanding of the truth that will ultimately be revealed, but all such efforts to articulate truth remain tentative and subject to transfiguration by the final epiphany he journeys in hope of experiencing.

The literary critic Roger Lundin draws on Irenaeus' doctrine of recapitulation, derived from biblical passages such as the first chapter of Ephesians, to describe the temporal, promise-fulfillment structure of language portrayed in Christ's life and adopted by early Christians.[16] While "a spatial orientation informs Plato's view of words," which relies on the categories of "*presence* and *absence*" and "*signifier* and *signified*," Irenaeus' account of Christ's recapitulation "shifts the emphasis from space to time, and it exchanges the certainty of presence for the hopefulness of promise." As Christ sums up or recapitulates all things, he thereby transforms their meaning. "To make transformation a central category of redemption," Lundin notes, "is to cast the question of word and thing, and of story and reality—myth and fiction—into a new framework."[17] This narrative framework for verbal signification causes the meaning of any statement to remain subject to revision by further speech or events in the unfolding story. And even as Christ's incarnation transforms all that came before, it also places all that comes after it under the sign of his promised second coming. Such words are verbal events that ramify forward and backward, transfiguring the meaning of everything else: significantly, the Hebrew term *dabar* in fact means both *word* and *event*.[18] The incarnation and the second coming become the paradigmatic events that demonstrate how a verbal event has the potential to ripple across a story or life and radically reconfigure the meaning of what has already occurred.

Pilgrimage with others toward some hoped-for epiphany enacts a faith in the transformative potential of verbal events. The conversations that the pilgrims in *Clarel* share along their journey remind both them and readers that no individual has a final grasp of truth; they talk with one another in an effort to correct and improve their understanding of various religious, cultural, and scientific disputes. This posture recalls our other examples from this section: Thoreau striding back and forth between complementary truths, Fuller orchestrating a conversation among different perspectives, Hester and Hawthorne befriending others despite their mistakes and errors. *Clarel*'s polyphonic form follows in this vein, and the indeterminacy of its conversations conveys the same set of implications that Mikhail Bakhtin argues is characteristic of Dostoevsky's mature novels: "*Nothing conclusive has yet taken place in the world, the ultimate word of the world and about the world has not yet been spoken, the world is open and free, everything is still in the future and will always be in the future.*" By withholding the "new word" that would resolve and transform the pilgrims' conversation, Melville invites readers to cultivate a patient hope for a word that has not yet been heard.[19]

One critique of such polyphonic indeterminacy—and I considered similar complaints about Fuller's conversational mode of writing—is that it leaves us lost in ambiguity and confusion. But as Lundin argues, "Bakhtin's point is decidedly not the Nietzschean claim that 'truths are illusions about which one has forgotten that this is what they are.' Instead of arguing that all truth claims are interpretations and all interpretations lies, Bakhtin is claiming that to know the truth we must hear it proclaimed and tested among a potential multitude of voices."[20] If conversation as such remains the goal, then there is a real danger of becoming lost in a pointless and unceasing dialogue—a "perpetuum mobile" of "endless dialogue"—that does not bring its participants nearer the truth or prepare them for a transformative epiphany.[21] Hence Lundin concludes by citing Hans Urs von Balthasar's theological observation that "dialogue can achieve something when both partners are looking in the same direction."[22] And some revelation must come from beyond their shared horizon for their words to be ultimately resolved into a harmony neither may have expected. This is the "eschatological context" that Alan Jacobs argues is essential for Bakhtin's model of human dialogue: "For Bakhtin, God is the Father who waits patiently but hopefully for the world's prodigal meanings to return to him and receive his blessing. Bakhtin implicitly invites us as readers to wait in patient hope for that consummation, and to participate, at first proleptically and then fully, in the 'homecoming festival.'"[23] Such patient hope clings to the possibility that despite the disagreements and the shortcomings that plague our current understanding, there will come a word—the Word—that will resolve the cacophony we perceive into an unforeseeable harmony.

Traversing the demanding dialogues of *Clarel* cultivates this patient hope in readers. And to some extent, the buildup of expectation and the delayed satisfaction that is inherent in all verbal (or musical) art fosters such patience.[24] Of course, some authors (or composers) deliberately frustrate such expectations: a paradigmatic example of this would be Beckett's *Waiting for Godot*.[25] Yet even Beckett's play depends on the temporal deferment of meaning, on an audience's willingness to wait to determine the final meaning of conversations and events until the play's conclusion. Responding to absurdist art, including Beckett's, George Steiner argues that these plays—and, indeed, all verbal making—still take place under "the question of God" and offer ways of inhabiting the "immensity of waiting" that defines our human condition.[26] Steiner's moving conclusion to *Real Presences* is worth quoting at length on this matter:

> There is one particular day in Western history about which neither historical record nor myth nor Scripture make report. It is a Saturday. And it has become the longest of days. We know of that Good Friday which Christianity holds to have been that of the Cross. But the non-Christian, the atheist, knows of it as well. This is to say that he knows of the injustice, of the interminable suffering, of the waste, of the brute enigma of ending, which so largely make up not only the historical dimension of the human condition, but the everyday fabric of our personal lives. We know, ineluctably, of the pain, of the failure of love, of the solitude which are our history and private

fate. We know also about Sunday. To the Christian, that day signifies an intimation, both assured and precarious, both evident and beyond comprehension, of resurrection, of a justice and a love that have conquered death. If we are non-Christians or non-believers, we know of that Sunday in precisely analogous terms. We conceive of it as the day of liberation from inhumanity and servitude. We look to resolutions, be they therapeutic or political, be they social or messianic. The lineaments of that Sunday carry the name of hope (there is no word less deconstructible).

But ours is a long day's journey of the Saturday. Between suffering, aloneness, unutterable waste on the one hand and the dream of liberation, of rebirth on the other. In the face of the torture of a child, of the death of love which is Friday, even the greatest art and poetry are almost helpless. In the Utopia of the Sunday, the aesthetic will, presumably, no longer have logic or necessity. The apprehensions and figurations in the play of metaphysical imagining, in the poem and the music, which tell of pain and of hope, of the flesh which is said to taste of ash and of the spirit which is said to have the savour of fire, are always Sabbatarian. They have risen out of an immensity of waiting which is that of man. Without them, how could we be patient?[27]

Steiner's Sabbatarian waiting, given Christ's claim that his death and resurrection fulfill "the sign of Jonah," aptly characterizes Peter Moe's hope for how memorizing Jonah's story might sustain him in loss and uncertainty: "Perhaps [it might teach me] to bide my time within the belly of the whale."[28]

The pilgrim Clarel models precisely this attitude of patient hope. He converses and travels through the utter confusion and dismay of Friday, yet despite the deaths of those he loves and the seemingly unresolvable questions he wrestles with, Clarel refuses to give up his quest. And in both *Moby-Dick* and *Clarel*, Melville rewards readers' patience, giving them glimpses of the eucatastrophic epiphany that the event of Easter promises.[29]

Stoics Astounded into Heaven

Near the end of *Moby-Dick*, Melville stages an exchange that demonstrates how the indeterminacy of verbal promises—the very indeterminacy that causes the frustration and confusion and despair on display in the chapter titled "The Doubloon"—makes such eucatastrophic redemption possible. As the ship cruises in search of the White Whale, Ahab comes upon the carpenter caulking a coffin, which he had recently built to Queequeg's specifications when the harpooner seemed at the point of death. Queequeg recovered and adopted the box as his sea chest. In his spare hours, he copied "the twisted tattooing on his body" onto the lid of this coffin-chest, so that it now bears the same unreadable, "mystical treatise on the art of attaining truth" inscribed on his body.[30] The carpenter is caulking the coffin-chest because it has been requisitioned for a third use after an unsettling tragedy befalls the *Pequod*: a lookout falls from the masthead, and though the crew drops the ship's life buoy to him, both lookout and life buoy—shriveled and cracked by the sun—sink into the ocean. Thus the carpenter is in the process of converting this coffin into a watertight vessel to serve as a replacement life buoy.

Ahab is scandalized by the carpenter so radically altering the meaning of what he had made: "Thou art as unprincipled as the gods, and as much of a jack-of-all trades." When he proceeds to pose a series of metaphysical questions to the carpenter, the carpenter responds, "Faith, sir, I've—" and is then interrupted by Ahab who demands to know what he means by "faith." "Why, faith, sir, it's only a sort of exclamation-like," the carpenter stammers in reply.[31] Melville foregrounds the link between verbal ambiguity—which threatens to erode our faith in words, one another, and God—and the ambiguity of matter whereby the same vessel can serve as a coffin, a chest, or a life buoy. Given such radical indeterminacy, perhaps no authentic meaning exists and there is no truth beyond what we subjectively project. It is this fear that causes the "indefiniteness" of the White Whale to shadow "forth the heartless voids and immensities of the universe" and so terrify Ishmael.[32] In the same vein, Ahab muses in the soliloquy that concludes his conversation with the carpenter, "Oh! how immaterial are all materials! What things real are there, but imponderable thoughts? Here now's the very dreaded symbol of grim death, by a mere hap, made the expressive sign of the help and hope of most endangered life. A life-buoy of a coffin! Does it go further? Can it be that in some spiritual sense the coffin is, after all, but an immortality-preserver! I'll think of that. But no."[33] Ahab may reject this fantastic surmise, but of course the Christian who bears a cross testifies that, by a mere hap, as it were, a dreaded symbol of grim death was transformed into the expressive sign of the help and hope of life. And at the end of the novel, this life buoy coffin saves Ishmael's life when its "cunning spring" releases it from the sinking *Pequod* to provide him a refuge from the sharks until the *Rachel* chances across him.[34] Melville thus reminds readers that the final meaning of any word or sign is not fixed until the end of the story and that surprising events can radically transform even the most grim signs.

Given this verbal possibility, Melville proffers images of foolish-seeming hope being rewarded by unexpected fulfillments. In the case of Ishmael's rescue, he is saved only because the *Rachel*'s captain continues searching the area where the boat that his son was in disappeared. Six or seven days after they last saw this boat, long after any reasonable hope of finding it, they recover Ishmael instead. This was not the fulfillment that the grieving father hoped for, but it was certainly a godsend to Ishmael. This recovery despite all odds recalls an earlier episode in the novel when Ishmael's whaling boat is lost in a fierce storm. Their situation is grim indeed:

> The oars were useless as propellers, performing now the office of life-preservers. So, cutting the lashing of the waterproof match keg, after many failures Starbuck contrived to ignite the lamp in the lantern; then stretching it on a waif pole, handed it to Queequeg as the standard-bearer of this forlorn hope. There, then, he sat, holding up that imbe-cile candle in the heart of that almighty forlornness. There, then, he sat, the sign and symbol of a man without faith, hopelessly holding up hope in the midst of despair. Wet, drenched through, and shivering cold, despairing of ship or boat, we lifted up our eyes as the dawn came on.[35]

In these dire circumstances, lost in a thick fog, they are unaccountably saved: "The ship had given us up, but was still cruising, if haply it might light upon some token of our perishing," when it runs over their boat, and the men jump out and are saved. Such a violent, salvific revelation rewards those who hopelessly hold up hope in the midst of despair, even if it also surprises and discomfits them with its transfiguring power.

Melville's novel does not try to make some reductive, rationalist argument for the efficacy of patient hope. And it certainly does not point to some technology or technique that will resolve the "immensity of waiting" that is our lot—no new invention from the printing press to the telegraph, from the encyclopedia to the map, from ChatGPT to Google can relieve us of this long Sabbatarian vigil. But by critiqu-ing both Ahab's efforts to render mystery perspicuous and controllable and Stubb's despairing refusal to account for any truth beyond his own appetites (as I discussed in chapters 3 and 6), Melville suggests that our proper response to verbal indeterminacy and the mystery of our human condition is to take up a posture of patient hope. If, like the captain of the *Rachel*, we continue questing even when hopeless, we will be ready to experience a eucatastrophe like the cross, one that looks like torture and death but comes to mean redemption and life. This is the hope of all pilgrims: that we will encounter a meaning that resignifies our lives. And the play of verbal meaning that is so often frustrating is also what makes such redemptive fulfillment a live possibility.

In a similar fashion, *Clarel* repeatedly foregrounds the foolishness of those who would place their hope in some new communications technology or some interpretive method that will supposedly ensure mutual understanding and comity. Those who trust in such solutions are mocked by the character Ungar, a "wandering Ishmael from the West" who is a bitter Confederate officer with Catholic and Native American ancestors (yes, he is trebly on the losing side of American interpretive conflicts).[36] Ungar mocks a fellow pilgrim who thinks that "the world [has] turned Christian." Against such blithe, progressive Whiggism, Ungar counters that Christ's teachings are often given lip service rather than taken to heart: despite being widely read, the Bible's religious teachings are "sundry texts, disowned in mart, / Light scratched, not graved on man's hard heart."[37] Ungar likewise disdains the "paper pact" of the U.S. Constitution, whose interpretive knots could only be "cut . . . with the sword" of internecine war.[38] American Christians—both Northern industrialists and Southern slaveholders—warped Christ's teachings in the tradition of the colonizing "Anglo-Saxons . . . [w]ho in the name of Christ and Trade / . . . Deflower the world's last sylvan glade!"[39] According to Ungar, all the education and sophisticated communication technologies now enjoyed only make modern people more susceptible to deception by those Ishmael would term "ostentatious smuggling verbalists"; these seeming improvements are "as the ring in the bull's nose / Whereby a pert boy turns and winds / This monster of a million minds."[40] Universal access to the Bible has had little influence on the way Americans treat one another, has failed to slow their exploitation of creation, and has not helped people actually heed its message. Instead, it has empowered demagogues to manipulate "this monster of a million minds." Industrial communication technologies cannot, on their own, sustain religious or political or cultural faith, and a focus on the words themselves—and various techniques to make them more accessible or more authoritative—can deflect attention from their purpose: to shape readers' minds, to reform their lives, and to foster a right relationship with God and with one another.[41] No technology can ensure such transformative verbal encounters.

The poem seems to confirm Ungar's despairing assessment. By its conclusion, Clarel's hope for any epiphany or even consolation has been thwarted. Clarel sets out on his pilgrimage after his Zionist friend Nathan is murdered. He leaves Nathan's wife Agar and their daughter Ruth—whom Clarel loves—to grieve this loss in private. But the first people the pilgrims encounter on their return to Jerusalem are a group of Jewish people furtively digging graves for Ruth and Agar, dead of either grief or fever. Clarel is thrown into paroxysms of sorrow, intensified when he is told that Ruth left no "last word" for him: she went to the grave in silence.[42] This tragedy elucidates Clarel's "monitory dream" on the previous night, when he felt himself "roofed with awful skies / Whose stars like silver nail-heads gleam / Which stud some lid over lifeless eyes."[43] In this foreboding vision, the stars become not gleams from the celestial sphere but nails in the claustrophobic dark of a coffin: death seems utterly final, leaving no hope of resurrection or even temporary comfort for those left behind.

Clarel, paralyzed by loss, lingers in Jerusalem as his friends depart and as Easter comes and goes. The pageantry of the Holy Week celebrations fails to penetrate his numbed heart, even on this special year when the eastern and western calendars converge and all Christians celebrate the resurrection on the same day. Like the disciples who wait in Jerusalem after Christ's ascension, Clarel remains until Pentecost. Even so, he is vouchsafed no fiery epiphany, and the last glimpse we get of him is at the rear of a procession winding along the Via Crucis that Christ walked to Golgotha. "Cross-bearers all," these people from around the world follow the same path that Christ did when he journeyed toward his death.[44] As he vanishes from readers' view, Clarel murmurs his despairing final words: "They wire the world—far under sea / They talk; but never comes to me / A message from beneath the stone."[45] Referring to the recently completed transatlantic telegraph cable—which was initially completed in 1858, soon failed, and was replaced in 1868 with a more reliable wire—Clarel contrasts the remarkable technological achievement that spreads words instantly across the world with the existential silence in which he dwells. No word emerges from Ruth's tomb or from Christ's, and there is certainly no telegraph or other miraculous-seeming technology that could carry a word from beyond the grave.

But the poem does not end with the despair so achingly articulated by Ungar and Clarel. Melville appends an astonishing epilogue whose pentameter lines hold out hope that the frustrations expressed in the compressed tetrameter of the poem's preceding seventeen-thousand-some lines may be resolved.[46] The narrator contrasts two different responses to the Sphinx whose ancient riddle remains unsolved by all the knowledge and technology of modern civilization. "Despair" chooses the path of cynical skepticism and "scrawls . . . his bitter pasquinade" on the unreadable face of this ancient statue.[47] Despair gives up on the possibility of meaning and indulges in shitposting. Yet Faith refuses Despair's cynicism and models the patient hope we saw Melville commend in *Moby-Dick*: Faith, "With blood warm oozing from her wounded trust, / Inscribes even on her shards of broken urns / The sign o' the cross—*the spirit above the dust!*"[48] Rather than defacing this inscrutable text out of frustration, Faith "turns" from Despair's "scrawl" and responds by marking her own body with her source of hope. As Paul does in 2 Corinthians, Melville figures us as earthen vessels, jars of clay, written on by Christ's redemptive blood. And if we always carry around in our bodies the death of Jesus, this is so that the life of Jesus might also be revealed in our bodies and in our words.[49] All of us, Melville's narrator suggests, can respond to frustration and uncertainty by living as cross-bearers who journey under this pilgrim's ensign.

Such a posture does not "solve" disagreement or ambiguity, but it enables us to converse with one another about our mysterious world in a kind of proleptic participation in the divine Word whose epiphany we wait. The narrator makes this christological hope explicit in the poem's remarkable conclusion:

> But through such strange illusions have they passed
> When in life's pilgrimage have baffled striven—
> Even death may prove unreal at the last,
> And stoics be astounded into heaven.
>
> Then keep thy heart, though yet but ill-resigned—
> Clarel, thy heart, the issues there but mind;
> That like the crocus budding through the snow—
> That like a swimmer rising from the deep—
> That like a burning secret which doth go
> Even from the bosom that would hoard and keep;
> Emerge thou mayst from the last whelming sea,
> And prove that death but routs life into victory.[50]

The pilgrim who strives, even though baffled, to the end may experience eucatastrophic transformation. Even stoics, the narrator tells Clarel, may be astounded into heaven.

The temporal movement of the pilgrim's slow progress enacts the process by which words, regardless of the technological medium they inhabit, might lead to transformed lives. The pilgrim continues no matter how bleak the circumstances seem, no matter how final his confusion or despair seems. He practices his faith by journeying step-by-step even when it would be easier to fall back on the jesting tone of the cynical, despairing skeptic. The pilgrim has not yet received the full revelation of meaning, yet he holds the ambiguous fragments loosely, fingering their sharp edges, piecing them together as he is able, waiting in hope for the final revelation of their form. And because the event of Christ's resurrection so radically transformed the instrument of torture into an emblem of hope, the pilgrim knows that this final revelation may be astonishing indeed.

Clarel serves as a reminder that truth seekers have always faced serious challenges. Con men of various stripes want us to see our current media ecosystem as unprecedented and determined: that is how they sell their services. Yet there are no technological or institutional shortcuts to the immensity of waiting that defines our human condition and our stuttering articulations of truth. The message from beneath the stone does not come in dots and dashes or in bits and bytes, but our grounds for hope today—and our means for practicing this hope—are the same as Clarel's. If even stoics may one day be astounded into heaven, we have time now to mull words whose promise we only dimly glimpse, to befriend those who have grievously sinned, to converse with others despite intractable disagreements, to walk step-by-step through discordant experiences. Such patient practices may seem a kind of imbecile candle, hopelessly holding out the hope of greater understanding in the midst of despair-inducing confusion. Yet they are practices in keeping with our condition as cross-bearing pilgrims, pilgrims who journey—baffled—in hope of a eucatastrophe that will transform our feeble words and erring lives into a harmony more beautiful than anything we can ask or imagine.

Epilogue

Melville's hope can, admittedly, seem rather bleak. Is there anything we can do while waiting for some eschatological eucatastrophe, or must we merely imitate Queequeg as he holds his lighted lantern aloft in a dark storm, hopelessly holding out hope in the midst of despair? I want to briefly offer two answers to this question: First, not looking for the wrong kinds of solutions is itself a salutary act. And second, the metaphors and practices of hope I consider in the third section of this book point toward real possibilities for making do along the margins of even an unhealthy media landscape.

To set the stage for these answers, let me briefly recapitulate the three stages this book's pilgrimage has traversed. In the first stage, we heard how optimistic readers imagined that industrial print and communication technologies might provide them with an unmediated, panoptic view of reality so they can manipulate it according to the judgment of their composing eye; they might render the Bible and other authoritative texts into private commodities that authorize their views of the world; they might enable them to organize or map the mysteries of the world and thereby solve life's ultimate questions of purpose; they might form the means of forging asymmetric intimacy with a vast audience; they might even enable one to boss the populace of an entire country. And those who expect such technologies to usher in utopia resort to despotism and coercion if their expectations are frustrated.

In the second movement, we heard how pessimistic readers experienced the effects of these efforts. They feared that industrial communications technologies would make them Loose-Fish, vulnerable to the wiles of predatory verbalists; they would macadamize the minds of those who habitually attend to the endless stream of trivia; they would commodify the souls of those who participate in the media marketplace; they would thingify human persons caught up in their webs of representation and control.

227

Those who see the utopian promise of powerful textual technologies and those who see their dystopian perils both have legitimate grounds for their expectations. Yet in the third movement, we considered subversive metaphors and practices that might help us imagine ways to make do along the margins of an industrial media ecosystem. These authors invite us to saunter outside of stereotyped conventions and so encounter wild, yet perhaps harmonious, forms of truth; they seek to facilitate conversations among disparate yet sympathetic participants; they urge us to befriend our morally flawed neighbors and imagine how we might contribute to their redemption; they invite us to journey as cross-bearers, in patient hope that our confusions and disagreements may one day be transfigured.

These practices of hope depend on the recognition that although textual technologies are not neutral, neither are they determinative. As Neil Postman reminds us, "no medium is excessively dangerous if its users understand what the dangers are. . . . This is an instance in which the asking of the questions is sufficient. To ask is to break the spell."[1] Asking these questions breaks the aura of inevitability that surrounds powerful new technologies and enables us to maintain "an epistemological and psychic distance from any technology, so that it always appears somewhat strange, never inevitable, never natural."[2] This distance inoculates us from trying to solve disagreements and confusion through some new technology or law or life hack. Disagreements are not a bug to be fixed but a reality to live with, and we live with them well to the extent that we prioritize relationships over power and the mutual pursuit of truth over our private appetites or preferences.

This is why none of the practices I have considered in the final third of this book are systemic or technocratic or scalable. There is no iron or silicon Paul that will be an infallible proclaimer of the gospel of truth and reason. And yet the cross-bearer's patient hope, the friend's faithful love, the interlocutor's earnest questions, the walker's complementary strides—all these are virtuous practices that can foster conviviality here and now without waiting for some inventor or politician to fix the ills that afflict our media ecosystem. These postures and practices may take different forms in different technological contexts, but they are the habits that characterize studious friends who exchange words with one another while journeying toward a fuller participation in truth.

If we can resist the seduction of devices or techniques that tempt us with the lure of easy solutions, we will be more open to embarking on these formative endeavors, endeavors that will require real effort on our part. AI chatbots and Wikipedia promise easy answers, but no app will make truth perspicuous to all and eliminate deep political or religious disagreements. When we turn away from these false solutions, we are freed to cultivate the practices and rituals and institutions that might help us inhabit the immensity of waiting that characterizes the human condition. We may be working "under conditions / That seem unpropitious," in T. S. Eliot's phrase, but the possibilities for practices that contribute to a convivial verbal culture remain.[3]

We can read slowly. We can wrestle with old books. We can memorize passages. We can discuss difficult texts with friends who interpret them differently. Further, we can contribute to communities of practice that honor and foster verbal virtues such as attention, magnanimity, care, and patience. The possibilities of such institutions can be glimpsed in Thoreau's wild woods where he walked out his intellectual difficulties, Fuller's conversations in the Peabody home where she challenged her interlocutors, Hester's cottage of comfort where she welcomed and counseled the wretched, and the road where Clarel and his fellow pilgrims conversed. Families, churches, classrooms, schools, neighborhoods, libraries, lyceums, and other sites of community can model and develop these virtuous forms of verbal engagement. People habituated in such communities might be capable of wisely navigating our desiccated media landscape and offering the balm of friendship and truth-seeking dialogue to those thirsty for genuine conviviality. As Wendell Berry writes in one of his poems, "This is no paradisal dream. / Its hardship is its possibility."[4]

Notes

Introduction

1 Herman Melville, *The Confidence-Man: His Masquerade*, ed. Hershel Parker, G. Thomas Tanselle, and Harrison Hayford (Evanston, Ill.: Northwestern University Press, 1988), 167. Melville is not the first to compare the printing press to the wine press. Since Gutenberg's printing press used the same technique as the much older wine press, many later authors have considered the links between these two apparently disparate uses for the press. *The Tempest*, for instance, contrasts Prospero's bookish, magical power with the power of Stephano's wine. Caliban is enslaved by both, and both undergird political orders that end up being oppressive. Stephano tells Trinculo to "kiss the book," referring to his bottle, and then has Caliban do the same: "Come, swear to that; kiss the book: I will furnish / it anon with new contents swear." The bottle, like the book, amplifies disorder and human emotions and restructures community. The play ends with the overthrow of both forms of power—the book and the bottle—and the promise of a new politics grounded in forgiveness. And Prospero's final speech invites viewers to participate in the power of forgiveness themselves; he implores the audience to pray for him. William Shakespeare, *The Tempest*, ed. Alden T. Vaughan and Virginia Mason Vaughan, 4th ed. (London: Arden Shakespeare, 2011), 2.2.143–44; epilogue, 15–18. Such prayer, such forgiveness, is a more promising foundation of healthy relationships than any technology. See also Marshall McLuhan's passing comments on these links in *The Gutenberg Galaxy: The Making of Typographic Man* (Toronto: University of Toronto Press, 2011), 167, 173.

2 Melville, *Confidence-Man*, 165. Francis Bacon also linked the power of the printing press to firearms: "The art of printing, gunpowder and the nautical compass, have changed the face and condition of things all over the globe." Francis Bacon, *The New Organon*, ed. Lisa Jardine and Michael Silverthorne, Cambridge Texts in the History of Philosophy (Cambridge: Cambridge University Press, 2000), 100.

3 Frank's claims are eerily reminiscent of the Reverend E. H. Chapin's toast given to "the Printing Press of the Age of Steam and Electricity" at the 1855 New York Book Publishers' Association. "Complimentary Fruit Festival of the New York Book Publishers' Association to Authors and Booksellers," *American Publishers' Circular and Literary Gazette*, 1855, 73. Chapin acknowledges the press can sometimes be misguided, but he figures it as being guided by Providence to bring benefits to all the world: "From its iron lips thousands take truth or error. . . . And if it engenders evil, it is the only vehicle through which the remedy can be poured into the world . . . Mainly, . . . on the whole, it is an agent of great and beneficent uses. . . . Human measures are defeated, methods fail, but God's own purposes

never; and the processes of his eternal righteousness and truth run in the iron grooves of the printing press."

4 Melville, *Confidence-Man*, 165–66. Frank's reference to the sovereign of England's title as "Defender of the Faith" is rather ironic given that Pope Leo X granted King Henry VIII this title after Henry published *Assertio Septem Sacramentorum*, an anti-Reformation polemic. Just nine years later, of course, Henry separated from Rome under famously dubious motives. If the printing press defends the faith in the same way that King Henry VIII did, it is not exactly a trustworthy ally.

5 Melville, *Confidence-Man*, 4.

6 Melville, *Confidence-Man*, 3–6.

7 Frank Mott notes that hoaxes proliferated after the industrialization of print made penny newspapers possible, which sought to boost sales by sensationalizing (or fabricating) news. Frank Luther Mott, "Facetious News Writing, 1833–1883," *Mississippi Valley Historical Review* 29, no. 1 (1942): 35–54. See also Alex Boese, *The Museum of Hoaxes: A History of Outrageous Pranks and Deceptions* (New York: Plume, 2003), 4–6, 51–76. In many respects, this contrast parallels the one Neil Postman draws between Huxley and Orwell at the beginning of *Amusing Ourselves to Death: Public Discourse in the Age of Show Business* (New York: Penguin, 1986), vii.

8 Karen Halttunen, *Confidence Men and Painted Women: A Study of Middle-Class Culture in America, 1830–1870* (New Haven: Yale University Press, 1986), 1–55; Boese, *Museum of Hoaxes*; Lynda Walsh, *Sins against Science: The Scientific Media Hoaxes of Poe, Twain, and Others* (Albany: SUNY Press, 2016).

9 C. S. Lewis, "On Obstinacy in Belief," in *The World's Last Night: And Other Essays* (New York: Harvest Books, 2002), 28.

10 Melville, *Confidence-Man*, 174–75.

11 Other studies also find instructive parallels between nineteenth-century American cultural debates over technology and today's challenges. Christina Bieber Lake, *Prophets of the Posthuman: American Fiction, Biotechnology, and the Ethics of Personhood* (Notre Dame, Ind.: University of Notre Dame Pess, 2014); Caleb Smith, *Thoreau's Axe: Distraction and Discipline in American Culture* (Princeton: Princeton University Press, 2023).

12 David Ramsay, *The History of the American Revolution*, vol. 2 (Philadelphia: R. Aitken & Son, 1789), 319. See Robert Parkinson's essay for a survey of later scholarly responses to Ramsay's claim, Parkinson, "Print, the Press, and the American Revolution," *Oxford Research Encyclopedia of American History*, published online September 3, 2015.

13 "Philadelphia Typographical Society," *Long-Island Patriot*, November 14, 1821.

14 For one diagnosis of this faith, see Henry Adams' famous chapter "The Dynamo and the Virgin," in *The Education of Henry Adams* (New York: Modern Library, 1999), 379–90. See also David E. Nye, *American Technological Sublime* (Cambridge, Mass.: MIT Press, 1996).

15 The most prominent proponent of this view was Ben Franklin. See Ralph Frasca, *Benjamin Franklin's Printing Network: Disseminating Virtue in Early America* (Columbia: University of Missouri Press, 2006).

16 Postman, *Amusing Ourselves to Death*, 31.

17 Mark A. Noll, *America's God: From Jonathan Edwards to Abraham Lincoln* (Oxford: Oxford University Press, 2002), 372–73. On the link between the Bible and the Constitution, Noll also cites Daniel Walker Howe, *The Political Culture of the American Whigs* (Chicago: University of Chicago Press, 1984), 23–24, 227, and Robert H. Wiebe, *Opening of American Society: From the Adoption*

of the Constitution to the Eve of Disunion (New York: Alfred A. Knopf, 1984), 308. See also Elisabeth L. Eisenstein, who links the printing press to Protestantism throughout her work, noting, "Tributes to the power of the press were more compatible with patriotic themes in Protestant realms" (*The Printing Press as an Agent of Change: Communications and Cultural Transformations in Early Modern Europe* [Cambridge: Cambridge University Press, 1980], 19). Edward S. Corwin declares, "The Reformation superseded an infallible Pope with an infallible Bible; the American Revolution replaced the sway of a king with that of a document." See Corwin, "The Higher Law Background of American Constitutional Law," *Harvard Law Review* 42, no. 2 (1929): 149. Michael Warner discusses the significance of the Constitution as a *printed* document rather than a manuscript in *The Letters of the Republic: Publication and the Public Sphere in Eighteenth-Century America* (Cambridge, Mass.: Harvard University Press, 1990), 97, 107–8.

18 The U.S. Constitution obviously has other important antecedents besides the printed Bible. Oliver O'Donovan gives one account of the theological origins of constitutionalism in *The Desire of the Nations* (Cambridge: Cambridge University Press, 1999), 233–42. Bruce Johansen traces some aspects of the U.S. Constitution back to Iroquois sources in *Forgotten Founders: How the American Indian Helped Shape Democracy* (Boston: Harvard Common Press, 1982).

19 Thomas Paine, *Common Sense, The Rights of Man, and Other Essential Writings of Thomas Paine*, ed. Sidney Hook (New York: Meridian, 1984), 154, 247–48.

20 "The Constitution of the United States of America" (1789; Washington, D.C.: U.S. Government Publishing Office, 2007), http://www.gpo.gov/fdsys/pkg/CDOC-110hdoc50/pdf/CDOC-110hdoc50.pdf.

21 Nathan O. Hatch, *The Democratization of American Christianity* (New Haven: Yale University Press, 1989), 7.

22 John M. Murrin, "A Roof without Walls: The Dilemma of American National Identity," in *Beyond Confederation: Origins of the Constitution and American National Identity*, ed. Richard R. Beeman, Stephen Botein, and Edward Carlos Carter (Chapel Hill: University of North Carolina Press, 1987), 333–48.

23 Noll, *America's God*, 195.

24 Noll (*America's God*, 20–21) also discusses a related development: the emergence of increasingly authoritative written confessions among American Protestants. In the absence of a central church hierarchy, written texts came to delimit the faith.

25 Noll, *America's God*, 370–73. See Hatch's analysis of the ways that Americans took *sola Scriptura* to extremes in ways that the earlier Reformers did not, in *Democratization of American Christianity*, 179–83.

26 Noll sees constitutionalism crystalizing in the 1830s and '40s, explaining, "It was certainly the case that widespread reverence for the written Scripture preceded widespread reverence for the written Constitution" (*America's God*, 372). This constitutionalism can also be seen in antebellum arguments over slavery, which were framed as arguments about the meaning of the Constitution. See Eric Foner, *Free Soil, Free Labor, Free Men: The Ideology of the Republican Party before the Civil War* (1970; repr., Oxford: Oxford University Press, 1995), 73–87.

27 Cathy N. Davidson, *Revolution and the Word: The Rise of the Novel in America*, expanded ed. (New York: Oxford University Press, 2004), 5.

28 Noll, *America's God*, 10, 93–113, 233–34; Hatch, *Democratization of American Christianity*, 28–29; Trish Loughran, *The Republic in Print: Print Culture in the Age of U.S. Nation Building, 1770–1870* (New York: Columbia University

234 Notes to Pages 9–10

Press, 2009), 37, 80. For the broader story of how common sense functioned in political discourse, see Sophia A. Rosenfeld, *Common Sense: A Political History* (Cambridge, Mass.: Harvard University Press, 2011).

29 Noll also calls this "a *methodological* common sense, or the assertion that truths about consciousness, the physical world, and religion could be authoritatively built by strict induction from the irreducible facts of experience" (*America's God*, 234).

30 George M. Marsden, "Everyone One's Own Interpreter? The Bible, Science, and Authority in Mid-Nineteenth Century America," in *The Bible in America: Essays in Cultural History*, ed. Nathan O. Hatch and Mark A. Noll (New York: Oxford University Press, 1982), 83. See also Charles Hodge, *Systematic Theology*, vol. 1 (Grand Rapids: Eerdmans, 1979), 1–17.

31 Bernard Bailyn and Jane N. Garrett, eds., *Pamphlets of the American Revolution, 1750–1765* (Cambridge, Mass.: Belknap Press, 1965); Bernard Bailyn, *The Ideological Origins of the American Revolution* (Cambridge, Mass.: Belknap Press of Harvard University Press, 2017); Robert G. Parkinson, *The Common Cause: Creating Race and Nation in the American Revolution* (Chapel Hill: University of North Carolina Press, 2016).

32 G. Thomas Tanselle, drawing on work done by Connery Lathem, concludes there were forty-four newspapers in 1775 and that this number remained roughly steady during the war, rising to fifty-eight in 1783. See G. Thomas Tanselle, "Some Statistics on American Printing, 1764–1783," in *The Press and the American Revolution*, ed. Bernard Bailyn and John B. Hench (Worcester, Mass.: American Antiquarian Society, 1980), 348. See also Parkinson, "Print, the Press, and the American Revolution," 9–14; Carol Sue Humphrey, *The American Revolution and the Press: The Promise of Independence*, Medill Visions of the American Press (Evanston, Ill.: Northwestern University Press, 2013), 24, 180; and Isaiah Thomas, *The History of Printing in America: With a Biography of Printers*, 2nd ed., Burt Franklin Bibliography and Reference Series, no. 62 (New York: B. Franklin, 1972), 17–18.

33 Humphrey, *American Revolution and the Press*, 202.

34 Winifred Gallagher, *How the Post Office Created America: A History* (New York: Penguin, 2017); Richard R. John, *Spreading the News: The American Postal System from Franklin to Morse* (Cambridge, Mass.: Harvard University Press, 1995).

35 Joyce Appleby, *Inheriting the Revolution: The First Generation of Americans* (Cambridge, Mass.: Belknap Press, 2001), 179–81, 239–41; Angela G. Ray, *The Lyceum and Public Culture in the Nineteenth-Century United States* (Lansing: Michigan State University Press, 2005).

36 David D. Hall, "The Uses of Literacy in New England, 1600–1850," in *Printing and Society in Early America*, ed. William Leonard Joyce et al. (Worcester, Mass.: American Antiquarian Society, 1983), 24.

37 Appleby, *Inheriting the Revolution*, 92.

38 As Appleby and others point out, print culture particularly thrived in New England and was relatively weaker in the southern states. Appleby, *Inheriting the Revolution*, 103–4, 241–50. See also Lawrence Buell, *New England Literary Culture: From Revolution through Renaissance*, Cambridge Studies in American Literature and Culture (Cambridge: Cambridge University Press, 1986). For the increasingly active roles that women played in writing and publishing, see Appleby, 96–99.

39 Shirley Wilson Logan, *Liberating Language: Sites of Rhetorical Education in Nineteenth-Century Black America* (Carbondale: Southern Illinois University

Press, 2008); Wilma King, *Stolen Childhood: Slave Youth in Nineteenth-Century America* (Bloomington: Indiana University Press, 2011); Christopher Hager, *Word by Word: Emancipation and the Act of Writing* (Cambridge, Mass.: Harvard University Press, 2013); Catherine Hobbs, ed., *Nineteenth-Century Women Learn to Write* (Charlottesville: University of Virginia Press, 1995); and Dale M. Bauer and Philip Gould, eds., *The Cambridge Companion to Nineteenth-Century American Women's Writing* (Cambridge: Cambridge University Press, 2001).

40 Mark Noll writes that "the burgeoning of newspapers and the popular press" played a role in the construction of a national culture, though his argument focuses on the role of evangelical ideas and organizations (*America's God*, 195). Benedict Anderson's seminal work on nationalism and print culture applies in many respects to America as well. See Benedict R. O'Gorman Anderson, *Imagined Communities: Reflections on the Origin and Spread of Nationalism*, rev. ed. (London: Verso, 2006).

41 Robert A. Gross and Mary Kelley, eds., *A History of the Book in America*, vol. 2, *An Extensive Republic: Print, Culture, and Society in the New Nation, 1790–1840* (Chapel Hill: University of North Carolina Press, 2014); Scott E. Casper et al., eds., *A History of the Book in America*, vol. 3, *The Industrial Book, 1840–1880* (Chapel Hill: University of North Carolina Press, 2009); Robert Hoe, *A Short History of the Printing Press and of the Improvements in Printing Machinery from the Time of Gutenberg Up to the Present Day* (New York: Robert Hoe, 1902); and Louis Dudek, *Literature and the Press: A History of Printing, Printed Media, and Their Relation to Literature* (Toronto: Ryerson Press, 1960).

42 Daniel Walker Howe enumerates some of these disruptive technologies: "The invention of electric telegraphy, coming near the close of the period treated here, represented a climactic moment in a widespread revolution of communications. Other features of this revolution included improvements in printing and paper manufacturing; the multiplication of newspapers, magazines, and books; and the expansion of the postal system (which mostly carried newspapers and commercial business, not personal letters). Closely related to these developments occurred a simultaneous revolution in transportation: the introduction of steamboats, canals, turnpikes, and railroads, shortening travel times and dramatically lowering shipping costs. How these twin revolutions transformed American life will be central to the story told here. Their consequences certainly rivaled, and probably exceeded in importance, those of the revolutionary 'information highway' of our own lifetimes." See Howe, *What Hath God Wrought: The Transformation of America, 1815–1848* (New York: Oxford University Press, 2007), 1–2. As Louis Dudek concurs, "Gutenberg's invention (printing from moveable types) has absorbed all the dramatic attention of historians. . . . But since 1800, the Industrial Revolution in Printing, far more overwhelming in its effects, in fact the true determinant of our present culture, has been virtually neglected" (*Literature and the Press*, 9). Tom Standage gives a telling example of the drastic changes that took place: in 1844 it took ten weeks to send a message from London to Bombay. Thirty years later it took just minutes via submarine telegraph cables. Standage concludes, writing in 1998, that "today we are repeatedly told that we are in the midst of a communications revolution. But the electric telegraph was, in many ways, far more disconcerting for the inhabitants of the time than today's advances are for us. If any generation has the right to claim that it bore the full bewildering, world-shrinking brunt of such a revolution, it is not us—it is our nineteenth-century forebears" (Standage, *The Victorian Internet: The Remarkable Story of the Telegraph and the Nineteenth Century's On-Line Pioneers* [New York: Walker, 1998], 102, 213).

43 J. B. Mitchell, "Address of Welcome," *Publishers Weekly*, vol. 10 (New York: F. Leypoldt, 1876), 167. For a discussion of the American Book Trade Association and this meeting, see Casper et al., *Industrial Book*, 1.

44 For a further discussion of this print, see Loughran, *Republic in Print*, 1–2.

45 Luke 2:14.

46 Standage, *Victorian Internet*, 186–87.

47 Horace Bushnell, for one, was not convinced by such rhetoric. As Nathan Hatch writes, "Bemused by this infatuation with the printed word, Horace Bushnell observed that Americans operated 'As if God would offer man a mechanical engine for converting the world, . . . or as if types of lead and sheets of paper may be the light of the world'" (*Democratization of American Christianity*, 126).

48 Hall, "Uses of Literacy in New England," 47, 44–45.

49 Joanne Freeman documents the congressional violence this fragmentation contributed to and describes how "national press coverage in the age of the telegraph" inflamed sectional disputes, in Freeman, *The Field of Blood: Violence in Congress and the Road to Civil War* (New York: Farrar, Straus and Giroux, 2018), 173; see also 184–85. See also John Nerone, "Newspapers and the Public Sphere," in Casper et al., *Industrial Book, 1840–1880*, 230–48.

50 Loughran, *Republic in Print*, 3.

51 Loughran, *Republic in Print*, 3–4. As others have noted, Loughran overstates the limitations of eighteenth-century print networks; just because the colonists did not have a fully-fledged, continentwide print culture does not mean that print was not essential in unifying the colonies. For one such critique of Loughran, see Parkinson, "Print, the Press, and the American Revolution," 16.

52 Loughran, *Republic in Print*, 18, 111–12. Michael Warner traces a similar progression, though he focuses less on technological shifts and more on ideological developments. He notes that the late eighteenth century displayed "a high degree of confidence in the transparency of language and the undifferentiated universality of print. . . . In the decades after ratification, however, a liberal discourse of rights increasingly regarded the state as an institution for accommodating the conflicting claims of persons, and defended persons by their economic self-interest and their privative relation to the state. The republican ideology of print eroded, and an official hermeneutics emerged" (*Letters of the Republic*, 114). Warner also points out that this shift had important consequences for antebellum literature: "It was of no small importance that the years in which literary culture was established in this country were also the years of protracted constitutional crisis. . . . [I]t became possible to locate in language the conflicted and mediated character of truth, nonetheless maintaining the authoritative character of that truth" (115).

53 Nathan O. Hatch, "Elias Smith and the Rise of Religious Journalism in the Early Republic," in Joyce et al., *Printing and Society in Early America*, 277. Hatch expands on this point in his book in describing the paradoxical effects of the Second Great Awakening: "Instead of fostering a unified, cohesive movement, it splintered American Christianity and magnified the diversity of institutions claiming to be the church. . . . The heart of the movement was a revolution in communications, preaching, print, and song; and these measures were instrumental in building mass popular movements" (*Democratization of American Christianity*, 226). George Marsden articulates a related irony: "Everything in the Common Sense Baconian system assumed the stability of truth which could be known objectively by careful observers in any age or culture. Almost all the other trends in nineteenth-century thought, however, pointed toward an opposite conclusion" ("Everyone One's Own Interpreter?" 92).

54 David McKitterick makes the broader point that many twentieth-century theorists of print read nineteenth-century technologies back into earlier cultures, in *Print, Manuscript, and the Search for Order, 1450–1830* (Cambridge: Cambridge University Press, 2003). In a complementary vein, Adrian Johns documents the messy, very *un*-industrial world of early book-making, in *The Nature of the Book: Print and Knowledge in the Making* (Chicago: University of Chicago Press, 1998). While both scholars single out Elizabeth Eisenstein for critique, Eisenstein does qualify her narrative regarding early print culture, noting that her claims about print's effects—dissemination, standardization, reorganization, data collection, preservation, and amplification and reinforcement—are comparative rather than absolute. Eisenstein, *Printing Press as an Agent of Change*, 71–129.

55 And these were not just American phenomena. Industrial print had similar effects elsewhere. See, for example, Chad Wellmon, *Organizing Enlightenment: Information Overload and the Invention of the Modern Research University* (Baltimore: Johns Hopkins University Press, 2015) and Dudek, *Literature and the Press*.

56 Hatch, *Democratization of American Christianity*, 36.

57 Eisenstein argues that early printing had a similar effect: "Thus when 'technology went to press' so too did a vast backlog of occult practices and formulas and few readers were able to discriminate between the two" (*Printing Press as an Agent of Change*, 272).

58 S. G. Goodrich, *Recollections of a Lifetime, or Men and Things I Have Seen: In a Series of Familiar Letters to a Friend, Historical, Biographical, Anecdotical, and Descriptive*, vol. 1 (New York: Miller, Orton and Mulligan, 1856), 86. David Hall quotes this passage and situates it within the broader technological and cultural shifts I have been describing, in "Uses of Literacy in New England," 20–23.

59 Raymond Williams, *The Country and the City* (New York: Oxford University Press, 1975), 9–12.

60 Ivan Illich, *Tools for Conviviality* (London: Marion Boyars, 2001), 6.

61 Illich, *Tools for Conviviality*, 2.

62 Illich, *Tools for Conviviality*, 7; see also 1–9, 84–85.

63 As Wendell Berry puts it, "It is easy for me to imagine that the next great division of the world will be between people who wish to live as creatures and people who wish to live as machines" (Berry, *Life Is a Miracle: An Essay against Modern Superstition* [New York: Counterpoint, 2001], 55).

64 This paragraph is adapted from a paragraph in Jeffrey Bilbro, *Reading the Times: A Literary and Theological Inquiry into the News* (Downers Grove, Ill.: IVP Academic, 2021), 2–3.

65 Louis Dudek makes a similar point in the British context: "Until at least the middle of the [nineteenth] century, it can probably be said that on the whole the newspapers in England were improving: the new papers and those taking up the leadership at each new stage were more responsible, better written, more professional and reliably informative. After that time professionalism was even greater and newspapers were designed more and more to interest their readers; but along with this gain in clarity, the new successful papers at each stage tended to create a spurious kind of news, to adopt a slicker and less solid style of journalese, and in general to concoct their matter so as to draw in the lowest common denominator among readers" (*Literature and the Press*, 40).

66 Langdon Winner, *The Whale and the Reactor: A Search for Limits in an Age of High Technology*, (Chicago: University of Chicago Press, 1989), 105. For more on the damaging effects of such assumptions, see Kentaro Toyama, *Geek Heresy:*

Rescuing Social Change from the Cult of Technology (New York: PublicAffairs, 2015).

67 Wael Ghonim, "Inside the Egyptian Revolution," filmed March 2011 in Cairo, TED video, https://www.ted.com/talks/wael_ghonim_inside_the_egyptian_revolution.

68 Wael Ghonim, "Let's Design Social Media That Drives Real Change," filmed December 2015 in Geneva, TED video, https://www.ted.com/talks/wael_ghonim _let_s_design_social_media_that_drives_real_change.

69 "Let's Design Social Media." See also Siva Vaidhyanathan, *Antisocial Media: How Facebook Disconnects Us and Undermines Democracy* (New York: Oxford University Press, 2018), 122–39; Zeynep Tufekci, *Twitter and Tear Gas: The Power and Fragility of Networked Protest* (New Haven: Yale University Press, 2017), 118–19.

70 Alexis C. Madrigal, "What Facebook Did to American Democracy," *Atlantic*, October 12, 2017, https://www.theatlantic.com/technology/archive/2017/10/what-facebook-did/542502/. See also the fuller analysis in Siva Vaidhyanathan's brilliant and disturbing book, *Antisocial Media*.

71 When Luther published ninety-nine theses against Scholastic theology two months earlier, they provoked no response and quickly fell into the dustbin of history. Andrew Pettegree, *Brand Luther: How an Unheralded Monk Turned His Small Town into a Center of Publishing, Made Himself the Most Famous Man in Europe—and Started the Protestant Reformation* (New York: Penguin, 2015), 51–52.

72 Tom Standage, "How Luther Went Viral," *Economist*, December 17, 2011, http://www.economist.com/node/21541719.

73 Pettegree, *Brand Luther*, 77.

74 Pettegree, *Brand Luther*, 104–6, 157–63.

75 Pettegree, *Brand Luther*, 210.

76 Pettegree, *Brand Luther*, 237.

77 Pettegree, *Brand Luther*, 235–44, 250.

78 Jacques Ellul, *Propaganda: The Formation of Men's Attitudes* (New York: Vintage, 1973), x.

79 Paul J. Griffiths, *Intellectual Appetite: A Theological Grammar* (Washington, D.C: Catholic University of America Press, 2009), 20.

80 Griffiths, *Intellectual Appetite*, 21.

81 See also Paul Griffiths' book on religious modes of reading, *Religious Reading: The Place of Reading in the Practice of Religion* (New York: Oxford University Press, 1999). Alan Jacobs develops this way of adjudicating between good and bad reading though he relies on a different set of Augustinian terms. As he puts it, "What makes the difference between a reading that is manipulative and selfish and one that is charitable? . . . Fundamentally, it is the reader's will that determines the moral form the reading takes: If the will is directed toward God and neighbor, it will in Augustinian terms exemplify *caritas*; if the will is directed toward the self, it will exemplify *cupiditas*" (*A Theology of Reading: The Hermeneutics of Love* [Boulder: Westview Press, 2001], 31). C. S. Lewis takes a similar approach when, in *An Experiment in Criticism* (Cambridge: Cambridge University Press, 1961), he distinguishes between readers who use works of art and those who receive them. Curious readers seek to "use" a text, to "do things with it." Yet studious readers recognize that "the first demand any work of art makes upon us is surrender. Look. Listen. Receive. Get yourself out of the way." (Lewis, *An Experiment in Criticism*, 19). For a phenomenological approach to the question of reading as an act of love, see Cassandra Falke, *The Phenomenology of Love and Reading* (New York: Bloomsbury, 2016). Karen

Swallow Prior makes a related distinction between reading for information and reading for formation in *On Reading Well* (Grand Rapids: Brazos, 2022), 14–30.

82 Illich, *Tools for Conviviality*, 11.

83 Illich, *Tools for Conviviality*, 73.

84 McLuhan, *Gutenberg Galaxy*, 280.

85 McLuhan, *Gutenberg Galaxy*, 281. See also Walter J. Ong, *The Presence of the Word: Some Prolegomena for Cultural and Religious History* (Minneapolis: University of Minnesota Press, 1981), 175.

86 Marshall McLuhan and Quentin Fiore, *The Medium Is the Massage: An Inventory of Effects* (Berkeley, Calif.: Gingko Press, 2001), 25.

87 Postman, *Amusing Ourselves to Death*, 160. See also Ong, *Presence of the Word*, 175. Alan Jacobs makes a similar point about the power of diagnosis in *How to Think: A Survival Guide for a World at Odds* (New York: Currency, 2017), 28–30.

88 Postman, *Amusing Ourselves to Death*, 10.

89 Postman, *Amusing Ourselves to Death*, 18. Postman makes a similar point in *Technopoly: The Surrender of Culture to Technology* (New York: Vintage, 1993): "New technologies alter the structure of our interests: the things we think *about*. They alter the character of our symbols: the things we think *with*. And they alter the nature of community: the arena in which thoughts develop" (20).

90 George Lakoff and Mark Johnson, *Metaphors We Live By* (Chicago: University of Chicago Press, 2003), 3.

91 Lakoff and Johnson, *Metaphors We Live By*, 239.

92 In a rather different vein, Mary Midgley's argument for the fundamental importance of myth supports this approach as well, in *The Myths We Live By* (New York: Taylor and Francis, 2011).

93 Alan Jacobs, "Attending to Technology: Theses for Disputation," *New Atlantis*, Winter 2016, 45.

94 Lakoff and Johnson, *Metaphors We Live By*, 234.

95 James Smith's *Cultural Liturgies* series, particularly the first two volumes, offers a complementary account of cultural formation through imagination and practice. James K. A. Smith, *Cultural Liturgies*, vol. 1, *Desiring the Kingdom: Worship, Worldview, and Cultural Formation* (Grand Rapids: Baker Academic, 2009); idem, *Cultural Liturgies*, vol. 2, *Imagining the Kingdom: How Worship Works* (Grand Rapids: Baker Academic, 2013).

96 Postman, *Amusing Ourselves to Death*.

97 Lakoff and Johnson, *Metaphors We Live By*, 204; see also 198–209.

98 Walter J. Ong, *Ramus, Method, and the Decay of Dialogue: From the Art of Discourse to the Art of Reason* (Chicago: University of Chicago Press, 2004), 313.

99 Ong, *Ramus, Method, and the Decay of Dialogue*, 315.

100 In imagining how to organize this book, I was also guided by the way Christina Bieber Lake orchestrates her masterful book, *Prophets of the Posthuman*, which considers the wisdom nineteenth-century American authors might offer for the ethical questions raised by modern medical technologies. And for more on the contrast between a map and a tour, see Peter Candler's reading of Michel de Certeau in *Theology, Rhetoric, Manuduction, or Reading Scripture Together on the Path to God* (Grand Rapids: Eerdmans, 2006), 41–51.

101 On the foolishness of looking to technological fixes for technological problems, see Illich, *Tools for Conviviality*, 8; Wendell Berry, "Solving for Pattern," in *The Gift of Good Land: Further Essays Cultural and Agricultural* (Berkeley, Calif.: Counterpoint, 2009), 134–47.

102 Isaiah 2:4; Michel de Certeau, *The Practice of Everyday Life*, trans. Steven Rendall (Berkeley: University of California Press, 1988), 18.

Twenty-Six Theses

1 My use of this form is also indebted to Alan Jacobs ("Attending to Theology"), though as my theses are followed by a book, I have not employed his method of following each thesis with a quote and commentary.

2 Francis Bacon, *The Philosophical Works of Francis Bacon*, ed. Robert Leslie Ellis, James Spedding, and John Robertson (London: George Routledge, 1905), 531.

1 Transparent Eyeballs

1 Ralph Waldo Emerson, *Nature*, in *The Collected Works of Ralph Waldo Emerson: Nature, Addresses, and Lectures*, ed. Robert Ernest Spiller et al. (Cambridge, Mass.: Harvard University Press, 1971), 10.

2 Louisa Thomas, "Emerson's Eyes," *Sewanee Review* 125, no. 4 (2017): 824.

3 I am using *panoptic* here in the sense that Michel Foucault develops in *Discipline and Punish: The Birth of the Prison*, trans. Alan Sheridan (New York: Pantheon, 1977). Bruno Latour's summary of Foucault's analysis indicates the link between Emerson's transparent eyeball and Foucault's account of "a new invisible power that sees everything about everyone." See Bruno Latour, "Drawing Things Together," in *Representation in Scientific Practice*, ed. Michael Lynch and Steve Woolgar (Cambridge, Mass.: MIT Press, 1990), 37.

4 Lawrence Buell tries to downplay the significance of this passage. He notes that it appears to suggest that the "body seems to play no part whatever in Emerson's theory." Buell, however, thinks this is a misreading: "To my ear such readings miss a deliberately comic bubbliness in the passage." Buell provides little evidence for his assessment, and I haven't seen any other scholars who read Emerson's tone here as comic or particularly bubbly. Lawrence Buell, *Emerson* (Cambridge, Mass.: Belknap Press of Harvard University Press, 2003), 94.

5 Thomas, "Emerson's Eyes," 822–23; Robert D. Richardson Jr., *Emerson: The Mind on Fire* (Berkeley: University of California Press, 1996), 63.

6 Thomas, "Emerson's Eyes," 823. See also Richardson Jr., *Emerson*, 71; Evelyn Barish, "The Moonless Night: Emerson's Crisis of Health, 1825–1827," in *Emerson Centenary Essays*, ed. Joel Myerson (Carbondale: Southern Illinois University Press, 1982), 4–8.

7 Emerson, *Nature*, 7.

8 Emerson, *Nature*, 23.

9 Charles Duhigg, "How Companies Learn Your Secrets," *New York Times*, February 16, 2012, https://www.nytimes.com/2012/02/19/magazine/shopping-habits.html; Michael Lewis, *Moneyball: The Art of Winning an Unfair Game*, (New York: W. W. Norton, 2004); Richard H. Thaler and Cass R. Sunstein, *Nudge: Improving Decisions about Health, Wealth, and Happiness*, rev. and exp. ed. (New York: Penguin, 2009).

10 Virginia Eubanks, *Automating Inequality: How High-Tech Tools Profile, Police, and Punish the Poor* (London: Picador, 2019); Matthew B. Crawford, "Algorithmic Governance and Political Legitimacy," *American Affairs Journal*, May 20, 2019, https://americanaffairsjournal.org/2019/05/algorithmic-governance-and-political-legitimacy/. Other examples abound: algorithms encode gender bias (Jeffrey Dastin, "Amazon Scraps Secret AI Recruiting Tool That Showed Bias against Women," *Reuters*, October 10, 2018, https://www.reuters.com/article/us-amazon-com-jobs-automation-insight-idUSKCN1MK08G); they reproduce

social inequity (Amit Katwala, "An Algorithm Determined UK Students' Grades. Chaos Ensued," *Wired*, August 15, 2020, https://www.wired.com/story/an-algorithm-determined-uk-students-grades-chaos-ensued/); they reify social and political valuations (Kate Crawford and Trevor Paglen, "Excavating AI," Excavating AI, September 19, 2019, https://www.excavating.ai); and they hallucinate in ways that could cause serious errors (Gernot Beutel, Eline Geerits, and Jan T. Kielstein, "Artificial Hallucination: GPT on LSD?" *Critical Care* 27, no. 1 [2023]: 148).

11 Colin Lecher, "A Healthcare Algorithm Started Cutting Care, and No One Knew Why," *Verge*, March 21, 2018, https://www.theverge.com/2018/3/21/17144260/healthcare-medicaid-algorithm-arkansas-cerebral-palsy.

12 For more on the shortcomings of this approach, see my review essay of Chris Bail's *Breaking the Social Media Prism*: Jeffrey Bilbro, "How Tech Reform Diminishes Us," *New Atlantis*, Winter 2022.

13 Ralph Waldo Emerson, *The Essays of Ralph Waldo Emerson*, ed. Alfred Riggs Ferguson and Jean Ferguson Carr (Cambridge, Mass.: Harvard University Press, 1987), 33.

14 Robert Mark Smith, "Orality and Typography: A Study of Contrasts in the Prose of Ralph Waldo Emerson" (PhD diss., University of Southwestern Louisiana, 1992), 1. Smith's dissertation probes some interesting lines of inquiry, but for the most part I focus on other typographical features of Emerson's imagination. For more on Emerson as an orator and powerful speaker, see Joel Porte, *In Respect to Egotism: Studies in American Romantic Writing* (Cambridge: Cambridge University Press, 1991), 108–9.

15 Hatch, *Democratization of American Christianity*, 179, 181–82. See also Paul Gutjahr, *An American Bible: A History of the Good Book in the United States, 1777–1880* (Stanford, Calif.: Stanford University Press, 2002), 95–96.

16 McLuhan, *Gutenberg Galaxy*, 164.

17 Walter J. Ong, *Orality and Literacy: The Technologizing of the Word*, New Accents (London: Routledge, 1991), 41.

18 Eisenstein, *Printing Press as an Agent of Change*, 124, see also 119 and 704.

19 Ralph Waldo Emerson, "Sermon CLXII ['The Lord's Supper']," in *Transcendentalism: A Reader*, ed. Joel Myerson (Oxford: Oxford University Press, 2000), 75, 77.

20 Emerson, "Sermon CLXII," 74–75.

21 Emerson, "Sermon CLXII," 76.

22 Emerson, "Sermon CLXII," 76.

23 Emerson, "Sermon CLXII," 74.

24 Emerson, "Sermon CLXII," 75.

25 Buell, *New England Literary Culture*, 202. See also Jeffrey Bilbro, *Loving God's Wildness: The Christian Roots of Ecological Ethics in American Literature* (Tuscaloosa: University of Alabama Press, 2015), 30–34.

26 Emerson, "The American Scholar," in *Collected Works*, 55–56.

27 Emerson, "Sermon CLXII," 72.

28 Emerson himself recognizes this relational reality elsewhere. See, for instance, his poem "Each and All," in *The Complete Works of Ralph Waldo Emerson: Poems* (Boston: Houghton, Mifflin, 1904), 4–6.

29 Hans Georg Gadamer, *Truth and Method*, trans. Joel Weinsheimer and Donald G. Marshall, 2nd rev. ed. (London: Sheed and Ward, 1999); Michael Polanyi, *The Tacit Dimension*, reissued ed. (Chicago: University of Chicago Press, 2009); and Raymond John Pierotti, *Indigenous Knowledge, Ecology, and Evolutionary Biology*, Indigenous Peoples and Politics (New York: Routledge, 2011).

30 Ong, *Presence of the Word*, 264.

31   Nicholas Carr, *The Shallows: How the Internet Is Changing the Way We Think, Read and Remember* (New York: W. W. Norton, 2011); Susan Greenfield, *Mind Change: How Digital Technologies Are Leaving Their Mark on Our Brains* (New York: Random House, 2015).

32   Emerson, *Essays*, 219.

33   Emerson, *Essays*, 239.

34   Emerson, *Nature*, 12.

35   Emerson, *Nature*, 31.

36   Emerson, *Nature*, 23. Roger Lundin also notes that Emerson's visual metaphors owe a debt to print technologies and the broader shifts that Ong traces. Roger Lundin, *Believing Again: Doubt and Faith in a Secular Age* (Grand Rapids: Eerdmans, 2009), 199–201.

37   Bacon, *New Organon*, 100.

38   Emerson, *Nature*, 25.

39   Emerson, *Nature*, 45.

40   *OED Online*, s.v. "Abracadabra, n. and Int.," accessed November 7, 2020, http://www.oed.com/view/Entry/539.

41   Emerson, *Nature*, 31–33, 45.

42   For more on the popularity of mesmerism and seances in the nineteenth century, see Bruce Mills, *Poe, Fuller, and the Mesmeric Arts: Transition States in the American Renaissance* (Columbia: University of Missouri Press, 2005); B. Bennett, *Transatlantic Spiritualism and Nineteenth-Century American Literature* (New York: Palgrave Macmillan, 2007); Emily Ogden, *Credulity: A Cultural History of US Mesmerism* (Chicago: University of Chicago Press, 2018).

43   Duhigg, "How Companies Learn Your Secrets."

44   Cal Newport, "What Kind of Mind Does ChatGPT Have?" *New Yorker*, April 13, 2023, https://www.newyorker.com/science/annals-of-artificial-intelligence/what-kind-of-mind-does-chatgpt-have.

45   Thaler and Sunstein, *Nudge*.

46   Martin Buber, *I and Thou*, trans. Walter Kaufmann (New York: Charles Scribner's Sons, 1970). Walter Ong gestures to this danger when he writes, "If we define reality in these terms [of extension, as mediated through sight], we become largely incapacitated for dealing with persons. Persons are potentialities, sources of power, and, although they may be extended in space, this is not what gives us our sense of them as persons, for extension in space is essentially passive. Persons, moreover, precisely as persons are eminently real" (*Presence of the Word*, 173–74).

47   Allen Tate, "Emily Dickinson," in *Emily Dickinson: A Collection of Critical Essays*, ed. Richard B. Sewall (Englewood Cliffs, N.J.: Prentice-Hall, 1963), 18.

48   Buell, *Emerson*, 70.

49   Lake, *Prophets of the Posthuman*, 2.

50   Lake, *Prophets of the Posthuman*, 4.

51   Emerson, *Nature*, 10.

52   Emerson, *Essays*, 261.

53   Emerson, *Essays*, 249.

54   Emerson, *Essays*, 265.

2 Men of Adamant

1   Nathaniel Hawthorne, "The Man of Adamant," in *The Snow Image and Uncollected Tales*, Centenary Edition of the Works of Nathaniel Hawthorne, vol. 11 (Columbus: Ohio State University Press, 1974), 162.

2   Hawthorne, "Man of Adamant," 163.

3   Thomas Jefferson, *The Jefferson Bible: The Life and Morals of Jesus of Naza-reth, Extracted Textually from the Gospels in Greek, Latin, French and English*, Smithsonian ed. (Washington, D.C.: Smithsonian Books, 2011).

4   Harry R. Rubenstein and Barbara Clark Smith, "History," in *Jefferson Bible*, 13, 30.

5   Albert Schweitzer, *The Quest of the Historical Jesus: A Critical Study of Its Progress from Reimarus to Wrede* (London: A. and C. Black, 1910), 4.

6   "Slave Bible from the 1800s Omitted Key Passages That Could Incite Rebel-lion," NPR, December 9, 2018, https://www.npr.org/2018/12/09/674995075/slave-bible-from-the-1800s-omitted-key-passages-that-could-incite-rebellion.

7   Gutjahr, *American Bible*, 176.

8   *Busy Dad's Bible: Daily Inspiration Even If You Only Have One Minute*, Box Lea ed. (Grand Rapids: Zondervan, 2010); Thomas Nelson, *Duck Commander Faith and Family Bible, Hardcover: Bible, New King James Version* (n.p.: Thomas Nelson, 2014); *1599 Geneva Bible: Patriot's Edition*, 2nd ed. (Power Springs, Ga.: Tolle Lege Press, 2021); *The Green Bible* (San Francisco: Harper-One, 2008).

9   David Lyle Jeffrey, "Our Babel of Bibles: Scripture, Translation, and the Pos-sibility of Spiritual Understanding," *Touchstone Magazine*, 2012, http://www.touchstonemag.com/archives/article.php?id=25-02-029-f.

10   Portions of these two paragraphs are adapted from my essay "Personal but Not Individual: How *The Saint John's Bible* Responds to Consumerism," in *"The Saint John's Bible" and Its Tradition: Illuminating Beauty in the Twenty-First Century*, ed. Jack R. Baker, Jeffrey Bilbro, and Daniel Train (Eugene, Ore.: Pick-wick, 2018), 122–35.

11   McLuhan, *Gutenberg Galaxy*, 180.

12   For more on this shift, see Ivan Illich, *In the Vineyard of the Text: A Commen-tary to Hugh's Didascalicon* (Chicago: University of Chicago Press, 1993) and Alberto Manguel, *A History of Reading* (New York: Penguin, 2014), 41–54.

13   Ong, *Presence of the Word*, 271.

14   McLuhan, *Gutenberg Galaxy*, 180, 186.

15   Eisenstein, *Printing Press as an Agent of Change*, 319.

16   Eisenstein, *Printing Press as an Agent of Change*, 326.

17   Quoted in Eisenstein, *Printing Press as an Agent of Change*, 325.

18   Ong, *Presence of the Word*, 272, emphasis original.

19   I am borrowing the terms "porous" and "buffered" from Charles Taylor's account. While Taylor does not focus on the role that communications media played in the development of the self, his narrative has intriguing parallels to Ong's. Charles Taylor, *A Secular Age* (Cambridge, Mass.: Belknap Press of Harvard University Press, 2007), 41–43.

20   Ong, *Presence of the Word*, 164.

21   Ong, *Presence of the Word*, 126.

22   Ong, *Ramus, Method, and the Decay of Dialogue*, 309–11. See also Ong, *Orality and Literacy*, 116–32.

23   Ong, *Ramus, Method, and the Decay of Dialogue*, 315.

24   Wellmon, *Organizing Enlightenment*, 43.

25   Noll, *America's God*, 4.

26   Hatch, *Democratization of American Christianity*, 179–83.

27   Hodge, *Systematic Theology*, 10.

28   Hodge, *Systematic Theology*, 183. Noll claims Hodges nuances this statement elsewhere, but he also points to Hodges as an exemplar of the commonsense, inductive mode of reading the Bible (*America's God*, 316–19).

29   Hodge, *Systematic Theology*, 15.

30 Hatch, *Democratization of American Christianity*.
31 Brian Yothers, "Terrors of the Soul: Religious Pluralism, Epistemological Dread, and Cosmic Exaltation in Poe, Hawthorne, and Melville," *Poe Studies/ Dark Romanticism: History, Theory, Interpretation* 39–40, nos. 1–2 (2006): 136. George Marsden makes a similar observation: "Everything in the Common Sense Baconian system assumed the stability of truth which could be known objectively by careful observers in any age or culture. Almost all the other trends in nineteenth-century thought, however, pointed toward an opposite conclusion" ("Everyone One's Own Interpreter?" 92). Drawing on one of these contrasting trends, Thomas Werge situates *Moby-Dick* in the Calvinist epistemic tradition of human depravity, one opposed to the optimistic, commonsense philosophy (Werge, "*Moby-Dick* and the Calvinist Tradition," *Studies in the Novel* 1, no. 4 [1969]: 484–506).
32 Hatch, *Democratization of American Christianity*, 41–42.
33 Thomas Paine, *The Age of Reason* (London: Freethought Publishing, 1889), 2.
34 Marsden, "Everyone One's Own Interpreter?" 79. Portions of the preceding paragraphs are adapted from my essay "The 'Art of Attaining Truth' in *Moby-Dick*: Print Technologies, Hermeneutics, and Castaway Readers," in *Above the American Renaissance: David S. Reynolds and the Spiritual Imagination in American Literary Studies*, ed. Harold K. Bush and Brian Yothers (Amherst: University of Massachusetts Press, 2018), 125–39.
35 John W. Nevin, quoted in Noll, *America's God*, 403.
36 Noll, *America's God*, 396. See also Noll's book on this subject, *The Civil War as a Theological Crisis*, Steven and Janice Brose Lectures in the Civil War Era (Chapel Hill: University of North Carolina Press, 2006).
37 Hawthorne, "Man of Adamant," 162.
38 Stephen Greenblatt, *Renaissance Self-Fashioning: From More to Shakespeare* (Chicago: University of Chicago Press, 2005), emphasis in original, 97.
39 Griffiths, *Intellectual Appetite*, 20.
40 Hawthorne, "Man of Adamant," 163–64.
41 Hawthorne, "Man of Adamant," 165–66.
42 Hawthorne, "Man of Adamant," 166–67.
43 Saint Augustine, *On Christian Teaching*, trans. R. P. H. Green (Oxford: Oxford University Press, 2008), 27.

3 Encyclopedists and Map-Plotters

1 Portions of this chapter, particularly the readings of *Moby-Dick*, are adapted from my essay "'Art of Attaining Truth' in *Moby-Dick*."
2 Herman Melville, *Moby-Dick: Or, The Whale*, ed. Harrison Hayford, Hershel Parker, and G. Thomas Tanselle, Writings of Herman Melville (Evanston, Ill.: Northwestern University Press, 1988), 480.
3 Melville, *Moby-Dick*, xv, xvii.
4 The Multigraph Collective, *Interacting with Print: Elements of Reading in the Era of Print Saturation* (Chicago: University of Chicago Press, 2018), 164.
5 Ong, *Orality and Literacy*, 72.
6 "About Google, Our Culture & Company News," Google.com, accessed December 5, 2020, about.google.com.
7 Ursula K. Heise, *Sense of Place and Sense of Planet: The Environmental Imagination of the Global* (Oxford: Oxford University Press, 2008), 67.
8 Wikipedia, s.v. "Wikipedia," version from December 4, 2020, https://en.wikipedia.org/w/index.php?title=Wikipedia&oldid=992347324.

9   Edward Osborne Wilson, *Consilience: The Unity of Knowledge* (New York: Vintage, 1999), 3, 7.

10 "What Is EOL?" *Encyclopedia of Life*, accessed December 5, 2020, https://naturalhistory.si.edu/research/eol.

11 For an extended critique of Wilson's hubris, see Berry, *Life*.

12 Two helpful studies of these kinds of responses to the information overload sparked by print are Ann Blair, *Too Much to Know: Managing Scholarly Information before the Modern Age* (New Haven: Yale University Press, 2010), and Wellmon, *Organizing Enlightenment*.

13 Wellmon, *Organizing Enlightenment*, 43.

14 Wellmon, *Organizing Enlightenment*, 88–90.

15 *Oxford English Dictionary*, "History of the OED," accessed December 8, 2020, https://public.oed.com/history/.

16 Multigraph Collective, *Interacting with Print*, 164. See also Gerald Strauss, who explains, "Clarity and logic of organization, the disposition of matter on the printed page became . . . almost an end in itself. It is a phenomenon familiar to a student of encyclopedic books of the late sixteenth century, relating to the increased fascination with the technical possibilities of typesetting and the great influence exerted by the methodology of Peter Ramus" (Strauss, "A Sixteenth-Century Encyclopedia: Sebastian Münster's *Cosmography* and Its Editions," in *From the Renaissance to the Counter-Reformation: Essays in Honour of Garrett Mattingly*, ed. Charles Howard Carter [London: Jonathan Cape, 1966], 152). For more on the role that Ramism plays in this development, see Ong, *Ramus, Method, and the Decay of Dialogue*.

17 As Ivan Illich argues, developments in indexing and page layout made books into "scrutable text[s]": "The book for the monastic reader was a discourse which you could follow, but into which you could not easily dip at a point of your choosing. Only after Hugh does easy access to a specific place become a standard procedure" (*In the Vineyard of the Text*, 94, 96).

18 Marsden, "Everyone One's Own Interpreter?" 83.

19 Hodge, *Systematic Theology*, 10.

20 Melville, *Moby-Dick*, xv–xvii.

21 Ann Moss, *Printed Commonplace-Books and the Structuring of Renaissance Thought* (Oxford: Clarendon Press, 1996), 275–76.

22 Melville, *Moby-Dick*, xvii.

23 Melville, *Moby-Dick*, xxiii.

24 Jonathan Cook comes to a similar conclusion regarding the effect of this prefatory matter: "The total of some eighty prose and poetic 'Extracts' subsequently reveal the whale as a universal presence in human history and an object of knowledge that, like the deity, eludes any fixed identity." In Cook, *Inscrutable Malice: Theodicy, Eschatology, and the Biblical Sources of* Moby-Dick (DeKalb: Northern Illinois University Press, 2012), 41.

25 Melville, *Moby-Dick*, 5.

26 Melville is likely in conversation with *Paradise Lost*'s allusions to the Narcissus myth. I consider the influence of Milton's view of interpretation on Margaret Fuller in "Learning to Woo Meaning from Apparent Chaos: Republican Interpreters, Milton, and the Ecological Form of *Summer on the Lakes*," in *Writing the Environment in Nineteenth-Century American Literature: The Ecological Awareness of Early Scribes of Nature*, Ecocritical Theory and Practice (Lanham, Md.: Lexington Books, 2015), 57–76.

27 Melville, *Moby-Dick*, 189.

28 Melville, *Moby-Dick*, 134.

246 | Notes to Pages 63–68

29 Melville, *Moby-Dick*, 136.
30 Melville, *Moby-Dick*, 137.
31 Melville, *Moby-Dick*, 145.
32 Melville, *Moby-Dick*, 455–56.
33 Gal 6:11; Exod 17:11–12; Melville, *Moby-Dick*, 456.
34 As Sandra Gustafson notes, "In the chapters following Ahab's speech on the quarterdeck, Melville uses dramatic form to depict the disintegration of the bond that Ahab has imposed on the crew, a formal choice that makes vividly apparent the tension between novelistic conventions and scenes of oratory." Gustafson, "Orality and Literacy in Transatlantic Perspective," *19: Interdisciplinary Studies in the Long Nineteenth Century*, no. 18 (2014): 7–8, https://19.bbk.ac.uk/article/id/1672/.
35 Melville, *Moby-Dick*, 199.
36 Donna Haraway, "Situated Knowledges: The Science Question in Feminism and the Privilege of Partial Perspective," *Feminist Studies* 14, no. 3 (1988): 581. For more on this "false perspectivism" and other assumptions inherent in modern cartography, see Matthew H. Edney, *Cartography: The Ideal and Its History* (Chicago: University of Chicago Press, 2019), 77.
37 Ong, *Orality and Literacy*, 72.
38 Illich, *In the Vineyard of the Text*, 37, 96. See also the opening chapter of Peter Candler's book in which he contrasts tour-like grammars of participation with maplike grammars of representation (*Theology, Rhetoric, Manuduction*, 21–40).
39 Elizabeth Eisenstein's work is seminal to this discussion. Eisenstein, *Printing Press as an Agent of Change*, 478–83. For an analysis of printed maps and national identity in early America, see Martin Brückner, *The Geographic Revolution in Early America: Maps, Literacy, and National Identity* (Chapel Hill: University of North Carolina Press, 2006). Benedict Anderson traces related developments in Siam (*Imagined Communities*, 171–73).
40 William T. Cavanaugh, *Theopolitical Imagination* (London: T&T Clark, 2002), 100–101.
41 My understanding of the significance of these contrasting ways of imagining space is indebted to Peter Candler, specifically, his *Theology, Rhetoric, Manuduction*, 21–40.
42 Loughran, *Republic in Print*, 233.
43 Loughran reads Colles' project rather differently than I do, comparing it to Enlightenment encyclopedias "in its attempt to create a 'systematized' approach to the entire circumference of the known physical world, an inclusive and incorporative system not only for mapping all known spaces, but for indexing all known things within those places as well." Loughran, *Republic in Print*, 297. While there is some explanatory power in her approach, particularly given the ambitions of Colles' project, the form his maps took shares more in common with older, itinerary maps than with modern cartography.
44 Joel Kovarsky, *The True Geography of Our Country: Jefferson's Cartographic Vision* (Charlottesville: University of Virginia Press, 2014), 17–18.
45 Kovarsky, *True Geography of Our Country*, 14–16.
46 Loughran, *Republic in Print*, 292.
47 "The Jefferson Grid (@the.Jefferson.Grid)," Instagram photo, accessed December 17, 2020, https://www.instagram.com/the.jefferson.grid/. See also Laura Bliss, "Photographing the American 'Grid,' One Square Mile Per Frame," *Bloomberg*, September 16, 2015, https://www.bloomberg.com/news/articles/2015-09-16/the -jefferson-grid-shows-the-american-west-through-one-square-mile-per-frame. The Jefferson grid has since become inactive; see Chris Bodenner, "Orbital View: Where'd You Go, Jefferson Grid?" *The Atlantic*, December 17, 2015, https://www

.theatlantic.com/national/archive/2015/12/orbital-view-whered-you-go-jefferson
-grid/625471/.

48 Samuel Otter, "Reading *Moby-Dick*," in *The New Cambridge Companion to Herman Melville*, ed. Robert S. Levine (Cambridge: Cambridge University Press, 2014), 73.

49 Melville, *Moby-Dick*, 199.

50 Quoted in Steven J. Dick, *Sky and Ocean Joined: The US Naval Observatory 1830–2000* (Cambridge: Cambridge University Press, 2003), 96.

51 Maury's charts, particularly his whale chart, were part of a new kind of map that emerged in the nineteenth century, one that, according to Susan Schulten, "focused on the distribution of phenomena rather than the landscape itself" (*Mapping the Nation: History and Cartography in Nineteenth-Century America* [Chicago: University of Chicago Press, 2012], 3).

52 Melville, *Moby-Dick*, 198.

53 Melville, *Moby-Dick*, 199.

54 Melville, *Moby-Dick*, 200.

55 Melville, *Moby-Dick*, 201.

56 Melville, *Moby-Dick*, 501.

57 Melville, *Moby-Dick*, 55.

58 Wilson, *Consilience*, 7.

59 Melville, *Moby-Dick*, 480.

4 Celebrities

1 Walt Whitman, *Leaves of Grass: A Textual Variorum of the Printed Poems*, ed. Sculley Bradley et al., Collected Writings of Walt Whitman (New York: New York University Press, 1980), 83–84. This poem later becomes "Poem of the Daily Work of the Workmen and Workwomen of These States," part of "Chants Democratic," and, after several other iterations, "A Song for Occupations." The opening portion that I have quoted was revised several times and then dropped in the 1881 version.

2 Robert D. Putnam, *Bowling Alone: The Collapse and Revival of American Community* (New York: Touchstone Books, 2001); Timothy P. Carney, *Alienated America: Why Some Places Thrive while Others Collapse* (New York: Harper, 2019).

3 Sherry Turkle, *Alone Together: Why We Expect More from Technology and Less from Each Other* (New York: Basic Books, 2012).

4 Jean M. Twenge, *iGen: Why Today's Super-Connected Kids Are Growing Up Less Rebellious, More Tolerant, Less Happy—and Completely Unprepared for Adulthood—and What That Means for the Rest of Us* (New York: Simon and Schuster, 2017), 79–80.

5 Julianne Holt-Lunstad, "The Potential Public Health Relevance of Social Isolation and Loneliness: Prevalence, Epidemiology, and Risk Factors," *Public Policy and Aging Report* 27, no. 4 (2017): 127–30.

6 Rupi Kaur, "@rupikaur_," Instagram photo, accessed April 27, 2021, https://www.instagram.com/rupikaur_/.

7 Seth Perlow, "The Handwritten Styles of Instagram Poetry," *Post45* (blog), September 17, 2019, https://post45.org/2019/09/the-handwritten-styles-of-instagram-poetry/.

8 David S. Reynolds, *Walt Whitman's America: A Cultural Biography* (New York: Vintage, 1996), 570.

9   Barrett Swanson, "The Anxiety of Influencers: Educating the TikTok Generation," *Harper's Magazine*, June 2021, https://harpers.org/archive/2021/06/tiktok-house-collab-house-the-anxiety-of-influencers/.

10 Ronald J. Zboray, *A Fictive People: Antebellum Economic Development and the American Reading Public* (New York: Oxford University Press, 1993), 111. Zboray cites, among others, Stephan Thernstrom, *The Other Bostonians: Poverty and Progress in the American Metropolis, 1880–1970* (Cambridge, Mass.: Harvard University Press, 2013), 221–32, and Donald H. Parkerson, "How Mobile Were Nineteenth-Century Americans?" *Historical Methods: A Journal of Quantitative and Interdisciplinary History* 15, no. 3 (1982): 99–109.

11 Patricia Kelly Hall and Steven Ruggles, "'Restless in the Midst of Their Prosperity': New Evidence on the Internal Migration of Americans, 1850–2000," *Journal of American History* 91, no. 3 (2004): 829–46.

12 Claude S. Fischer, "Ever-More Rooted Americans," *City and Community* 1, no. 2 (2002): 177–98.

13 Zboray, *Fictive People*, 111.

14 Zboray, *Fictive People*, 113.

15 Zboray, *Fictive People*, 113.

16 Zboray, *Fictive People*, 71.

17 Anderson, *Imagined Communities*.

18 Zboray, *Fictive People*, 120.

19 Zboray, *Fictive People*, 78–79. Nathan Beacom offers one account of how similar dynamics play out in a digital age in "The Community Community," *Comment Magazine*, September 7, 2023, https://comment.org/the-community-community/.

20 Zboray, *Fictive People*, 121.

21 Zboray, *Fictive People*, 82.

22 Whitman, in Bradley et al., *Leaves of Grass*, 83–84.

23 Reynolds, *Walt Whitman's America*, 574.

24 Ed Folsom, "Whitman Making Books/Books Making Whitman: A Catalog and Commentary," Walt Whitman Archive, 2005, http://whitmanarchive.org/criticism/current/anc.00150.html.

25 Whitman, in Bradley et al., *Leaves of Grass*, 333. Whitman echoes this sentiment in "So Long," with which several editions of *Leaves of Grass* conclude: "Dear friend whoever you are take this kiss, / I give it especially to you, do not forget me," 452.

26 Whitman, in Bradley et al., *Leaves of Grass*, 452.

27 Whitman, in Bradley et al., *Leaves of Grass*, 549.

28 Ted Genoways, "'One Goodshaped and Wellhung Man': Accentuated Sexuality and the Uncertain Authorship of the Frontispiece to the 1855 Edition of *Leaves of Grass*," in *Leaves of Grass: The Sesquicentennial Essays*, ed. Susan Belasco, Ed Folsom, and Kenneth M. Price (Lincoln: University of Nebraska Press, 2007), 89.

29 Multigraph Collective, *Interacting with Print*, 143.

30 Eisenstein, *Printing Press as an Agent of Change*, 121.

31 Genoways, "'One Goodshaped and Wellhung Man'," 98; Folsom, "Whitman Making Books."

32 Reynolds, *Walt Whitman's America*, 535.

33 Folsom, "Whitman Making Books."

34 Walt Whitman, *The Correspondence*, vol. 3, *1876–1885*, ed. Edwin Haviland Miller (New York: NYU Press, 2007), 243.

35 Whitman, *Correspondence*, 226.

36 Whitman, in Bradley et al., *Leaves of Grass*, 78.
37 Folsom, "Whitman Making Books."
38 Reynolds, *Walt Whitman's America*, 367.
39 Buell, *Emerson*, 23.
40 Reynolds, *Walt Whitman's America*, 344, 362.
41 Reynolds, *Walt Whitman's America*, 362.
42 Reynolds, *Walt Whitman's America*, 356.
43 Walt Whitman, *Leaves of Grass and Other Writings*, ed. Michael Moon (New York: W. W. Norton, 2002), 473.
44 Whitman, in Bradley et al., *Leaves of Grass*, 204.
45 Whitman, in Bradley et al., *Leaves of Grass*, 12.
46 Whitman, in Bradley et al., *Leaves of Grass*, 17.
47 Whitman, in Bradley et al., *Leaves of Grass*, 1.
48 Reynolds, *Walt Whitman's America*, 49.
49 Whitman, in Bradley et al., *Leaves of Grass*, 20, 21.
50 Reynolds, *Walt Whitman's America*, 231.
51 Reynolds, *Walt Whitman's America*, 308.
52 Whitman, in Bradley et al., *Leaves of Grass*, 197–98.
53 Whitman, in Bradley et al., *Leaves of Grass*, 209.
54 Whitman, *Leaves of Grass and Other Writings*, 637.
55 Wilfred M. McClay, *The Masterless: Self and Society in Modern America* (Chapel Hill: University of North Carolina Press, 2000), 6–7.
56 McClay, *Masterless*, 54.
57 McClay, *Masterless*, 54.
58 McClay, *Masterless*, 72.
59 Sherry Turkle, "Connected, but Alone?" Filmed February 2012, TED video, https://www.ted.com/talks/sherry_turkle_connected_but_alone; idem, *Alone Together*.

5 Benevolent Bosses

1   Mark Twain, *A Connecticut Yankee in King Arthur's Court*, ed. Bernard L. Stein (Berkeley: University of California Press, 1979), 303.
2   Twain, *Connecticut Yankee*, 308.
3   Twain, *Connecticut Yankee*, 429.
4   Melville, *Confidence-Man*, 165–66.
5   Ghonim, "Let's Design Social Media."
6   Tufekci, *Twitter and Tear Gas*, 119.
7   Toyama, *Geek Heresy*, 3.
8   Toyama, *Geek Heresy*, 5.
9   Toyama, *Geek Heresy*, 6–7.
10 Toyama, *Geek Heresy*, 8–14.
11 Twain, *Connecticut Yankee*, 160.
12 Twain, *Connecticut Yankee*, 98.
13 Twain, *Connecticut Yankee*, 118.
14 Twain, *Connecticut Yankee*, 120.
15 Benjamin Rush, *A Plan for the Establishment of Public Schools and the Diffusion of Knowledge in Pennsylvania; To Which Are Added Thoughts upon the Mode of Education, Proper in a Republic. Addressed to the Legislature and Citizens of the State* (Philadelphia: Thomas Dobson, 1786), 11.
16 Warner, *Letters of the Republic*, 128.

17 Noah Webster, *A Collection of Essays and Fugitiv Writings: On Moral, Historical, Political and Literary Subjects* (Boston: I. Thomas and E. T. Andrews, 1790), 24.
18 Quoted in Foner, *Free Soil, Free Labor, Free Men*, 39. Foner provides further examples of these sentiments in the antebellum years.
19 Rush, *Plan for the Establishment of Public Schools*, 27.
20 Warner, *Letters of the Republic*, 129.
21 Twain, *Connecticut Yankee*, 160, 476.
22 Melville, *Confidence-Man*, 165–66.
23 Justin Kaplan, *Mr. Clemens and Mark Twain* (New York: Simon and Schuster, 1966), 285.
24 Jerome Loving, *Mark Twain: The Adventures of Samuel L. Clemens* (Berkeley: University of California Press, 2011), 274.
25 Kaplan, *Mr. Clemens and Mark Twain*, 287.
26 Kaplan, *Mr. Clemens and Mark Twain*, 303.
27 Everett Emerson, *Mark Twain, a Literary Life* (Philadelphia: University of Pennsylvania Press, 2017), 166.
28 Loving, *Mark Twain*, 250; Twain, *Connecticut Yankee*, 50.
29 Jim Rasenberger, *Revolver: Sam Colt and the Six-Shooter That Changed America* (New York: Scribner, 2020).
30 Kaplan, *Mr. Clemens and Mark Twain*, 284, 283.
31 Twain, *Connecticut Yankee*, 369.
32 Jeffrey Bilbro, "'That Petrified Laugh': Mark Twain's Hoaxes in the West and Camelot," *Journal of Narrative Theory* 41, no. 2 (2011): 204–34; Loving, *Mark Twain*, 298. Although Kaplan identifies Hank with Twain, his reading of the novel is otherwise quite perceptive. Kaplan, *Mr. Clemens and Mark Twain*, 297.
33 Jacobs, *How to Think*, 28–29. See also McLuhan, *Gutenberg Galaxy*, 280; Postman, *Amusing Ourselves to Death*, 160.
34 Twain, *Connecticut Yankee*, 48.
35 Twain, *Connecticut Yankee*, 50.
36 Twain, *Connecticut Yankee*, 53.
37 For a fuller analysis of how this novel functions as a hoax, see Lawrence I. Berkove, "*A Connecticut Yankee*: A Serious Hoax," *Essays in Arts and Sciences* 19 (May 1990): 28–44; Bilbro, "'That Petrified Laugh.'"
38 This is a standard trope of Gothic literature, and Nathaniel Hawthorne adapts it for *The Scarlet Letter: A Romance*, which we will turn to in chapter 12.
39 Twain, *Connecticut Yankee*, 102.
40 Twain, *Connecticut Yankee*, 105.
41 Twain, *Connecticut Yankee*, 71.
42 Twain, *Connecticut Yankee*, 262.
43 Twain, *Connecticut Yankee*, 167, 624, 267.
44 Twain, *Connecticut Yankee*, 255.
45 Twain, *Connecticut Yankee*, 275.
46 Twain, *Connecticut Yankee*, 276.
47 Twain, *Connecticut Yankee*, 303.
48 Twain, *Connecticut Yankee*, 304.
49 Twain, *Connecticut Yankee*, 306.
50 Multigraph Collective, *Interacting with Print*, 97.
51 Twain, *Connecticut Yankee*, 300.
52 Twain, *Connecticut Yankee*, 115, 113.
53 Twain, *Connecticut Yankee*, 160.
54 Twain, *Connecticut Yankee*, 288.

55 Kaplan, *Mr. Clemens and Mark Twain*, 300.
56 Twain, *Connecticut Yankee*, 127.
57 Twain, *Connecticut Yankee*, 444.
58 Twain, *Connecticut Yankee*, 123.
59 Twain, *Connecticut Yankee*, 443.
60 Twain, *Connecticut Yankee*, 469.
61 Twain, *Connecticut Yankee*, 475.
62 Twain, *Connecticut Yankee*, 478.
63 Peter Arnett, "Major Describes Move," *New York Times*, March 15, 1968.
64 Twain, *Connecticut Yankee*, 492.

6 Loose Fish

1   Eisenstein, *Printing Press as an Agent of Change*, 153.
2   Melville, *Moby-Dick*, 396.
3   Melville, *Moby-Dick*, 396.
4   Ian McGuire, "'Who Ain't a Slave?' 'Moby Dick' and the Ideology of Free Labor," *Journal of American Studies* 37, no. 2 (2003): 302.
5   Melville, *Moby-Dick*, 397–98.
6   Vaidhyanathan, *Antisocial Media*, 99. The standard account of these developments in our digital era is Shoshana Zuboff, *The Age of Surveillance Capitalism: The Fight for a Human Future at the New Frontier of Power* (New York: PublicAffairs, 2020).
7   Cathy O'Neil, *Weapons of Math Destruction: How Big Data Increases Inequality and Threatens Democracy* (New York: Crown, 2017), 71–72.
8   O'Neil, *Weapons of Math Destruction*, 76.
9   O'Neil, *Weapons of Math Destruction*, 70.
10 For another example of this, see Amazon Halo, which conducted emotional analyses of its users that many feared would be used to target them with advertisements. Amazon later discontinued the Halo. Austin Carr, "Amazon's New Wearable Will Know If I'm Angry. Is That Weird?" *Bloomberg*, August 31, 2020, https://www.bloomberg.com/news/newsletters/2020-08-31/amazon-s-halo-wearable-can-read-emotions-is-that-too-weird; Chris Welch, "Inside Amazon's Canceled Plan to Make Halo a Fitness Success," *Verge*, May 1, 2023, https://www.theverge.com/2023/5/1/23704825/amazon-halo-canceled-features-ai-training-apple-watch.
11 Melville, *Confidence-Man*, 4.
12 Zygmunt Bauman, *Liquid Modernity* (Cambridge: Polity, 2000).
13 A classic account here is Robert Nisbet, *The Quest for Community: A Study in the Ethics of Order and Freedom* (Wilmington, Del: Intercollegiate Studies Institute, 2010).
14 Zygmunt Bauman, *Does Ethics Have a Chance in a World of Consumers?* Institute for Human Sciences Vienna Lecture Series (Cambridge, Mass.: Harvard University Press, 2008), 14.
15 Wilfred McClay traces these developments in his rich historical study, *Masterless*.
16 Melville, *Moby-Dick*, 573.
17 Kovarsky, *True Geography of Our Country*, 114–17. For a through account of *Johnson v. M'Intosh* and its legal legacy, see Blake A. Watson's comprehensive study, *Buying America from the Indians: Johnson v. McIntosh and the History of Native Land Rights* (Norman: University of Oklahoma Press, 2012).

18 My use of the concept of *legibility* here is indebted to James Scott. James C. Scott, *Seeing like a State: How Certain Schemes to Improve the Human Condition Have Failed* (New Haven: Yale University Press, 1999).

19 William T. Cavanaugh, *Migrations of the Holy: God, State, and the Political Meaning of the Church* (Grand Rapids: Eerdmans, 2011), 39–40.

20 Loughran, *Republic in Print*, 149, 181–82, 243–44.

21 Foner, *Free Soil, Free Labor, Free Men*, 17.

22 Foner, *Free Soil, Free Labor, Free Men*, 31–32.

23 McGuire, "'Who Ain't a Slave?'" 290. This fear became more pronounced after the Panic of 1857. Foner, *Free Soil, Free Labor, Free Men*, 24–25.

24 Significantly, the manifold ties of civil society also seem to have contributed to support for greater legal rights for free blacks. Foner notes that most racist states were those with the most fluid economies and societies: "Where the social order was least stratified—as in the frontier states of Kansas, California, and Oregon—legal discrimination was most severe. Thus, paradoxically, the very social mobility for which the West has been celebrated may have tended to exaggerate racial prejudice." Foner, *Free Soil, Free Labor, Free Men*, 262.

25 Ishmael's warnings about the fate of Loose-Fish should not be taken as Melville's tacit support of Southern slavery. There are rhetorical parallels between the arguments of an apologist such as George Fitzhugh and Melville's critique of free labor ideology, and Foner provides a helpful overview of such Southern critiques of Northern society, in *Free Soil, Free Labor, Free Men*, 66–69. Melville, however, was deeply critical of racial slavery and was concerned about the common assumptions shared by these two apparently opposed systems. For further analysis of these common assumptions, see Marvin Fisher's essay, which situates some of Melville's other writings in the economic, racial, and technological conversations of the 1850s. Fisher concludes that "despite his use of an argument which was itself a rationalization favoring slavery, Melville never seems the least sympathetic to slavery. Instead he seems to see domination and subjugation as a lamentable fact of human existence; and any of the forces which subject man to a condition of marked inferiority—whether naval discipline, economic pressures, ideas of class and caste, theological insistence on human depravity—thereby coerce his will and render him a slave" ("Melville's 'Bell-Tower': A Double Thrust," *American Quarterly* 18, no. 2 [1966]: 207). See also Jason Frank, who contrasts Melville to Fitzhugh and argues that Melville's tragic political insight is that "America's defining ideal of freedom as autonomy engenders the material and spiritual forms of domination that mark American history and mar its democratic futures" ("American Tragedy: The Political Thought of Herman Melville," in *A Political Companion to Herman Melville* (Lexington: University Press of Kentucky, 2013), 7).

26 Bauman, *Does Ethics Have a Chance?* 58.

27 McGuire, "'Who Ain't a Slave?'" 293.

28 Noll, *America's God*, 173.

29 Hatch, *Democratization of American Christianity*, 11.

30 Hatch, *Democratization of American Christianity*, 208.

31 Hatch, *Democratization of American Christianity*, 183.

32 Ellul, *Propaganda*, 91.

33 Ellul, *Propaganda*, 92.

34 Melville, *Moby-Dick*, 121.

35 Ellul, *Propaganda*, 92.

36 Hatch, *Democratization of American Christianity*, 183.

37 These political dynamics in particular have been often noted, and many commentators have pointed to the links Melville establishes between Ahab and the

populist president Andrew Jackson. Alan Heimert, "Moby-Dick and American Political Symbolism," *American Quarterly* 15, no. 4 (1963): 498–534; McGuire, "'Who Ain't a Slave?'" 291.

38 Melville, *Moby-Dick*, 169.

39 Melville, *Moby-Dick*, 536, 568.

40 Melville, *Moby-Dick*, 430.

41 Melville, *Moby-Dick*, 431.

42 Melville, *Moby-Dick*, 433.

43 Melville, *Moby-Dick*, 297.

44 Melville, *Moby-Dick*, 434.

45 Melville, *Moby-Dick*, 435.

46 McGuire, "'Who Ain't a Slave?'" 293.

47 Roger Lundin, *The Promise of Hermeneutics* (Grand Rapids: Eerdmans, 1999), 42.

48 Melville, *Moby-Dick*, 492.

49 Roger Lundin, *Beginning with the Word: Modern Literature and the Question of Belief* (Grand Rapids: Baker Academic, 2014), 216.

50 Melville, *Moby-Dick*, 573.

7 Macadamized Minds

1 Portions of the following analysis of Thoreau's metaphors are adapted from chapter 2 of my book *Reading the Times*.

2 Henry David Thoreau, *Reform Papers*, ed. Wendell Glick, Writings of Henry D. Thoreau (Princeton: Princeton University Press, 1973), 173.

3 Kathryn Schulz, "Why Do We Love Henry David Thoreau?" *New Yorker*, October 12, 2015, https://www.newyorker.com/magazine/2015/10/19/pond-scum; Laura Dassow Walls, *Henry David Thoreau: A Life* (Chicago: University of Chicago Press, 2017).

4 Walls, *Henry David Thoreau*, 449–56.

5 Thoreau, *Reform Papers*, 172.

6 Cory Doctorow, "Writing in the Age of Distraction," *Locus Magazine* (blog), January 2009, http://www.locusmag.com/Features/2009/01/cory-doctorow-writing-in -age-of.html, quoted in Alan Jacobs, "Habits of Mind in an Age of Distraction," *Comment*, Summer 2016; Linda Stone, "Continuous Partial Attention," *Linda Stone* (blog), November 30, 2009, https://lindastone.net/2009/11/30/beyond-simple-multi -tasking-continuous-partial-attention/.

7 Greenfield, *Mind Change*; Carr, *Shallows*.

8 Carr, *Shallows*, 48.

9 While Neil Postman takes care to qualify his arguments by averring that "at no point do I care to claim that changes in media bring about changes in the structure of people's minds or changes in their cognitive capacities," he would likely revise this statement in light of the work documented by Carr, Greenfield, and others. Postman, *Amusing Ourselves to Death*, 27.

10 Caitlin Flanagan, "You Really Need to Quit Twitter," *Atlantic*, July 5, 2021, https://www.theatlantic.com/ideas/archive/2021/07/twitter-addict-realizes -she-needs-rehab/619343/. For variations on this theme, see Andrew Sullivan, "My Distraction Sickness—and Yours," *New York Magazine*, September 16, 2016, https://nymag.com/intelligencer/2016/09/andrew-sullivan-my-distraction -sickness-and-yours.html; Alan Jacobs, *The Pleasures of Reading in an Age of Distraction* (New York: Oxford University Press, 2011).

11   Maryanne Wolf, *Reader, Come Home: The Reading Brain in a Digital World* (New York: HarperCollins, 2018), 39.
12   Postman, *Amusing Ourselves to Death*, 29, 61.
13   Eisenstein, *Printing Press as an Agent of Change*, 130; Reynolds, *Walt Whitman's America*, 195–96; Donna Dennis, *Licentious Gotham: Erotic Publishing and Its Prosecution in Nineteenth-Century New York* (Cambridge, Mass.: Harvard University Press, 2009).
14   Goodrich, *Recollections of a Lifetime*, 86.
15   For Hegel's quote and further analysis of his view of history, see Anderson, *Imagined Communities*, 35. I discuss Hegel's view of history and the news further in chapter 4 of *Reading the Times*.
16   Appleby, *Inheriting the Revolution*, 99–100.
17   Dudek, *Literature and the Press*, 66. See also the Heidlers' analysis of the role newspapers played in Andrew Jackson's 1824 campaign: "The sheer number of American newspapers—861 by 1828—marked a significant increase from even the 1824 contest. . . . The use of newspapers in the campaign of 1828 was the most revolutionary aspect of a revolutionary year in American politics. Partisan newspapers enlisted in campaigns openly and avidly, and their editors could be strident or subtle, the former sounding alarms over the fate of the republic should it fall into the wrong hands, the latter falsely lamenting the need to point out the unsavory nature of an opponent. Operatives working for centrally controlled campaigns called on newspaper editors the way modern sales representatives drop in on clients, systematically lining up support and making sure everyone stayed in line. Meanwhile, because they were cheaper to produce and inexpensive or free to mail, the reach and influence of newspapers gave those wielding legislative power or executive contracts unique ability to direct the sentiments of the entire country as newspapers became just another form of traditional political tracts. The power of such organizing principles was incalculable." In David S. Heidler and Jeanne T. Heidler, *The Rise of Andrew Jackson: Myth, Manipulation, and the Making of Modern Politics* (New York: Basic Books, 2018), 303–4.
18   There was plenty of backlash to this news consumption. In a poem published in Goodrich's 1835 gift book, *Token and Atlantic Souvenir*, the author celebrates the beauty and serenity of the White Mountains and contrasts this with the noise and confusion brought by the newspaper:

> The morning comes not with a lying sheet
>   Telling of party strife and party throes,
> No evening transcript of the guilty street,
>   Echoes the day's disasters, follies, woes.
>
> . . .
>
> No minions of the press, who cull the street
>   For news, like wasps along a ruined wall,
> And if, perchance, some lonely flower they meet,
>   Instead of honey, only gather gall.

In S. G. Goodrich, ed., *The Token and Atlantic Souvenir: A Christmas and New Year's Present* (Boston: Charles Bowen, 1835), 160–61.
19   "The Magnetic Telegraph—Some of Its Results," in *Littell's Living Age*, vol. 6 (Boston: T. H. Carter, 1845), 194–95.
20   Standage, *Victorian Internet*, 83.
21   Greeley's view of the telegraph was quite common. For other examples, see Shannon L. Thomas, "'What News Must Think When Pondering': Emily Dickinson,

the *Springfield Daily Republican*, and the Poetics of Mass Communication," *Emily Dickinson Journal* 19, no. 1 (2010): 72–74. When a more successful transatlantic cable was laid in 1866, it too was met with outlandish praise. Edward Thornton, the British ambassador to America, toasted the cable as the bearer of universal peace: "What can be more likely to effect [peace] than a constant and complete intercourse between all nations and individuals in the world? Steam [power] was the first olive branch offered to us by science. Then came a still more effective olive branch—this wonderful electric telegraph, which enables any man who happens to be within reach of a wire to communicate instantaneously with his fellow men all over the world." Another toast at the same celebration called the transatlantic "telegraph wire, the nerve of international life, transmitting knowledge of events, removing causes of misunderstanding, and promoting peace and harmony throughout the world." Standage, *Victorian Internet*, 90–91.

22 Oliver Wendell Holmes, "Bread and the Newspaper," *Atlantic*, September 1861, 348.

23 Holmes, "Bread and the Newspaper," 347.

24 *OED Online*, s.v. "Consensus, n.," accessed July 13, 2022, https://www.oed.com/view/Entry/39516.

25 Loughran, *Republic in Print*; Noll, *Civil War as a Theological Crisis*.

26 Nathaniel Hawthorne, "Chiefly about War Matters," *Atlantic*, July 1, 1862, https://www.theatlantic.com/magazine/archive/1862/07/chiefly-about-war-matters/306159/.

27 Henry David Thoreau, *Walden*, ed. J. Lyndon Shanley, Writings of Henry D. Thoreau (Princeton: Princeton University Press, 1971), 105.

28 Thoreau, *Walden*, 102.

29 Thoreau, *Reform Papers*, 178–79.

30 Griffiths, *Intellectual Appetite*, 20.

31 Thoreau, *Reform Papers*, 169–70.

32 Ben Smith, "How TikTok Reads Your Mind," *New York Times*, December 6, 2021, https://www.nytimes.com/2021/12/05/business/media/tiktok-algorithm.html.

33 Nicole Blanchett Neheli, "Here's How Metrics and Analytics Are Changing Newsroom Practice," JSource, February 20, 2019, https://j-source.ca/article/heres-how-metrics-and-analytics-are-changing-newsroom-practice/.

34 For more on this problem, see Twenge, *iGen*, 66.

35 Thoreau, *Reform Papers*, 172.

36 Thoreau, *Walden*, 105; idem., *Walden and Civil Disobedience* (New York: Penguin Classics, 1983), 150.

37 Thoreau, *Walden*, 100–101; idem., *Walden and Civil Disobedience*, 146.

38 Thoreau, *Walden*, 107; idem., *Walden, and Civil Disobedience*, 153.

39 Holmes, "Bread and the Newspaper," 347.

40 Thoreau, *Reform Papers*, 172.

41 Multigraph Collective, *Interacting with Print*, 251.

42 For one exploration of this culture, see Caleb Smith's monograph, *Thoreau's Axe*. I find his readings of various nineteenth-century texts on attention provocative, though—for reasons my own argument makes clear—only partially satisfying.

43 Thoreau, *Walden*, 75–76. For a history of American philanthropy—and a critique of the turn it took in the nineteenth century—see Jeremy Beer, *The Philanthropic Revolution: An Alternative History of American Charity* (Philadelphia: University of Pennsylvania Press, 2015).

44 Charles Dickens, *Bleak House* (Oxford: Oxford University Press, 1998), 44ff. Adam Gurri borrows Dickens' metaphor for his analysis of "telescopic morality,"

in Gurri, "Free Yourself from the Telescopic Morality Machine," *Front Porch Republic* (blog), December 9, 2014, https://www.frontporchrepublic.com/2014/12/free-telescopic-morality-machine/.
45   Thoreau, *Walden*, 52.
46   Postman, *Amusing Ourselves to Death*, 67–68.
47   Thoreau, *Reform Papers*, 177.
48   Thoreau, *Walden*, 97.
49   Thoreau, *Reform Papers*, 173.

8 Commodities

1   Emily Dickinson, *The Poems of Emily Dickinson: Variorum Edition*, ed. R. W. Franklin (Cambridge, Mass.: Harvard University Press, 1998), 303. All Dickinson poems in this chapter will be cited by the number assigned by Franklin (e.g., FP 303).
2   Dickinson, FP 788.
3   Emily Dickinson, *The Letters of Emily Dickinson*, ed. Thomas H. Johnson and Theodora Ward (Cambridge, Mass.: Belknap Press, 1965), 404–5.
4   Thomas Herbert Johnson, *Emily Dickinson: An Interpretive Biography* (Cambridge, Mass.: Belknap Press, 1955), 112.
5   Ivan Illich and David Cayley, *The Rivers North of the Future: The Testament of Ivan Illich as Told to David Cayley* (Toronto: House of Anansi Press, 2005), 210–11.
6   Justin E. H. Smith, "It's All Over," *Point Magazine*, January 3, 2019, https://thepointmag.com/examined-life/its-all-over/.
7   Smith, "It's All Over." For more on the way "self-knowledge through numbers" quantifies and commodifies the self, see the work of Deborah Lupton: Lupton, *The Quantified Self* (Cambridge: Polity, 2016), and idem., *Data Selves: More-than-Human Perspectives* (Cambridge: Polity, 2019).
8   Scott, *Seeing like a State*, 77. For another description of these dynamics in both government and corporations, see Jill Lepore, *If Then: How One Data Company Invented the Future* (London: John Murray, 2020).
9   Portions of the preceding paragraphs are adapted from my review essay of Chris Bail's book *Breaking the Social Media Prism: How to Make Our Platforms Less Polarizing* (Bilbro, "How Tech Reform Diminishes Us"). See this essay for a further exploration of these dynamics.
10   Paul Schor, *Counting Americans: How the US Census Classified the Nation* (New York: Oxford University Press, 2017), 10.
11   Kenneth Prewitt, *What Is "Your" Race? The Census and Our Flawed Efforts to Classify Americans* (Princeton: Princeton University Press, 2013).
12   Schor, *Counting Americans*, 43–51.
13   Gerald J. Baldasty, *The Commercialization of News in the Nineteenth Century* (Madison: University of Wisconsin Press, 1992), 4. Baldasty's book charts this multifaceted transition, and my account throughout this section is indebted to his analysis.
14   Baldasty, *Commercialization of News*, 9.
15   Baldasty, *Commercialization of News*, 79.
16   Baldasty, *Commercialization of News*, 63.
17   Baldasty, *Commercialization of News*, 66–69.
18   Dickinson, FP 272.
19   Thomas, "What News Must Think When Pondering," 64–67.
20   Thomas, "What News Must Think When Pondering," 65.
21   Dickinson, FP 1091.

22 For a wonderful exposition of her poetry in regard to her "nimble" belief, see Roger Lundin's study *Emily Dickinson and the Art of Belief* (Grand Rapids: Eerdmans, 1998).

23 Dickinson, FP 466.

24 Marissa Grunes, "Open Interiority: Emily Dickinson, Augustine, and the Spatial Self," *Women's Studies* 47, no. 3 (2018): 353.

25 Dickinson, FP 407.

26 Dickinson, FP 1211.

27 Robert Carroll and Stephen Prickett, eds., *The Bible: Authorized King James Version* (New York: Oxford University Press, 2008); Ps 46:10.

28 For a glimpse of such convocation, see my account of the "convocated self" in Wendell Berry's fiction: *Virtues of Renewal: Wendell Berry's Sustainable Forms* (Lexington: University Press of Kentucky, 2019), 135–55.

29 Dickinson, FP 1002.

30 Dickinson, FP 319.

31 Dickinson, *Letters of Emily Dickinson*, 411.

32 James McIntosh, "Dickinson's Kinetic Religious Imagination," *Religion and Literature* 46, no. 1 (2014): 144.

33 Certeau, *Practice of Everyday Life*, 18.

34 Thoreau, *Walden*, 19.

35 Smith, "It's All Over."

36 Buber, *I and Thou*.

37 Dickinson, *Letters of Emily Dickinson*, 680.

38 Christopher N. Phillips, *The Hymnal: A Reading History* (Baltimore: Johns Hopkins University Press, 2018), 201.

39 Much has been written on Dickinson's use of the hymn tradition. In addition to Phillips, Victoria N. Morgan explores these connections at length, noting that "traditionally, the hymn is used to give voice to the imagined or real congregation alongside that of the hymn writer," so they are at once communal and deeply personal (*Emily Dickinson and Hymn Culture: Tradition and Experience* [Abingdon: Routledge, 2016], 4–5).

40 Dickinson, FP 454. See also Phillips' discussion of this poem in *Hymnal*, 202–4.

41 Dickinson, *Letters of Emily Dickinson*, 385.

42 Dickinson, FP 512.

43 Dickinson, FP 569.

44 Richard Benson Sewall, *The Life of Emily Dickinson* (Cambridge, Mass.: Harvard University Press, 1994), 678–94; Jamie Fuller, "An Emily Dickinson Reading List," *Lapham's Quarterly*, August 13, 2018, https://www.laphamsquarterly.org/roundtable/emily-dickinson-reading-list; Michael West, "Emily Dickinson's Ambrosian Nights with Christopher North," *Harvard Library Bulletin* 5, no. 1 (1994): 67–71.

45 Dickinson, FP 640.

46 Dickinson, FP 519.

9 Slaves

1 See also, for instance, the ways in which Phyllis Wheatley was conscripted into debates over the intelligence of African people. Jeffrey Bilbro, "Who Are Lost and How They're Found: Redemption and Theodicy in Wheatley, Newton, and Cowper," *Early American Literature* 47, no. 3 (2012): 582–83.

2 David W. Blight, *Frederick Douglass: Prophet of Freedom* (New York: Simon and Schuster, 2020).

3 Frederick Douglass, *Frederick Douglass: Autobiographies*, ed. Henry Louis Gates (New York: Library of America, 1994), 366.
4 Maurice O. Wallace and Shawn Michelle Smith, "Framing the Black Solder: Image, Uplift, and the Duplicity of Pictures," in *Pictures and Progress: Early Photography and the Making of African American Identity* (Durham, N.C.: Duke University Press, 2012), 253.
5 Douglass, *Frederick Douglass*, 366. For more on these dynamics, see Blight, *Frederick Douglass*, 145–50.
6 Douglass, *Frederick Douglass*, 367.
7 Douglass, *Frederick Douglass*, 367.
8 Martin Luther Jr. King, "Where Do We Go from Here?" speech given in Atlanta, Georgia, August 16, 1967, available via Stanford University, Martin Luther King, Jr., Research and Education Institute, https://kinginstitute.stanford.edu/where-do-we-go-here.
9 John Stauffer et al., *Picturing Frederick Douglass: An Illustrated Biography of the Nineteenth Century's Most Photographed American* (New York: Liveright, 2015), lx; Zoe Trodd, "A Renaissance-Self: Frederick Douglass and the Art of Remaking," in *The Cambridge Companion to the Literature of the American Renaissance*, ed. Christopher N. Phillips (Cambridge: Cambridge University Press, 2018), 192.
10 Stauffer et al., *Picturing Frederick Douglass*, 127.
11 Stauffer et al., *Picturing Frederick Douglass*, 129.
12 Stauffer et al., *Picturing Frederick Douglass*, xiii.
13 Trodd, "Renaissance-Self," 192.
14 Eunsun Cho, "The Social Credit System: Not Just Another Chinese Idiosyncrasy," *Journal of Public and International Affairs*, May 1, 2020, https://jpia.princeton.edu/news/social-credit-system-not-just-another-chinese-idiosyncrasy.
15 Nicole Kobie, "The Complicated Truth about China's Social Credit System," *Wired UK*, July 6, 2019, https://www.wired.co.uk/article/china-social-credit-system-explained.
16 Danielle L. Couch, Priscilla Robinson, and Paul A. Komesaroff, "COVID-19—Extending Surveillance and the Panopticon," *Journal of Bioethical Inquiry* 17, no. 4 (2020): 809–14; Garance Burke et al., "Police Seize on COVID-19 Tech to Expand Global Surveillance," AP News, December 20, 2022, https://apnews.com/article/technology-police-government-surveillance-covid-19-3f3f348d176bc7152a8cb2dbab2e4cc4.
17 Justin E. H. Smith, "Permanent Pandemic: Will COVID Controls Keep Controlling Us?" *Harper's Magazine*, May 11, 2022, https://harpers.org/archive/2022/06/permanent-pandemic-will-covid-controls-keep-controlling-us/.
18 Zuboff, *Age of Surveillance Capitalism*, 8.
19 James C. Scott, *Against the Grain: A Deep History of the Earliest States* (New Haven: Yale University Press, 2017), vi.
20 Olaudah Equiano and Vincent Carretta, *The Interesting Narrative and Other Writings: Revised Edition* (New York: Penguin Classics, 2003); Helen Keller, *The Story of My Life* (Garden City, N.Y.: Doubleday, 1954); Lamin Sanneh, *Summoned from the Margin: Homecoming of an African* (Grand Rapids: Eerdmans, 2012); Malala Yousafzai and Christina Lamb, *I Am Malala: The Girl Who Stood Up for Education and Was Shot by the Taliban* (New York: Back Bay Books, 2015).
21 Scott, *Against the Grain*, 141.
22 Scott, *Against the Grain*, 148–49.
23 Scott, *Against the Grain*, 142.
24 Scott, *Against the Grain*, 30.

25 On these dynamics, see also Gary Snyder's account of how writing contributed to transforming "a free, untaxed, self-sustaining people . . . into a serf or slave populace, whose hard-earned surplus is taken by force to support a large class of non-producers" (Snyder, *The Great Clod: Notes and Memoirs on Nature and History in East Asia* [Berkeley, Calif.: Counterpoint, 2016], 26–27). Wendell Berry discusses these dynamics and their implications for slavery in the American context in *The Need to Be Whole: Patriotism and the History of Prejudice* (Cincinnati: Shoemaker, 2022), 365–67.

26 Caitlin Rosenthal, *Accounting for Slavery: Masters and Management* (Cambridge, Mass.: Harvard University Press, 2019).

27 Anderson, *Imagined Communities*, 56.

28 Willie James Jennings, *The Christian Imagination: Theology and the Origins of Race* (New Haven: Yale University Press, 2010), 59, 64.

29 Loughran, *Republic in Print*, 368–69.

30 Loughran, *Republic in Print*, 378.

31 Loughran, *Republic in Print*, 410.

32 McClay, *Masterless*, 54.

33 Loughran, *Republic in Print*, 368–69.

34 Loughran, *Republic in Print*, 433.

35 Loughran, *Republic in Print*, 442–43.

36 As Eric Foner points out, during the antebellum years African Americans were discriminated against more in the socially fluid western states than in regions such as the Northeast where communal identities had been better established: "Paradoxically, the very social mobility for which the West has been celebrated may have tended to exaggerate racial prejudice" (*Free Soil, Free Labor, Free Men*), 262. Willie Jennings provides the fullest historical and theological account of how the loss of geographic identity facilitates the exploitation of racial minorities in *Christian Imagination*. For a twenty-first-century meditation on the benefits of such geographic identity for African Americans—and others—see bell hooks, *Belonging: A Culture of Place* (New York: Routledge, 2008). Wendell Berry also traces these dynamics at length In *Need to Be Whole*.

37 Jennings, *Christian Imagination*, 290.

38 Equiano and Carretta, *Interesting Narrative and Other Writings*, 159.

39 Equiano and Carretta, *Interesting Narrative and Other Writings*, 266.

40 Vincent Carretta, *Equiano, the African: Biography of a Self-Made Man* (Athens: University of Georgia Press, 2005), 207.

41 Equiano and Carretta, *Interesting Narrative and Other Writings*, 178.

42 Carretta, *Equiano, the African*, 212.

43 Carretta, *Equiano, the African*, 366. For more on Equiano's marketing savvy, see Willie Jennings, *Christian Imagination*, 189.

44 Carretta, *Equiano, the African*, 350–54.

45 Douglass, *Frederick Douglass*, 37.

46 Douglass, *Frederick Douglass*, 42.

47 Several scholars emphasize the alienating effects of literacy and Douglass' efforts to wield "white" language without becoming merely its puppet. For a representative set of arguments regarding this tension, see Robert B. Stepto, "Narration, Authentication, and Authorial Control in Frederick Douglass' Narrative of 1845," in *Afro-American Literature: The Reconstruction of Instruction*, ed. Dexter Fisher and Robert B. Stepto (New York: Modern Language Association of America, 1979), 178–91; Thad Ziolkowski, "Antitheses: The Dialectic of Violence and Literacy in Frederick Douglass's *Narrative* of 1845," in *Critical Essays on Frederick Douglass*, ed. William L. Andrews (Boston: G. K. Hall, 1991), 148–65; Houston A. Baker Jr., *The Journey Back: Issues in Black*

Literature and Criticism (Chicago: University of Chicago Press, 1984), 34–46. Daniel Royer's analysis shows some of the ways that Douglass uses his literacy to foster "intersubjective community," in "The Process of Literacy as Communal Involvement in the Narratives of Frederick Douglass," *African American Review* 28, no. 3 (1994): 363–74.

48 Douglass, *Frederick Douglass*, 53.
49 Douglass, *Frederick Douglass*, 70–71.
50 Royer, "Process of Literacy as Communal Involvement," 373.
51 Douglass, *Frederick Douglass*, 67.
52 Douglass, *Frederick Douglass*, 78.
53 Douglass, *Frederick Douglass*, 89.
54 Douglass, *Frederick Douglass*, 95.
55 Blight, *Frederick Douglass*, 93.
56 Douglass, *Frederick Douglass*, 96.
57 Blight, *Frederick Douglass*, 94. For more on the background of *The Columbian Orator*, see Blight, *Frederick Douglass*, 43–44.
58 Blight, *Frederick Douglass*, 183–88, 217–27.
59 Douglass, *Frederick Douglass*, 708.
60 Blight, *Frederick Douglass*, 236, 284–86.
61 Stauffer et al., *Picturing Frederick Douglass*, 140.
62 "Magnetic Telegraph."
63 Matt Richtel, "A Silicon Valley School That Doesn't Compute," *New York Times*, October 22, 2011, https://www.nytimes.com/2011/10/23/technology/at-waldorf -school-in-silicon-valley-technology-can-wait.html; Matthew Jenkin, "Tablets out, Imagination in: The Schools That Shun Technology," *Guardian*, December 2, 2015, https://www.theguardian.com/teacher-network/2015/dec/02/schools -that-ban-tablets-traditional-education-silicon-valley-london.

10 Walkers

1 Illich, *Tools for Conviviality*, xii–xiii.
2 Albert Borgmann, *Technology and the Character of Contemporary Life: A Philosophical Inquiry* (Chicago: University of Chicago Press, 1987). Andy Crouch applies and develops Borgmann's central concepts in his book on living as persons and finding ways to use digital technologies to deepen relationships rather than replace them. See Crouch, *The Life We're Looking For: Reclaiming Relationship in a Technological World* (New York: Convergent Books, 2022). See also Ursula Franklin's account of the contrast between prescriptive technologies and holistic ones, in *The Real World of Technology* (Toronto: House of Anansi, 1999), 10–11. In summarizing the insights of John Ruskin, Illich, and Franklin, Alan Jacobs concludes that "there are technologies that liberate human creativity, that enable human power, and, by contrast, technologies that enslave us, that force our very being into conformity with their codes and structures" ("John Ruskin: Fit the Third and Last," *New Atlantis* [blog], May 28, 2018, https://www .thenewatlantis.com/text-patterns/john-ruskin-fit-third-and-last). By pointing out the similarities among these different authors, however, I do not mean to imply their varying terms and conclusions are without significant differences; Borgmann, for instance, critiques Illich's notion of conviviality (in *Technology and the Character of Contemporary Life*, 167–68), and my use of both emphasizes some aspects of their arguments while downplaying the features of their analysis that I find less helpful.
3 Illich, *Tools for Conviviality*, 73.

4   My use of "making do" comes from Michel de Certeau, *Practice of Everyday Life*, 18. For an expanded discussion of this definition of hope, see my chapter in *Virtues of Renewal* on Wendell Berry's definition of this virtue (81–99). His account more or less parallels that of Christopher Lasch, *The True and Only Heaven: Progress and Its Critics* (New York: Norton, 1991), 14, 80–81. For a helpful survey of different modes of technological determinism, see L. M. Sacasas' description of the "Borg Complex" in Sacasas, "Borg Complex: A Primer," *L.M. Sacasas* (blog), March 1, 2013, https://thefrailestthing.com/2013/03/01/borg-complex-a-primer/.

5   Postman, *Amusing Ourselves to Death*, 10, 18. Alan Jacobs makes the same claim in a related context in *How to Think*, 28–30.

6   Lakoff and Johnson, *Metaphors We Live By*, 239.

7   Certeau, *Practice of Everyday Life*, 18. As Certeau argues, such make do does not depend on large-scale, systemic changes: "The actual order of things is precisely what 'popular' tactics turn to their own ends, without any illusion that it will change any time soon. Though elsewhere it is exploited by a dominant power or simply denied by an ideological discourse, here order is *tricked* by an art" (26).

8   Henry David Thoreau, *Excursions*, ed. Joseph J. Moldenhauer, Writings of Henry D. Thoreau (Princeton: Princeton University Press, 2007), 185.

9   Thoreau, *Excursions*, 189.

10 Henry David Thoreau, entry for August 19, 1851, *Journal*, ed. Leonard N. Neufeldt and Nancy Craig Simmons, Writings of Henry D. Thoreau (Princeton: Princeton University Press, 1981), 378–79.

11 Thoreau, *Excursions*, 202.

12 Thoreau, *Excursions*, 203.

13 Thoreau, *Excursions*, 214.

14 Thoreau, *Excursions*, 185.

15 My understanding of the philosophical and theological implications of musical harmony is indebted to the work of Jeremy S. Begbie. See, for example, his essay "Room of One's Own? Music, Space, and Freedom," in *A Peculiar Orthodoxy: Reflections on Theology and the Arts* (Grand Rapids: Baker Academic, 2018), 145–80. For more on the implications of this auditory metaphor see Ong, *Presence of the Word* and Hartmut Rosa, *Resonance: A Sociology of Our Relationship to the World*, trans. James Wagner (Cambridge: Polity, 2021).

16 Thoreau, *Excursions*, 215.

17 Thoreau, *Walden*, 1971, 53. For an elaboration of such accounting, see Ivan Illich's short book on the inequalities and inefficiencies of more rapid, energy-intensive forms of transportation, *Energy and Equity*, Ideas in Progress (New York: Harper and Row, 1974).

18 The exact origin of the phrase is disputed: some attribute it to Augustine, and others say it comes from Diogenes' response to an argument about whether motion is possible. See Paul Theroux, *The Tao of Travel: Enlightenments from Lives on the Road* (Boston: Houghton Mifflin Harcourt, 2011), 131; Rebecca Solnit, *Wanderlust: A History of Walking* (New York: Penguin, 2001), 27. *OED Online*, s.v. "Solvitur Ambulando, Phr.," accessed February 16, 2023, https://www.oed.com/view/Entry/184399. The phrase has now taken on a broader meaning to refer to other questions for which experience or practice provides the best response.

19 John Muir, *A Thousand-Mile Walk to the Gulf* (Boston: Houghton Mifflin, 1916); Wendell Berry, *This Day: Collected and New Sabbath Poems 1979–2012* (Berkeley, Calif.: Counterpoint, 2013), xxi; Chris Arnade, *Dignity: Seeking Respect in Back Row America* (New York: Penguin, 2019); and Garnette Cadogan,

"Walking while Black," *Literary Hub* (blog), July 8, 2016, https://lithub.com/walking-while-black/.

20 Solnit, *Wanderlust*, 29. For more examples of those who proclaim the virtues of walking, see Arianna Huffington, "Hemingway, Thoreau, Jefferson and the Virtues of a Good Long Walk," *HuffPost*, August 29, 2013, https://www.huffpost.com/entry/hemingway-thoreau-jeffers_b_3837002, and Gracy Olmstead, "The Art of the Stroll," *American Conservative*, August 14, 2018, https://www.theamericanconservative.com/articles/the-art-of-the-stroll/. I develop some of these benefits more fully elsewhere. See Bilbro, *Reading the Times*, 165–69.

21 Thoreau, *Reform Papers*, 74.

22 Thoreau, *Walden*, 100–101.

23 Thoreau, *Walden*, 105.

24 George Adolf Kubler, *A Short History of Stereotyping* (Brooklyn, N.Y.: Brooklyn Eagle Commercial Printing Department, 1927), 14–41; Harris B. Hatch and A. A. Stewart, *Electrotyping and Stereotyping, a Primer of Information about the Processes of Electrotyping and Stereotyping*, Typographic Technical Series for Apprentices, part 1, no. 15 (Chicago: Committee on Education, United Typothetae of America, 1918), 46–48.

25 Michael Winship, "Publishing *The Scarlet Letter* in the Nineteenth-Century United States," in *The Scarlet Letter: Complete Text with Introduction, Historical Contexts, Critical Essays*, by Nathaniel Hawthorne, ed. Rita Gollin (Boston: Houghton Mifflin, 2002), 70–72.

26 *OED Online*, s.v. "Stereotype, n. and Adj.," accessed March 10, 2023, https://www.oed.com/view/Entry/189956. Thoreau also uses this technology as a metaphor for ideas or emotions of permanent and lasting value. See Henry David Thoreau, *A Week on the Concord and Merrimack Rivers*, ed. Carl Hovde (Princeton: Princeton University Press, 1980), 92, 274, 343.

27 Thoreau, *Walden*, 8.

28 Thoreau, *Walden*, 318.

29 Thoreau, *Walden*, 324.

30 Thoreau, *Walden*, 324–25.

31 For a parallel account of Thoreau's language, see Stanley Cavell's description of doubling in *Walden* in *The Senses of Walden* (Chicago: University of Chicago Press, 1992).

32 Thoreau, *Walden*, 64–65.

33 William Blake et al., *The Complete Poetry and Prose of William Blake*, rev. ed. (Garden City, N.Y: Anchor, 1982), 34.

34 James Shanley's research on *Walden*'s manuscripts demonstrates Thoreau's careful construction of its organization: "As he took over his raw material, Thoreau broke it up, changed it in detail, developed it, and finally ordered it so that he might offer his hearers and readers, not the immediate, random, and intermittent notes of a journal, but a reflected-on and consciously shaped re-creation of his experience." See James Lyndon Shanley and Henry David Thoreau, *The Making of Walden: With the Text of the First Version* (Chicago: University of Chicago Press, 1957), 23. Even so, many have found the book shapeless, perhaps most famously James Russell Lowell: *The Writings of James Russell Lowell*, vol. 1 (Boston: Houghton, Mifflin, 1890), 370. F. O. Matthiessen, A. E. Elmore, and Shanley—among others—all propose various organizing principles, and my own view most closely follows Elmore, who points out the book does not really follow a seasonal pattern and that many chapters form contrasting pairs. F. O. Matthiessen, *American Renaissance: Art and Expression in the Age of Emerson and Whitman* (New York: Oxford University Press, 1968), 166–71; Shanley and

Thoreau, *Making of Walden*, 74–91; A. E. Elmore, "Symmetry out of Season: The Form of 'Walden,'" *South Atlantic Bulletin* 37, no. 4 (1972): 19–23,; and Lawrence Buell, *The Environmental Imagination: Thoreau, Nature Writing, and the Formation of American Culture* (Cambridge, Mass.: Harvard University Press, 1995), 118–26. As I see it, even the seasonal aspect of the book contributes to its study of complementary contrasts; the warmth and growth of summer stand against the cold solitude of winter; the withdrawal and decay of fall stand against the hope and new life of spring.

35   Thoreau, *Walden*, 140.

36   Thoreau, *Walden*, 9.

37   Shanley sees this "comic interlude" as a way of "descen[ding] from the level of 'Higher Laws.'" Shanley and Thoreau, *Making of Walden*, 80; Thoreau, *Walden*, 223–25.

38   Thoreau, *Walden*, 80.

39   Thoreau, *Walden*, 98. Thoreau's image here borrows from Heb 4:12, where the biblical author imagines Jesus, who in John 14:6 calls himself the truth, as a sword who divides soul and spirit, joints and marrow (see thesis 3).

40   Thoreau, *Walden*, 272.

41   The auditory metaphor here is vital. As Walter Ong demonstrates, the dominance of the visual sense engendered by writing and print contributes to a more isolated and alienated self-understanding: "Sight isolates, sound incorporates. Whereas sight situates the observer outside what he views, at a distance, sound pours into the hearer. . . . The auditory ideal . . . is harmony, a putting together" (Ong, *Orality and Literacy*, 71). Ong also expounds upon the implications of these different primary senses in *The Presence of the Word*, where he notes that "sound reciprocates" in ways the visual cannot (122). Further, the auditory metaphor does not collapse difference into a compromise or consonance—harmony and resonance *sustain* difference. See Rosa, *Resonance*, 165, 447.

42   Thoreau, *Walden*, 122.

43   Thoreau, *Walden*, 92.

44   Thoreau, *Walden*, 306–9.

45   The classic reading of this scene and its relationship to Thoreau's earlier discussion of the railroad is Leo Marx's *The Machine in the Garden: Technology and the Pastoral Ideal in America* (New York: Oxford University Press, 1964), 242–65. I discuss the significance of this scene at greater length as elsewhere as well, Bilbro, *Loving God's Wildness*, 45–47. While the details vary, most critics concur that Thoreau concludes his experiment at Walden should be judged a success. Buell, *Environmental Imagination*, 245–49; Marx, *Machine*, 243; Sargent Bush, "The End and Means in Walden: Thoreau's Use of the Catechism," *ESQ: A Journal of the American Renaissance* 31, no. 1 (1985): 8; Gordon V. Boudreau, *The Roots of Walden and the Tree of Life* (Nashville: Vanderbilt University Press, 1990), 3.

46   Rosa can illuminate Thoreau's work despite his passing critique of Thoreau for contributing "to the evolution of a cultural attitude in which the experience of nature has become a refuge for a purely extra-ordinary and purely contemplative relationship to the world" (*Resonance*, 279). Rosa's misreading of *Walden* does not substantively detract from his insightful exploration of the possibilities of restoring resonant relationships with others, the world, and God. Rosa defines resonance in terms of "the quality of one's *relationship to the world*, i.e. the ways in which one experiences and positions oneself with respect to the world" (*Resonance*, 3). See also Hartmut Rosa, *The Uncontrollability of the World*, trans. James Wagner (Cambridge: Polity, 2020).

47 Carl R. Trueman, "A Critical Theorist Worth Reading," *First Things*, September 7, 2021, https://www.firstthings.com/web-exclusives/2021/09/a-critical-theorist-worth-reading.
48 Thoreau, *Walden*, 282.
49 Rosa argues this capacity to act meaningfully, which he terms "self-efficacy," comes from a resonant relationship with reality (*Resonance*, 158–64).
50 Thoreau, *Walden*, 290.
51 Ong, *Presence of the Word*, 150. As Ong goes on to claim, "Truth, permanent though it is, is formally accessible to man primarily in terms of an intellectual event, not in terms of a diagram" (159). See also the way that Rosa situates his work within a broader set of thinkers pursuing the "notion that not subjects and objects, but dynamic relationships and referentialities might form the basic material of reality" (*Resonance*, 36).

11 Conversationalists

1 Thoreau, *Walden*, 241.
2 Charles Capper, *Margaret Fuller: An American Romantic Life*, vol. 1, *The Private Years* (New York: Oxford University Press, 1994), 338.
3 As quoted in Joel Myerson, ed., *Critical Essays on Margaret Fuller*, Critical Essays on American Literature (Boston: G. K. Hall, 1980), 5.
4 Portions of the readings in this chapter of Fuller's *Summer on the Lakes, in 1843* are adapted from my essay on Fuller and Milton, see Bilbro, "Learning to Woo Meaning."
5 Margaret Fuller, *Summer on the Lakes, in 1843* (Urbana: University of Illinois Press, 1990), 101.
6 Fuller, *Summer*, 78.
7 Charles Capper, *Margaret Fuller: An American Romantic Life*, vol. 2, *The Public Years* (New York: Oxford University Press, 2010), 135–36.
8 Fuller, *Summer*, 78–79.
9 Fuller, *Summer*, 80–82.
10 Josef Pieper, *Abuse of Language, Abuse of Power* (San Francisco: Ignatius Press, 1992), 36.
11 Ray, *Lyceum and Public Culture*; Tom F. Wright, *The Cosmopolitan Lyceum: Lecture Culture and the Globe in Nineteenth-Century America* (Amherst: University of Massachusetts Press, 2013).
12 Nathan Beacom, "Lyceums: Places to Think with Neighbors," in *The Liberating Arts: Why We Need Liberal Arts Education*, ed. Jeffrey Bilbro, Jessica Hooten Wilson, and David Henreckson (Walden, N.Y.: Plough, 2023), 183.
13 Capper, *Margaret Fuller*, vol. 1, 294.
14 Fuller's conversations can be seen as akin to the Junto that Ben Franklin formed in Philadelphia. See Benjamin Franklin, *The Autobiography of Benjamin Franklin*, ed. Leonard W. Labaree et al. (New Haven: Yale University Press, 1964), 116–19.
15 L. D. Burnett has suggested that Fuller's penchant for conversation parallels the contemporary podcasting form (Burnett, "Margaret Fuller's 'Conversations' for a Digital Age?" Society for U.S. Intellectual History, June 17, 2017, https://s-usih.org/2017/06/margaret-fullers-conversations-for-a-digital-age/). This is a perceptive comparison, but a podcast listener has less opportunity to participate in the discussion than does a member of a book club or a Catherine Project group.

16 Zena Hitz, "The Catherine Project," in Bilbro, Wilson, and Henreckson, *Liberating Arts*, 56. For another endeavor with a related but different approach, see the debates that Braver Angels organizes: Leah Libresco Sargeant, "Students Brave the Heat," *Plough*, August 22, 2023, https://www.plough.com/en/topics/life/relationships/students-brave-the-heat.

17 Capper, *Margaret Fuller*, vol. 2, 17.

18 Dudek, *Literature and the Press*, 137.

19 Capper, *Margaret Fuller*, vol. 2, 16–18.

20 Peter Mommsen, "Small Magazines as Educational Communities," in Bilbro, Wilson, and Henreckson, *Liberating Arts*, 195. For other accounts of the contributions that small magazines can make to the public conversation, see Bilbro, *Reading the Times*, 170–74; Anne Snyder, "Respecting Reality," in Bilbro, Wilson, and Henreckson, *Liberating Arts*, 61–63; and David Heddendorf, "Blowing Up the Bert: The Outside Story," *Front Porch Republic* (blog), August 20, 2018, https://www.frontporchrepublic.com/2018/08/blowing-up-the-bert-the-outside-story/.

21 Rosa, *Uncontrollability of the World*, 31.

22 Cass R. Sunstein, "The Law of Group Polarization" (working paper, John M. Olin Law and Economic Working Paper, no. 91, University of Chicago Law School, Chicago, December 1999), 3–4.

23 David French, *Divided We Fall: America's Secession Threat and How to Restore Our Nation* (New York: St. Martin's, 2020), 64–65.

24 Vaidhyanathan, *Antisocial Media*, 85. The notion that social media creates "filter bubbles" or "echo chambers" is somewhat overplayed. In fact, people who get their news online tend to be more aware of competing perspectives and positions than others. However, the agonistic and simplistic form such online discourse tends to take precludes careful listening and thoughtful response. For more on these dynamics, see Bilbro, *Reading the Times*, 138–42.

25 Ivan Illich, *Celebration of Awareness: A Call for Institutional Revolution* (New York: Doubleday, 1970), 134.

26 Capper, *Margaret Fuller*, vol. 1, 290–306.

27 Capper, *Margaret Fuller*, vol. 1, 297–306.

28 Berry, *Need to Be Whole*, 24. I expound on Berry's views regarding the conditions for genuine conversation in my review of this book, in "Practicing Authentic Conversation," *Front Porch Republic* (blog), October 4, 2022, https://www.frontporchrepublic.com/2022/10/practicing-authentic-conversation/.

29 Capper, *Margaret Fuller*, vol. 2, 49–55.

30 R. I. M. Dunbar, *Grooming, Gossip, and the Evolution of Language* (Cambridge, Mass.: Harvard University Press, 1998), 76–77.

31 Margaret Fuller, *The Letters of Margaret Fuller: 1839–1841*, vol. 2 (Ithaca: Cornell University Press, 2018), 104. See also Capper, *Margaret Fuller*, vol. 1, 296.

32 Multigraph Collective, *Interacting with Print*, 85–88.

33 Blake Bronson-Bartlett, "Writing with Pencils in the Antebellum United States: Language, Instrument, Gesture," *American Literature* 92, no. 2 (2020): 203; Capper, *Margaret Fuller*, vol. 1, 296.

34 James Freeman Clarke, *James Freeman Clarke: Autobiography, Diary and Correspondence* (Boston: Houghton, Mifflin, 1891), 143–44.

35 Nancy Craig Simmons, "Margaret Fuller's Boston Conversations: The 1839–1840 Series," *Studies in the American Renaissance* (1994): 200.

36 Clarke, *James Freeman Clarke*, 143. See also Capper, *Margaret Fuller*, vol. 1, 299.

37 Simmons, "Margaret Fuller's Boston Conversations," 196.

38 Capper, *Margaret Fuller*, vol. 1, 335.

39 Capper, *Margaret Fuller*, vol. 1, 336–37.

40 Thoreau, *Walden*, 104, 105.

41 *Dial* (n.p.: Weeks, Jordan, 1841), 10; Capper, *Margaret Fuller*, vol. 2, 6–8.

42 Capper, *Margaret Fuller*, vol. 2, 4.

43 Capper, *Margaret Fuller*, vol. 1, 298.

44 Perry Miller and Margaret Fuller, *Margaret Fuller, American Romantic: A Selection from Her Writings and Correspondence* (Ithaca: Cornell University Press, 1970), 116. Similarly, James Freeman Clarke calls it "a portfolio of sketches" (qtd. in Myerson, *Critical Essays*, 2). And Arthur Brown claims "*Summer on the Lakes* lacks systematic arrangement" in *Margaret Fuller*, Twayne's United States Authors Series, no. 48 (New York: Twayne, 1964), 125. Margaret Vanderhaar Allen concludes, "Fuller never solved the problem of form for herself and never found the best vehicle for her expression" (*The Achievement of Margaret Fuller* [University Park: Pennsylvania State University Press, 1979], 70). More perceptive is the assessment of William Stowe, who concludes that "rather than composing a polemic, she invites serious conversation" ("'Busy Leisure': Margaret Fuller, Nature, and Vacation Writing," *Interdisciplinary Studies in Literature and Environment* 9, no. 1 [2002]: 39). In a similar vein, Bell Gale Chevigny supports such a reading by identifying the primacy of dialogue and conversation for Fuller's epistemology: "As dialogue is the only reliable basis of thought for Fuller, so is it the privileged form of intellectual and social interaction" ("'Cheat Me [On] by No Illusion': Margaret Fuller's Cultural Critique and Its Legacies," in *Margaret Fuller's Cultural Critique*, ed. Fritz Fleischmann, Early American Literature and Culture through the American Renaissance, no. 3 [New York: Peter Lang, 2000], 32.)

45 Fuller, *Summer*, 3.

46 The poem is by James Clarke. In a letter to Emerson, Fuller explained that she wanted to include this poem and several letters to make her chapter "a kind of letter box." While critics cite this as evidence of its lack of formal coherence, Fuller goes on to claim "when I have once concocted any such little plan, I am in a fever till I get it arranged," implying that her "letter box" would follow a deliberate structure. Margaret Fuller, *The Letters of Margaret Fuller*, ed. Robert N. Hudspeth, 6 vols. (Ithaca: Cornell University Press, 1983), 159.

47 Fuller, *Summer*, 44–45.

48 Fuller, *Summer*, 46.

49 Fuller, *Summer*, 47. Clearly, this perception justifies white settlement at the expense of the Native Americans who, while they did not settle the land according to European standards, certainly used the land. In fact, their use of fire likely played a role in shaping the prairie, so the painter was ironically correct to note that it looked like the work of man's hand. William M. Denevan, "Foreword," in *Imperfect Balance: Landscape Transformations in the Precolumbian Americas*, ed. David Lewis Lentz, The Historical Ecology Series (New York: Columbia University Press, 2000), xvii–xx.

50 Fuller, *Summer*, 48–49.

51 Several scholars have pointed out the parallels between Mariana and Fuller, noting their similar experiences at boarding school. Megan Marshall, *Margaret Fuller: A New American Life* (Boston: Mariner Books, 2014), 30–33; John Matteson, *The Lives of Margaret Fuller: A Biography* (New York: W. W. Norton, 2013), 56; Meg McGavran Murray, *Margaret Fuller, Wandering Pilgrim* (Athens: University of Georgia Press, 2008), 52–53. Yet Charles Capper warns against interpreting this sketch too autobiographically, and because Fuller does

not present it here as autobiographical, I read the story for its function within her larger narrative. See Capper, *Margaret Fuller*, vol. 1, 81–82.

52   Fuller, *Summer*, 51–55.
53   Fuller, *Summer*, 57.
54   Fuller, *Summer*, 59.
55   Fuller, *Summer*, 61, 64.
56   Fuller, *Summer*, 64–65.

12 Friends

1   Nathaniel Hawthorne, *The Scarlet Letter*, Centenary Edition of the Works of Nathaniel Hawthorne, vol. 1 (Columbus: Ohio State University Press, 1963), 126.
2   Hawthorne later alludes to this part of the biblical account as well. Hawthorne, *Scarlet Letter*, 217.
3   2 Sam 11–12. For more on the significance of this biblical narrative and for an in-depth exposition of a Christian account of words in which the "final centrality of the Person . . . , in a world of imperfect speech and imperfect deeds, makes *metanoia* rather than *gnosis* the redemptive goal of poetry as a human instrument," see David Lyle Jeffrey, *People of the Book: Christian Identity and Literary Culture* (Grand Rapids: Eerdmans, 1996), 360, 378.
4   For more on how we might rightly befriend voices from the past, see Alan Jacobs, *Breaking Bread with the Dead: A Reader's Guide to a More Tranquil Mind* (New York: Penguin, 2020), and Jeffrey Bilbro, "The Liberating Potential of Knowing the Past," in Bilbro, Wilson, and Henreckson, *Liberating Arts*, 106–15.
5   P. G. Maxwell-Stuart, *The Chemical Choir: A History of Alchemy* (New York: Continuum, 2012).
6   Hawthorne, *Scarlet Letter*, 64.
7   Anne Applebaum, "The New Puritans," *Atlantic*, August 31, 2021, https://www.theatlantic.com/magazine/archive/2021/10/new-puritans-mob-justice-canceled/619818/.
8   Thoreau, *Walden*, 140.
9   Sherry Turkle, *Reclaiming Conversation: The Power of Talk in a Digital Age* (New York: Penguin, 2016), 9–11. See also Ray Oldenburg, *Great Good Place: Cafés, Coffee Shops, Bookstores, Bars, Hair Salons, and Other Hangouts at the Heart of a Community*, 3rd ed. (New York: Marlowe, 1999); and Patrick J. Deneen, "A Republic of Front Porches," *Front Porch Republic* (blog), March 3, 2009, https://www.frontporchrepublic.com/2009/03/front-porch-republic/.
10   In a review of *Breaking the Social Media Prism*, I provide a fuller account of some of the dynamics in digital culture that contribute to a reductive view of human persons (Bilbro, "How Tech Reform Diminishes Us"). For more analysis of how these contemporary dynamics shape political polarization, as individuals make public gestures to express individual identities rather than engage in the messy work of institution building, see Lilliana Mason, *Uncivil Agreement: How Politics Became Our Identity* (Chicago: University of Chicago Press, 2018), and Eitan Hersh, *Politics Is for Power: How to Move beyond Political Hobbyism, Take Action, and Make Real Change* (New York: Scribner, 2020).
11   There is a growing awareness of the value in friendly modes of public thinking and writing. This is a bit different from the kind of personal friendship that Hawthorne values, but it is certainly related. Rita Felski and Kathleen Fitzpatrick are perhaps the most prominent proponents of this mode of engagement: see Rita Felski, *The Limits of Critique* (Chicago: University of Chicago Press, 2015),

and Kathleen Fitzpatrick, *Generous Thinking: A Radical Approach to Saving the University* (Baltimore: Johns Hopkins University Press, 2021).

12 For a wise consideration of the risks and transformations entailed by friendship, see David Henreckson's essay "Venturing Our Selves," *Comment Magazine*, July 7, 2022, https://comment.org/venturing-our-selves/.

13 "How Political Opposites Became Best Friends | Robert George & Cornel West at WashU | April 2019," October 26, 2022, YouTube video, https://www.youtube.com/watch?v=jky-nZE30nI.

14 Collin Hansen, "What Happened to Historian Molly Worthen?" Gospelbound, accessed July 4, 2023, https://www.thegospelcoalition.org/podcasts/gospelbound/happened-molly-worthen/.

15 Dwane Brown, "How One Man Convinced 200 Ku Klux Klan Members to Give Up Their Robes," *NPR*, August 20, 2017, https://www.npr.org/2017/08/20/544861933/how-one-man-convinced-200-ku-klux-klan-members-to-give-up-their-robes.

16 hooks, *Belonging*.

17 Berry, *Need to Be Whole*, 38. In both this book and in earlier essays, particularly "Sex, Economy, Freedom, and Community," Berry argues that the public discourse around issues such as racism and sexual propriety has become dysfunctional precisely because the middle space of friendship and community has been eroded. See Berry, "Sex, Economy, Freedom, and Community," in *Sex, Economy, Freedom and Community: Eight Essays* (New York: Pantheon, 1993), 117–73.

18 Richard Wilbur, *New and Collected Poems* (San Diego: Mariner Books, 1989), 73.

19 The classic source on medieval biblical exegesis is Henri de Lubac, *Medieval Exegesis: The Four Senses of Scripture* (Grand Rapids: Eerdmans, 1998). In addition to Walter Ong's analysis cited below, see Peter Harrison for one narration of the shift from interpretive methods that sought polyphonic meanings to those in search of univocal significance., in *The Bible, Protestantism, and the Rise of Natural Science* (Cambridge: Cambridge University Press, 2001), 30–31. For more on Puritan allegory, see Thomas H. Luxon, *Literal Figures: Puritan Allegory and the Reformation Crisis in Representation* (Chicago: University of Chicago Press, 1995).

20 Ong, *Presence of the Word*, 46.

21 Ong, *Presence of the Word*, 138.

22 Patricia Crain, *The Story of A: The Alphabetization of America from "The New England Primer" to "The Scarlet Letter"* (Stanford, Calif.: Stanford University Press, 2000), 33.

23 Crain, *Story of A*, 91.

24 Hawthorne, *Scarlet Letter*, 106.

25 Hawthorne, *Scarlet Letter*, 110. This scene apparently draws on historical precedent. David Hall notes, "From time to time the Massachusetts government would order house-to-house inspections to see if every family owned a Bible; and there were similar inspections of children's knowledge of the catechism" ("Uses of Literacy in New England," 26).

26 Ong, *Presence of the Word*, 300.

27 Hawthorne, *Scarlet Letter*, 67.

28 Hawthorne, *Scarlet Letter*, 130.

29 Hawthorne, *Scarlet Letter*, 192.

30 Hawthorne, *Scarlet Letter*, 132, 144, 215.

31 Hawthorne, *Scarlet Letter*, 190. Many critics have noted the symbolism of the woods or forests in Hawthorne's stories. They should not be simply identified with evil, but they are places where witches gather and the moral clarity of society becomes dim and questionable. Marina Boonyaprasop, *Hawthorne's Wilderness: Nature and Puritanism in Hawthorne's "The Scarlet Letter" and "Young Goodman Brown"* (Hamburg: Anchor Academic Publishing, 2013); Steven Petersheim, *Rethinking Nathaniel Hawthorne and Nature: Pastoral Experiments and Environmentality* (Lanham, Md.: Lexington Books, 2020), 45–82.

32 Hawthorne, *Scarlet Letter*, 181.
33 Hawthorne, *Scarlet Letter*, 198.
34 Mark Twain, *Adventures of Huckleberry Finn*, ed. Victor Fischer and Lin Salamo (Berkeley: University of California Press, 2003), 362.
35 Hawthorne, *Scarlet Letter*, 199, 219, 214.
36 Hawthorne, *Scarlet Letter*, 254.
37 Hawthorne, *Scarlet Letter*, 81.
38 Hawthorne, *Scarlet Letter*, 83.
39 Hawthorne, *Scarlet Letter*, 32.
40 Hawthorne, *Scarlet Letter*, 158–59.
41 Hawthorne, *Scarlet Letter*, 169.
42 Hawthorne, *Scarlet Letter*, 263.
43 Hawthorne, *Scarlet Letter*, 16, 15.
44 Hawthorne, *Scarlet Letter*, 18.
45 Hawthorne, *Scarlet Letter*, 9–10.
46 Hawthorne, *Scarlet Letter*, 10.
47 Hawthorne, *Scarlet Letter*, 34.
48 Hawthorne, *Scarlet Letter*, 37.
49 Hawthorne, *Scarlet Letter*, 33.
50 For more on ambiguity and the need for interpretation in Hawthorne's novel, see Millicent Bell's analysis. Unlike Bell, however, I think Hawthorne is quite clear in inviting readers to read with the attitude of what Bell identifies as the "pious man's" patient hope for the "ultimate revelation" that will resolve the inevitable ambiguities of life. Millicent Bell, "The Obliquity of Signs: *The Scarlet Letter*," *Massachusetts Review* 23, no. 1 (1982): 9–26.
51 Hawthorne, *Scarlet Letter*, 259.
52 Applebaum, "New Puritans."

13 Cross-Bearers

1 Hawthorne, *Scarlet Letter*, 264. *Gules* is the heraldic term for the color red.
2 Herman Melville, *Clarel: A Poem and Pilgrimage in the Holy Land*, ed. Hayford Harrison et al., (Evanston: Northwestern University Press, 1991), 823. The quotation comes from George Sandys' *A Relation of a Journey Begun An: Dom: 1610*, and the context for Melville's familiarity with this and other sources regarding the ensign is detailed in the notes of this Northwestern-Newberry edition of *Clarel*.
3 Andrew Delbanco, *Melville: His World and Work* (New York: Vintage, 2006), 285, 287.
4 Christopher N. Phillips, *Epic in American Culture: Settlement to Reconstruction* (Baltimore: Johns Hopkins University Press, 2012), 281.
5 Melville, *Clarel*, 1.6.19–20.
6 Delbanco, *Melville*, 279; Melville, *Clarel*, 531, 538.
7 Sacasas, "Borg Complex."

8   Graeme Wood, "How Bronze Age Pervert Charmed the Far Right," *Atlantic*, August 3, 2023, https://www.theatlantic.com/magazine/archive/2023/09/bronze -age-pervert-costin-alamariu/674762/.

9   Melville, *Clarel*, 4.34.43.

10 For more on the theological background to this claim, see Jeffrey, *People of the Book*, 378.

11 Melville, *Clarel*, 4.2.50–124.

12 Melville, *Moby-Dick*, 480–81. Interestingly, Queequeg's "mark" that he uses to sign the ship's papers is a Jerusalem cross (*Moby-Dick*, 89).

13 Peter Wayne Moe, *Touching This Leviathan* (Corvallis: Oregon State University Press, 2021), 65.

14 Moe, *Touching This Leviathan*, 74.

15 For further reflections on the power of memorizing religious or literary texts, see Ellen Condict, "It's Time to Rediscover the Power of Poetry," *American Conservative*, September 20, 2019, https://www.theamericanconservative.com/its-time -to-rediscover-the-power-of-poetry/.

16 For more on this debate, see Paul Ricoeur's essay "Structure, Word, Event," in *The Conflict of Interpretations*, ed. Don Ihde (Evanston: Northwestern University Press, 1974), 79–98. Lundin puts Ricoeur's argument in the context of other work on a theological hermeneutic that questions the explanatory power of structuralism (*Beginning with the Word*, 96–101).

17 Lundin, *Beginning with the Word*, 179–80.

18 Jeffrey C. K. Goh, *Christian Tradition Today: A Postliberal Vision of Church and World* (Louvain: Peeters, 2000), 303.

19 Mikhail Bakhtin, *Problems of Dostoevsky's Poetics*, trans. Caryl Emerson (Minneapolis: University of Minnesota Press, 1984), 166, italics in original.

20 Lundin, *Believing Again*, 167.

21 Bakhtin, *Problems of Dostoevsky's Poetics*, 230.

22 Hans Urs von Balthasar, *Theo-Drama: Theological Dramatic Theory*, vol. 1, *Prolegomena*, trans. Graham Harrison (San Francisco: Ignatius Press, 1989), 36; Lundin, *Believing Again*, 170.

23 Jacobs, *Theology of Reading*, 97.

24 On the centrality of patience for Christian hope, see also Balthasar's theological work on drama and history. He summarizes the necessity for patience thus: "God intended man to have *all* good, but in his, God's, time; and therefore all disobedience, all sin, consists essentially in breaking out of time. Hence the restoration of order by the Son of God had to be the annulment of that premature snatching at knowledge, the beating down of the hand outstretched toward eternity, the repentant return from a false, swift transfer of eternity to a true, slow confinement in time. Hence the importance of patience in the New Testament, which becomes the basic constituent of Christianity, more central, even than humility: the power to wait, to persevere, to hold out, to endure to the end, not to transcend one's own limitations, not to force issues by playing the hero or the titan, but to practice the virtue that lies beyond heroism: the meekness of the Lamb which is *led*" (Hans Urs von Balthasar, *A Theology of History*, reissued ed. [San Francisco: Ignatius Press, 1994], 36–37).

25 Samuel Beckett, *Waiting for Godot: A Tragicomedy in Two Acts* (New York: Grove Press, 2011).

26 Roger Lundin offers a significant qualification to Steiner's view of our condition as Sabbatarian in *Believing Again*, 257–63. Even though we live after the

resurrection, however, we await the eschatological second coming of Christ, so the human condition remains, to a significant extent, Sabbatarian in Steiner's sense.

27 George Steiner, *Real Presences* (Chicago: University of Chicago Press, 1991), 230–32.

28 Matt 12:39; Moe, *Touching This Leviathan*, 74.

29 My use of "eucatastrophe" follows J. R. R. Tolkien's famous definition of his neologism in *Tree and Leaf* (London: HarperCollins UK, 2012), 68–70.

30 Melville, *Moby-Dick*, 480.

31 Melville, *Moby-Dick*, 527–29.

32 Melville, *Moby-Dick*, 195.

33 Melville, *Moby-Dick*, 528.

34 Melville, *Moby-Dick*, 573.

35 Melville, *Moby-Dick*, 225.

36 Melville, *Clarel*, 4.10.186.

37 Melville, *Clarel*, 4.18.162–63.

38 Melville, *Clarel*, 4.5.87, 4.5.91.

39 Melville, *Clarel*, 4.9.117, 123, 125.

40 Melville, *Moby-Dick*, 398; idem, *Clarel*, 4.10.107–9.

41 In fact, as Jeffrey points out, drawing on Søren Kierkegaard, an obsession with reading and discussing and interpreting texts can be a means of evading their import. There is a world of difference between "criticism of a text and radical accountability to it" (*People of the Book*, 13–14).

42 Melville, *Clarel*, 4.30.98.

43 Melville, *Clarel*, 4.29.150–52.

44 Melville, *Clarel*, 4.34.43.

45 Melville, *Clarel*, 4.35.51–53. For more on the telegraph and the hype surrounding it, see Standage, *Victorian Internet*, 74–91.

46 *Clarel*'s epilogue has provoked strong, contradictory opinions from critics. Some, like Christopher Phillips, are content to note that it surprises readers: "As in the epilogue to *Moby-Dick*, the hope of finding life in the midst of death leaves the reader off balance" (*Epic in American Culture*, 282). Bryan Short sees the epilogue as fitting, but he also argues it is not integral to the poem's structure: "Redemption comes second hand in Melville's curiously buoyant epilogue. It is here that Melville redefines organic form in order to escape the objective decorum of his narrative. Like the palinode of a Medieval allegory or the epilogue of an Elizabethan play, the *Clarel* epilogue removes Melville's conclusion from the context of the tale. Clarel is left alone shouldering a greater burden than ever; none of his friends can comfort him; but Melville blithely tells us that things are not so bad." And Short concludes it expresses "Melville's faith in literature." See Bryan C. Short, "Form as Vision in Herman Melville's *Clarel*," *American Literature* 50, no. 4 (1979): 558, 568. Jeff Wheelwright simply does not find the epilogue convincing, stating that after reading it, "We are not consoled" ("The Skeptical Pilgrim: Melville's *Clarel*," *Public Domain Review*, accessed August 9, 2023, https://publicdomainreview.org/essay/the-skeptical-pilgrim-melvilles-clarel/). As my analysis makes plain, I think the epilogue articulates an explicitly religious hope that is consistent with Melville's other writings and with the pilgrimage portrayed in the poem.

47 Melville, *Clarel*, 4.35.7.

48 Melville, *Clarel*, 4.35.9–11.

49 Carroll and Prickett, *Bible*, 2 Cor 3:3, 4:6–12.

50 Melville, *Clarel*, 4.35.23–34.

Epilogue

1 Postman, *Amusing Ourselves to Death*, 161.
2 Postman, *Technopoly*, 185.
3 T. S Eliot, *Collected Poems, 1909–1962* (New York: Harcourt Brace Jovanovich, 1991), 189.
4 Wendell Berry, *New Collected Poems* (Berkeley, Calif.: Counterpoint, 2012), 218.

Bibliography

1599 Geneva Bible: Patriot's Edition. 2nd ed. Power Springs, Ga.: Tolle Lege Press, 2021.

"About Google, Our Culture & Company News." Google.com. Accessed December 5, 2020. about.google.com.

Adams, Henry. "The Dynamo and the Virgin." In *The Education of Henry Adams*, 379–90. New York: Modern Library, 1999.

Allen, Margaret Vanderhaar. *The Achievement of Margaret Fuller.* University Park: Pennsylvania State University Press, 1979.

Anderson, Benedict R. O'Gorman. *Imagined Communities: Reflections on the Origin and Spread of Nationalism.* Rev. ed. London: Verso, 2006.

Applebaum, Anne. "The New Puritans." *Atlantic*, August 31, 2021. https://www.theatlantic.com/magazine/archive/2021/10/new-puritans-mob-justice-canceled/619818/.

Appleby, Joyce. *Inheriting the Revolution: The First Generation of Americans.* Cambridge, Mass.: Belknap Press, 2001.

Arnade, Chris. *Dignity: Seeking Respect in Back Row America.* New York: Penguin, 2019.

Arnett, Peter. "Major Describes Move." *New York Times*, March 15, 1968.

Augustine, Saint. *On Christian Teaching.* Translated by R. P. H. Green. Oxford: Oxford University Press, 2008.

Bacon, Francis. *The New Organon.* Edited by Lisa Jardine and Michael Silverthorne. Cambridge Texts in the History of Philosophy. Cambridge: Cambridge University Press, 2000.

———. *The Philosophical Works of Francis Bacon.* Edited by Robert Leslie Ellis, James Spedding, and John Robertson. London: George Routledge, 1905.

Bailyn, Bernard. *The Ideological Origins of the American Revolution.* Cambridge, Mass.: Belknap Press of Harvard University Press, 2017.

Bailyn, Bernard, and Jane N. Garrett, eds. *Pamphlets of the American Revolution, 1750–1765.* Cambridge, Mass.: Belknap Press, 1965.

Baker, Houston A., Jr. *The Journey Back: Issues in Black Literature and Criticism.* Chicago: University of Chicago Press, 1984.

Bakhtin, Mikhail. *Problems of Dostoevsky's Poetics.* Translated by Caryl Emerson. Minneapolis: University of Minnesota Press, 1984.

Baldasty, Gerald J. *The Commercialization of News in the Nineteenth Century.* Madison: University of Wisconsin Press, 1992.

Balthasar, Hans Urs von. *A Theology of History.* Reissued ed. San Francisco: Ignatius Press, 1994.

———. *Theo-Drama: Theological Dramatic Theory.* Vol. 1, *Prolegomena.* Translated by Graham Harrison. San Francisco: Ignatius Press, 1989.

Barish, Evelyn. "The Moonless Night: Emerson's Crisis of Health, 1825–1827." In *Emerson Centenary Essays*, edited by Joel Myerson, 1–16. Carbondale: Southern Illinois University Press, 1982.

Bauer, Dale M., and Philip Gould, eds. *The Cambridge Companion to Nineteenth-Century American Women's Writing.* Cambridge: Cambridge University Press, 2001.

Bauman, Zygmunt. *Does Ethics Have a Chance in a World of Consumers?* Institute for Human Sciences Vienna Lecture Series. Cambridge, Mass.: Harvard University Press, 2008.

———. *Liquid Modernity.* Cambridge: Polity, 2000.

Beacom, Nathan. "The Community Community." *Comment Magazine*, September 7, 2023. https://comment.org/the-community-community/.

———. "Lyceums: Places to Think with Neighbors." In Bilbro, Wilson, and Henreckson, *Liberating Arts*, 181–84.

Beckett, Samuel. *Waiting for Godot: A Tragicomedy in Two Acts.* New York: Grove Press, 2011.

Beer, Jeremy. *The Philanthropic Revolution: An Alternative History of American Charity.* Philadelphia: University of Pennsylvania Press, 2015.

Begbie, Jeremy S. "Room of One's Own? Music, Space, and Freedom." In *A Peculiar Orthodoxy: Reflections on Theology and the Arts*, 145–80. Grand Rapids: Baker Academic, 2018.

Bell, Millicent. "The Obliquity of Signs: *The Scarlet Letter.*" *Massachusetts Review* 23, no. 1 (1982): 9–26.

Bennett, B. *Transatlantic Spiritualism and Nineteenth-Century American Literature.* New York: Palgrave Macmillan, 2007.

Berkove, Lawrence I. "*A Connecticut Yankee*: A Serious Hoax." *Essays in Arts and Sciences* 19 (1990): 28–44.

Berry, Wendell. *Life Is a Miracle: An Essay against Modern Superstition.* New York: Counterpoint, 2001.

———. *New Collected Poems.* Berkeley, Calif.: Counterpoint, 2012.

———. "Sex, Economy, Freedom, and Community." In *Sex, Economy, Freedom and Community: Eight Essays*, 117–73. New York: Pantheon, 1993.

———. "Solving for Pattern." In *The Gift of Good Land: Further Essays Cultural and Agricultural*, 134–47. Berkeley, Calif.: Counterpoint, 2009.

———. *The Need to Be Whole: Patriotism and the History of Prejudice.* Cincinnati: Shoemaker, 2022.

———. *This Day: Collected and New Sabbath Poems 1979–2012.* Berkeley, Calif.: Counterpoint, 2013.

Beutel, Gernot, Eline Geerits, and Jan T. Kielstein. "Artificial Hallucination: GPT on LSD?" *Critical Care* 27, no. 1 (2023): 148.

Bilbro, Jeffrey. "The 'Art of Attaining Truth' in *Moby-Dick*: Print Technologies, Hermeneutics, and Castaway Readers." In *Above the American*

Renaissance: David S. Reynolds and the Spiritual Imagination in American Literary Studies, edited by Harold K. Bush and Brian Yothers, 125–39. Amherst: University of Massachusetts Press, 2018.

———. "How Tech Reform Diminishes Us." *New Atlantis*, Winter 2022.

———. "Learning to Woo Meaning from Apparent Chaos: Republican Interpreters, Milton, and the Ecological Form of *Summer on the Lakes*." In *Writing the Environment in Nineteenth-Century American Literature: The Ecological Awareness of Early Scribes of Nature*, 57–76. Ecocritical Theory and Practice. Lanham, Md.: Lexington Books, 2015.

———. "The Liberating Potential of Knowing the Past." In Bilbro, Wilson, and Henreckson, *Liberating Arts*, 106–15.

———. *Loving God's Wildness: The Christian Roots of Ecological Ethics in American Literature*. Tuscaloosa: University of Alabama Press, 2015.

———. "Personal but Not Individual: How *The Saint John's Bible* Responds to Consumerism." In *"The Saint John's Bible" and Its Tradition: Illuminating Beauty in the Twenty-First Century*, edited by Jack R. Baker, Jeffrey Bilbro, and Daniel Train, 122–35. Eugene, Ore.: Pickwick, 2018.

———. "Practicing Authentic Conversation." *Front Porch Republic* (blog), October 4, 2022. https://www.frontporchrepublic.com/2022/10/practicing -authentic-conversation/.

———. *Reading the Times: A Literary and Theological Inquiry into the News*. Downers Grove, Ill.: IVP Academic, 2021.

———. "'That Petrified Laugh': Mark Twain's Hoaxes in the West and Camelot." *Journal of Narrative Theory* 41, no. 2 (2011): 204–34.

———. *Virtues of Renewal: Wendell Berry's Sustainable Forms*. Lexington: University Press of Kentucky, 2019.

———. "Who Are Lost and How They're Found: Redemption and Theodicy in Wheatley, Newton, and Cowper." *Early American Literature* 47, no. 3 (2012): 561–89.

Bilbro, Jeffrey, Jessica Hooten Wilson, and David Henreckson, eds. *The Liberating Arts: Why We Need Liberal Arts Education*. Walden, N.Y.: Plough, 2023.

Blair, Ann. *Too Much to Know: Managing Scholarly Information before the Modern Age*. New Haven: Yale University Press, 2010.

Blake, William, David V. Erdman, Harold Bloom, and William Golding. *The Complete Poetry and Prose of William Blake*. Rev. ed. Garden City, N.Y: Anchor, 1982.

Blight, David W. *Frederick Douglass: Prophet of Freedom*. New York: Simon and Schuster, 2020.

Bliss, Laura. "Photographing the American 'Grid,' One Square Mile Per Frame." *Bloomberg*, September 16, 2015. https://www.bloomberg.com/ news/articles/2015-09-16/the-jefferson-grid-shows-the-american-west -through-one-square-mile-per-frame.

Boese, Alex. *The Museum of Hoaxes: A History of Outrageous Pranks and Deceptions*. New York: Plume, 2003.

Boonyaprasop, Marina. *Hawthorne's Wilderness: Nature and Puritanism in Hawthorne's "The Scarlet Letter" and "Young Goodman Brown."* Hamburg: Anchor Academic Publishing, 2013.

Borgmann, Albert. *Technology and the Character of Contemporary Life: A Philosophical Inquiry*. Chicago: University of Chicago Press, 1987.

Boudreau, Gordon V. *The Roots of Walden and the Tree of Life*. Nashville: Vanderbilt University Press, 1990.

Bronson-Bartlett, Blake. "Writing with Pencils in the Antebellum United States: Language, Instrument, Gesture." *American Literature* 92, no. 2 (2020): 199–227.

Brown, Arthur William. *Margaret Fuller*. Twayne's United States Authors Series, no. 48. New York: Twayne, 1964.

Brown, Dwane. "How One Man Convinced 200 Ku Klux Klan Members To Give Up Their Robes." *NPR*. August 20, 2017. https://www.npr.org/2017/08/20/544861933/how-one-man-convinced-200-ku-klux-klan-members-to-give-up-their-robes.

Brückner, Martin. *The Geographic Revolution in Early America: Maps, Literacy, and National Identity*. Chapel Hill: University of North Carolina Press, 2006.

Buber, Martin. *I and Thou*. Translated by Walter Kaufmann. New York: Charles Scribner's Sons, 1970.

Buell, Lawrence. *Emerson*. Cambridge, Mass.: Belknap Press of Harvard University Press, 2003.

———. *The Environmental Imagination: Thoreau, Nature Writing, and the Formation of American Culture*. Cambridge, Mass.: Harvard University Press, 1995.

———. *New England Literary Culture: From Revolution through Renaissance*. Cambridge Studies in American Literature and Culture. Cambridge: Cambridge University Press, 1986.

Burke, Garance, Josef Federman, Huizhong Wu, Krutika Pathi, and Rod McGuirk. "Police Seize on COVID-19 Tech to Expand Global Surveillance." AP News, December 20, 2022. https://apnews.com/article/technology-police-government-surveillance-covid-19-3f3f348d176bc7152a8cb2dbab2e4cc4.

Burnett, L. D. "Margaret Fuller's 'Conversations' for a Digital Age?" Society for U.S. Intellectual History, June 17, 2017. https://s-usih.org/2017/06/margaret-fullers-conversations-for-a-digital-age/.

Bush, Sargent. "The End and Means in Walden: Thoreau's Use of the Catechism." *ESQ: A Journal of the American Renaissance* 31, no. 1 (1985): 1–10.

Busy Dad's Bible: Daily Inspiration Even If You Only Have One Minute. Box Lea ed. Grand Rapids: Zondervan, 2010.

Cadogan, Garnette. "Walking while Black." *Literary Hub* (blog), July 8, 2016. https://lithub.com/walking-while-black/.

Candler, Peter M., Jr. *Theology, Rhetoric, Manuduction, or Reading Scripture Together on the Path to God*. Grand Rapids: Eerdmans, 2006.

Capper, Charles. *Margaret Fuller: An American Romantic Life*. Vol. 1, *The Private Years*. New York: Oxford University Press, 1994.

———. *Margaret Fuller: An American Romantic Life*. Vol. 2, *The Public Years*. New York: Oxford University Press, 2010.

Carney, Timothy P. *Alienated America: Why Some Places Thrive while Others Collapse*. New York: Harper, 2019.

Carr, Austin. "Amazon's New Wearable Will Know If I'm Angry. Is That Weird?" *Bloomberg*, August 31, 2020. https://www.bloomberg.com/news/newsletters/2020-08-31/amazon-s-halo-wearable-can-read-emotions-is-that-too-weird.

Carr, Nicholas. *The Shallows: How the Internet Is Changing the Way We Think, Read and Remember*. New York: W. W. Norton, 2011. Reissued as *The Shallows: What the Internet Is Doing to Our Brains*. 2nd ed. New York: Norton, 2020.

Carretta, Vincent. *Equiano, the African: Biography of a Self-Made Man*. Athens: University of Georgia Press, 2005.

Carroll, Robert, and Stephen Prickett, eds. *The Bible: Authorized King James Version*. New York: Oxford University Press, 2008.

Casper, Scott E., Jeffrey D. Groves, Stephen W. Nissenbaum, and Michael Winship. *A History of the Book in America*. Vol. 3, *The Industrial Book, 1840–1880*. Chapel Hill: University of North Carolina Press, 2009.

Cavanaugh, William T. *Migrations of the Holy: God, State, and the Political Meaning of the Church*. Grand Rapids: Eerdmans, 2011.

———. *Theopolitical Imagination*. London: T & T Clark, 2002.

Cavell, Stanley. *The Senses of Walden*. Chicago: University of Chicago Press, 1992.

Certeau, Michel de. *The Practice of Everyday Life*. Translated by Steven Rendall. Berkeley: University of California Press, 1988.

Chevigny, Bell Gale. "'Cheat Me [On] by No Illusion': Margaret Fuller's Cultural Critique and Its Legacies." In *Margaret Fuller's Cultural Critique*, edited by Fritz Fleischmann, 27–41. Early American Literature and Culture through the American Renaissance, no. 3. New York: Peter Lang, 2000.

Cho, Eunsun. "The Social Credit System: Not Just Another Chinese Idiosyncrasy." *Journal of Public and International Affairs*, May 1, 2020. https://jpia.princeton.edu/news/social-credit-system-not-just-another-chinese-idiosyncrasy.

Clarke, James Freeman. *James Freeman Clarke: Autobiography, Diary and Correspondence*. Boston: Houghton, Mifflin, 1891.

"Complimentary Fruit Festival of the New York Book Publishers' Association to Authors and Booksellers." *American Publishers' Circular and Literary Gazette*. 1855.

Condict, Ellen. "It's Time to Rediscover the Power of Poetry." *American Conservative*, September 20, 2019. https://www.theamericanconservative.com/its-time-to-rediscover-the-power-of-poetry/.

"The Constitution of the United States of America." 1789. Reprinted as amended, Washington, D.C.: U.S. Government Publishing Office, 2007. http://www.gpo.gov/fdsys/pkg/CDOC-110hdoc50/pdf/CDOC-110hdoc50.pdf.

Cook, Jonathan A. *Inscrutable Malice: Theodicy, Eschatology, and the Biblical Sources of* Moby-Dick. DeKalb: Northern Illinois University Press, 2012.

Corwin, Edward S. "The Higher Law Background of American Constitutional Law." *Harvard Law Review* 42, no. 2 (1929): 149–85.

Couch, Danielle L., Priscilla Robinson, and Paul A. Komesaroff. "COVID-19— Extending Surveillance and the Panopticon." *Journal of Bioethical Inquiry* 17, no. 4 (2020): 809–14.

Crain, Patricia. *The Story of A: The Alphabetization of America from "The New England Primer" to "The Scarlet Letter."* Stanford, Calif.: Stanford University Press, 2000.

Crawford, Kate, and Trevor Paglen. "Excavating AI." Excavating AI, September 19, 2019. https://www.excavating.ai.

Crawford, Matthew B. "Algorithmic Governance and Political Legitimacy." *American Affairs Journal*, May 20, 2019. https://americanaffairsjournal .org/2019/05/algorithmic-governance-and-political-legitimacy/.

Crouch, Andy. *The Life We're Looking For: Reclaiming Relationship in a Technological World.* New York: Convergent Books, 2022.

Dastin, Jeffrey. "Amazon Scraps Secret AI Recruiting Tool That Showed Bias against Women." *Reuters*, October 10, 2018. https://www.reuters.com/ article/us-amazon-com-jobs-automation-insight-idUSKCN1MK08G.

Davidson, Cathy N. *Revolution and the Word: The Rise of the Novel in America.* Expanded ed. New York: Oxford University Press, 2004.

Delbanco, Andrew. *Melville: His World and Work.* New York: Vintage, 2006.

Deneen, Patrick J. "A Republic of Front Porches." *Front Porch Republic* (blog), March 3, 2009. https://www.frontporchrepublic.com/2009/03/front -porch-republic/.

Denevan, William M. "Foreword." In *Imperfect Balance: Landscape Transformations in the Precolumbian Americas*, edited by David Lewis Lentz, xvii–xx. The Historical Ecology Series. New York: Columbia University Press, 2000.

Dennis, Donna. *Licentious Gotham: Erotic Publishing and Its Prosecution in Nineteenth-Century New York.* Cambridge, Mass.: Harvard University Press, 2009.

Dial, the. N.p.: Jordan Weeks, 1841.

Dick, Steven J. *Sky and Ocean Joined: The US Naval Observatory 1830–2000.* Cambridge: Cambridge University Press, 2003.

Dickens, Charles. *Bleak House.* Oxford: Oxford University Press, 1998.

Dickinson, Emily. *The Letters of Emily Dickinson.* Edited by Thomas H. Johnson and Theodora Ward. Cambridge, Mass.: Belknap Press, 1965.

———. *The Poems of Emily Dickinson: Variorum Edition.* Edited by R. W. Franklin. Cambridge, Mass.: Harvard University Press, 1998.

Doctorow, Cory. "Writing in the Age of Distraction." *Locus Magazine* (blog), January 2009. http://www.locusmag.com/Features/2009/01/cory-doctorow -writing-in-age-of.html.

Douglass, Frederick. *Frederick Douglass: Autobiographies.* Edited by Henry Louis Gates. New York: Library of America, 1994.

Dudek, Louis. *Literature and the Press: A History of Printing, Printed Media, and Their Relation to Literature.* Toronto: Ryerson Press, 1960.

Duhigg, Charles. "How Companies Learn Your Secrets." *New York Times*, February 16, 2012, https://www.nytimes.com/2012/02/19/magazine/shopping -habits.html.

Dunbar, R. I. M. *Grooming, Gossip, and the Evolution of Language*. Cambridge, Mass.: Harvard University Press, 1998.

Edney, Matthew H. *Cartography: The Ideal and Its History*. Chicago: University of Chicago Press, 2019.

Eisenstein, Elizabeth L. *The Printing Press as an Agent of Change: Communications and Cultural Transformations in Early Modern Europe*. Cambridge: Cambridge University Press, 1980.

Eliot, T. S. *Collected Poems, 1909–1962*. New York: Harcourt Brace Jovanovich, 1991.

Ellul, Jacques. *Propaganda: The Formation of Men's Attitudes*. New York: Vintage, 1973.

Elmore, A. E. "Symmetry out of Season: The Form of 'Walden.'" *South Atlantic Bulletin* 37, no. 4 (1972): 18.

Emerson, Everett. *Mark Twain, a Literary Life*. Philadelphia: University of Pennsylvania Press, 2017.

Emerson, Ralph Waldo. *The Collected Works of Ralph Waldo Emerson: Nature, Addresses, and Lectures*. Edited by Robert Ernest Spiller, Alfred Riggs Ferguson, Joseph Slater, and Jean Ferguson Carr. Cambridge, Mass.: Harvard University Press, 1971.

———. *The Complete Works of Ralph Waldo Emerson: Poems*. Boston: Houghton, Mifflin, 1904.

———. *The Essays of Ralph Waldo Emerson*. Edited by Alfred Riggs Ferguson and Jean Ferguson Carr. Cambridge, Mass.: Harvard University Press, 1987.

———. "Sermon CLXII ['The Lord's Supper']." In *Transcendentalism: A Reader*, edited by Joel Myerson, 68–78. Oxford: Oxford University Press, 2000.

Equiano, Olaudah, and Vincent Carretta. *The Interesting Narrative and Other Writings: Revised Edition*. New York: Penguin Classics, 2003.

Eubanks, Virginia. *Automating Inequality: How High-Tech Tools Profile, Police, and Punish the Poor*. London: Picador, 2019.

Falke, Cassandra. *The Phenomenology of Love and Reading*. New York: Bloomsbury, 2016.

Felski, Rita. *The Limits of Critique*. Chicago: University of Chicago Press, 2015.

Fischer, Claude S. "Ever-More Rooted Americans." *City and Community* 1, no. 2 (2002): 177–98.

Fisher, Marvin. "Melville's 'Bell-Tower': A Double Thrust." *American Quarterly* 18, no. 2 (1966): 200–207.

Fitzpatrick, Kathleen. *Generous Thinking: A Radical Approach to Saving the University*. Baltimore: Johns Hopkins University Press, 2021.

Flanagan, Caitlin. "You Really Need to Quit Twitter." *Atlantic*, July 5, 2021. https://www.theatlantic.com/ideas/archive/2021/07/twitter-addict-realizes -she-needs-rehab/619343/.

Folsom, Ed. "Whitman Making Books/Books Making Whitman: A Catalog and Commentary." Walt Whitman Archive, 2005. http://whitmanarchive .org/criticism/current/anc.00150.html.

Foner, Eric. *Free Soil, Free Labor, Free Men: The Ideology of the Republican Party before the Civil War.* 1970. Reprint. Oxford: Oxford University Press, 1995.

Foucault, Michel. *Discipline and Punish: The Birth of the Prison.* Translated by Alan Sheridan. New York: Pantheon, 1977.

Frank, Jason. "American Tragedy: The Political Thought of Herman Melville." In *A Political Companion to Herman Melville*, 1–20. Lexington: University Press of Kentucky, 2013.

Franklin, Benjamin. *The Autobiography of Benjamin Franklin.* Edited by Leonard W. Labaree, Ralph L. Ketcham, Helen C. Boatfield, and Helene Fineman. New Haven: Yale University Press, 1964.

Franklin, Ursula M. *The Real World of Technology.* Toronto: House of Anansi, 1999.

Frasca, Ralph. *Benjamin Franklin's Printing Network: Disseminating Virtue in Early America.* Columbia: University of Missouri Press, 2006.

Freeman, Joanne B. *The Field of Blood: Violence in Congress and the Road to Civil War.* New York: Farrar, Straus and Giroux, 2018.

French, David. *Divided We Fall: America's Secession Threat and How to Restore Our Nation.* New York: St. Martin's, 2020.

Fuller, Jamie. "An Emily Dickinson Reading List." *Lapham's Quarterly*, August 13, 2018. https://www.laphamsquarterly.org/roundtable/emily -dickinson-reading-list.

Fuller, Margaret. *The Letters of Margaret Fuller.* Edited by Robert N. Hudspeth. 6 vols. Ithaca: Cornell University Press, 1983.

———. *The Letters of Margaret Fuller: 1839–1841.* Vol. 2. Ithaca: Cornell University Press, 2018.

———. *Summer on the Lakes, in 1843.* Urbana: University of Illinois Press, 1990.

Gadamer, Hans Georg. *Truth and Method.* Translated by Joel Weinsheimer and Donald G. Marshall. 2nd rev. ed. London: Sheed and Ward, 1999.

Gallagher, Winifred. *How the Post Office Created America: A History.* New York: Penguin, 2017.

Genoways, Ted. "'One Goodshaped and Wellhung Man': Accentuated Sexuality and the Uncertain Authorship of the Frontispiece to the 1855 Edition of *Leaves of Grass*." In *Leaves of Grass: The Sesquicentennial Essays*, edited by Susan Belasco, Ed Folsom, and Kenneth M. Price, 87–123. Lincoln: University of Nebraska Press, 2007.

Ghonim, Wael. "Inside the Egyptian Revolution." Filmed March 2011 in Cairo. TED video. https://www.ted.com/talks/wael_ghonim_inside_the_egyptian _revolution.

———. "Let's Design Social Media That Drives Real Change." Filmed December 2015 in Geneva. TED video, 2015. https://www.ted.com/talks/ wael_ghonim_let_s_design_social_media_that_drives_real_change.

Goh, Jeffrey C. K. *Christian Tradition Today: A Postliberal Vision of Church and World.* Louvain: Peeters, 2000.

Goodrich, S. G. *Recollections of a Lifetime, or Men and Things I Have Seen: In a Series of Familiar Letters to a Friend, Historical, Biographical, Anecdotical, and Descriptive.* Vol. 1. New York: Miller, Orton and Mulligan, 1856.

Goodrich, S. G., ed. *The Token and Atlantic Souvenir: A Christmas and New Year's Present.* Boston: Charles Bowen, 1835.

Green Bible, The. San Francisco: HarperOne, 2008.

Greenblatt, Stephen. *Renaissance Self-Fashioning: From More to Shakespeare.* Chicago: University of Chicago Press, 2005.

Greenfield, Susan. *Mind Change: How Digital Technologies Are Leaving Their Mark on Our Brains.* New York: Random House, 2015.

Griffiths, Paul J. *Intellectual Appetite: A Theological Grammar.* Washington, D.C: Catholic University of America Press, 2009.

———. *Religious Reading: The Place of Reading in the Practice of Religion.* New York: Oxford University Press, 1999.

Gross, Robert A., and Mary Kelley, eds. *A History of the Book in America.* Vol. 2, *An Extensive Republic: Print, Culture, and Society in the New Nation, 1790–1840.* Chapel Hill: University of North Carolina Press, 2014.

Grunes, Marissa. "Open Interiority: Emily Dickinson, Augustine, and the Spatial Self." *Women's Studies* 47, no. 3 (2018): 350–71.

Gurri, Adam. "Free Yourself from the Telescopic Morality Machine." *Front Porch Republic* (blog), December 9, 2014. https://www.frontporchrepublic.com/2014/12/free-telescopic-morality-machine/.

Gustafson, Sandra M. "Orality and Literacy in Transatlantic Perspective." *19: Interdisciplinary Studies in the Long Nineteenth Century*, no. 18 (2014). https://19.bbk.ac.uk/article/id/1672/.

Gutjahr, Paul. *An American Bible: A History of the Good Book in the United States, 1777–1880.* Stanford, Calif: Stanford University Press, 2002.

Hager, Christopher. *Word by Word: Emancipation and the Act of Writing.* Cambridge, Mass.: Harvard University Press, 2013.

Hall, David D. "The Uses of Literacy in New England, 1600–1850." In Joyce et al., *Printing and Society in Early America*, 1–47.

Hall, Patricia Kelly, and Steven Ruggles. "'Restless in the Midst of Their Prosperity': New Evidence on the Internal Migration of Americans, 1850–2000." *Journal of American History* 91, no. 3 (2004): 829–46.

Halttunen, Karen. *Confidence Men and Painted Women: A Study of Middle-Class Culture in America, 1830–1870.* New Haven: Yale University Press, 1986.

Hansen, Collin. "What Happened to Historian Molly Worthen?" Gospelbound. Accessed July 4, 2023. https://www.thegospelcoalition.org/podcasts/gospelbound/happened-molly-worthen/.

Haraway, Donna. "Situated Knowledges: The Science Question in Feminism and the Privilege of Partial Perspective." *Feminist Studies* 14, no. 3 (1988): 575–99.

Harrison, Peter. *The Bible, Protestantism, and the Rise of Natural Science.* Cambridge: Cambridge University Press, 2001.

Hatch, Harris B., and A. A. Stewart. *Electrotyping and Stereotyping, a Primer of Information about the Processes of Electrotyping and Stereotyping.*

Typographic Technical Series for Apprentices, part 1, no. 15. Chicago: Committee on Education, United Typothetae of America, 1918.

Hatch, Nathan O. *The Democratization of American Christianity*. New Haven: Yale University Press, 1989.

———. "Elias Smith and the Rise of Religious Journalism in the Early Republic." In Joyce et al., *Printing and Society in Early America*, 250–77.

Hawthorne, Nathaniel. "Chiefly about War Matters." *Atlantic*, July 1, 1862. https://www.theatlantic.com/magazine/archive/1862/07/chiefly-about-war-matters/306159/.

———. *The Scarlet Letter*. Centenary Edition of the Works of Nathaniel Hawthorne, vol. 1. Columbus: Ohio State University Press, 1963.

———. *The Snow Image and Uncollected Tales*. Centenary Edition of the Works of Nathaniel Hawthorne, vol. 11. Columbus: Ohio State University Press, 1974.

Heddendorf, David. "Blowing Up the Bert: The Outside Story." *Front Porch Republic* (blog), August 20, 2018. https://www.frontporchrepublic.com/2018/08/blowing-up-the-bert-the-outside-story/.

Heidler, David S., and Jeanne T. Heidler. *The Rise of Andrew Jackson: Myth, Manipulation, and the Making of Modern Politics*. New York: Basic Books, 2018.

Heimert, Alan. "Moby-Dick and American Political Symbolism." *American Quarterly* 15, no. 4 (1963): 498–534.

Heise, Ursula K. *Sense of Place and Sense of Planet: The Environmental Imagination of the Global*. Oxford: Oxford University Press, 2008.

Henreckson, David. "Venturing Our Selves." *Comment Magazine*, July 7, 2022. https://comment.org/venturing-our-selves/.

Hersh, Eitan. *Politics Is for Power: How to Move beyond Political Hobbyism, Take Action, and Make Real Change*. New York: Scribner, 2020.

Hitz, Zena. "The Catherine Project." In Bilbro, Wilson, and Henreckson, *Liberating Arts*, 56–58.

Hobbs, Catherine, ed. *Nineteenth-Century Women Learn to Write*. Charlottesville: University of Virginia Press, 1995.

Hodge, Charles. *Systematic Theology*. Vol. 1. Grand Rapids: Eerdmans, 1979.

Hoe, Robert. *A Short History of the Printing Press and of the Improvements in Printing Machinery from the Time of Gutenberg Up to the Present Day*. New York: Robert Hoe, 1902.

Holmes, Oliver Wendell. "Bread and the Newspaper." *Atlantic*, September 1861, 346–52.

Holt-Lunstad, Julianne. "The Potential Public Health Relevance of Social Isolation and Loneliness: Prevalence, Epidemiology, and Risk Factors." *Public Policy and Aging Report* 27, no. 4 (2017): 127–30.

hooks, bell. *Belonging: A Culture of Place*. New York: Routledge, 2008.

Howe, Daniel Walker. *The Political Culture of the American Whigs*. Chicago: University of Chicago Press, 1984.

———. *What Hath God Wrought: The Transformation of America, 1815–1848*. New York: Oxford University Press, 2007.

"How Political Opposites Became Best Friends | Robert George & Cornel West at WashU | April 2019." October 26, 2022. YouTube video. https://www.youtube.com/watch?v=jky-nZE30nI.

Huffington, Arianna. "Hemingway, Thoreau, Jefferson and the Virtues of a Good Long Walk." *HuffPost*, August 29, 2013. https://www.huffpost.com/entry/hemingway-thoreau-jeffers_b_3837002.

Humphrey, Carol Sue. *The American Revolution and the Press: The Promise of Independence*. Medill Visions of the American Press. Evanston, Ill.: Northwestern University Press, 2013.

Illich, Ivan. *Celebration of Awareness: A Call for Institutional Revolution*. New York: Doubleday, 1970.

———. *Energy and Equity*. Ideas in Progress. New York: Harper and Row, 1974.

———. *In the Vineyard of the Text: A Commentary to Hugh's Didascalicon*. Chicago: University of Chicago Press, 1993.

———. *Tools for Conviviality*. London: Marion Boyars, 2001.

Illich, Ivan, and David Cayley. *The Rivers North of the Future: The Testament of Ivan Illich as Told to David Cayley*. Toronto: House of Anansi Press, 2005.

Jacobs, Alan. "Attending to Technology: Theses for Disputation." *New Atlantis*, Winter 2016, 16–45.

———. *Breaking Bread with the Dead: A Reader's Guide to a More Tranquil Mind*. New York: Penguin, 2020.

———. "Habits of Mind in an Age of Distraction." *Comment*, Summer 2016.

———. *How to Think: A Survival Guide for a World at Odds*. New York: Currency, 2017.

———. "John Ruskin: Fit the Third and Last." *New Atlantis* (blog), May 28, 2018. https://www.thenewatlantis.com/text-patterns/john-ruskin-fit-third-and-last.

———. *The Pleasures of Reading in an Age of Distraction*. New York: Oxford University Press, 2011.

———. *A Theology of Reading: The Hermeneutics of Love*. Boulder: Westview Press, 2001.

Jefferson, Thomas. *The Jefferson Bible: The Life and Morals of Jesus of Nazareth, Extracted Textually from the Gospels in Greek, Latin, French and English*. Smithsonian ed. Washington, D.C.: Smithsonian Books, 2011.

Jeffrey, David Lyle. "Our Babel of Bibles: Scripture, Translation, and the Possibility of Spiritual Understanding." *Touchstone Magazine*, 2012. http://www.touchstonemag.com/archives/article.php?id=25-02-029-f.

———. *People of the Book: Christian Identity and Literary Culture*. Grand Rapids: Eerdmans, 1996.

Jenkin, Matthew. "Tablets out, Imagination in: The Schools That Shun Technology." *Guardian*, December 2, 2015. https://www.theguardian.com/teacher-network/2015/dec/02/schools-that-ban-tablets-traditional-education-silicon-valley-london.

Jennings, Willie James. *The Christian Imagination: Theology and the Origins of Race*. New Haven: Yale University Press, 2010.

Johansen, Bruce. *Forgotten Founders: How the American Indian Helped Shape Democracy*. Boston: Harvard Common Press, 1982.

John, Richard R. *Spreading the News: The American Postal System from Franklin to Morse*. Cambridge, Mass.: Harvard University Press, 1995.

Johns, Adrian. *The Nature of the Book: Print and Knowledge in the Making*. Chicago: University of Chicago Press, 1998.

Johnson, Thomas Herbert. *Emily Dickinson: An Interpretive Biography*. Cambridge, Mass.: Belknap Press, 1955.

Joyce, William Leonard, David D. Hall, Richard D. Brown, and John B. Hench, eds. *Printing and Society in Early America*. Worcester, Mass.: American Antiquarian Society, 1983.

Kaplan, Justin. *Mr. Clemens and Mark Twain*. New York: Simon and Schuster, 1966.

Katwala, Amit. "An Algorithm Determined UK Students' Grades. Chaos Ensued." *Wired*, August 15, 2020. https://www.wired.com/story/an-algorithm -determined-uk-students-grades-chaos-ensued/.

Kaur, Rupi. "@rupikaur_." Instagram photo. Accessed April 27, 2021. https:// www.instagram.com/rupikaur_/.

Keller, Helen. *The Story of My Life*. Garden City, N.Y.: Doubleday, 1954.

King, Martin Luther, Jr. "Where Do We Go from Here?" Speech given in Atlanta, Georgia, August 16, 1967. Available via Stanford University, Martin Luther King, Jr., Research and Education Institute. https://kinginstitute .stanford.edu/where-do-we-go-here.

King, Wilma. *Stolen Childhood: Slave Youth in Nineteenth-Century America*. Bloomington: Indiana University Press, 2011.

Kobie, Nicole. "The Complicated Truth about China's Social Credit System." *Wired UK*, July 6, 2019. https://www.wired.co.uk/article/china-social-credit -system-explained.

Kovarsky, Joel. *The True Geography of Our Country: Jefferson's Cartographic Vision*. Charlottesville: University of Virginia Press, 2014.

Kubler, George Adolf. *A Short History of Stereotyping*. Brooklyn, N.Y.: Brooklyn Eagle Commercial Printing Department, 1927.

Lake, Christina Bieber. *Prophets of the Posthuman: American Fiction, Biotechnology, and the Ethics of Personhood*. Notre Dame, Ind.: University of Notre Dame Press, 2014.

Lakoff, George, and Mark Johnson. *Metaphors We Live By*. Chicago: University of Chicago Press, 2003.

Lasch, Christopher. *The True and Only Heaven: Progress and Its Critics*. New York: Norton, 1991.

Latour, Bruno. "Drawing Things Together." In *Representation in Scientific Practice*, edited by Michael Lynch and Steve Woolgar, 19–68. Cambridge, Mass.: MIT Press, 1990.

Lecher, Colin. "A Healthcare Algorithm Started Cutting Care, and No One Knew Why." *Verge*, March 21, 2018. https://www.theverge.com/2018/3/21/ 17144260/healthcare-medicaid-algorithm-arkansas-cerebral-palsy.

Lepore, Jill. *If Then: How One Data Company Invented the Future*. London: John Murray, 2020.

Lewis, C. S. *An Experiment in Criticism*. Cambridge: Cambridge University Press, 1961.

———. "On Obstinacy in Belief." In *The World's Last Night: And Other Essays*, 13–30. New York: Harvest Books, 2002.

Lewis, Michael. *Moneyball: The Art of Winning an Unfair Game*. New York: W. W. Norton, 2004.

Logan, Shirley Wilson. *Liberating Language: Sites of Rhetorical Education in Nineteenth-Century Black America*. Carbondale: Southern Illinois University Press, 2008.

Loughran, Trish. *The Republic in Print: Print Culture in the Age of U.S. Nation Building, 1770–1870*. New York: Columbia University Press, 2009.

Loving, Jerome. *Mark Twain: The Adventures of Samuel L. Clemens*. Berkeley: University of California Press, 2011.

Lowell, James Russell. *The Writings of James Russell Lowell*. Vol. 1. Boston: Houghton, Mifflin, 1890.

Lubac, Henri de. *Medieval Exegesis: The Four Senses of Scripture*. Grand Rapids: Eerdmans, 1998.

Lundin, Roger. *Beginning with the Word: Modern Literature and the Question of Belief*. Grand Rapids: Baker Academic, 2014.

———. *Believing Again: Doubt and Faith in a Secular Age*. Grand Rapids: Eerdmans, 2009.

———. *Emily Dickinson and the Art of Belief*. Grand Rapids: Eerdmans, 1998.

———. *The Promise of Hermeneutics*. Grand Rapids: Eerdmans, 1999.

Lupton, Deborah. *Data Selves: More-than-Human Perspectives*. Cambridge: Polity, 2019.

———. *The Quantified Self*. Cambridge: Polity, 2016.

Luxon, Thomas H. *Literal Figures: Puritan Allegory and the Reformation Crisis in Representation*. Chicago: University of Chicago Press, 1995.

Madrigal, Alexis C. "What Facebook Did to American Democracy." *Atlantic*, October 12, 2017. https://www.theatlantic.com/technology/archive/2017/10/what-facebook-did/542502/.

Manguel, Alberto. *A History of Reading*. New York: Penguin, 2014.

Marsden, George M. "Everyone One's Own Interpreter? The Bible, Science, and Authority in Mid-Nineteenth Century America." In *The Bible in America: Essays in Cultural History*, edited by Nathan O. Hatch and Mark A. Noll, 79–100. New York: Oxford University Press, 1982.

Marshall, Megan. *Margaret Fuller: A New American Life*. Boston: Mariner Books, 2014.

Marx, Leo. *The Machine in the Garden: Technology and the Pastoral Ideal in America*. New York: Oxford University Press, 1964.

Mason, Lilliana. *Uncivil Agreement: How Politics Became Our Identity*. Chicago: University of Chicago Press, 2018.

Matteson, John. *The Lives of Margaret Fuller: A Biography*. New York: W. W. Norton, 2013.

Matthiessen, F. O. *American Renaissance: Art and Expression in the Age of Emerson and Whitman*. New York: Oxford University Press, 1968.

Maxwell-Stuart, P. G. *The Chemical Choir: A History of Alchemy*. New York: Continuum, 2012.

McClay, Wilfred M. *The Masterless: Self and Society in Modern America*. Chapel Hill: University of North Carolina Press, 2000.

McGuire, Ian. "'Who Ain't a Slave?' 'Moby Dick' and the Ideology of Free Labor." *Journal of American Studies* 37, no. 2 (2003): 287–305.

McIntosh, James. "Dickinson's Kinetic Religious Imagination." *Religion and Literature* 46, no. 1 (2014): 144–49.

McKitterick, David. *Print, Manuscript, and the Search for Order, 1450–1830*. Cambridge: Cambridge University Press, 2003.

McLuhan, Marshall. *The Gutenberg Galaxy: The Making of Typographic Man*. Toronto: University of Toronto Press, 2011.

McLuhan, Marshall, and Quentin Fiore. *The Medium Is the Massage: An Inventory of Effects*. Berkeley, Calif.: Gingko Press, 2001.

Melville, Herman. *Clarel: A Poem and Pilgrimage in the Holy Land*. Edited by Hayford Harrison, Alma A. MacDougall, Hershel Parker, and G. Thomas Tanselle. Evanston: Northwestern University Press, 1991.

———. *The Confidence-Man: His Masquerade*. Edited by Hershel Parker, G. Thomas Tanselle, and Harrison Hayford. Evanston: Northwestern University Press, 1988.

———. *Moby-Dick: Or, The Whale*. Edited by Harrison Hayford, Hershel Parker, and G. Thomas Tanselle. Writings of Herman Melville. Evanston, Ill.: Northwestern University Press, 1988.

Midgley, Mary. *The Myths We Live By*. New York: Taylor and Francis, 2011.

Miller, Perry, and Margaret Fuller. *Margaret Fuller, American Romantic: A Selection from Her Writings and Correspondence*. Ithaca: Cornell University Press, 1970.

Mills, Bruce. *Poe, Fuller, and the Mesmeric Arts: Transition States in the American Renaissance*. Columbia: University of Missouri Press, 2005.

Mitchell, J. B. "Address of Welcome." *Publishers Weekly*, vol. 10, 167. New York: F. Leypoldt, 1876.

Moe, Peter Wayne. *Touching This Leviathan*. Corvallis: Oregon State University Press, 2021.

Mommsen, Peter. "Small Magazines as Educational Communities." In Bilbro, Wilson, and Henreckson, *Liberating Arts*, 193–97.

Morgan, Victoria N. *Emily Dickinson and Hymn Culture: Tradition and Experience*. Abingdon: Routledge, 2016.

Moss, Ann. *Printed Commonplace-Books and the Structuring of Renaissance Thought*. Oxford: Clarendon Press, 1996.

Mott, Frank Luther. "Facetious News Writing, 1833–1883." *Mississippi Valley Historical Review* 29, no. 1 (1942): 35–54.

Muir, John. *A Thousand-Mile Walk to the Gulf*. Boston: Houghton Mifflin, 1916.

Multigraph Collective, The. *Interacting with Print: Elements of Reading in the Era of Print Saturation*. Chicago: University of Chicago Press, 2018.

Murray, Meg McGavran. *Margaret Fuller, Wandering Pilgrim*. Athens: University of Georgia Press, 2008.

Murrin, John M. "A Roof without Walls: The Dilemma of American National Identity." In *Beyond Confederation: Origins of the Constitution and American National Identity*, edited by Richard R. Beeman, Stephen Botein, and Edward Carlos Carter, 333–48. Chapel Hill: University of North Carolina Press, 1987.

Myerson, Joel, ed. *Critical Essays on Margaret Fuller*. Critical Essays on American Literature. Boston: G. K. Hall, 1980.

Neheli, Nicole Blanchett. "Here's How Metrics and Analytics Are Changing Newsroom Practice." JSource, February 20, 2019. https://j-source.ca/article/heres-how-metrics-and-analytics-are-changing-newsroom-practice/.

Nelson, Thomas. *Duck Commander Faith and Family Bible, Hardcover: Bible, New King James Version*. N.p.: Thomas Nelson, 2014.

Nerone, John. "Newspapers and the Public Sphere." In *A History of the Book in America*, vol. 3, *The Industrial Book, 1840–1880*, edited by Scott E. Casper, Jeffrey D. Groves, Stephen W. Nissenbaum, and Michael Winship, 230–48. Chapel Hill: University of North Carolina Press, 2009.

Newport, Cal. "What Kind of Mind Does ChatGPT Have?" *New Yorker*, April 13, 2023. https://www.newyorker.com/science/annals-of-artificial-intelligence/what-kind-of-mind-does-chatgpt-have.

Nisbet, Robert. *The Quest for Community: A Study in the Ethics of Order and Freedom*. Wilmington, Del.: Intercollegiate Studies Institute, 2010.

Noll, Mark A. *America's God: From Jonathan Edwards to Abraham Lincoln*. Oxford: Oxford University Press, 2002.

———. *The Civil War as a Theological Crisis*. Steven and Janice Brose Lectures in the Civil War Era. Chapel Hill: University of North Carolina Press, 2006.

Nye, David E. *American Technological Sublime*. Cambridge, Mass.: MIT Press, 1996.

O'Donovan, Oliver. *The Desire of the Nations*. Cambridge: Cambridge University Press, 1999.

Ogden, Emily. *Credulity: A Cultural History of US Mesmerism*. Chicago: University of Chicago Press, 2018.

Oldenburg, Ray. *Great Good Place: Cafés, Coffee Shops, Bookstores, Bars, Hair Salons, and Other Hangouts at the Heart of a Community*. 3rd ed. New York: Marlowe, 1999.

Olmstead, Gracy. "The Art of the Stroll." *American Conservative*, August 14, 2018. https://www.theamericanconservative.com/articles/the-art-of-the-stroll/.

O'Neil, Cathy. *Weapons of Math Destruction: How Big Data Increases Inequality and Threatens Democracy*. New York: Crown, 2017.

Ong, Walter J. *Orality and Literacy: The Technologizing of the Word*. New Accents. London: Routledge, 1991.

———. *The Presence of the Word: Some Prolegomena for Cultural and Religious History*. Minneapolis: University of Minnesota Press, 1981.

———. *Ramus, Method, and the Decay of Dialogue: From the Art of Discourse to the Art of Reason*. Chicago: University of Chicago Press, 2004.

Otter, Samuel. "Reading *Moby-Dick*." In *The New Cambridge Companion to Herman Melville*, edited by Robert S. Levine, 68–84. Cambridge: Cambridge University Press, 2014.

Oxford English Dictionary. "History of the OED." Accessed December 8, 2020. https://public.oed.com/history/.

Paine, Thomas. *The Age of Reason.* London: Freethought Publishing, 1889.

———. *Common Sense, The Rights of Man, and Other Essential Writings of Thomas Paine.* Edited by Sidney Hook. New York: Meridian, 1984.

Parkerson, Donald H. "How Mobile Were Nineteenth-Century Americans?" *Historical Methods: A Journal of Quantitative and Interdisciplinary History* 15, no. 3 (1982): 99–109.

Parkinson, Robert G. *The Common Cause: Creating Race and Nation in the American Revolution.* Chapel Hill: University of North Carolina Press, 2016.

———. "Print, the Press, and the American Revolution." *Oxford Research Encyclopedia of American History.* Published online September 3, 2015.

Perlow, Seth. "The Handwritten Styles of Instagram Poetry." *Post45* (blog), September 17, 2019. https://post45.org/2019/09/the-handwritten-styles-of-instagram-poetry/.

Petersheim, Steven. *Rethinking Nathaniel Hawthorne and Nature: Pastoral Experiments and Environmentality.* Lanham, Md.: Lexington Books, 2020.

Pettegree, Andrew. *Brand Luther: How an Unheralded Monk Turned His Small Town into a Center of Publishing, Made Himself the Most Famous Man in Europe—and Started the Protestant Reformation.* New York: Penguin, 2015.

"Philadelphia Typographical Society." *Long-Island Patriot*, November 14, 1821.

Phillips, Christopher N. *Epic in American Culture: Settlement to Reconstruction.* Baltimore: Johns Hopkins University Press, 2012.

———. *The Hymnal: A Reading History.* Baltimore: Johns Hopkins University Press, 2018.

Pieper, Josef. *Abuse of Language, Abuse of Power.* San Francisco: Ignatius Press, 1992.

Pierotti, Raymond John. *Indigenous Knowledge, Ecology, and Evolutionary Biology.* Indigenous Peoples and Politics. New York: Routledge, 2011.

Polanyi, Michael. *The Tacit Dimension.* Reissued ed. Chicago: University of Chicago Press, 2009.

Porte, Joel. *In Respect to Egotism: Studies in American Romantic Writing.* Cambridge: Cambridge University Press, 1991.

Postman, Neil. *Amusing Ourselves to Death: Public Discourse in the Age of Show Business.* New York: Penguin, 1986.

———. *Technopoly: The Surrender of Culture to Technology.* New York: Vintage, 1993.

Prewitt, Kenneth. *What Is "Your" Race? The Census and Our Flawed Efforts to Classify Americans.* Princeton: Princeton University Press, 2013.

Prior, Karen Swallow. *On Reading Well.* Grand Rapids: Brazos, 2022.

Putnam, Robert D. *Bowling Alone: The Collapse and Revival of American Community*. New York: Touchstone Books, 2001.

Ramsay, David. *The History of the American Revolution*. Vol. 2. Philadelphia: R. Aitken & Son, 1789.

Rasenberger, Jim. *Revolver: Sam Colt and the Six-Shooter That Changed America*. New York: Scribner, 2020.

Ray, Angela G. *The Lyceum and Public Culture in the Nineteenth-Century United States*. Lansing: Michigan State University Press, 2005.

Reynolds, David S. *Walt Whitman's America: A Cultural Biography*. New York: Vintage, 1996.

Richardson, Robert D., Jr. *Emerson: The Mind on Fire*. Berkeley: University of California Press, 1996.

Richtel, Matt. "A Silicon Valley School That Doesn't Compute." *New York Times*, October 22, 2011. https://www.nytimes.com/2011/10/23/technology/at-waldorf-school-in-silicon-valley-technology-can-wait.html.

Ricoeur, Paul. *The Conflict of Interpretations*. Edited by Don Ihde. Evanston: Northwestern University Press, 1974.

Rosa, Hartmut. *Resonance: A Sociology of Our Relationship to the World*. Translated by James Wagner. Cambridge: Polity, 2021.

———. *The Uncontrollability of the World*. Translated by James Wagner. Cambridge: Polity, 2020.

Rosenfeld, Sophia A. *Common Sense: A Political History*. Cambridge, Mass.: Harvard University Press, 2011.

Rosenthal, Caitlin. *Accounting for Slavery: Masters and Management*. Cambridge, Mass.: Harvard University Press, 2019.

Royer, Daniel J. "The Process of Literacy as Communal Involvement in the Narratives of Frederick Douglass." *African American Review* 28, no. 3 (1994): 363–74.

Rubenstein, Harry R., and Barbara Clark Smith. "History." In *Jefferson Bible*, 11–35.

Rush, Benjamin. *A Plan for the Establishment of Public Schools and the Diffusion of Knowledge in Pennsylvania; To Which Are Added Thoughts upon the Mode of Education, Proper in a Republic. Addressed to the Legislature and Citizens of the State*. Philadelphia: Thomas Dobson, 1786.

Sacasas, L. M. "Borg Complex: A Primer." *L.M. Sacasas* (blog), March 1, 2013. https://thefrailestthing.com/2013/03/01/borg-complex-a-primer/.

Sanneh, Lamin. *Summoned from the Margin: Homecoming of an African*. Grand Rapids: Eerdmans, 2012.

Sargeant, Leah Libresco. "Students Brave the Heat." *Plough*, August 22, 2023. https://www.plough.com/en/topics/life/relationships/students-brave-the-heat.

Schor, Paul. *Counting Americans: How the US Census Classified the Nation*. New York: Oxford University Press, 2017.

Schulten, Susan. *Mapping the Nation: History and Cartography in Nineteenth-Century America*. Chicago: University of Chicago Press, 2012.

Schulz, Kathryn. "Why Do We Love Henry David Thoreau?" *New Yorker*, October 12, 2015. https://www.newyorker.com/magazine/2015/10/19/pond -scum.

Schweitzer, Albert. *The Quest of the Historical Jesus: A Critical Study of Its Progress from Reimarus to Wrede*. London: A. and C. Black, 1910.

Scott, James C. *Against the Grain: A Deep History of the Earliest States*. New Haven: Yale University Press, 2017.

———. *Seeing like a State: How Certain Schemes to Improve the Human Condition Have Failed*. New Haven: Yale University Press, 1999.

Sewall, Richard Benson. *The Life of Emily Dickinson*. Cambridge, Mass.: Harvard University Press, 1994.

Shakespeare, William. *The Tempest*. Edited by Alden T. Vaughan and Virginia Mason Vaughan. 4th ed. London: Arden Shakespeare, 2011.

Shanley, James Lyndon, and Henry David Thoreau. *The Making of Walden: With the Text of the First Version*. Chicago: University of Chicago Press, 1957.

Short, Bryan C. "Form as Vision in Herman Melville's *Clarel*." *American Literature* 50, no. 4 (1979): 553–69.

Simmons, Nancy Craig. "Margaret Fuller's Boston Conversations: The 1839–1840 Series." *Studies in the American Renaissance* (1994): 195–226.

"Slave Bible from the 1800s Omitted Key Passages That Could Incite Rebellion." NPR, December 9, 2018. https://www.npr.org/2018/12/09/674995075/slave-bible-from-the-1800s-omitted-key-passages-that-could -incite-rebellion.

Smith, Ben. "How TikTok Reads Your Mind." *New York Times*, December 6, 2021. https://www.nytimes.com/2021/12/05/business/media/tiktok -algorithm.html.

Smith, Caleb. *Thoreau's Axe: Distraction and Discipline in American Culture*. Princeton: Princeton University Press, 2023.

Smith, James K. A. *Cultural Liturgies*. Vol. 1, *Desiring the Kingdom: Worship, Worldview, and Cultural Formation*. Grand Rapids: Baker Academic, 2009.

———. *Cultural Liturgies*. Vol. 2, *Imagining the Kingdom: How Worship Works*. Grand Rapids: Baker Academic, 2013.

Smith, Justin E. H. "It's All Over." *Point Magazine*, January 3, 2019. https://thepointmag.com/examined-life/its-all-over/.

———. "Permanent Pandemic: Will COVID Controls Keep Controlling Us?" *Harper's Magazine*, May 11, 2022. https://harpers.org/archive/2022/06/permanent-pandemic-will-covid-controls-keep-controlling-us/.

Smith, Robert Mark. "Orality and Typography: A Study of Contrasts in the Prose of Ralph Waldo Emerson." PhD diss., University of Southwestern Louisiana, 1992.

Snyder, Anne. "Respecting Reality." In Bilbro, Wilson, and Henreckson, *Liberating Arts*, 61–63.

Snyder, Gary. *The Great Clod: Notes and Memoirs on Nature and History in East Asia*. Berkeley, Calif.: Counterpoint, 2016.

Solnit, Rebecca. *Wanderlust: A History of Walking*. New York: Penguin, 2001.

Standage, Tom. "How Luther Went Viral." *Economist*, December 17, 2011. http://www.economist.com/node/21541719.

———. *The Victorian Internet: The Remarkable Story of the Telegraph and the Nineteenth Century's On-Line Pioneers*. New York: Walker, 1998.

Stauffer, John, Zoe Trodd, Celeste-Marie Bernier, Henry Louis Gates Jr., and Kenneth B. Morris Jr. *Picturing Frederick Douglass: An Illustrated Biography of the Nineteenth Century's Most Photographed American*. New York: Liveright, 2015.

Steiner, George. *Real Presences*. Chicago: University of Chicago Press, 1991.

Stepto, Robert B. "Narration, Authentication, and Authorial Control in Frederick Douglass' Narrative of 1845." In *Afro-American Literature: The Reconstruction of Instruction*, edited by Dexter Fisher and Robert B. Stepto, 178–91. New York: Modern Language Association of America, 1979.

Stone, Linda. "Continuous Partial Attention." *Linda Stone* (blog), November 29, 2009. https://lindastone.net/2009/11/30/beyond-simple-multi-tasking -continuous-partial-attention/.

Stowe, William W. "'Busy Leisure': Margaret Fuller, Nature, and Vacation Writing." *Interdisciplinary Studies in Literature and Environment* 9, no. 1 (2002): 25–43.

Strauss, Gerald. "A Sixteenth-Century Encyclopedia: Sebastian Münster's *Cosmography* and Its Editions." In *From the Renaissance to the Counter-Reformation: Essays in Honour of Garrett Mattingly*, edited by Charles Howard Carter, 145–63. London: Jonathan Cape, 1966.

Sullivan, Andrew. "My Distraction Sickness—and Yours." *New York Magazine*, September 16, 2016. https://nymag.com/intelligencer/2016/09/andrew -sullivan-my-distraction-sickness-and-yours.html.

Sunstein, Cass R. "The Law of Group Polarization." John M. Olin Law and Economic Working Paper, no. 91, University of Chicago Law School, Chicago, Ill., December 1999.

Swanson, Barrett. "The Anxiety of Influencers: Educating the TikTok Generation." *Harper's Magazine*, June 2021. https://harpers.org/archive/2021/06/ tiktok-house-collab-house-the-anxiety-of-influencers/.

Tanselle, G. Thomas. "Some Statistics on American Printing, 1764–1783." In *The Press and the American Revolution*, edited by Bernard Bailyn and John B. Hench, 315–63. Worcester, Mass.: American Antiquarian Society, 1980.

Tate, Allen. "Emily Dickinson." In *Emily Dickinson: A Collection of Critical Essays*, edited by Richard B. Sewall, 16–27. Englewood Cliffs, N.J.: Prentice-Hall, 1963.

Taylor, Charles. *A Secular Age*. Cambridge, Mass.: Belknap Press of Harvard University Press, 2007.

Thaler, Richard H., and Cass R. Sunstein. *Nudge: Improving Decisions about Health, Wealth, and Happiness*. Rev. and exp. ed. New York: Penguin, 2009.

"The Jefferson Grid (@the.Jefferson.Grid)." Instagram photo. Accessed December 17, 2020, https://www.instagram.com/the.jefferson.grid/.

"The Magnetic Telegraph—Some of Its Results." In *Littell's Living Age*, vol. 6, 194–95. Boston: T. H. Carter, 1845.

Thernstrom, Stephan. *The Other Bostonians: Poverty and Progress in the American Metropolis, 1880–1970*. Cambridge, Mass.: Harvard University Press, 2013.

Theroux, Paul. *The Tao of Travel: Enlightenments from Lives on the Road*. Boston: Houghton Mifflin Harcourt, 2011.

Thomas, Isaiah. *The History of Printing in America: With a Biography of Printers*. 2nd ed. Burt Franklin Bibliography and Reference Series, no. 62. New York: B. Franklin, 1972.

Thomas, Louisa. "Emerson's Eyes." *Sewanee Review* 125, no. 4 (2017): 822–32.

Thomas, Shannon L. "'What News Must Think When Pondering': Emily Dickinson, the *Springfield Daily Republican*, and the Poetics of Mass Communication." *Emily Dickinson Journal* 19, no. 1 (2010): 60–79.

Thoreau, Henry David. *Excursions*. Edited by Joseph J. Moldenhauer. Writings of Henry D. Thoreau. Princeton: Princeton University Press, 2007.

———. *Journal*. Edited by Leonard N. Neufeldt and Nancy Craig Simmons. Writings of Henry D. Thoreau. Princeton: Princeton University Press, 1981.

———. *Reform Papers*. Edited by Wendell Glick. Writings of Henry D. Thoreau. Princeton: Princeton University Press, 1973.

———. *Walden*. Edited by J. Lyndon Shanley. Writings of Henry D. Thoreau. Princeton: Princeton University Press, 1971.

———. *Walden and Civil Disobedience*. New York: Penguin Classics, 1983.

———. *A Week on the Concord and Merrimack Rivers*. Edited by Carl Hovde. Princeton: Princeton University Press, 1980.

Tolkien, J. R. R. *Tree and Leaf*. London: HarperCollins UK, 2012.

Toyama, Kentaro. *Geek Heresy: Rescuing Social Change from the Cult of Technology*. New York: PublicAffairs, 2015.

Trodd, Zoe. "A Renaissance-Self: Frederick Douglass and the Art of Remaking." In *The Cambridge Companion to the Literature of the American Renaissance*, edited by Christopher N. Phillips, 189–204. Cambridge: Cambridge University Press, 2018.

Trueman, Carl R. "A Critical Theorist Worth Reading." *First Things*, September 7, 2021. https://www.firstthings.com/web-exclusives/2021/09/a-critical-theorist-worth-reading.

Tufekci, Zeynep. *Twitter and Tear Gas: The Power and Fragility of Networked Protest*. New Haven: Yale University Press, 2017.

Turkle, Sherry. *Alone Together: Why We Expect More from Technology and Less from Each Other*. New York: Basic Books, 2012.

———. "Connected, but Alone?" Filmed February 2012. TED video. https://www.ted.com/talks/sherry_turkle_connected_but_alone.

———. *Reclaiming Conversation: The Power of Talk in a Digital Age*. Reprint ed. New York: Penguin, 2016.

Twain, Mark. *Adventures of Huckleberry Finn*. Edited by Victor Fischer and Lin Salamo. Berkeley: University of California Press, 2003.

———. *A Connecticut Yankee in King Arthur's Court*. Edited by Bernard L. Stein. Berkeley: University of California Press, 1979.

Twenge, Jean M. *iGen: Why Today's Super-Connected Kids Are Growing Up Less Rebellious, More Tolerant, Less Happy—and Completely Unprepared for Adulthood—and What That Means for the Rest of Us.* New York: Simon and Schuster, 2017.

Vaidhyanathan, Siva. *Antisocial Media: How Facebook Disconnects Us and Undermines Democracy.* New York: Oxford University Press, 2018.

Wallace, Maurice O., and Shawn Michelle Smith. "Framing the Black Solder: Image, Uplift, and the Duplicity of Pictures." In *Pictures and Progress: Early Photography and the Making of African American Identity*, 244–66. Durham, N.C.: Duke University Press, 2012.

Walls, Laura Dassow. *Henry David Thoreau: A Life.* Chicago: University of Chicago Press, 2017.

Walsh, Lynda. *Sins against Science: The Scientific Media Hoaxes of Poe, Twain, and Others.* Albany: SUNY Press, 2016.

Warner, Michael. *The Letters of the Republic: Publication and the Public Sphere in Eighteenth-Century America.* Cambridge, Mass.: Harvard University Press, 1990.

Watson, Blake A. *Buying America from the Indians: Johnson v. McIntosh and the History of Native Land Rights.* Norman: University of Oklahoma Press, 2012.

Webster, Noah. *A Collection of Essays and Fugitiv Writings: On Moral, Historical, Political and Literary Subjects.* Boston: I. Thomas and E. T. Andrews, 1790.

Welch, Chris. "Inside Amazon's Canceled Plan to Make Halo a Fitness Success." *Verge*, May 1, 2023. https://www.theverge.com/2023/5/1/23704825/amazon-halo-canceled-features-ai-training-apple-watch.

Wellmon, Chad. *Organizing Enlightenment: Information Overload and the Invention of the Modern Research University.* Baltimore: Johns Hopkins University Press, 2015.

Werge, Thomas. "*Moby-Dick* and the Calvinist Tradition." *Studies in the Novel* 1, no. 4 (1969): 484–506.

West, Michael. "Emily Dickinson's Ambrosian Nights with Christopher North." *Harvard Library Bulletin* 5, no. 1 (1994): 67–71.

"What Is EOL?" *Encyclopedia of Life.* Accessed December 5, 2020. https://naturalhistory.si.edu/research/eol.

Wheelwright, Jeff. "The Skeptical Pilgrim: Melville's *Clarel*." *Public Domain Review.* Accessed August 9, 2023. https://publicdomainreview.org/essay/the-skeptical-pilgrim-melvilles-clarel/.

Whitman, Walt. *The Correspondence.* Vol. 3, *1876–1885*. Edited by Edwin Haviland Miller. New York: NYU Press, 2007.

———. *Leaves of Grass: A Textual Variorum of the Printed Poems.* Edited by Sculley Bradley, Harold W. Blodgett, Arthur Golden, and William White. Collected Writings of Walt Whitman. New York: New York University Press, 1980.

———. *Leaves of Grass and Other Writings.* Edited by Michael Moon. New York: W. W. Norton, 2002.

Wiebe, Robert H. *Opening of American Society: From the Adoption of the Constitution to the Eve of Disunion.* New York: Alfred A. Knopf, 1984.

Wikipedia. s.v. "Wikipedia." Version from December 4, 2020. https://en.wikipedia.org/w/index.php?title=Wikipedia&oldid=992347324.

Wilbur, Richard. *New and Collected Poems.* San Diego: Mariner Books, 1989.

Williams, Raymond. *The Country and the City.* New York: Oxford University Press, 1975.

Wilson, Edward Osborne. *Consilience: The Unity of Knowledge.* New York: Vintage, 1999.

Winner, Langdon. *The Whale and the Reactor: A Search for Limits in an Age of High Technology.* Chicago: University of Chicago Press, 1989.

Winship, Michael. "Publishing *The Scarlet Letter* in the Nineteenth-Century United States." In *The Scarlet Letter: Complete Text with Introduction, Historical Contexts, Critical Essays,* by Nathaniel Hawthorne, edited by Rita Gollin, 68–76. Boston: Houghton Mifflin, 2002.

Wolf, Maryanne. *Reader, Come Home: The Reading Brain in a Digital World.* New York: HarperCollins, 2018.

Wood, Graeme. "How Bronze Age Pervert Charmed the Far Right." *Atlantic,* August 3, 2023. https://www.theatlantic.com/magazine/archive/2023/09/bronze-age-pervert-costin-alamariu/674762/.

Wright, Tom F. *The Cosmopolitan Lyceum: Lecture Culture and the Globe in Nineteenth-Century America.* Amherst: University of Massachusetts Press, 2013.

Yothers, Brian. "Terrors of the Soul: Religious Pluralism, Epistemological Dread, and Cosmic Exaltation in Poe, Hawthorne, and Melville." *Poe Studies/Dark Romanticism: History, Theory, Interpretation* 39–40, no. 1–2 (2006): 136–44.

Yousafzai, Malala, and Christina Lamb. *I Am Malala: The Girl Who Stood Up for Education and Was Shot by the Taliban.* New York: Back Bay Books, 2015.

Zboray, Ronald J. *A Fictive People: Antebellum Economic Development and the American Reading Public.* New York: Oxford University Press, 1993.

Ziolkowski, Thad. "Antitheses: The Dialectic of Violence and Literacy in Frederick Douglass's *Narrative* of 1845." In *Critical Essays on Frederick Douglass,* edited by William L. Andrews, 148–65. Boston: G. K. Hall, 1991.

Zuboff, Shoshana. *The Age of Surveillance Capitalism: The Fight for a Human Future at the New Frontier of Power.* New York: PublicAffairs, 2020.

Index